The Games Presidents Play

The Games Presidents Play

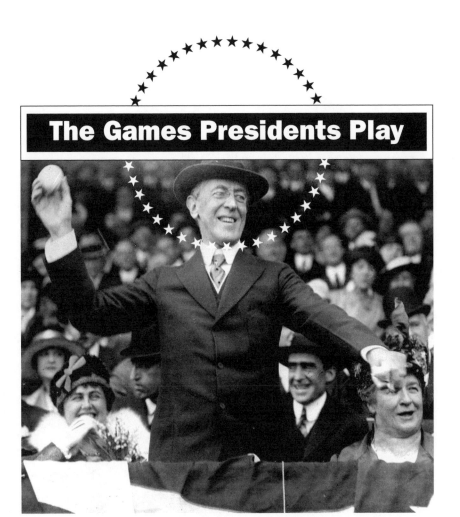

★ SPORTS AND THE PRESIDENCY ★

John Sayle Watterson

THE JOHNS HOPKINS UNIVERSITY PRESS

BALTIMORE

The Johns Hopkins University Press
2715 North Charles Street
Baltimore, Maryland 21218-4363
www.press.jhu.edu

Library of Congress Cataloging-in-Publication Data
Watterson, John Sayle.
The games presidents play : sports and the presidency / John Sayle Watterson.
p. cm.
Includes bibliographical references and index.
ISBN 0-8018-8425-x (hardcover : alk. paper)
1. Presidents—Sports—United States. 2. Sports and state—United States.
I. Title.
E176.1.W347 2006
973.09′9—dc22   2006005556

A catalog record for this book is available from the British Library.

To Martha and Emily

★ ★ ★
Contents

Preface *ix*

Introduction *1*

PART I. FOUNDATIONS
Chapter 1. In the Beginning *9*
Chapter 2. The Sporting Frontier *20*
Chapter 3. Barely Visible to Press and Public *27*

PART II. THE MAN WHO CHANGED EVERYTHING
Chapter 4. Theodore Roosevelt: Climbing the Mountain *37*
Chapter 5. Sports and the Presidency: The Founding Father *47*
Chapter 6. Inside TR's Sporting Presidency *63*

PART III. SPORTS: ACCEPTABLE BUT NOT REQUIRED
Chapter 7. William Howard Taft: A Large Legacy *75*
Chapter 8. Woodrow Wilson: More than Just a Game *91*
Chapter 9. Warren Harding: The Wager He Didn't Win *107*
Chapter 10. Calvin Coolidge: Grace, under Pressure *119*
Chapter 11. Herbert Hoover: No Place to Hide *133*
Chapter 12. Franklin Delano Roosevelt:
Politically and Physically Challenged *149*

PART IV. FLIGHT FROM WASHINGTON
Chapter 13. Harry S Truman: Striding—and Flying—into History *173*
Chapter 14. Dwight D. Eisenhower: Hero under Assault *185*
Chapter 15. John F. Kennedy: Swimming into Politics *201*
Chapter 16. Lyndon Johnson: The Games He Didn't Play *217*

PART V. IN THE PUBLIC EYE

Chapter 17. Richard Nixon: Show Me a Good Loser . . . 229

Chapter 18. Gerald Ford: The Pigskin President 245

Chapter 19. Jimmy Carter: More than Meets the Eye 261

Chapter 20. Ronald Reagan: Creating a Sports Legend 275

Chapter 21. George H. W. Bush: TR Revisited 293

PART VI. NEW PLAYERS, OLD GAMES

Chapter 22. Bill Clinton: Oh, How He Played the Game 311

Chapter 23. George W. Bush: From Bush Leagues to the Majors 323

Conclusion 337

Appendix: Ranking the Presidents 355

Notes 361

Suggested Reading 385

Index 395

Preface

In the winter of 2001, when I began research on this book, Bill Clinton had just left the presidency and George W. Bush had recently taken the oath of office.

For a historian of contemporary sport, I could not ignore the parallels of the old and new presidents. Clinton played golf with a disregard for the rules that seemed to mirror his behavior in Monicagate. Bush, on the other hand, used his highly visible position as managing partner of the Texas Rangers to catapult himself into Texas politics. Many people questioned whether playing fast and loose with the rules of golf was presidential and whether baseball was a proper preparation for the highest office in the land.

Several thoughts intrigued me as I began digging into my topic. Sports and political character might be more intimately connected than is commonly acknowledged. Presidential sports might even influence a president's career and his approach to foreign and domestic policy. Furthermore, through sports and games, presidents can create a positive image and schmooze with those who can be of use. And, of course, presidents use games and sports for rest and recreation.

Visiting presidential libraries, I concluded that sports indeed matter. I also found that archivists working for the National Archives and Records Administration in presidential libraries and repositories were remarkably familiar with the sports and physical regimens of the presidents. Many libraries have even organized their materials so that sports can easily be accessed. I never felt as if I were given short shrift because I chose sports and games rather than foreign or economic policy. In fact, archivists went to great pains to obtain oral histories, materials that were in other libraries, and photos that fit my needs.

Although I discuss eighteenth- and nineteenth-century presidents, readers will find that I spend far more time on more recent presidents, beginning with Theodore Roosevelt. The reason is simple: These presidents generally showed more interest in sports and used their sports—and games—for personal and political purposes. George W. Bush's sporting presidency is almost too close at hand to evaluate. Yet newspaper articles on Bush are constantly calling attention to his athletic obsessions. Because sports contributed to his rise to power—and, since then, to the macho climate of the Bush White House—I could hardly neglect him. Now his second term has given me more to write about and a clearer view of his attitude toward sports.

As for the title, the reader should be aware that it does not refer to simply athletics, sports, and traditional games. Increasingly, the games that presidents play are just that—political games, carefully designed to burnish and shape presidential images and to send a message that the commander in chief, like many of his fellow Americans, is a sports fan. Richard Nixon's ill-advised forays into sports may have caused people to view cynically his all-star teams, his suggestions to NFL coaches, and *Air Force One* flights to high-profile football and baseball games. But Nixon was hardly the first and surely not the last to use sports politically. And wasn't it also possible that his sporting antics stemmed from his sincere and intense interest in sports that manifested itself so clearly when he was a third-string lineman on the Whittier College football team?

Although much of my research and writing has taken place at my home in Charlottesville, Virginia, I would like to thank those who helped me both near and far. My thanks go out to the numerous members of research staffs who assisted me at presidential libraries, presidential homes and sites, at the National Archives repositories at College Park, Maryland, and Laguna Beach, California, and at the Library of Congress. This includes the NARA archivists at the many presidential libraries and presidential sites who worked with me to obtain the photos I needed. Among the others who deserve to be acknowledged are Cynthia Bittinger, Philander Chase, Wallace Dailey, Alvah Drew, Frank Grizzard, Mike Greco, Michael Lansing, Brian MacDonald, William McNitt, George Rugg, Alexandria Searls, Diane Sheth, Kenneth Thompson, and Martha Williams. I would like to thank University Librarian Karin Wittenborg and her staff at the University of Virginia Library; the books and articles that I found there kept my research alive. The Miller Center of Public Affairs at the University of Virginia, especially its library, also proved to be a valuable resource.

Other people also rendered assistance. I was fortunate to have interviews with President Gerald Ford and former coach Darrell Royal of the Texas Longhorns. Edward J. Renehan and Kathleen Dalton also assisted me in working toward publication. C. Brian Kelly of Charlottesville looked at my chapters in their early stages and made helpful suggestions. Susan Langenkamp deserves several votes of thanks for serving as my editor as I wrote the book; her editorial judgment and advice were indispensable. Once again, Robert J. Brugger of the Johns Hopkins University Press showed an interest in my manuscript, as he did with my history of college football, and was instrumental in its publication.

More than anyone else, my wife, Yvonne, supported this project and believed in it after I was ready to give up. I only wish that my mother, Emily Timberlake Watterson, who had an M.A. in history from Duke University and was a lover of both history and sports, had lived long enough to read this book.

The Games Presidents Play

Introduction

In October 1905 President Theodore Roosevelt held a luncheon for the war-ring athletic potentates from Harvard, Yale, and Princeton. The meeting was the first time a president had intervened in a sporting controversy. Though Roosevelt had not played football, he was a football enthusiast and had a plan to reform the then controversial sport.

If Roosevelt was a football enthusiast, what games engaged the interests of other presidents, and, just as important, what other games and sports did they play? Richard Nixon, once a third-string lineman for Whittier College, placed a call to George Allen, coach of the Washington Redskins. The Red-skins were playing the San Francisco Forty-niners in the NFL playoffs, and Nixon had a play for Allen. On the following day, Allen saw his opportunity. Late in the second quarter, the Redskins faced a second down and six yards to go on the Forty-niners' eight-yard line. Allen used the flanker reverse play that Nixon had suggested. The result was a thirteen-yard loss; the Redskins failed to score and lost the game 24-20.

Nixon's ill-advised foray seems perfectly natural, especially if you are com-mander in chief. After all, isn't this just a presidential version of call-in sports shows or virtual sports on the Internet? Or did Nixon's play calling and schmoozing with sports figures provide more clues to his character? Might his use of sports be another way of courting voters or appealing to the "silent American"?

The sports played by presidents turn out to be just as interesting as presi-dential play calling. Further research on Teddy Roosevelt revealed a president who revitalized himself by scaling cliffs in Rock Creek Valley, boxing and wrestling in the White House, and riding on horseback ninety miles into a howling gale. For weeks at a time, Woodrow Wilson went with his personal physician across the Potomac to northern Virginia to play a few holes of awful golf. Herbert Hoover played a game similar to volleyball with a medicine ball on the South Lawn of the White House before breakfast. And Jimmy Carter ran in Rock Creek Park and, with First Lady Rosalynn, explored trout streams near Camp David.

Many presidents played golf, but their style of play differed radically.

Dwight D. Eisenhower flew to Augusta, where he had a house on the golf course; he played golf so fanatically that once, in a spasm of anger, he threw a club at his personal physician. In contrast, John F. Kennedy in his infrequent outings enjoyed the company of his golf partners and, though a talented athlete, seldom complained about bad holes.

The games that chief executives played as presidents can be fascinating and useful to understanding presidential character. Just as intriguing are the sports and games that engaged future presidents in their formative years. Woodrow Wilson, who never played football, coached winning teams at Princeton and Wesleyan. Dwight Eisenhower and Gerald Ford played and coached football. Was it possible that the managerial ability gained in coaching transferred to their politics and presidencies? Jimmy Carter was a high school tennis player who carried his interest in the game and his tendency to micromanage to the White House tennis courts. Harry Truman relaxed by playing raucous games of poker with his political cronies and friends. Of the twentieth-century presidents, only Franklin Roosevelt was unable to participate actively in sports such as golf and hunting while in office. Yet FDR's experience with polio relates an athletic story equally important. Other presidents used sports because of medical conditions, but none so dramatically as FDR. In spite of disability or lack of ability, sport can play a formative role in a president's character.

Some presidents displayed their athletic ability in military settings. Presidents from George Washington to the first George Bush won their spurs in combat. Other presidents who commanded troops and achieved well-publicized military victories rode into politics or into the White House. To be sure, most of the generals, including Washington, Jackson, and Grant, served before 1900. Yet the twentieth-century presidency has also had its share of military veterans and war heroes who used their war experiences to burnish their political image.

Public policy can translate into sports and vice versa. Thomas Jefferson invested in what was one of the most extreme ventures in the nation's history when he promoted the three-year exploration of the Louisiana Purchase by Meriwether Lewis and William Clark. Teddy Roosevelt carried his enthusiasm for the strenuous life into the public arena through conservation. Both Herbert Hoover and Franklin Roosevelt helped to bring about the Skyline Drive in the Blue Ridge Mountains of Virginia. Several times, the Olympics have competed for the attention of presidents, most memorably during the Carter administration.

Broadly defined, presidential sports are sometimes pivotal in bringing about change. A Ping Pong match in China proved to be the improbable beginning of Richard Nixon's dramatic rapprochement with Communist China. Ironically, despite its highly political nature, this was one sports event that the president chose not to attend. Yet its effect continues to be felt in the twenty-first century.

Increasingly, sports have defined the presidency itself. Sports stars and celebrities either are guests at the White House or receive awards or calls from the president. Presidents fly to pro-am tournaments or schedule one-on-one rounds with the Masters or U.S. Open champions. Or they fly to high-profile events such as the Daytona 500 or the NCAA basketball championship game. Sporting interests help to define the presidents, and they use sports to connect with the electorate.

In recent years, the presidency has become more sports-friendly and the public more tolerant of sporting activities. The still vibrant memories of Theodore Roosevelt's antics might suggest that TR began a trend that has continued over the past century. But the public sports presidency that had begun early in the last century with a spurt of energy and verve appeared to have withered on the vine by midcentury. TR's successors rarely entertained athletes at the White House or did much more than throw out the first ball at Griffith Stadium at the beginning of the baseball season. Weekends away from the White House usually took place on the presidential yacht, the *Williamsburg*, or at Shangri-La (soon-to-become Camp David) in the Catoctin Mountains of Maryland. TR's scrambling, horseback rides, and tennis games on the White House courts appeared to be the eccentricities of a single, madcap chief executive. For that matter, Teddy Roosevelt's reputation had fallen into disrepute—his sports were merely an extension of what was regarded as an eccentric, egotistical, and war-mongering personality.

When Franklin Roosevelt died in 1945, the sporting presidency had reached a low ebb. Because of FDR's paralyzed limbs, he could not exercise his legs for sports except when he was swimming. He could fish and watch sports, but he could barely do more—in World War II, he seldom exercised at all. And the new president, Harry Truman, preferred poker to active sports and merely walked or swam for exercise.

In the years immediately after World War II, sports seemed to be merely a minor footnote to the twentieth-century presidency. Indeed the Great Depression and the war had such an overarching importance that sports hardly counted in politics. When Herbert Hoover exercised, he hid from the public. Sports had merely provided weekend diversions or early morning exercise. The last serious golfing president had been Warren Harding, whose reputation was in shambles. Camping and tramping, hunting and fishing, swimming in Rock Creek and the Potomac were no longer possible in the Washington area, at least for presidents. The growth of government under the New Deal and during World War II had changed Washington from a sleepy southern outpost into an extension of the eastern corridor. It would have required an oracle to have foreseen the growth of the sports presidency in the second half of the twentieth century and its transformation by some presidents into a facsimile of Teddy Roosevelt's sports presidency—not to mention the realization that sports could be useful politically or that sports in excess could be used as a political issue.

The second half of the twentieth century would produce nearly fifty years of presidents whose sporting lives were deeply affected by the Great Depression or World War II. President Eisenhower, who had been a mere colonel at the outset of the war, would bring his golf obsession, honed by playing with first-class golfers on fine courses, to the South Lawn of the White House. John F. Kennedy, Richard Nixon, and Ronald Reagan would put their early enthusiasm for football and baseball—or wartime feats such as Kennedy's World War II swim in the South Pacific—to political uses in the presidency. Almost all of them would invite sporting celebrities or teams to the White House or actually travel to sporting events to watch or participate. The grounding of the sports presidency in presidents whose sports enthusiasms developed or whose reputations rested on the era of depression and war created an expectation that presidents would be athletes—and even the least athletic at first glance, such as Jimmy Carter or Bill Clinton, proved to have sporting obsessions.

By the end of the century, the sports presidency had veered close to the frenetic and versatile version of Teddy Roosevelt. No one scrambled in Rock Creek Park or swam the creek in the buff. Yet at least one president would suggest that he might become an "Oyster Bay kind of guy." The presidents who did not play before the cameras (most of them) often watched football on television and occasionally were televised or spoke before the cameras at the Olympics or at other big-time sporting events.

In some ways, the uses (and abuses) of sports by later twentieth-century presidents would go far beyond TR. As we look beyond midcentury, the unfinished sports presidency, begun with such gusto in 1901, reemerges. To be sure, no more marathon horseback rides or death-defying scrambles up jagged cliffs, but flights of fancy and reality that made sports and games into presidential drama and melodrama.

Although our focus on the sporting presidency deals primarily with the twentieth century, the story would be incomplete if the eighteenth and nineteenth centuries were neglected. In contrast to modern presidents, in the first 112 years of the American republic, sports played a less conspicuous role in the lives of White House occupants. From 1789 to 1901, the sports and games of the presidents normally took place in their younger years or before they reached the presidency. At first glance, these activities had little to do with their public lives. Jackson's ownership of racehorses and Abraham Lincoln's feats of strength tell us little about their presidencies or their political appeal.

From a different perspective, the games and sports of these earlier presidents provide glimpses of talents and traits that would carry them to power or even the shadowy outlines of what they would become as president. Occasionally, it is possible to catch sight of sporting activities they pursued during their presidencies or afterward.

Before the age of steam and the internal-combustion engine, the ability to manage and ride horses was an avenue to gaining a political following. The officer on horseback sat godlike above the foot soldiers. The troops on foot knew him only by his profile on horseback or by accounts of his heroics in battle. It is no mystery that generals who achieved success on horseback rode into the presidency. Most of these men, in their initial combat experience, showed impressive athletic prowess in the saddle.

The first example was George Washington. Washington's height and strength were well known. He literally towered over most of his contemporaries. What is most remarkable is that our first president began as a land surveyor without military training. How did this relatively untutored gentleman farmer become the father of his country?

Washington's strength was not simply in his character and charisma. His athleticism clearly contributed to the American presidency. The best-known and most powerful office in the world began not during the deliberations of Congress in 1776 or at the Philadelphia convention of 1787. Instead, it first appeared many years earlier in 1754 on a battlefield in what is today western Pennsylvania. Without Washington's superb athletic performance in this battle near the present site of Pittsburgh, it is unlikely that Washington would have ridden into American history as its first president. Indeed, without Washington, it's doubtful that the presidency, as we know it, would ever have been born.

Foundations

In the Beginning

George Washington: First in Sports

George Washington may have been the most talented athlete of all our presidents. In both war and peace, he demonstrated remarkable endurance and strength. Standing almost six foot three and weighing more than two hundred pounds, Washington had muscular arms and remarkable agility, especially on horseback.

At the age of twenty-two, Washington was a major in the Virginia militia when his men attacked a French military unit, triggering the French and Indian War. That would set the stage for the American Revolution and for Washington's future renown.

In 1754 he was serving under British general Edward Braddock, who was sent to dislodge the French from the headwaters of the Ohio River. Barely ten miles from their destination, Fort Duquesne (present-day Pittsburgh), they were ambushed by a force of French and Indians. Washington threw himself into the thick of the battle, carrying messages on horseback from Braddock to his commanders. Upon orders from the seriously wounded Braddock, the eager young horseman rode beyond the river to try to stop the flight of the badly mauled regulars.

Twice during the afternoon, Washington had horses shot out from under him and four times musket balls passed through his clothing without wounding him. He managed to keep his head in the midst of a scene that grew more and more chaotic and deadly.

He helped out wherever he could. One onlooker was amazed at his prodigious strength. He saw Washington take hold of a brass fieldpiece (a cannon) as if it were a stick. Washington moved furiously as he ripped the sheet lead from the touchhole, putting one hand on the muzzle, the other on the breach. According to the account, "he pulled with this, and he pushed with that, and wheeled it around as if it had been nothing."[1]

After he helped to reorganize the retreating troops, Washington rode all night and into the next morning to summon a Colonel Dunbar for wagons, medical supplies, and provisions. As he rode through the darkness, the cries and groans of soldiers rent the night. He was enveloped by "the gloom & horror of which was not a little increased by the impervious darkness occasioned by the close shade of this woods," he wrote. When he arrived at Colonel Dunbar's headquarters, he had been in the saddle for nearly twenty-four hours (later, during the Revolution, he would stay in the saddle forty-eight hours when the British attacked Long Island). He rode back with Dunbar and helped bury General Braddock, who had died of his wounds.[2]

The stories of Washington's physical prowess later morph into legend and myth, though never beyond the realm of possibility.

Did he throw a stone or a silver dollar across the Rappahannock River or to the top of Virginia's Natural Bridge? Whether a true story or myth, what is certain is that it has everything to do with Washington's reputation for having astonishing strength. As proof that myths never die, Walter Johnson—"the big train"—the legendary pitcher for the Washington Senators and one of the greatest in major league history, reportedly threw a silver dollar across the Rappahannock River on Washington's Birthday in 1936.[3]

Washington was also a sports spectator. Like all other Virginia gentlemen, Washington was steeped in social functions that surrounded horse racing, and he recorded his love of the sport in his diaries. In the early part of the eighteenth century, the Virginia, Maryland, and Pennsylvania gentry organized jockey clubs, probably the first groups of sports enthusiasts in America. In the 1770s Washington traveled to Annapolis and Philadelphia for the races, which were held over several days, always with fine dining, fancy dress balls, and gambling. Big crowds came eager for the horses and to see and to be seen: "there was a prodigious concourse of spectators and considerable sums were depending on the contest of each day."[4]

Washington played cards in the evening at the Assembly House on the Duke of Gloucester Street in Williamsburg. While the front room was for dancing, the men gathered in the back to play cards and drink. Because he knew other young men who had gone bankrupt gambling, Washington was moderate in his card playing and kept careful records of his losses and occasional winnings.

The members of Philadelphia's jockey club read like a "who's who" of Pennsylvania society, an eastern network of prominent sportsmen. Washington hobnobbed with governors, prominent merchants, and politicians, as well as with a Scottish immigrant, William Alexander, Lord Stirling, so called because he had claim to a Scottish title of nobility. Alexander was to become one of Washington's generals, serving under him during the soon-to-erupt American Revolution.

At home, Washington thrived on fox hunting. Washington's riding to the hounds was wild and unruly, a far cry from the ritual of riders in scarlet pursuing the quarry across well-cultivated fields and hedgerows. Sometimes he hunted pheasants, duck, and even deer. A rider of remarkable speed and endurance, Washington had few equals but he didn't hunt with just anyone. His journals suggest a routine to his hunting: "Rid [sic] out with my gun," "went pheasant hunting," "went a-gunning up the Creek," "went a hunting with Jackie Custis [stepson] & catched a bitch fox after three hours chace."[5]

It wasn't always horses. One story has Washington wrestling the strongest man in the region, possibly at a tavern in Berryville, Virginia, where travelers, especially teamsters, came to refresh themselves and spend the night. According to the story, Washington was sitting quietly reading a book, perhaps a book on surveying. When "the strong man" hired at such taverns to wrestle teamsters repeatedly pestered and taunted him, he slammed shut his book and, still wearing his coat, confronted "the champion." The two were soon "grappling" with each other: "the struggle was fierce but momentary, for, said the vanquished hero of the arena, in Washington's lion-like grasp, 'I became powerless, and was hurled to the ground with a force that seemed to jar the very marrow of my bones.'" Amid the shouting and cheers, Washington went back to his book.[6]

Years later, Washington, watching some younger men who were tossing a heavy iron bar (they probably had wagered on the outcome), ambled over, picked it up, and hurled it farther than any of them. He smiled indulgently: "You perceive, young gentlemen, that my arm yet retains some portion of the vigor of my earlier days," and this was when he was about forty years old.[7]

Washington's sporting career was too often interrupted by his military and public duties. In the first years of the Revolution, British Lord Howe frequently foiled Washington's strategic plans and managed to outmaneuver him. Yet hunting and war, in their strategy and planning, sometimes resemble each other, as when Washington took the offensive at the Battle of Germantown. Appropriately, Washington was known as the "fox" by the British, though at Germantown he outfoxed himself.

The commander ordered his troops on the move before dawn to surprise the British who had driven him from Philadelphia. As if moving in for the kill, he put four columns in motion, and one of the columns reached the

British outposts, forcing their forward garrisons quickly back. Unfortunately, the attack bogged down, some units fired on each other in an early instance of friendly fire, and Washington ended up retreating with his army to Valley Forge where he went into winter quarters.

Earlier at Morristown, New Jersey, a French visitor reported that Washington was throwing a ball with younger officers. Was the father of his country playing an early form of baseball? Did he play "ball" at Valley Forge?

Washington was best known as the commanding figure on horseback. Mounted as he was, Washington was visible to his troops because he could be seen by men on foot. Still, it was his officers, the ones he played "ball" with, who worshiped him and were ready to give him dictatorial powers in 1783 when government seemed to be breaking down. Instead, Washington squelched these plots. His election as the first president under the Constitution in 1789 demonstrated the universal respect in which he was held. Only because it was understood that Washington would become the first president did delegates to the ratifying conventions agree to endow the government with powers that seemed to contradict the ideals of the Revolution.

By eighteenth-century standards, Washington had passed middle age when he was president. While he was still large and imposing, the years on horseback and feats of athletic prowess were largely behind him. One exception occurred when, as president-elect, he rode from Mount Vernon to New York City, the temporary capital, among jubilant citizens, who fired cannons, rang bells, and threw flowers in the road. Washington merely had to appear dignified and presidential in the saddle on the long and fatiguing ride. According to one Washington scholar, "up to his sixty-eighth year, he mounted a horse with surprising agility, and rode with the ease and gracefulness of his earlier years."[8]

In a final campaign, Washington would once again mount his horse. In 1794 he led a force to suppress the Whiskey Rebellion, a protest against a federal excise tax by farmers in western Pennsylvania. Because the rebels quickly fled, Washington had only to ride slightly over a hundred miles to Carlisle, the last time he commanded troops. "It also turned out to be the first and only time," writes Joseph Ellis, "a sitting American president led troops in the field."[9]

Among his many other "firsts," Washington would set a precedent for subsequent chief executives who reached the presidency as a result of their military achievements or, more precisely, their feats of leadership on horseback.

One point is clear: were it not for his athleticism at the Battle of Monongahela in 1754, it is unlikely that Washington would have ascended the military and political ladder to become President George Washington, father of his country.

★

Thomas Jefferson: Hurdling into History

Thomas Jefferson, the intellectual statesman, rarely gets mentioned in the same breath as General George Washington as an athlete or sportsman. Instead, Jefferson is recognized as a writer, an intellectual, a diplomat, and a statesman—and with good reason. At the age of thirty-three, Jefferson authored the Declaration of Independence, easily the most famous document in American history. He served as minister to France, governor of Virginia, secretary of state, vice-president, and president. A century and a half after Jefferson left the presidency, John F. Kennedy once praised a group of Nobel Prize winners in the White House as the most distinguished group of intellects ever assembled at the White House, except for when Thomas Jefferson dined there alone.

It may come as a surprise, therefore, that Jefferson was tall, strong, and in his way athletic. While he never rode into battle, he could stay in the saddle for three or four hours at a time. He had a collection of weapons, many of which he acquired while ambassador to France in the 1780s. Although he spent much of his time reading and writing, he engaged in physical exercise for at least two hours each day. His preference was to walk—and once he wrote that he knew no one who lived to an advanced age who didn't engage in walking. He remained active into his late sixties, though he confessed by then that he could no longer walk a mile.

As a young man, Jefferson was bred to the life of a country squire. Once, the story goes, he was sent as a boy into the woods by Peter Jefferson, his father, to bag wild game. Already efficient in the use of his time, Jefferson supposedly took a turkey from a pen, tied it to a tree with his garter, and shot it. Then he rode home in triumph with his quarry. History does not record his father's reaction.

When Jefferson was twenty-five, he jotted in his account book: "Won at shooting 1/3." A later shooting match had the same result: he lost two out of three. He occasionally ordered weapons and probably carried them when he traveled. He recommended that his nephew, while walking, carry a gun, presumably to blast away at squirrels or rabbits that crossed his path. "As to species of exercise, I advise the gun," he wrote to his nephew Peter Carr.

"While this gives moderate exercise to the body, it gives boldness, enterprise, and independence to the mind." Occasionally, he also mentioned fishing, as on a trip to Lake Champlain and Lake George in the 1780s or on outings at the falls of the Schuylkill River, five miles above Philadelphia—or at a dam near his home at Monticello.[10]

That said, Jefferson far preferred exercise to sport. In 1990, when Jefferson's own University of Virginia was ranked number one in the college football polls, a clever cartoonist drew a caricature of Jefferson hunched over the Declaration penning "Hoos [Virginia's athletic nickname] Number one," while a bored colleague implores, "sit down Jefferson." In truth, Jefferson would have recoiled at college football, especially at *his* university. "Games played with the ball and other of that nature are too violent for the body and stamp no character on the mind," he wrote Peter Carr in August 1785. In the same letter, Jefferson, who was minister to France, strongly recommended walking. "Habituate yourself to walk very far," he advised; "no one knows, til he tries, how easily a habit of walking is acquired." So what if you had never walked three miles. In a month, he optimistically predicted, "you will be able to walk fifteen to twenty without tiring."[11]

Less than a month later, Jefferson suffered possibly the worst sports injury in pre-presidential history while taking a walk with a female friend. A widower, the American ambassador to France had become infatuated with the seductive Maria Cosway, wife of an artist and herself an artist. On a beautiful September afternoon, Jefferson was engaged in walking and conversing with Maria in Paris when he tried to jump over a fence. No longer a youthful athlete, the forty-three-year-old Jefferson fell on his wrist in what proved to be a compound fracture. In intense pain, the stoic Jefferson completed the four-mile walk to his lodgings, talking quietly to his companion. Unable to sleep, he called for the "surgeons." The French doctors erroneously diagnosed the injury as a dislocated wrist, failing to set the mangled bones. When the swelling and pain persisted, he could not sleep or, for that matter, use his right hand. The little writing that he did in the months that followed had to be done laboriously with his left hand.

In February 1787, still suffering, Jefferson departed on a trip to the baths at Aix in Provence, hoping that the warm and curative waters would heal his wrist. Though the waters did him little good, he went from Aix to Italy, his only trip to a country from which he derived so many of his architectural ideas. After two years, the wrist and hand had still not mended. "I have forever lost the use of my hand except that I can write," he remarked, "and a swelled and crooked fingers still remaining months after the accident make me fear that I still do not know the worst of it." To strengthen his wrist, he resorted to working with a dumbbell.[12]

In a lifetime of spills and falls, many of them from horses, Jefferson continued to exercise on horseback, long after he ceased to walk for exercise. He boasted to John Adams that he could ride to his plantation, Poplar Forest, near Lynchburg, Virginia, ninety miles in the saddle in three or four hours—but could not walk a mile. By 1820 he wrote to Adams: "I can walk but little; but I ride six or eight miles a day without fatigue. . . . Our university [Jefferson's University of Virginia], four miles distant, gives me frequent exercise." In 1822, nearly eighty, he broke his left arm in a fall down the stairs at Monticello. Now he had "two crippled wrists," and a page of writing was nearly a day's work.[13]

Jefferson's wrist injury in Paris was one of the most severe sustained by any president—short of a gunshot wound—but it did not affect his political career. After returning from France, he served as secretary of state, vice-president, and president. He learned to write reasonably well, at first with his left hand and then with his partially healed right hand. Later he acquired a polygraph, a primitive copier, to keep a record of his correspondence, perhaps to reduce his need to copy by hand or to help keep a record of his correspondence. Yet it continued to bother him. Scholars long puzzled as to why Jefferson sold a number of his law books in 1795. After all, he spent large amounts of money acquiring the books and used them extensively, including for tutoring law students. Evidently these "large format books" were difficult for Jefferson to handle after his wrist injury. Instead, he bought a collection of smaller books, which were easier to lift.[14]

One wonders if he could have penned a document as long as the Declaration of Independence, done in several drafts fully ten years before his injury, after his accident in 1786. Or, if in composing the critical passages, the discomfort in writing would have interfered with the result.

While Jefferson was not a presidential sportsman, he did preside over a project that involved great athleticism and endurance. In 1804 he commissioned Meriwether Lewis to explore the vast Louisiana territory recently purchased from France. The Lewis and Clark expedition from 1804 to 1806 was the most successful government-commissioned expedition of the nineteenth century (and perhaps of our entire history), equivalent to America's trip to the moon in 1969. The trip upriver on the Missouri, hunting for food and collecting natural specimens, and the crossing of the Rocky Mountains demonstrated incredible fortitude. Jefferson's vision contributed to one of the most remarkable demonstrations of all-around athleticism. It is doubtful that the twentieth-century feats of aviation and ballooning—even the conquest of Mount Everest—were as impressive as physical accomplishments either by single individuals or members of a group.

It more than redeemed the folly of the broken wrist.

John Quincy Adams: Potomac Fever

John Quincy Adams, the eldest son of Jefferson's friend and, for a time, his adversary, President John Adams, lived a remarkable life as a son of the American Revolution. Accompanying his father to Paris in 1778 at the age of eleven, John Quincy quickly learned to write and speak French. When Adams was sent to Amsterdam, young John Quincy acquired ice skates so he could skate on canals—a sign of his athletic interests.

At the age of fifteen, he accompanied Adams's secretary, Francis Dana, to Russia, to translate French into English for the American envoy (French was the language of the Russian court). During his stay abroad, he spent time in Paris conversing with Jefferson and even had a brief stay in England when his father was appointed the first minister to the court of George III. A few years later, he returned to the United States to attend Harvard, afterward embarking on a legal, diplomatic, and political career.

Although he resembled his balding, rotund father, the son was far more athletic and even engaged in a sport that was considered extreme for his time. In an age when few Americans knew how to swim, John Quincy Adams was a strong and daring swimmer who braved the hazardous tidal currents of the Potomac River.

Adams was called back by James Monroe in 1817 from London, where he was ambassador, to become secretary of state. The dour Adams, who frowned on frivolity and lacked his father's proud and argumentative personality, seems an unlikely candidate for a sporting president. When he was appointed to the peace commission in Brussels to negotiate an end to the War of 1812, he appeared to lack any capacity for relaxing with his fellow commissioners. His colleagues were convivial politicians like Henry Clay, who liked to cap off their diplomatic duties by playing cards into the wee hours. Adams went to bed about the time the games were beginning and arose before daylight as the games were ending.

Yet he made the most of his early mornings, many of them devoted to physical exercise. As secretary of state—and as president—he continued his habit of rising early to read, write, and exercise. Sometimes he would walk or jog four miles in laps from the White House to the Capitol. Other times he would go horseback riding.

When the weather warmed up, he would walk briskly to the Potomac with his servant Antoine. Then he would strip off his clothes and plunge into the water. The New York politician Thurlow Weed, who went out to catch a glimpse of the president, observed "a gentleman, in nankeen pantaloons and a blue pea jacket, walking rapidly from the White House toward the river. . . . I moved off to a respectful distance. The President began to disrobe before he reached a tree on the brink of the river, where he deposited his clothes, and then plunged in head first and struck out fifteen or twenty rods, swimming rapidly and turning occasionally upon his back, seeming as much at ease in that element as upon terra firma." And all this before sunrise![15]

On July 8, 1823, he was swimming when suddenly a breeze came up making the swim more difficult. "It sometimes occurs to me," he confided in his diary, "that exercise and amusement . . . is with constant risk of life." On his fifty-seventh birthday, he swam for an hour with Antoine—the Potomac bridge as his goal. After a half hour, Adams saw that he and Antoine were being swept toward the middle of the river. He turned back, and fifteen minutes later he came ashore at the rock where he had left his clothes. Following his swim, he met with President James Monroe and worked on the document that would later become known as the Monroe Doctrine—possibly the most important foreign policy pronouncement in American history.[16]

In 1825, after being elected president with fewer popular votes than the national hero Andrew Jackson, Adams carried his sporting pastimes with him into the presidency. His latest innovation was swimming with his clothes on. One morning that first summer, Adams asked Antoine to row him fully clothed toward the far shore in an abandoned boat they had come across. But soon the boat sprung a leak, and then up came a breeze from the northeast spinning the boat out of control. The two men began to swim for shore. With his clothes on "and while struggling for life and grasping for breath, I had ample leisure to reflect on my own indiscretion." He barely made it to shore. When he staggered onto the river bank, he shed his shirt, "which had filled with water and hung like two fifty-six pound weights upon my arms." Rumors circulated that the president had been drowned. "By the mercy of God, our lives were spared, and no injury befell our persons," the shaken chief executive wrote.[17]

For the remainder of his term, Adams treated swimming in the Potomac more cautiously. Rather than danger, his early morning swims resulted in embarrassment. Once, he came ashore to find that his clothes had been stolen, so the president was forced to hail a boy who was instructed to hurry to the White House and return with proper garb. Another time, a Baltimore newspaper owner and reporter, Anne Royall, the iron lady of early American journalism, followed Adams to his favorite rock, and, when he was in the water, planted herself atop his clothes. "Come here," she cried, and when he was standing on the muddy bottom of the Potomac, she demanded an interview. Undaunted by the dignity—or lack of dignity—of the presidency, she turned deaf ears to Adams's pleas that he be allowed to get dressed, threatening to scream if he tried to get out of the water. Standing waist-deep in the Potomac, the humbled Adams gave surely the most unusual interview in American presidential history to the determined young newspaperwoman.[18]

After his near fatal attempt to swim fully clothed and the awkward moments at river's edge, Adams was temporarily chastened. He played billiards, did his early-morning jogs, and took up gardening. Nevertheless, Adams was unique among nineteenth-century presidents in his penchant for risk taking, both physical and political. When he was in his seventies, long after he had left the presidency and was serving in the House of Representatives, he appeared before the Supreme Court in the celebrated *Amistad* case. His arguments helped win freedom for the African slaves who had rebelled against their Spanish masters and steered their ship into American waters. Adams also engaged in a personally heroic campaign against southern slaveholders in Congress, a one-man struggle that led to a gag rule prohibiting discussion of slavery on the floor of Congress. "Old Man Courage," as he was called, would outlast the vendetta of the southern slaveholders. The gag rule was repealed in 1844.

Once in the summer of 1846, when Adams was seventy-nine, he decided to swim once again in the Potomac. Three boys who had left their clothes at *his* rock exclaimed, "there is old John Quincy Adams." Adams returned two days later at dawn, and no one had put their clothes on his favorite rock. It could have been his last swim. On February 23, 1848, less than two years after that last recorded dip in the Potomac, he collapsed on the floor of Congress. He died two days later.[19]

Long before Adams's death, a new presidential era began. Henceforth, the presidents were less cultivated and less connected with the politics of the American Revolution or the early republic. More often, the men who occupied the White House arose from the frontier or were expatriate southerners or midwesterners who lived outside the original thirteen colonies. Often they grew up on the frontier and had experience fighting in wars against Native

Americans or hunting and fishing in the vast woodlands and inland rivers. The sporting White House, in which the presidents engaged in physical exercise or outdoor sports, had not yet arrived, but some of the presidents had as younger men engaged lustily in the sporting life.

2

The Sporting Frontier

Andrew Jackson: From the Stables to the White House

Andrew Jackson, whose career of fighting on the frontier stretched from the Revolution to the War of 1812, would be the second general on horseback to arrive at the White House.

While still a young man, he began studying law and also cultivating some of the wealthy men in town by being a true authority on horses and, later, by being a very successful owner of racehorses. Although Jackson had the reputation of being a wild young man, his lifelong love of horses gave him a solid foundation. Jackson not only owned and raced horses, but also made his living from the winnings. He was the first president to make a living from sports (the others: Theodore Roosevelt, who wrote about the outdoors; Gerald Ford, a Yale football coach; Ronald Reagan, a sports announcer; and George W. Bush, an owner of the Texas Rangers).

The young Jackson walked a fine line between wildness bordering on delinquency and the good-ol'-boy sporting culture of the upper classes. Someone who remembered the wild-haired youth described Jackson as "the most roaring, rollicking, game-cocking, horse-racing, card-playing, mischievous fellow that ever lived in Salisbury [North Carolina]." A woman who learned that Jackson was a candidate for the presidency could hardly believe the news. *"Jackson? Andrew Jackson:* The Jackson who used to live in Salisbury? Why, when he was here he was such a rake that my husband would not bring him into the house! It is true, he *might* have taken him out to the stable to weigh horses for a race, and might drink a glass of whiskey with him *there*. Well, if Andrew Jackson can be President, anybody can!"[1]

Jackson also enjoyed cockfighting. One can imagine that this macho sport appealed to Jackson's wild instincts. But breeding and racing horses were among his real passions, another of which was vengeance. Jackson's temper could turn violent when he was provoked, and horse racing was all too likely to lead to blood feuds—matters of honor that had to be settled by duels with pistols.

Later an ambitious lawyer, politician, and landowner in Nashville, Jackson married Rachel Donelson under circumstances that were to vex them both. Rachel had been married and deserted by an earlier husband. Both Jackson and Rachel believed that her husband had obtained a divorce. Months later, they learned that he had not done so until after they were married. They immediately hurried to a justice of the peace and were married a second time in a civil ceremony. For the rest of their lives, stories dogged them both, and Rachel was branded an "adulteress" by Jackson's enemies. Jackson, whose love for Rachel and temper were both legendary, seldom let these slanders go without seeking revenge.

In 1805 Jackson's magnificent thoroughbred Truxton was to race against Ploughboy, owned by Joseph Erwin. The purse was $2,000, and the penalty if either party forfeited would be $800. Ploughboy came up lame the day before the race, and so Erwin had to pay Jackson. While waiting for the debt to be paid, the matter escalated into a war of words over money—and character. But it consisted mainly of verbal thrusts until Jackson received word that Charles Dickinson, Erwin's son-in-law, had insulted his wife Rachel.

Jackson flew into a rage and challenged Dickinson to a duel. Dickinson was not only a dandy but was also reputedly one of the best shots in Tennessee. Not surprisingly, such face-offs were deadly—few duelists missed their target at thirty feet or less. To be sure, duels were occasionally settled before the pistols were discharged—or partially settled, when one of the parties fired into the air, as Alexander Hamilton did in his fatal meeting with Aaron Burr. But Jackson regarded a duel as a fight to the death.

The two combatants took their positions. Dickinson aimed for Jackson's heart and squeezed the trigger, while Jackson, standing ramrod straight, withheld his fire. Amazingly, Jackson did not topple to the ground when struck. He barely flinched, though Dickinson's shot had entered his rib cage near his heart. "Great God, have I missed him?" Dickinson cried.[2]

Jackson could now make his point in a nonlethal way. He could have aimed into the air or disabled him with a shot to the arm or leg—but only if he were someone other than Andrew Jackson. Instead, he carefully aimed at Dickinson's midsection and squeezed the trigger, but the weapon did not fire. He was then allowed to reset the hammer, aim, and fire. His shot struck Dickinson just below the ribs. Jackson left the field with a doctor, his shoe filling with blood. "I believe he has pinked me a little," he confided. Hardly an accurate description, as he had come within inches of being killed. Indeed his steely will was never more evident than in his duel with the young dandy. "I would have hit him," he said, "if he had shot me through the brain." Dickinson survived through the day only to die an agonizing death at nine that evening.[3]

Did Jackson's duel have anything to do with sport or define him as an athlete? While no one today mourns their passing, these encounters did require steady nerves and skill with firearms. Not a contest for the novice or unskilled, since the inexperienced duelist would likely be the one lying dead or bleeding to death on the ground. Compared with boxing and wrestling, dueling could be described as extreme sport.

Jackson carried the souvenir of his duel next to his heart for the rest of his life, causing him periodic medical traumas. In June 1833, while touring New England as president, Jackson was seized by one of these attacks. He would begin coughing and hemorrhaging. The bullet had caused an abscess, which would unpredictably flare up.

His remarkable victory against the British at the Battle of New Orleans in 1815 made him a national figure, who was then reinvented as a presidential contender. At New Orleans, the iron-nerved general commanded an army of Indian fighters, pirates, African Americans, and volunteers that killed 2,037 British while losing only 13 men. The battle actually took place several weeks after the war's formal end, but neither Jackson nor the British had heard the news. What might have been a thrust by the enemy into the recently acquired Louisiana Purchase was nipped in the bud. After this battle, the British never again put troops ashore in American territory—or, for that matter, allowed their army and navy to be dragged into a war against the former colonies.

Whether Jackson's known athletic abilities contributed to his remarkable capacity to command is difficult to know for sure. Yet, like Washington, his skill with horses contributed to his spectacular career. Like Washington, he rode into the presidency as a military hero.

★

Abraham Lincoln: Strong as an Ox

During Jackson's presidency, Abraham Lincoln was establishing himself as a lawyer in New Salem, Illinois. The images we have of Lincoln show a tall, ungainly, and somber character, nothing that would suggest athletic ability and skill.

But Lincoln's intellect is only part of the story. While Lincoln built a career on mastery of the law, he was also known for his physical skills. While living in New Salem, he played town ball (the ancestor of baseball) and quoits (a game that resembled horseshoes), and he was an accomplished swimmer. Unlike the solitary John Quincy Adams or the wild man Andrew Jackson, Lincoln was more sociable than competitive. Lincoln never hunted or engaged in duels; he attended horse races but neither bred nor bet on horses; and, unlike Jackson, he neither drank nor used tobacco.

Abraham Lincoln was known far and wide for his prodigious strength. Once a local gang led by the menacing Jack Armstrong taunted the lean and gangly stranger, challenging him to a wrestling match. A contemporary described Armstrong as "a man in the prime of life, square built, muscular and strong as an ox." When Lincoln agreed to fight, people flocked to town, and many wagered on the outcome. According to eyewitnesses, Lincoln caught Armstrong in a hold, but his adversary broke loose. Armstrong then caught Lincoln by the leg and nearly threw him. In turn, Lincoln grabbed Armstrong by the throat and pushed him at arm's length. One spectator claimed that Lincoln, after failing to throw Armstrong, set him down and said, "Jack, let's quit—I can't throw you—you can't throw me." The wrestling match fought to a draw resulted in a lifelong friendship between Lincoln and Armstrong, and Lincoln would later defend Armstrong's son in a dramatic murder trial.[4]

One farmer recalled that Lincoln in his twenties could lift a thousand pounds. And, if this sounds exaggerated, his friend John Short, who worked with him in the fields, testified that Abe could husk twice as much corn as he could.

In 1840, when he stood for election to the state legislature, a Democrat challenged Lincoln to a test of strength. "'See here Lincoln,'" he said, "'if you can throw this cannon ball further than we Can, We'll vote for you.'" Lincoln picked it up: "'Well, boys, if thats all I have to do I'll get your votes.'" He swung around as if hurling a shot put and heaved it four to six feet, farther by far than anyone else.[5]

So many times it was Lincoln's humor and simple logic that helped him prevent fights or crude pranks. "When a fight was on hand, Abe used to say to me, 'Let's go and stop it. Tell a joke, a story. Say something humorous and end the fight in a good laugh,'" one of his friends recalled. Once, when Jack Armstrong induced an old man to roll down a hill in a barrel for a gallon of whiskey, Lincoln intervened and halted it. Another time, Armstrong called a newcomer a liar, a son of a bitch, and a coward. The two men squared off, but then they agreed to let Lincoln arbitrate. "Jack, if you were a stranger in a strange place as this man is," Lincoln told him, "and you were called d—d liar & c—What would you do?" Armstrong replied that he would hit him. "Well then, Jack," Lincoln reasoned, "this man has done no more to you than you would have done to him." Armstrong conceded the point, and the fight was prevented.[6]

As a young lawyer, Lincoln became a skillful chess player. While playing with his friend Judge Samuel Treat, one of Lincoln's sons came to call him home for dinner. After a half hour, the boy came again, probably sent by Lincoln's wife, Mary. When his father failed to acknowledge him, the child kicked the chess board and pieces into the air. Calmly, Lincoln got up, took his son's hand, and went home to dinner. "Well, Judge," he said as he was leaving, "I reckon we'll have to finish this game some other time."[7]

Although Lincoln had no time for sports as president, he often played a game called fives in the years before his election. Like handball, the players would strike the ball with their hands against a wall. Lincoln was playing the game most of the day before his nomination to the presidency. "This game makes my shoulders feel well," he commented.[8]

Lincoln's sports call attention to his character traits—sociability, ambition, competitiveness, and sense of fair play. In much the same way as he reacted when his son kicked over the chess game, letting fly all the pieces, Lincoln was able as president to pick up the pieces after military defeats and begin again.

When he was young, he did his best to break up frontier brawls; as president, he tried mightily to prevent the secession of the southern states in 1861. His peaceable nature and penchant for reconciling hostile parties, not to mention his physical strength and endurance, serve as symbols of his character and herald his success in seeing the crisis of secession through to the end, while briefly extending a hand of friendship to the vanquished.

★

Ulysses Grant: Born to Ride

Lincoln's favorite general, Ulysses Grant, was also born near the frontier—in southern Ohio in the 1820s. As a farm boy, he displayed one exceptional talent: he could break, train, and ride horses, almost any horse. Even at West Point, he achieved a reputation in only one category—horsemanship. At his graduation in 1843, the riding instructor raised the jumping bar above his own head and called out Grant's name. Cadet Grant rode his horse to the far end of the hall, paused, and thundered toward the barrier. "The horse increased his pace," one observer recalled, "and measured his strides for the great leap before him, bounded into the air, and cleared the bar, carrying the rider as if man and beast were welded together." Grant's record stood for twenty-five years.[9]

During the war with Mexico, four years later, his regiment came under withering fire from the enemy, and Grant volunteered to carry a message to division headquarters. In a brilliant display of trick riding that might have come from a western movie, Grant hooked one foot around the cantle of his saddle, one arm around the neck of his horse, and raced through the streets at full speed. "It was only at street crossings," he remembered, "that my horse came under fire, but these I crossed at such a flying rate that generally I was past and under cover of the next block of houses before the enemy fired."[10]

But Grant's horsemanship proved of no value during the tedium of garrison duty following the war. Soon boredom and loneliness led him to drink too much, and finally he resigned from the army, yearning to be with his wife Julia and their children. Nor did his innate skill with horses equip Grant to earn a living in civilian life, something that Grant failed at before and after the Civil War.

It was only as a soldier that his horsemanship served Grant well. He never acquired the mystique of the glamorous general on horseback like Washington and Robert E. Lee. But none was more accomplished with horses, both handling and riding, than Ulysses Grant. And this was quickly apparent in the Civil War as he rapidly rose to the rank of general. At the Battle of Shiloh, a Confederate attack took Grant and his staff by surprise, placing his army in danger of being decisively beaten and its ranks decimated. Immediately, the general rode his horse at breakneck speed to confer with each of his commanders, to assess his army's predicament, and to rearrange its defenses. Merely waiting for others to deliver him the information would never do for Grant. He and his horse, glued together and racing point to point, turned disaster into victory.

But even the best horsemen can have mishaps. Following the Confederate surrender at Vicksburg, Grant went to New Orleans where a military review was held in his honor. The shrill sound of a railway locomotive spooked his horse, and the animal fell on Grant. He was knocked unconscious and taken to a nearby hospital. "My leg was swollen from the knee to the thigh, and the swelling, almost to the point of bursting, extended along the body to the armpit," he wrote. "The pain proved almost beyond endurance. I lay in the hotel something over a week without being able to turn myself in bed."[11]

In the years after the Civil War, he rarely rode. Yet his interest in horses continued. He had part-ownership in a racehorse, and he once raced his coach-in-four against President Andrew Johnson, whom he would follow to the presidency. According to another story, he was stopped for driving his coach on Pennsylvania Avenue at an excessive speed and forced to pay a five-dollar fine. At Long Branch, a newly built resort on the New Jersey coast, he lent respectability to the newly created Monmouth Park where he went to the racetrack and wagered on the races.

Grant's shift from the man on horseback to the prosperous Victorian gentleman attending races at chic resorts captures the changing nature of the presidency. In an age when most Americans grew up on farms or in small towns, it was hardly surprising that presidents developed hunting, fishing, and riding skills. As adults and sometimes as presidents, these childhood anglers, squirrel hunters, and horse handlers evolved into something more polished—the gentleman sportsman. Some of the presidents spent their leisure on the waters and woods of northern New York and New England. The majority of presidents from Grant to McKinley also spent most of their summers vacationing near the ocean. The three Republicans who followed Grant—Hayes, Garfield, and Arthur—all frequented the fashionable resorts on the New Jersey shore.

Grant may have been the first president—or, more precisely, former president, to swing at a golf ball. While in England on his—and his wife Julia's—trip around the world, he tried out the game that had recently arrived from Scotland. Watching a golf match, he agreed to try a swing. After putting the ball on the turf, he swung and missed. When he tried a second time, he missed the ball. The old soldier made still another futile attempt—after three strikes, and not even a foul ball, he gave up. Grant is then said to have remarked: "It seems to be good exercise, but may I ask what is the ball for?"[12]

The farm boy who performed on horseback as if he were welded to the animal failed to become the first president to hit a golf ball. In the next twenty years, presidents and ex-presidents would swing at the golf ball more frequently, if only slightly more successfully.

3

Barely Visible to Press and Public

The presidents in the late 1800s may have been visible, but their sports were normally hidden from view. In the nineteenth century, sports still bore the imprint of childish games or, in the case of boxing, were regarded as symptoms of moral degeneracy. Yet the games of our presidents, as Grant's later years demonstrate, were evolving into a sporting presidency that would become visible—even the source of news and controversy—during the terms of Theodore Roosevelt and William Howard Taft.

The list of presidents from Grant to William McKinley shows a decline in the rough-and-tumble types and the emergence of gentlemen sportsmen. Many of these public men learned to appreciate the outdoors growing up on farms or in small towns or when traveling out west. After he went on a hunting trip to Texas as a young man, Rutherford Hayes recorded in his diary: "Deer, cattle, cranes, wild geese, brant, ducks, plover, prairie hens, and Lord knows what else often in sight at the same time."[1]

As president, Hayes was criticized for purchasing a set of boxwood croquet balls at government expense for the exorbitant price of six dollars. No doubt he got more exercise and less criticism from riding horseback, doing exercises when he got up in the morning, and walking in the White House hallways after dinner. After his single term in office, he had time for duck hunting near his home in Upper Sandusky (now Fremont), Ohio. He also watched his grandchildren play baseball and ride bicycles.

When these men were in the White House, most of them took their families, as Grant had done, to the New Jersey beaches, where they went to the races, attended balls, and stuck their toes in the ocean. The upper middle class invented the summer vacation that transported them from the stifling heat and humidity of eastern cities to the nearby beaches. The result was the golden age of the Victorian seaside resorts. Besides summer vacations at the seashore, there were still the lakes and rivers of the mountains in upstate New York and New England, which lent themselves to cool nights and sporting pursuits.

★

Chester Arthur: Spoilsman as a Sportsman

Vice-President Chester Arthur became president in 1881 when the recently inaugurated James Garfield was shot by an assassin. A fashionable gentleman, he was also a dedicated fisherman. Indeed, he was, according to historian John Reiger, "reputedly one of the finest fly-casters and salmon anglers America has ever produced." Arthur, a widower, tall and debonair, had gained a reputation as a machine politician—a "spoilsman" in the language of the Gilded Age—and his presidency began with the expectation of corruption. Yet, once in office, he surprised everyone by helping to pass the landmark Civil Service Reform Act of 1883, which created the federal civil service system.[2]

Ever since Ulysses Grant designated Yellowstone as a national park, the park's mission had remained ambiguous. And the park itself was endangered by private developers taking out leases on parklands. To gain support for his struggle to protect the park, Senator George Vest of Wyoming invited Arthur to visit Yellowstone. Arthur had already shown interest in protecting public lands and in solving what was called the "Indian Problem." The desire to extend property and civil laws to Indian reservations resulted in the Dawes Act, which sadly led to the sale of Indian lands and to the exploitation of their national resources.[3]

Arthur, who suffered from bouts of ill health and at the time was feeling acutely the burdens of high office, agreed to Vest's invitation. It was a chance to go where no other president had set foot and to experience the majestic scenery of Yellowstone in a way that few late nineteenth- or even early twentieth-century visitors were able to do. On his trek by horseback across the park, Arthur fished regularly for trout while others in the presidential party hunted for deer and bear. They reached the snow line, experienced the thin, bracing air and chilly nights, and saw meadows of wildflowers adorning the mountainsides. Spectacular opportunities for fishing abounded. One evening, Arthur and Vest, between the two of them, caught 105 pounds of fish.

On August 25 they reached the Upper Geyser basin, where the president saw Old Faithful put on its hourly show. From the lower part of the park, they viewed the jagged peaks of the Grand Tetons, or "Titans," as one reporter referred to them. According to newspaper reports, the president rose at six o'clock and rode on horseback each day for thirty miles through the valleys and across the high mountains. The pack train that accompanied the president numbered 175 horses and mules, and the expedition was commanded by the Civil War cavalry hero General Phil Sheridan. Couriers rode back and forth to keep Arthur in touch with the outside world.[4]

After three weeks of breathtaking scenery, fishing, hunting, horseback riding, and healthy outdoor living, the party arrived at a spur line where the president boarded a train that took him to the Northern Pacific Railroad and back toward Chicago. Arthur had blazed a pioneering path to the Rocky Mountains that other presidents, most famously Theodore Roosevelt, would follow.

Unfortunately for Arthur, political appearances on his return trip sapped his vitality—shaking hands with large crowds of party faithful was always fatiguing—and his health continued to deteriorate. He died in 1886, the year after he left office.

★

Grover Cleveland: Never Met a Fish He Didn't Like

In 1885 President Grover Cleveland left the White House for the funeral of Ulysses S. Grant in New York. The former president had been plunged into bankruptcy when his banking firm failed in 1884. In the final year of his life, he had battled lung cancer while he raced to finish his memoirs so that his family would be provided for. He barely made his deadline, and the book was a postmortem success.

Grover Cleveland—the first Democrat to occupy the White House since before the Civil War—had been elected on a reform platform. After his first four months in office, the bachelor president fled the heat of Washington to the Adirondacks, stopping in New York for Grant's funeral. A fisherman and hunter, Cleveland had already combed the Potomac near the capital for the best fishing spots. Now, as he retreated to Saranac Lake in the depths of the upstate New York wilderness, he left orders that he was not to be disturbed. A lone cabinet member was left in Washington to cover for Cleveland and other government officials. The newspapers soon reported that Cleveland was "lost" in the wilderness, leading to speculation that the president was ailing.

A lone reporter sent by the *New York Post* tracked Cleveland and his party of hunters and fishermen to their remote and crude cabin near the lake. Normally the president had no love for meddlesome newspaper reporters. When this solitary reporter appeared one morning at breakfast, he was warmly greeted and invited to join the presidential party. Grover Cleveland was a large man, more than three hundred pounds in his prime, and the breakfast reflected his appetite. "The meal consisted of broiled venison, baked potatoes, hot biscuits, and tea with condensed milk," the reporter wrote. "It was served on a rough board supported on stakes. Large logs were used as chairs." He added: "Everything was primitive in the extreme."[5]

Some members of the party hunted, but Cleveland fished. Still, the party spent evenings that could not have been quiet. Cleveland had a reputation as a hard drinker and, in his youth, as a tavern brawler in his hometown of Buffalo, New York. Another observer—a college student—who went through their camp soon after their departure saw a number of bottles piled nearby; "some of the bottles were water-bottles—and some were not," in the words of Cleveland's biographer, Allan Nevins.[6]

Cleveland grew up in the pre–Civil War period when game and fish were abundant and the northern woods were largely unspoiled. Years before he became president, he and his friends formed a fishing club. The members bought an island in Lake Ontario and built a handsome clubhouse. Each member had a boat and an oarsman, and behind the procession came a steam yacht with supplies. The club kept count of the day's catch—muskies, black bass, and yellow pike. Each fish was rated by degree of difficulty, and points were assigned. Prizes were awarded at the end of the season. Cleveland was the first commodore of the club and won the prize one year for the grand point total. "Yes, he was as lucky fishing as he has been in everything else," one member wrote, "but then you want to remember that he attended strictly to business when he sat down to it."[7]

Cleveland in 1886 married Frances Folsom, the daughter of his late law partner, Oscar Folsom (he had actually been her guardian). Frances, a recent graduate of Wells College, stepped into the role of First Lady at the tender age of twenty-two. Two months after they were married, Cleveland took Frances on one of his last trips to Saranac Lake. The president spent most of August and September fishing and hunting—and Frances managed to endure the black flies and primitive facilities.

This was Cleveland's final fling at a rustic vacation. Now the first couple looked for a not-so-quite-remote retreat and found at length the perfect location at Buzzards Bay on the neck of Cape Cod. Here the president could fish and putter about his small farm, Gray Gables, which was far enough from towns and railroads that the Clevelands could enjoy privacy without being "lost" in the wilderness.[8]

Cleveland's love of the outdoors translated into mild measures for reform. Though he never went west, he was protective of government lands. When he learned that railroads and cattle interests had illegally appropriated Native American and government lands, he took the complaints seriously. He acted to expel the cattlemen and restore lands illegally appropriated by railroads for homesteading. He opposed the slaughter of game, just as he did the theft of Indian lands, but he failed to propose federal laws that would protect wildlife.

One reason for his inaction may have been that Cleveland never saw the majesty of the forests and wildlife in the mountain West that the business interests were so rapaciously spoiling. His wilderness was the forest and streams of eastern America—and the small but safe perimeter around his rustic cabin. During two Cleveland terms (separated by four years), Congress took no action to extend government refuges. Yellowstone Park, created by Ulysses Grant, would barely survive the rapacious logging, mining, and railroad interests during the first two decades of its existence.

Benjamin Harrison: A Small Sporting Legacy

In 1889, the diminutive Benjamin Harrison of Indiana took the presidential oath and forced President Grover Cleveland to step aside for a term. A brilliant lawyer and an eloquent speaker, the hunched-over president had so little warmth that his political handlers were reluctant to let him meet the public. "I did not want him to freeze it out of them with his hand-shaking," one of Harrison's aides explained after hustling the candidate away after his speech. Barely defeating Cleveland (he received fewer popular votes, but won more electoral votes), Harrison served only one term as president.[9]

Historians have paid little attention to Harrison. With his sour as vinegar personality, he seems to have held the present as well as the past at arm's length. Yet, the reptilian president was a warm-blooded sportsman. Harrison enjoyed duck, quail, and squirrel hunting. During his four years in office, he hunted duck along the rivers and beside the marshes near the nation's capital. Once out of office in 1893, he bought a camp in the Adirondacks where he fished for trout. Back home in Indiana, he had more opportunities for squirrel and duck hunting, and later he would hunt for duck on a trip to California. To keep in shape between trips, he acquired an exercise apparatus known as the Whitney Home Gymnasium and had it installed at his home in Indianapolis.

On a visit to California, he attended a college baseball game at Leland Stanford, Jr. University, which had only recently opened its doors. When the shy ex-president neglected to pay his fifty cents for admission, the Stanford manager—future president Herbert Hoover—walked up to the stands to collect the fee. Harrison gave Hoover—former president to future president—a dollar and refused to take the change. When Hoover protested, Harrison said that they could consider it as an advance against other games he might attend.

Obscure as his presidency was, sandwiched between Grover Cleveland's two terms, Harrison and his secretary of the interior, John Noble, were remarkably active in helping to protect natural resources. Though Noble was not a hunter, he had been persuaded to act by two lobbyists for preservation—future president Theodore Roosevelt and outdoorsman George Grinnell—who pled their case for safeguarding the lands bordering Yellowstone National Park from logging interests. Once Noble approached Harrison, he found him receptive; with the president's approval, a plan was presented to Congress to withdraw forests from the public domain and set aside the first forest preserves adjoining Yellowstone.

In 1895 Harrison became the first president—technically the first former president—to take up golf (Ulysses Grant had hardly given it a sporting chance). Former president is an important—even crucial—distinction because the public surely would have ridiculed a president who regularly poked the ball around a manicured cow pasture. If golf playing proved healthy for John D. Rockefeller at his Pocantico Hills Estate, why not for former presidents? Benjamin Harrison, whose first wife had died while he was president, married the young woman who had cared for Mrs. Harrison in her final illness. Rejuvenated by his late romance, Harrison joined the new Country Club of Indiana and took lessons from the club professional. He bought a golfing outfit of knickerbockers and canvas shoes, and for a short time became an avid golfer (his scores are not recorded). A hundred years before Bill Clinton was giving—and taking—his infamous mulligans, the country club movement had its first post-presidential convert.

Two years after Harrison played his first golf, William McKinley would become the first sitting president to play golf. After trying the game in upstate New York and again in Hot Springs, Virginia, he gave it up. According to golf historian Don Van Natta Jr., his aides thought it would play poorly with the American public.[10]

A bit of doggerel parodied his brief affair with golf.

What degradation may there be
What loss of manly dignity
In coldly driving off the tee?
Or is it that, perhaps, you know
Your limbs, I mean the ones below
In heather stocking clad, would show
But thinly
McKinley.[11]

William McKinley and his adviser Mark Hanna also witnessed a football game between Yale and Princeton when McKinley was governor of Ohio, not long before he ran for president. Unlike Woodrow Wilson and Theodore Roosevelt, future presidents who watched and even managed football, neither McKinley or Hanna was familiar with the game. McKinley kept turning to his friend, bewildered, asking what was taking place. Hanna himself admitted that he too was bewildered. At length, McKinley confessed to Hanna that the whole thing reminded him of the country boy who exclaimed, "They didn't have no game; they got into a scrap and kept fightin' all the time when they ought to have been playin' ball." Apocryphal or not, it points ahead—like golf—to the soon-to-change presidential sporting culture.[12]

Normally sports and games embraced by the presidents reflected the recreations that they had adopted in their youth and young manhood. Befitting the culture of the Virginia gentry, George Washington rode to the hounds and displayed his skill on horseback. Thomas Jefferson went on horseback to and from his plantation at Monticello and walked in Paris. John Quincy Adams, who had spent much of his life abroad, broke the mold by swimming and jogging. Andrew Jackson learned to make his way in the world through horse racing and dueling. Abraham Lincoln engaged in frontier and small-town sports but also learned to play chess. A number of presidents, beginning with Andrew Johnson in 1866 and including Ulysses Grant, who entertained the Cincinnati Redstockings, the first outright professional team, either watched baseball games or invited teams to visit the White House. Grover Cleveland greeted John L. Sullivan, the bare-knuckle heavyweight champion, in a receiving line at the White House.

As the politicians became Victorian men of fashion, they adopted the outward trappings of wealthy sportsmen. Sometimes, like Ulysses Grant, they indulged their love of horse racing and gambling by going to racetracks in Monmouth or Saratoga, wearing stylish clothes. Or, if they liked to fish, they might go to fishing camps—or, in Grover Cleveland's case, to the coast of Massachusetts once Congress adjourned. Chester Arthur, the accidental reformer-president, broke precedent by traveling west to Yellowstone rather than east to his normal fishing haunts. Arthur's trip would prove a forerunner of the western trips before, during, and after presidents served in office.

Yet something that we take for granted was missing from the sports of the men who became president. Few presidents cared to build their political or personal lives around sports after moving into the White House. Practically none of them, even those who fished and hunted, actually created an agenda that included sports.

Sports such as baseball, hiking, or wrestling were an outlet for younger men, and most presidents were in their fifties by the time they climbed to the top of the "greasy pole." To create a sporting presidency, a younger occupant of the White House was required. Theodore Roosevelt would meet this requirement in more ways than one. As the British ambassador would say of Roosevelt, "you must always remember that the president is about six."[13]

To paraphrase the poet William Wordsworth, the boy was father of the man.

The Man Who Changed Everything

*Theodore Roosevelt playing football in the 1890s with the Roosevelt cousins
at his estate in Oyster Bay, New York. Nearsighted and asthmatic, TR never played
college football himself but lauded it as a manly game. In 1905, as president he attempted
to reform the brutality and lack of sportsmanship in football by calling a conference
of advisers from Harvard, Yale, and Princeton, a move that brought to the fore long-
simmering controversies in the college game. Daughter Alice and son Ted are in the
foreground. Courtesy of Theodore Roosevelt Collection, Houghton Library,
Harvard University, Cambridge, Massachusetts.*

4

Theodore Roosevelt
Climbing the Mountain

Theodore Roosevelt, a name synonymous with power, status, intellectual curiosity, and energy, introduced a new era in the sporting presidency. In his attitudes, habits, and sporting interests, Roosevelt marks a clear departure from his predecessors—youths who were rural strong men, horse traders, and solitary swimmers, or farm boys whose hunting, fishing, and riding crystallized into fashionable presidential sports.

Although many of Roosevelt's interests belong to the athletic culture of the earlier century, he was actually a forerunner. More than anyone, he represents a melding of sports and politics that has now become commonplace. As president, his life of active pursuits would raise athletic and outdoor sports to a level never before associated with the presidency. Yet TR not only initiated the twentieth-century sporting presidency but also took it to a level that has never been matched.

Just as he was a political maverick, throwing a scare into the powers-that-be, he also grew into a sporting maniac who literally wore out his sporting companions and competitors.

★

Hunting and Hiking

Born in 1858, Teddy Roosevelt and his brother watched Lincoln's funeral cortege from a window of the family's fashionable townhouse in New York City. Roosevelt's post–Civil War generation stood on the threshold between the disappearing frontier and the emerging urban society. Not only had this generation missed the Civil War, but it was also about to witness the end of the frontier. For those who wanted adventure, the buffalo hunts and open range were waning. And, as gentlemen sportsmen, they would become increasingly aware that the abundant fish and wildlife species that had once inhabited the eastern woods were visibly diminished.

Still Roosevelt refused to acknowledge that the frontier, *his frontier,* had disappeared. He sought pockets of wilderness where the frontier still existed. He hunted the final buffalo, plunged into the cattle ranches of the Great Plains, disappeared into wild tracts of wilderness in pursuit of grizzlies, and researched and wrote a multivolume history of the American West. He not only celebrated the conquest of the frontier, but he also saved portions of it for future generations. As president, Roosevelt set aside great tracts of land for national forests and preserves. Similarly, while he relished his personal wilderness experiences, he augmented public resources by making significant donations to the Smithsonian and the American Museum of Natural History.

Curiously, Theodore Roosevelt's first hunting experience was not on the flyways of the Hudson or Mississippi, but rather on the Nile. His father, Theodore Roosevelt Sr., took the family on travels abroad, and at fourteen "Tedee" was given a gun—and a pair of glasses. Nearsighted and puny, but tough in the ways of the outdoors, Roosevelt would exemplify throughout his life the will to engage in sport, no matter what the obstacles.

As a youngster, Roosevelt was no ordinary teen blasting away indiscriminately at small game, but rather a budding ornithologist and taxidermist who identified and mounted the birds he shot. Like other wellborn Victorian sportsmen, he combined an enthusiasm for killing animals with a detailed knowledge of the targeted natural species.

Despite bouts of asthma, which often made his life miserable, Roosevelt also was an active hiker and mountain climber. After some bullies tormented the scrawny boy on a stagecoach trip, Theodore's father hired a trainer and installed a gymnasium on the back porch of the Roosevelt townhouse and arranged for boxing lessons. Although the bantam-weight teenager did learn to box and wrestle, the chest-expanding and muscle-building exercises did little. When he was seventeen, Theodore stood five foot eight and weighed 124 pounds (later in life his weight would balloon to well over 200).

The regimen that his father pushed the sickly boy to undertake would eventually make him the leading sporting and political figure of his generation and contribute to the rugged image he projected as president. With keen intelligence and dogged determination, he worked to compensate for his slight build and asthmatic condition with truly remarkable energy and bottomless wells of enthusiasm. In his first year at Harvard, his diary was filled with references to physical activity, especially boxing and wrestling. He devoted two-and-a-half hours every afternoon to physical exercise. In October 1877 brief references in his diary show a grimly determined Roosevelt. October 8: "Threw Davis wrestling." October 12: "Threw Ellis wrestling." October 18: "Boxed with

Arthur Hooper. Even. Beat Ellis wrestling." October 22: "Beat Hooper boxing, and also Ellis." November 3: "Hooper beat me badly boxing. I beat Ellis & Brooks." December 15: "Gave red-haired Coolidge a tremendous thrashing in the gymnasium boxing." The insecurity of the scrawny boy bred a determination to succeed that carried over into everything he ever attempted—at Harvard and beyond.[1]

Even though Roosevelt threw himself into becoming a skilled boxer and spent hours learning the art of self-defense, his real passion was hunting. At the end of 1876, his "game bag" tally included 1 buck, 10 duck, 12 snipe, 3 grouse, 6 plover, 4 gray squirrel, 52 trout, and 120 "snapping mackerel." Each year he would add numbers and variety to his hunting tallies.[2]

Roosevelt also learned to play conventional and fashionable sports, notably tennis, recently imported from England. His enthusiasm for this genteel, upper-class sport coincided with the flowering of his sexual and social interests. He wrote in his journals about playing tennis with numerous young men and women, but one of his female companions made a deep impression. Alice Lee, the daughter of Boston blue bloods, loved games such as tennis and was quite good at them. In the winter, Alice was an occasional tobogganing partner. In his junior year, Alice became his heartthrob. With typical Roosevelt resolution, he decided to win her hand. On his first attempt at proposing, he was pleased with himself that she didn't turn him down. As with hunting, he kept firing, sometimes wildly, until he bagged his quarry.

He and Alice were married on October 27, 1880, after he had graduated from Harvard, but not before Roosevelt and his brother Elliott took a final bachelor hunting trip out in the American West. In those days, one could get to the "West" by going to Ohio, Indiana, or Illinois. While staying in spare farmhouses with farm families, they shot prairie chicken, grouse, and quail, often walking the fields in driving rain. "We are dressed about as badly as mortals could be," Teddy wrote, "with our cropped heads, unshaven faces, dirty gray shirts, still dirtier yellow trowsers and cowhide boots." Who would have guessed that this hastily planned trip to the Midwest was the modest beginning of TR's love affair with the American West?[3]

As a newlywed husband, Roosevelt walked six miles a day and drove Alice through Central Park in a horse-drawn sleigh. Upon finishing his spring term at Columbia Law School, Roosevelt took his bride on the fashionable grand tour of Europe. In Switzerland, he could not resist the challenge of mountain climbing. After ascending two smaller peaks, followed by the Jungfrau, he scaled the fifteen-thousand-foot Matterhorn, first conquered only two decades earlier. No wonder Alice didn't attempt to accompany him!

Just before his Harvard graduation, a doctor told Roosevelt that he had a bad heart and that he should avoid strenuous exercise. Roosevelt replied without hesitation: "Doctor, I am going to do all the things you tell me not to do. If I've got to live the sort of life you have described, I don't care how short it is." And he ignored the doctor's advice so completely and, for most of his adult life, so successfully that it appeared that he had been misdiagnosed—until his heart began to show signs of stress about the time he left the presidency.[4]

In 1883 Roosevelt went to the Badlands of North Dakota where he threw himself into a frantic quest to kill a buffalo. That he was bent on destroying one of the few remnants of this species did not deter him. For seven days, he led his reluctant guides across the moonscape terrain of the Badlands in torrential rains in pursuit of the elusive buffalo. He finally bagged one, and afterward he returned to Manhattan. But now he was determined to establish himself as a rancher on the Dakota prairie.

Governor Grover Cleveland of New York would soon have reason to know the name Theodore Roosevelt. Barely out of Harvard and bored by law school, Roosevelt was elected to the New York Assembly where he rose meteorically in state politics to become a leader of the Republican reformers (he also found a young boxer to spar with in his free time). In his first term as an assemblyman, Roosevelt became Governor Cleveland's Republican ally in passing civil service reform. If Grover Cleveland and Theodore Roosevelt had compared notes—and perhaps they did—they would have found that they were both avid outdoorsmen. While Cleveland was inert and phlegmatic, Roosevelt was a doer, whether he was pounding the podium on behalf of legislative reform or pursuing grizzlies. Unlike Grover Cleveland, the youthful Roosevelt preferred hunting to fishing—he could not sit still in a boat.

Once, when Roosevelt left a legislative session, he stopped at a saloon near the Capitol, a favorite haunt of legislators. He encountered a veteran Democratic politician, John Costello, drinking with friends. Costello began to insult the dandified Roosevelt, calling him a "damned little dude." Roosevelt then removed his spectacles and decked Costello with his patented Harvard punches. When Costello got up, Roosevelt hit him again and still another time. Then Roosevelt ordered him to wash up and said that he would then buy him a beer.

"When you're in the presence of gentlemen, conduct yourself like a gentleman," he told Costello before buying him a beer and then forcing him to down his cup of humiliation.[5]

Elected to a second one-year term, he resumed his duties in Albany with the same frenetic energy, but on Valentine's Day 1884 a tragedy occurred that would change the course of his life. After two years of marriage, Alice became pregnant, but instead of happiness, childbirth was to bring tragedy into the Roosevelt household. As she gave birth to Roosevelt's daughter Alice on February 14, Alice unexpectedly died of complications produced by Bright's disease—on the same day and in the same house that Roosevelt's mother, Mittie, died. "And, when my heart's dearest died," the benumbed Theodore wrote, "the light went out of my life for ever." He never wrote or spoke of that terrible day or of his first wife again. He immersed himself hyperactively in state politics at Albany and fought at the Republican convention of 1884 for a reform ticket. And soon afterward, he left for the Dakota Badlands. "Black care [depression]," he wrote, "rarely sits behind a rider whose pace is fast enough." And, as his biographer Kathleen Dalton points out, he would live his life at a very rapid pace.[6]

For a year, Roosevelt, the sportsman, would pour his physical energies into the life of a cowboy. Becoming a part of the booming cattle frontier, he learned to stay for hours in the saddle, rounding up and branding cattle, getting caught in a cattle stampede, and coping with the lawless rabble that came his way.

Roosevelt fell in the middle between a gentleman sportsman and one of the many gentlemen novices who flocked to the Northern Plains looking for a quick fortune. Just as the cowboy depended on his athleticism in and out of the saddle, Roosevelt drew upon his years of physical training—boxing, wrestling, and shooting—to earn his spurs.

Despite his inexperience, he won the grudging respect of the hard-bitten natives of Little Missouri. The transplanted French nobleman, the Marquis de Meres, who like Roosevelt was trying to make a fortune raising cattle, once sent one of his protégés, local cattle boss Jake Maunders, to intimidate Roosevelt, but the dude would have none of it. Roosevelt rode to Maunders's shack, knocked on the door, and let him know where matters stood. "I understand that you have threatened to kill me on sight. I have come over to see when you want to begin the killing and to let you know that, if you have anything to say against me, now is the time for you to say it." That ended that.[7]

His best-known tangle with a gun-toting bully came in the barroom of a small hotel where Roosevelt went to eat. He heard gunshots and saw the ruffian, a gun in each hand, shooting at the clock. As soon as he saw Roosevelt, he cried out: "Four eyes is going to treat." Four eyes laughed with the edgy crowd, sat down, and tried to avoid the bully. But Yosemite Sam came at him with a gun in each hand. It was "high noon" at Little Missouri.

"Well if I've got to, I've got to," Roosevelt said as he got to his feet and punched the man with a right to the side of the jaw, followed by a left, and then another right. The guns fired wildly, and the man toppled over. The featherweight from Harvard had proved that he could throw a punch when it counted. All of that wrestling and boxing again, as in Albany, proved useful. Roosevelt's stock among the local population soared.[8]

And he hunted. He had hardly been in the Badlands for a month when he and his ranch managers and hunting companions, Bill Sewall and Wilmot Dow, embarked on a hunting trip to the Big Horn Mountains of Wyoming. Here was Roosevelt's chance to take on larger game. Finding the tracks of a grizzly, they quickly began their pursuit, and the next day picked up the bear's giant footprints. Roosevelt came upon his quarry ten steps off. He drew a bead on his target and pulled the trigger. "Half rising up, the huge beast fell over on his side in death throes, the ball having gone into his brain, striking as fairly between the eyes as if the distance had been measured by a carpenter's rule." At about twelve hundred pounds and measuring nearly nine feet in length, this grizzly was a "mature" beast, as Roosevelt termed it. Killing grizzlies was part and parcel of Roosevelt's love of blood sport. And, like his other encounters with grizzlies and cougars, hunting in the West seems to have whetted his appetite for larger game as well as for the most dangerous game.[9]

He had missed the Civil War, but he would get his chance to lead an old-fashioned assault against the enemy. His experience as a rough rider on the Northern Plains would lead to the near legendary charge with the Rough Riders of the Spanish-American War at San Juan Hill in 1898—and would propel the hunter-politician into the White House.

In a less obvious way, Roosevelt's hunting experiences set the stage for his crusade on behalf of conserving forests and wildlife. Reconciling the hunting of grizzlies and buffalo with conservation has led some purists to regard Roosevelt as a bogus conservationist. And true, at first glance, Roosevelt hardly strikes us as the poster boy for wildlife preservation. Yet, as a youth Roosevelt had made a hobby of collecting and mounting specimens. He could identify literally hundreds of bird calls. While he participated in blood sport, he respected his adversary. He was well aware of threats to the environment, even if he wanted a piece of the action.

When Roosevelt returned to New York in September 1885, he gradually began his reentry into political life. He had made peace with his tragedy of the previous year or, at least, was prepared to move beyond it. In November he became secretly engaged to his childhood friend and sweetheart, Edith Carow; they would be married in December 1886 in London. While she was not as athletic as Alice, Edith understood her husband's need for strenuous sport—and she offered him companionship on rides and walks, and once accompanied him on a trip to the Badlands.

Roosevelt, the scrawny youth, had grown into the frame that indoor gyms had denied him. Bronzed and bleached, he had filled out around the neck and shoulders. Like a football player in weight training, his neck and upper torso bulged with muscle. His voice had lost the peculiar eastern falsetto that amused and irritated his college classmates and political cronies. Though he would always speak in a high-pitched voice, he now had a more commanding speech that was far more mainstream American. Even his health, which had alternated between asthmatic attacks and a weak heart, had improved dramatically. Descriptions of Roosevelt after his western sojourn referred to him as "rugged." He had won his bet with the physician at Harvard who predicted an early death if he tried to lead an active life.

In 1889 the standoffish Hoosier, Benjamin Harrison, became president. Theodore Roosevelt campaigned actively for the presidential ticket, and Harrison grudgingly rewarded Roosevelt by appointing him to the Civil Service Commission. For the next four years, he would irritate the little man in the White House and the Republican leadership by criticizing appointments and by flushing out the worst of the spoilsmen.

Yet, in spite of the president's distaste for Roosevelt, Harrison and his secretary of the interior, John Noble, were remarkably active in helping to preserve natural resources. As we have seen, Noble listened sympathetically to George Bird Grinnell and Theodore Roosevelt. Convinced by their arguments, the secretary got Harrison's approval of a plan to let the president withdraw forests from the public domain. Noble also insisted on a last-minute change that would have enduring impact on Yellowstone by setting aside a forest preserve adjoining Yellowstone National Park. Logging in and around the park was halted.

★

The Most Dangerous Game

With the explosion of the battleship Maine in the Havana harbor in 1898, the American public and Roosevelt wanted war. The growing crisis in Cuba threatened to bring about the American intervention that he favored. With the Spanish colonial masters fighting a counterinsurgency against Cuban rebels, Roosevelt hoped to see the United States take its place among the great powers. He also yearned to experience for himself the heady experience of leading troops into combat. His father, the first Theodore Roosevelt, had hired a substitute in the Civil War. His son would wipe that stain from the family's escutcheon.

When Congress agreed to raise several voluntary cavalry regiments from cowboys and hunters of the West to reinforce the regular Army, Roosevelt and his friend Leonard Wood seized their opportunity. Together Roosevelt and Wood had spent hours kicking the football and walking in the wild areas near Washington. They talked about the coming war with Spain and how to prepare for it. When Congress declared war, they wasted no time. Roosevelt left his position as assistant secretary of the Navy. Wood, a former Army surgeon and Indian fighter, was commissioned as a colonel and Roosevelt as a lieutenant colonel.

To add a little polish to their band of rough-and-ready westerners, the two Harvard grads recruited a number of athletes from Harvard, Yale, and Princeton and from eastern athletic clubs, along with a scattering of New York policemen. They were joined by a few politicians and General Fitz Lee, Robert E. Lee's nephew. In spite of their designation as cavalry, the regiment ended up in Cuba without horses—all except for Wood and Roosevelt.

The "Rough Riders" began their march on June 22 and continued into a deserted village. On July 1 the Army was poised before San Juan Hill, the last obstacle to Santiago; for Roosevelt, it was the "great day of my life." While the generals had only a fuzzy idea of what was happening that day, the volunteers and especially Roosevelt acted decisively. Roosevelt got his orders to join with a regular unit, though no one knew where the unit was located. Unable to locate Wood, Roosevelt received orders to move up a smaller hill neglected in the planning for the battle. He pushed his men as quickly as possible to the front. Roosevelt resembled the head of a TV crew hell-bent to get to the scene of an impending disaster. When the Rough Riders reached the regular Army unit, the brash, battle-hungry volunteer colonel spurred his horse up the hill as he tried to keep order in the chaotic attack. Halfway up the hill, he ran into a roll of barbed wire. Dismounting, he clambered over the barbed wire and led the charge on foot to the hilltop. The Spaniards fled their trenches. On top, the Americans found a massive kettle for sugar refining, which gave protection against the fire from the Spanish guns and provided a name for the hill they had just stormed.[10]

The nation's best-known war correspondent, Richard Harding Davis, spared no praise: "Roosevelt, mounted high on horseback, and charging the rifle-pits at a gallop and quite alone, made you feel that you would like to cheer." He wore a sombrero decorated with a blue polka-dot handkerchief, which, Davis recalled, "floated out straight behind his head like a guidon." Roosevelt and his men won the battle as they might have won a game, by simply ignoring the size and strength of the opposing team.[11]

There was a lull after the troops reached the top of newly christened Kettle Hill. Spanish fire poured onto them from the commanding Spanish positions, and the troops took cover behind the kettle. In the meantime, other units were scrambling up the larger San Juan Hill. With a shout, Roosevelt sprang into action. He climbed over the rolls of wire fence and started to join the infantry to advance up the hill on foot toward the Spanish fortifications. With Spanish shells crashing around them, few of the men heard their colonel. Accompanied by a mere handful of men, Roosevelt became a moving target for the Spanish riflemen and artillery. Sensing his predicament, he raced back to his men and got their attention by asking if they were cowards. He succeeded. Now his troops followed him racing through the high grass. Most of the Spanish troops abandoned their trenches, but Roosevelt fired his pistol at one of two enemy soldiers. He killed, well probably killed—even Roosevelt wasn't sure if it was his shot—his first and only two-legged quarry. But he was not inclined to be modest in public when it came to blood sport. "I killed a Spaniard with my own hand," he reported, "like a jackrabbit."[12]

Based on what happened—or didn't happen—to Roosevelt that day, someone might have said that the bullet hadn't been made that would kill Roosevelt. One of his troop commanders, a hard-bitten former lawman named Bucky O'Neill, was recklessly exposing himself to Spanish fire. His men implored him to get down. "Captain, a bullet is sure to hit you," one of his sergeants said. "Sergeant, the Spanish bullet isn't made that will kill me," O'Neill boasted. A few moments later, as he was turning around, a bullet went through his mouth and emerged from the back of his head.[13]

George Washington, who made his reputation on the Monongahela, assigned his own survival to Providence. Roosevelt was surely as fortunate as Washington in surviving the unusual risks of San Juan Hill, but unlike the first president he never again went to war. The death and carnage during this charge, while it made for a remarkable day in his life, may have made Roosevelt somewhat more sober. Though he would proudly watch his sons march off to France in 1917, Roosevelt as president never took the country to the brink of war. The advocate of national expansion and the romantic who lusted for combat would turn into a measured statesman. Indeed, the sportsman-soldier won the Nobel Peace Prize only eight years after he led the charge up San Juan Hill.

The Battle of San Juan Hill was more than enough to make TR into a national figure. First, it led to his election as governor of New York in the fall of 1898 and from there to a place on the national ticket as the Republican candidate for vice-president with President William McKinley.

His sporting interests as vice-president and president mirrored those of his earlier years. Roosevelt, one of his era's best-known participants in ultimate sports, had a need to stalk and kill wild game, to push himself to the limit, and to exceed his own expectations. Roosevelt was the undersized boy who challenged everyone and everything. He was competitive in all he did, especially outdoor sports. And for his country and its resources, this personal quest broadened into a national crusade.

But by Roosevelt's presidency, automobiles had begun to replace horses, though Roosevelt would remain a man on horseback who loved riding and insisted on traveling in horse-drawn carriages. Like his contemporaries, he played tennis (though not golf) and polo, and exercised daily on horseback. Yet TR never quite fit into the formal mold of an eastern aristocrat. Just as he had done in his father's house, Roosevelt would transform the White House into a sporting arena, while the District of Columbia and the wild spots in and around it became the equivalent of Roosevelt's backyard frontier. Although the media heard more than they saw of Roosevelt's sporting pursuits, they would use their growing capacity for image building to publicize the president's sporting exploits. Roosevelt's hunting and hiking trips across the West, mixed with political appearances, would create a sporting persona for the president. Politics and sports would forever be joined at the hip.

Presidents change and times change, but since the days of Theodore Roosevelt, sports as a central theme of presidential character has become a norm for presidential behavior as well as a vehicle for public relations. To be sure, TR's high energy approach to his sporting interests and to his politics has not yet been matched by any other president in its scope and intensity, but only reproduced in pieces of the whole. The Roosevelt revolution, though unique, is still representative of something at once new and enduring in presidential politics.

5

Sports and the Presidency
The Founding Father

The young vice-president Theodore Roosevelt was mountain climbing in the Adirondacks when he got a message that President McKinley was near death.

Thinking that McKinley was out of danger after an assassination attempt in Buffalo, he had gone to the hunting lodges near Tawahaus, New York, one of his favorite wilderness areas. Roosevelt had climbed to the summit of Mount Marcy, the highest peak of the Adirondacks. The next morning, while resting on a mountain shelf, he caught sight of a man coming out of the woods, a messenger who bore the news that McKinley's condition had worsened. Roosevelt rushed down the mountain and to a local train station for the unexpected return trip to Buffalo.

By the time he arrived, the president was dead. Roosevelt immediately took the oath of office—at forty-two, the youngest man ever to ascend to the presidency and surely the most physically active. In the next seven-and-a-half years, Roosevelt would establish a number of firsts as president: the first to travel abroad during his presidency; the first to submerge in a submarine; the first to use the Sherman Antitrust Act to prosecute a monopoly; the first to invite an African American, Booker T. Washington, to dine at the White House; the first to act as mediator between warring powers; and, not least, the first president to use sports extensively for political purposes.

Roosevelt's outdoor sports and sporting activities served a far broader purpose than mere recreation. He used his well-publicized hunting and camping trips to familiarize people with the idea of conservation, or what today we call environmentalism. Not by accident, his sporting and hiking excursions allowed him to make important political contacts and to speak all over the country, and conversely his political tours almost always included some rugged outdoor activities.

At home he played regularly—and strenuously. He hiked, swam, rode, wrestled, and boxed in Washington and "scrambled" in the rough woods and

One of many cartoons inspired by Roosevelt's failed bear hunt in Mississippi, where he was reported to have spared the life of a bear brought into camp by his hosts. Here TR in his Rough Rider uniform spares the Good Trust bear but has slain Bad Trust—a caricature of Roosevelt's philosophy toward monopolies. Roosevelt's hunt led to Teddy's bear, or the teddy bear, represented by the cub in the right background. TR embodied not just the great white hunter but also the hunter-sportsman and would later make conservation the hallmark of his presidency. Library of Congress, Washington, D.C.

creeks nearby. The once scrawny Roosevelt, who never ventured nearer a football field than the sidelines, met with sports potentates at the White House to plead for less brutality and more stringent rules in college football, then an amazingly freewheeling and uncontrolled sport.

His lifelong passion for sport was all the more remarkable because of the accidents he suffered while he was president, some resulting from sports. In the fall of 1902, a runaway trolley car in Pittsfield, Massachusetts, slammed into Roosevelt's horse-drawn coach, killing his secret service agent and throwing Roosevelt to the pavement. Roosevelt suffered a leg injury that required surgery and weeks in a wheelchair. This injury never ceased to give him problems, in part because he kept reinjuring his leg through his strenuous pursuits. As soon as he was out of his wheelchair, the president was anxious to test his strength and quickly resumed his pursuit of sports.

Roosevelt had a well-formulated theory of sport when he entered the White House. Like many wellborn, eastern sportsmen and intellectuals, he believed that Americans had become too sedentary. "We were producing in our leisure and in our sedentary lives," he wrote, "a type of man not much above the Bengalee baboo." He also believed that if America was to defend itself and to assume a larger power role in the world, it would have to produce more vital and vigorous young men. "I preach to you, then, my countrymen," he said, "that our country calls not for the life of ease but for the strenuous life."[1]

This president would practice what he preached.

Hunting for Votes

His sporting enthusiasms would transfer seamlessly to the vice-presidency and then the presidency. If he wasn't boxing, he was hunting or hiking.

In January 1901, before becoming vice-president, he went to Colorado for a cougar hunt where he dismounted from his horse and, with his knife, stabbed a wounded cougar to death. Several months later, he attended Colorado's twenty-fifth statehood anniversary and also tacked on a wolf hunt and a fishing trip on the White River.

In November 1902, only fourteen months after he had taken the presidential oath of office, he traveled to Mississippi, ostensibly on a bear hunt. Roosevelt had already shaken up American politics with his unusual White House guests, his attacks on an American monopoly, and the outrageous stories the press reported about his hunting exploits. What Roosevelt considered a bungled bear hunting trip to Mississippi led to the first twentieth-century presidential sporting legend—President Roosevelt and the Teddy Bear.

Though he did want to kill a bear, Roosevelt also had his sights set on the 1904 Republican nomination. He needed the support of influential southern Republicans, few as they were, at the Republican convention in 1904, and he sought out Republican-appointed officeholders. Because African Americans were then overwhelmingly Republican, he argued against the biased laws and constitutional provisions that kept them from voting. But, as a moderate whose mother hailed from the South and who was ready to put the Civil War behind him, he also sought to attract whites in the hope of stitching together a tapestry of a different species of Republican.

The politics proved easier than the Mississippi bear hunt. Desperate to find a bear for the president—any bear—his hunting guide managed to capture an old, lame, undersized black bear. As a sportsman, Roosevelt was disgusted at the idea of shooting the pathetic beast. So the bear was mercifully dispatched back into the woods from whence it came or possibly was killed by its captors. In spite of his love of hunting—and killing—TR despised the slaughter of animals. When he taught his son Archie to hunt, he insisted that the rabbit must be running before the boy shot his rifle.

The bear story, as it evolved, portrayed a kinder and gentler president who showed kindness to animals and bears especially. In short, this virile and manly president had a soft heart. And though, in reality, Roosevelt regarded bears as varmints, worthwhile only as a hunter's quarry, the bear story worked to the president's advantage. A cartoonist for the *Washington Evening Star* cranked out a drawing depicting Roosevelt, the great hunter, standing front and center with a visibly grateful black bear in the background. Gradually the cartoonists reduced the bear to a cuddly cub tied up behind the campfire. In turn, a Brooklyn candy-store owner began selling "Teddy's Bear" and the teddy bear was born.

But Roosevelt saw only the downside of this failed sojourn in the Mississippi woods. He was particularly irritated at the press. Not that this was the era of the paparazzi. But Roosevelt wanted to hunt without the press and to have the press on his own terms. He began to realize that image was a difficult thing to manage, as were his hosts, who were determined to turn the expedition into a picnic. "There were plenty of bears," Roosevelt wrote, "and if I had gone alone or with one companion, I would have gotten one or two."[2]

Bear hunting aside, Roosevelt's outdoor activities would reflect his maturing commitment to conservation. Though he never lost his love for blood sports, Roosevelt experienced a change of viewpoint as a result of a conversation with George Grinnell in 1885. Grinnell, who later helped TR to persuade Secretary Noble to preserve Yellowstone, was a gentleman sportsman, an editor of *Field and Stream*, and an early advocate for conserving wildlife. The encounter occurred when Roosevelt stormed into Grinnell's office and confronted him about several unflattering remarks in a review of Roosevelt's book, *Hunting Trips of a Ranchman*. Impressed by Grinnell's firm grasp of western wildlife (he had accompanied General Custer's 1874 expedition to the Dakota Territory), Roosevelt acknowledged that commercial hunters were slaughtering the wildlife on the western plains. Together he and Grinnell organized the Boone and Crocket Club (Grinnell had already founded the Audubon Society) with Roosevelt as its first president. It consisted of well-born easterners like Roosevelt and Grinnell who believed both in hunting and in the preservation of large game.

Besides George Grinnell, Roosevelt became acquainted with another young easterner, Gifford Pinchot, the chief forester of the United States. Educated at Yale and trained in scientific forestry in Germany, Pinchot's brand of conservation had more to do with using timber reserves intelligently and far less with preserving vast tracts of pristine wilderness. Though devoted to outdoor pastimes like fishing, Pinchot was not as dedicated to nature's aesthetic values or, for that matter, to the wilderness-wildlife ecosystem. After serving as the forester on George W. Vanderbilt's twenty-thousand-acre estate in North Carolina, Pinchot became the chief forester of the United States. In the late 1890s, he also became a friend and later a tennis partner of Theodore Roosevelt.

When Roosevelt became president, he was in a position to pursue the campaign to save both wildlife and forests. To be sure, he never entirely subscribed to Pinchot's philosophy of using the forests solely for utilitarian purposes—that is, intelligent and planned harvesting and reforesting. Nevertheless, as president, he would enlarge the national forest reserves, placing 150 million acres into what became known as national forests.

In 1903 President Roosevelt planned an ambitious trip that would take him to the far ends of continental United States. He would visit numerous states and communities where people had never seen a sitting president. To relax from public appearances, he planned several stops where he could go camping and observe, if not hunt, wildlife. He enlisted John Burroughs, another of his many literary friends, to accompany him on the first leg of the western journey. Their destination would be Yellowstone Park.

Burroughs's books were widely read, and he was admired for his knowledge of birds and was well known to the public. Roosevelt, who in college had considered a career as a naturalist, easily gravitated to literary naturalists, and his extensive knowledge of birds, trees, and large game meant that he could talk intelligently with Grinnell and Burroughs.

Technically Roosevelt could have hunted in Yellowstone, and apparently he considered doing just that. He wrote to the superintendent of the park months before asking about the possibility of killing mountain lions in the park. When the word got out that Roosevelt intended to hunt, newspaper editorials protested in a chorus of criticism. "The image of the President of the United States thundering through a wilderness preserve with shotgun in hand," the *New York Times* objected, "is not one we care to contemplate." Roosevelt realized that hunting might convey the wrong impression. To counter his gaffe, Roosevelt invited Burroughs, the good, gray-bearded naturalist, to accompany him. It would be, he wrote his son Ted, like "the town's prize burglar attended by the Methodist parson."[3]

The trip was more about politics than conservation or wildlife. As he worked his way west, the president met with welcoming committees, paraded through downtown Chicago, attended dinners as the guest of honor, and made speeches. "He usually spoke from eight to ten times every twenty-four hours, sometimes for only a few minutes from the rear platform of his private car, at others for an hour or more in some large hall," Burroughs wrote. The naturalist who led a quiet life away from politics was awed by the turnouts. "The throng that greeted him in the vast Auditorium in Chicago—that rose and waved and waved again," he declared, "was one of the grandest human spectacles I ever witnessed." The trip also took them to the president's old haunts such as the settlements of Medora and Little Missouri near the Badlands of North Dakota, where he had lost a great deal of money in the cattle boom of 1880.[4]

When they reached Yellowstone, the president left his secret service agents, personal physician, and secretary behind—and, wary of newspaper reporters after the Mississippi bear hunt, banished them from the park. Burroughs and Roosevelt spent two weeks in the park visiting many of the sights that Chester Arthur had seen in 1885 and, indeed, that the president had visited ten years earlier. At end of their trek, Roosevelt parted company with Burroughs who continued on a speaking tour. "Oom" (Dutch for uncle) John had proved a pleasant companion—flexible enough to endure TR's bouts of narcissism and flattered to be traveling with the president of the United States. Roosevelt had shrewdly chosen a popular author identified in the public mind with the love of nature, especially birds. By his presence, Burroughs bolstered Roosevelt's image as a political figure who was in Yellowstone to celebrate its natural grandeur, not to blast away at large predators. Burroughs, in turn, was able to turn this experience and other contacts with the president into a book, *Camping and Tramping with Roosevelt.*

Burroughs praised Roosevelt's commitment to nature as well as his camaraderie, although he had trouble keeping up with the frantic pace of the president. Once the president and the sixty-six-year-old naturalist borrowed some skis from the soldiers stationed at Yellowstone and, like two boys out on a lark, raced downhill while taking falls in the snow. Unfortunately, Burroughs, who was growing weary of the president's frantic pace, fell head-first into a snowbank and had to be pulled upright when someone arrived with a ski pole.

Good intentions aside, Roosevelt had difficulty restraining his hunting instincts. Once, he dismissed his military guard and plunged into the woods for a day. There were sounds of gunshots, and when he returned, he had a cartridge burn on his cheek. Presumably he was only targeting "varmints." The public never heard of his brief fall from grace because he had banned the media and, anyway, Burroughs, the "parson," provided a convenient cover.

Roosevelt continued on his trip to Yosemite in California, where he met with John Muir, a naturalist and author, more of a rock hugger than a tree- or bear-hugging sportsman like TR. As founder of the Sierra Club, a marathon hiker, and a naturalist with a profound reverence for the untrammeled wilderness, Muir would be far better known to future generations than Burroughs. In spite of the president's plea to avoid political discussions, Muir lectured Roosevelt on the need to preserve all of Yosemite, including the basin known as Hetch Hetchy, the proposed site for the San Francisco reservoir that would later set off a bitter controversy between Muir and Pinchot. Muir's interests extended to rocks, stones, and trees; unlike Roosevelt, he had no interest in birds, let alone hunting, which no doubt made their relations less chummy than those of Burroughs and the president.

The president's tour lasted for more than two months, and most of it was drearily political. The only other stop that rivaled Yellowstone and Yosemite was the Grand Canyon, where Roosevelt mixed with a group of Rough Riders and politicians. In spite of the time away from Washington—and Edith—the trip allowed him to make a personal inventory of the West's natural resources and bond with the constituencies that would determine his future in the election of 1904.

In a less obvious way, the trip indirectly contributed to his preservation of the nation's imperiled wilderness. Out of his presidency would come five new national parks—Crater Lake in Oregon, Wind Cave in South Dakota, Platt in Oklahoma, Sully Hill in North Dakota, and Mesa Verde in Colorado. He also established four extensive game reserves in Oklahoma, Arizona, Washington, and Montana. The game reserve in Montana, established his last day in office, would be home to small herds of buffalo, the same animal that Roosevelt—and his brother Elliott—had helped hunt to the brink of extinction in the early 1880s.

Roosevelt's trips in 1902 and 1903 added a luster to the sporting presidency. Those to Yellowstone and Yosemite stand out as far more important than the whistle-stops and schmoozing with local Republicans—and far more precedent setting. Other presidents, including Roosevelt's successor, William Howard Taft, and his cousin Franklin Roosevelt, embarked on political tours to distant states and scenic locations. Later presidents, who had Air Force One at their disposal, combined their sports interests, usually golf, with political junkets to strategic states. One president, Richard Nixon, would turn Roosevelt's active athletic presidency into a sports *spectator* presidency, using sports events and personalities to burnish his never-quite-sporting image. But none ever equaled Theodore Roosevelt as a presidential sportsman.

Compared with that of later presidents, the Roosevelt sporting presidency was hardly imperial. He did not set sail for Caribbean islands as did his cousin Franklin Roosevelt or travel a thousand miles, as Richard Nixon was to do, to crown a national college football champion. He occasionally took his family members along when he rowed to a camp site at his home in Oyster Bay, New York. Presidents have rarely cared to endure the harsh conditions that Roosevelt experienced. But, like Roosevelt, they have combined politics with sports.

Indeed, political appearances connected with sporting events such as attending the Army-Navy football game or meeting with sports teams and celebrities—even later trips by train and plane to sporting venues such as golfing meccas—all have their origins in Theodore Roosevelt's athletic presidency.

★

Hitting the Line Hard

Organized sports rarely invite presidential intervention. Yet, in October 1905, Theodore Roosevelt, who had never played football, invited two representatives each from Harvard, Yale, and Princeton to discuss the brutality and lack of sportsmanship in the college pastime. The meeting came in response to a plea from the president's friend, Endicott ("Cotty") Peabody, headmaster of Groton School.

Roosevelt had previously been a staunch champion of football. In 1895 he wrote Yale's Walter Camp, "the father of American football," affirming his support for the controversial sport. Having suffered broken shoulders in rounding up cows and concussions playing polo, he had no objection to the physical punishment that football exacted. His injunction to youngsters: "Hit the line hard; don't foul and don't shirk, but hit the line hard!"[5]

He and Peabody may have read the same investigative, muckraking articles in *McClure's Magazine* in the summer of 1905. Reporter Henry Beach Needham, one of TR's many "friends," had criticized the abuses of the amateur code by eastern schools, including Harvard and Yale. Needham described how eastern universities ransacked the prep schools—and other colleges—for promising talent and how they found ways to reward outstanding players, either with money or in kind. He even described instances of intentional violence. One of the most blatant led to the broken collarbone of an African American player for Dartmouth who was "put out of business" in the first few minutes of the Dartmouth-Princeton game.[6]

To an audience packed into Harvard's Memorial Hall, Roosevelt gave a blistering commencement speech at his twenty-fifth Harvard reunion. He condemned both the lack of sportsmanship in football and unethical practices in business. Speaking before an overflow crowd of 2,500, he urged those in the graduating class to apply college ideals to their future careers and to avoid becoming "glorified pawn brokers." (No pawnbrokers were present to give their side of the story.)[7]

Needham's articles and Roosevelt's speech may have influenced Peabody. In September he wrote a letter to Roosevelt asking him to call a conference of eastern colleges to discuss the brutality and lack of sportsmanship in football. With one son, Kermit, playing football at Groton and the other, Ted, about to try out for the Harvard freshman team, the president was especially interested in football. In the summer of 1905, he had successfully arbitrated the Russo-Japanese War. Why not college football?

A persistent rumor holds that Roosevelt threatened to issue an edict that he would shut down football if the colleges refused to make reforms. That was certainly not the case. Roosevelt could no more abolish football than he could eliminate the colleges that sponsored the teams, except perhaps at the military academies. Anyway, he believed in football just as he believed in free enterprise and the American military—two institutions that he criticized during his presidency. "I would rather see my boys play it," he declared, "than see them play any other." As he did in public life, he attacked excesses in order to restore a balance. So it was with football.[8]

Roosevelt held his meeting at the White House on October 9, 1905, the Monday after the start of the college football season. His goal was to keep the meeting small and informal. He invited only the six delegates, two from each of the most prestigious schools—Harvard, Yale, and Princeton. These three schools, which in college football were like Notre Dame, Oklahoma, and Southern California in the mid-twentieth century, could provide, the president believed, the leadership necessary to restore fair play. In 1905 football did not have the elaborate organizations and highly paid coaching staffs, and the salaries of the highest paid coaches—Columbia and Harvard—barely topped six thousand dollars. Because he was a Harvard graduate, Roosevelt also invited Secretary of State Elihu Root, a Yale grad, to keep the scales from tilting in favor of Harvard.

The meeting began with a luncheon in the White House dining room. To make his point in an evenhanded way, the president cited examples of unsportsmanlike play by each of the colleges. He deplored the practice of coaching players to injure their opponents. After lunch, he led the group to the White House porch where he instructed them to continue the discussions while he attended to work. When he returned, he asked the six gridiron gurus to draft a statement on their trip home pledging their schools to carry out "in letter and in spirit the rules of the game."[9]

Roosevelt's intervention resulted in a wave of publicity. On October 10 an editorial in the *New York Times* commented favorably on his intervention. "Having ended the war in the Far East, grappled with the railroad rate question . . . prepared for his tour of the South and settled the attitude of his administration toward Senator Foraker, President Roosevelt to-day took up another question of vital interest to the American people. He started a campaign for reform in football." Roosevelt later remarked that he found his attempts to resolve the conflicts in football more complicated than his recent efforts in arbitrating the Russo-Japanese War. Certainly his intervention proved less successful.[10]

Far from elevating the tone of football, Roosevelt's intervention only focused public scrutiny on the game—and, for the worse, because it uncorked criticisms that had been bottled up for more than a decade. As it turned out, the 1905 season brought about an unprecedented number of recorded fatalities and injuries (though all but three deaths took place outside the college game) and led to a radical reform of the rules before the next season began.

The brutality and unsportsmanlike play that the president had hoped to keep at bay was emblazoned across the sports pages of major daily newspapers. In the Harvard-Yale freshman game, the president's own son, Ted, the smallest player on the Harvard line, had his nose broken. At first, Teddy was proud of his son's gritty performance. Pride turned to concern when he learned that Ted had gone to a doctor in Boston for surgery. Unlike her husband, Edith Roosevelt blamed Yale for intentionally singling out the president's son—and "putting him out of business."

In the Harvard-Yale varsity game, a brutal act made a mockery of the White House meeting. Fielding a Yale punt, Harvard back Francis Burr called for a fair catch, only to have two Yale players run into him at full speed breaking Burr's nose and knocking him out of the game. The official, an instructor at the Naval Academy, failed to call a penalty. Normally at loggerheads, Roosevelt and President Charles Eliot of Harvard for once agreed—Paul Dashiell, the official, had been derelict in his duty. Roosevelt, who was Dashiell's boss as commander in chief, held up his appointment as a tenured professor while he made pointed inquiries. Chastened by his failed attempt in October, Roosevelt never directly involved himself in the storm of criticism that broke into the open after the end of the season. He had learned that presidents have less influence over sports than they do over foreign conflicts.

Why did Roosevelt feel so strongly about a game that he had never played?

Like other patrician intellectuals and sportsmen, Roosevelt felt that American boys were going through a crisis of manhood. He believed that these molly-coddles ("mama's boys") were cozened by doting mothers who permitted them to grow up effete and sedentary. Roosevelt coupled this notion with his dark forebodings about the swelling hordes in the underdeveloped world as well as the threats of rapacious rulers, such as Kaiser Wilhelm of Germany, in more advanced countries. How could Americans take their place on the world stage—a stage that he had helped to erect in 1898—if they produced a generation of weaklings? Rugged sports like football were his antidote. His friends—and guests at the White House—included rough-hewn boxers such as John L. Sullivan and Frank Fitzsimmons.

That said, Roosevelt's intervention in organized sports has practically no parallel with the possible exception of Franklin Roosevelt's injunction to Commissioner Kenesaw Mountain Landis to continue major league baseball in World War II and Bill Clinton's failed attempt to settle the baseball strike of 1994–95. Other than baseball and football, only the Olympics have galvanized a president. Jimmy Carter would use an Olympic boycott in 1980 to bludgeon the Soviets. Unlike Carter, Roosevelt refused to be drawn into an international sporting controversy.

Not that he didn't have his chance. In 1904 Roosevelt turned down an invitation from Pierre Coubertin, the founder of the modern Olympics, to be president of the Olympiad in St. Louis. It was just as well; the Olympics didn't draw many foreign athletes, and visitors were far more interested in the spectacle and excitement of the St. Louis World's Fair. Again, four years later, during the London games, Roosevelt kept his distance and was careful not to be drawn into an Olympic dispute. The brouhaha began when the American flag bearer refused to dip the flag when he passed the royal box. The British spectators saw this as an affront to the king and queen and a political gesture that should not be ignored. To be sure, many on the U.S. team were Irish Americans who opposed British rule in Ireland. Later, in the 400-meter track event, the British judges disqualified a Cornell athlete, J. C. Carpenter, accusing him of elbowing and blocking. Old rivalries die hard, especially in athletics.

To Americans—and to Roosevelt—it appeared that the British were blatantly biased against the Americans. An even more controversial incident occurred near the end of the marathon. As the runners neared the Olympic stadium and the finish line, the leader—Dorando Pietri, an Italian—had barely enough strength to stagger into the stadium, let alone reach the finish line. Not far behind in second place was Johnny Hayes, an Irish American runner. When Pietri collapsed on the track, sympathetic officials carried him across the line. Up went the Italian flag, and the queen awarded Pietri the gold medal. After the Americans protested, the International Olympic Committee gave the race to Hayes, but the British press lambasted the Americans as poor sports and poor losers.

Roosevelt agreed with the American press and public. When an American magazine, *Outlook*, took the British side against Carpenter, Roosevelt objected publicly. He had a young cousin at Yale who had competed against Carpenter at Cornell. "He says that he is a good, straight fellow and that there has never been a suspicion of crookedness about him," Roosevelt insisted. He was also familiar with the tug-of-war event, for which the British officials allowed their own team to wear hobnails and steel plates in their shoes but required the Americans to wear nongripping-type shoes.[11]

All in all, these controversies ignited a journalistic free-for-all, made worse by the British embassy publishing the grievances against the American athletes. Roosevelt, even though he viewed this display of British "fair play" as patently unfair, refused to leap into the fray. "I have seen these athletic rows again and again," he wrote the British ambassador, "and when they have once started, time and silence are the only sure remedies."[12]

Even so, Roosevelt greeted the American team at Oyster Bay. Congratulating Johnny Hayes: "This is fine, fine, and I am so glad a New York boy won the Marathon," he bubbled. "By George, I am so glad to see all you boys." Roosevelt's greeting of an American team of athletes soon became a presidential tradition. But beyond giving warm greetings and a hearty handshake, Roosevelt was careful to keep his distance. What seemed like a fiery cauldron was simply a tempest in a teapot.[13]

★

Beyond the Beltway

In January 1909 Teddy Roosevelt was a lame-duck president but there was nothing lame, weak, or unambiguous about the test of strength and endurance that he meted out to his military commanders before he left office. Roosevelt had earlier expressed his displeasure with colonels and majors who were "wholly incapable of undergoing any sustained physical exertion and were not able to even ride at any speed a moderately good horse."[14]

Given the president's remarkable stamina and fierce competitiveness, it's not surprising that some of his peers couldn't keep up. Just as the president was bemoaning the military's fitness, General J. Franklin Bell suggested that the president invite the War College and the General Staff to take a hike through Rock Creek Valley. Perhaps Bell was hoping to demonstrate his own fitness against the frailties of the others, but nothing of the kind occurred. During the outing, Bell lagged behind Roosevelt and had to stop several times to catch his breath. To make matters even worse, near the end of the hike, the president scaled a sixty-foot cliff, while many of the others avoided the climb altogether by making a detour. Upon descending the far side, the president "stepped off the bank about four or five feet high, up to his chest in about as cold water as I ever felt," an aide reported.[15]

Roosevelt considered military officers different from portly diplomats, and he demanded that they be fit enough to go into combat at a moment's notice. Roosevelt issued an executive order to the Army and Navy requiring a fifty-mile hike over three days and, for mounted troops, a ninety-mile ride, also to be completed in three days. Grumbling among the officers got back to the president, so he decided to do the ninety-mile ride himself, thinking that his example should stop the grumbling once and for all. His personal physician, Admiral Presley Rixey, had initially suggested that he—Rixey—make the ride. The president now insisted that he, too, should ride to Warrenton, Virginia, fifty miles away—and back. No wonder his daughter Alice once commented that "he wanted to be the bride at every wedding and the corpse at every funeral."[16]

Thus, on a dark and frigid January dawn, the expedition began. Roosevelt himself confided to his military aide, Archie Butt, that he was dreading the ride. But he felt that the backbiters would force his successor Taft to rescind his fitness order unless he made a dramatic gesture. If the order was too severe, well, they would soon know. The cavalry were to provide fresh mounts for Roosevelt and his party at several locations on the fifty-mile ride to War-renton and back home again. From the first moments, the riders bent into a full winter gale. TR's loyal aide and companion, Archie Butt, wrote, "the roads were the very worst I have ever seen, the weather execrable and the horses, with the exception of those we owned ourselves, about as bad and rough as it was possible to turn out from a cavalry post."[17]

Reaching the Potomac and slowly crossing the frozen bridge into Virginia, the roads soon deteriorated. Furrowed into frozen mud, they kept the horses from trotting, except for brief stretches when they could gallop. Periodically they were met with fresh horses, but the quality of their mounts rapidly deteriorated. Typically, while everyone was immersed in his own misery, Roosevelt was exuberantly telling stories, shouting over the roar of the wind. He regaled his comrades with tales of his youth, his mother, the Civil War. When the party reached Warrenton, the whole town turned out to meet the half-frozen entourage led by the high-octane president. A brief speech, a quick meal, and off they went on their return home, riding into a fierce winter storm. "The wind was blowing a gale and the ice cut our faces so that I thought mine must certainly be bleeding," Archie Butt wrote. Ice had begun to coat the president's spectacles, blinding him. His horse wandered off the road into a ditch, but luckily the horse did not stumble or toss Roosevelt out of the saddle.[18]

At long last, the lights of Washington provided light enough to guide them through the inky darkness. The sleet turned to snow, which covered the ice and enabled the horses to make better time. After nearly seventeen hours, they reached Aqueduct Bridge (now Memorial Bridge). A carriage had been ordered to meet them, and the streets of Washington were icy and dangerous. But the president refused to stop until they reached their final destination. "By George, we will make it to the White House with our horses," he exclaimed, "even if we have to lead them [by the reins]."[19]

The adventure was pure Teddy—the boy-man who needed to prove his virility. No sitting president had been so outrageously physical before or after, or, for that matter, needed or wanted to be. In truth, no president after Roosevelt would have been permitted—for personal safety and national security reasons—to attempt such a hazardous feat.

Roosevelt's bravado would not go unnoticed by future generations. During the Kennedy administration, the story of Roosevelt's ultimatum to the military surfaced. The result was a call to the military—and administration officials—to set an example to show their fitness by making a fifty-mile hike. Some younger members of Kennedy's best and brightest, including Attorney General Robert Kennedy, hiked fifty miles from Washington to Camp David. Young President Jack Kennedy, hobbled by a bad back and suffering from Addison's disease, may even have wished them all a fond farewell, knowing that they could look for him in his presidential limo at their destination.

★

TR: Tree Hugger

In considering American sporting presidents, and in particular Teddy Roosevelt with his intense interest in all things natural, the reader may become perplexed. Is Roosevelt to be vilified for his love of hunting and of killing hundreds of animals for the pure sport of it? Or does he deserve unqualified praise for his significant and real contributions to America's hundreds of wildlife refuges, national parks, and bird sanctuaries? With Roosevelt, separating the gentleman sportsman from the conservationist is next to impossible. The two tendencies grew out of the same enthusiasm for wildlife and the outdoors. Only Teddy's blood lust looms slightly larger than life because he managed to become president, to write extensively of his hunting adventures, and ultimately to gaze down on America from Mount Rushmore.

No wonder he considered a career as a naturalist when he was an undergraduate at Harvard. When he was outside his rustic cabin south of Charlottesville, Virginia, in 1907, Roosevelt spotted a small flock of passenger pigeons flying over. He reported this sighting to his friend and famed ornithologist John Burroughs. Though Roosevelt had seen only twelve birds, the sighting was significant. Thirty years before, flocks numbering more than 2 billion had darkened the skies. But, sadly, wholesale slaughter had decimated the species. Things were such that in 1913, in a Cincinnati, Ohio, zoo, the last passenger pigeon died, eliciting a heartfelt tribute from TR.

Historians have argued at length whether Roosevelt truly cared about preserving forests and wildlife. Some environmentalists have accused him of caring only for an environment that could be harvested like a farmer's crop—an apt comparison that Roosevelt and Pinchot often used to sell their foresting programs. To be sure, no one ever suggested that Roosevelt was a tree—or rock—hugger of the likes of John Muir. He was not, but the mature Roosevelt did care about preserving wildlife and wild places. In 1902 he began the first bird sanctuary at Pelican Island in the St. John's River in northern Florida. Commercial hunters were slaughtering exotic birds for their plumage. The Pelican Island preserve would stop that and would lead to many more wildlife refuges.

As a lifelong hunter, Roosevelt found indiscriminate killing distasteful. While a Harvard student, he wrote to a classmate, "as you know, I don't approve of too much slaughter." During his presidency, Roosevelt created fifty-one wildlife preserves. From his earliest days, his interest in hunting, mounting specimens, and identifying birds flowed from his very comprehensive reading and study of nature, as well as his extensive "field work." The vast increase in protected forest lands during Roosevelt's administration was part of his conservation ethic. Here was a president who was willing to act decisively to get his way, even if he had to play an occasional shell game with Congress.[20]

In 1907 a rider on an agricultural appropriations bill would have forbidden the president from creating further forest preserves in the Pacific Northwest. In the ten days before the bill went into effect, Roosevelt established twenty-one new forest preserves consisting of 16 million acres. He wanted to keep these lands from falling into the hands of "lumber syndicates" and to "keep them unimpaired for the benefit of children now growing up to inherit the land." Thanks to his foresight, the children of whom he spoke and their children would be able to use these lands as unfettered areas for recreation, leisure, and pure appreciation of nature.[21]

Before Roosevelt left office on March 3, 1909, he held a White House conference of governors and government officials on the topic of conservation. But he was also busy making plans for the biggest hunt of his life—a safari to East Africa to hunt tigers, rhinos, and elephants. Again Roosevelt believed in doing nothing by half; the conservationist-hunter went with his son Kermit to kill but also to collect and bring back thousands of specimens of Africa's grandest and most exotic wildlife for the Smithsonian Institute.

Big, bigger, biggest! Teddy believed in doing nothing by half.

From the very beginning, Roosevelt's pursuit of the "strenuous life" had taken its toll. What some people might find amusing was for Roosevelt a test of will. A wild ride through a snowstorm, dangling on a rope above a raging river, slogging through icy waters might be dramatic moments for the media—and historians—but they exacted a price from this highly active, sporting president. The press sometimes found the first president Bush's hyperactive sporting life excessive; yet neither the energy that the senior Bush devoted to sports nor the risks that he took ever approached Roosevelt's. One can only imagine what the media would do today if they had a Teddy Roosevelt to follow—it wouldn't take the *New York Times* or the *Washington Post* long to find TR just a little crazy.

During his presidency, Roosevelt dominated the news with his hunting, horseback rides, his memorable phrases, opinions, travels, friendships, and audacious thrusts into controversies that traditionally lay outside the presidential realm. And, by so doing, Roosevelt camouflaged his own inevitable compromises and shortcomings as president. His hold on the presidency, while secure, was never quite as secure as he would have liked. But because public attention was focused on his colorful personality and his personal exploits, his presidency seemed all the more potent and effective.

This was the sports presidency that was visible to press and public. Inside the White House, across Rock Creek Valley, and at Oyster Bay, New York, the indefatigable Roosevelt competed in a more private and personal sporting arena.

Inside TR's Sporting Presidency

Unlike his well-publicized hunting trips, much of Teddy Roosevelt's daily exercise took place closer to home. Beginning with Ulysses Grant, presidents normally left the White House for two or three months each summer to escape the sweltering heat in Washington. Likewise, Roosevelt and Edith along with their five children went to their Long Island home, Sagamore Hill, where the breezes off Long Island Sound made the summer far more bearable.

There, or in Washington, the Roosevelt family reflected the vigor and high voltage of the president. Although Edith Roosevelt was not as energetically athletic—how could she be?—she did share her husband's love for the outdoors. At Oyster Bay, Edith and Theodore rowed around Long Island Sound, rode horseback together, and enjoyed many hours of bird watching. In addition, the youthful first couple's five energetic children kept both the domestic White House and the summer White House lively and newsworthy.

Roosevelt's daughter Alice, from his first marriage to Alice Lee, who was seventeen when he became president, had the evanescent beauty of her mother (the song "Alice Blue Gown" was written in her honor) and the energy of her father. Then there were Ted, Kermit, Archie, and Quentin and daughter Ethel. All the boys shared their father's enthusiasm for sports and outdoor interests and kept an array of wildlife in the White House, including alligators—and even Ethel occasionally joined in the childhood high jinks. Not to mention the president's pillow fights in the White House with his two youngest, Archie and Quentin.

With their father's encouragement, Archie and Quentin also became hands-on naturalists—in other words, they captured and kept whatever they could get their hands on. When the president returned from his two-month western trip in 1903, he brought a baby badger from Kansas. The boys found turtles and snakes, which they kept at the White House. To his father's amusement, Quentin had a "very friendly King snake" and two smaller snakes in

Theodore Roosevelt posing with the "tennis cabinet," those insiders who joined him on the White House tennis court. An all-season player, the president attacked tennis with the same vigor and intensity that he scaled cliffs and rode horseback in Rock Creek Valley. Among those in the photo are Captain Archie Butt, Chief Forester Gifford Pinchot, future secretary of war and state Henry Stimson, French ambassador Jules Jusserand, Yale football great Pudge Heffelfinger, Secretary of the Interior James Garfield, Secretary of State (and TR classmate at Harvard) Robert Bacon. Some of those pictured were TR's playmates in other pursuits. Missing is son Ted who played when he "blew into town." Courtesy of Theodore Roosevelt Collection, Houghton Library, Harvard University, Cambridge, Massachusetts.

their collection. One day he burst into his father's office as he was meeting with Attorney General Charles Bonaparte. Quentin dropped the two small snakes in his father's lap. In the meantime, the king snake was trying to devour the smaller snakes. Then the boy raced into the next room where two congressmen were waiting and presented them with his trophies. Roosevelt could hardly keep from laughing.[1]

One of the favorite outdoor sports for Roosevelt and his boys was a game called point to point. Beginning from a fixed point, often in Rock Creek Valley (now Rock Creek Park) in Washington or at Sagamore Hill on Long Island, the participants had to walk up, across, and through whatever stood in their way. It was a purer form of what the president called "scrambling," hikes through rugged terrain on which the president often led unsuspecting diplomats and visitors.

Compared with today's presidents, the chief executive had a flexible schedule. There were days when Roosevelt's desk calendar was empty (in the early 1900s, visitors could still walk into the White House and ask to see the president). Roosevelt organized his days so that he played tennis three times each week—a relatively relaxed schedule for TR (once, in his twenties, he had played ninety-one games in a single day). The men who played alongside or against the president—at least thirty in seven years—were dubbed the "tennis cabinet." Among the participants whose names appear most frequently were Bob Bacon, assistant secretary of state (and briefly secretary of state); chief forester Gifford Pinchot; James Garfield, secretary of the interior; and even young Ted, when he "blew" into town. Occasionally, one of Roosevelt's favorite sporting diplomats, French ambassador Jules Jusserand, played as well.

According to his son Ted, the president played tennis in an unorthodox, cramped style. "He gripped the racket way up the handle with his index finger pointed along the back," he recalled. "When he served he didn't throw the ball into the air but held it in his left hand and hit it in between his fingers," Ted explained. Despite his serve and his ballooning weight, Ted recalled that his father "played a surprisingly good game."[2]

The games were vigorously contested, and no slackers were tolerated. Once, just as a doubles match began, the rains descended in full force. Instead of stopping play, they all played even harder. The balls wouldn't bounce, and the players were slipping and falling. By the third set, things became farcical. "While people looking on might think us insane," Roosevelt remarked, "yet we could get just as much exercise playing water tennis as water polo," and good exercise at that.[3]

★

Living on the Edge

Frequently, the president took a party of political cronies or diplomats on hikes through the untamed land of Rock Creek Valley or along the banks of the Potomac.

Roosevelt made the woods, trails, creeks, rivers, and craggy cliffs and rock formations into his own wilderness preserve. Here he would ride with Edith, hike through the woods, scale the slippery and treacherous cliffs, and swim in the nude. Roosevelt used *his* physical stamina to test the mettle of the people around him. It not only gave him an insight into their character but also provided a platform to show off his own prowess.

His disregard of danger and fatigue was a lifelong characteristic. On a hunting trip to Montana in 1886, Roosevelt encountered a waterfall so striking that he wanted to photograph it. Jack Willis, his hunting guide, "tied two one hundred-foot lariats together, made one end fast to a tree and looped the other to a tree." Then they lowered him into the canyon so that he could take his photo of this grand sight. After he had taken three shots, he called for his friends to haul him up. But the men on top could not budge him. As a result, Roosevelt dangled over the stream and falls for two hours until Willis devised a method to rescue him "without losing the camera or his life."[4]

When Teddy Roosevelt invoked a West African proverb to illustrate his approach to the Monroe Doctrine—"Speak softly and carry a big stick"—the words could also apply to "single stick," a jousting game that he played with his old friend General Leonard Wood. After his trolley accident in 1902, he wrote to his son Kermit: "General Wood is acting as my playmate now." No more scrambling or equestrian activities in Rock Creek Valley, for the present. "We put on heavily padded helmets, breastplates, and gauntlets," the president reported, as if he were preparing for a medieval tournament, "and wrap both towels around our necks, and then we turn to and beat one another like carpets." Single stick gave Roosevelt all the high impact exercise he could handle while his leg was still healing.[5]

During his presidency, Roosevelt kept to his hiking and climbing, rowing, and swimming even if it had to be mostly confined to the rough terrain in and around Washington. "It is whispered," wrote William Bayard Hale, "that he leads some of his companions a pretty chase—for few people at Washington keep themselves in training as does the President." Sir Mortimer Durand, the British ambassador, was "a bad walker and unable to climb," according to the president. Not surprisingly, Durand had his own version: "We drove out to a wooded valley with streams running through it, and then he made me struggle through bushes and over rocks for two hours and a half, at an impossible speed." When Durand got stuck in the rocks, Roosevelt had to grab him by the collar to "haul him up."[6]

In Jules Jusserand, the French ambassador, Roosevelt found someone who could match him in hiking, tennis, and horsemanship—the president rode practically every day. Once, Jusserand arrived at the White House in his silk hat and full dress ready for a midafternoon promenade. Instead, he found himself in the countryside, probably Rock Creek Valley, with the president scrambling through the woods and underbrush. Jusserand became quite out of breath as the party moved across the fields at a feverish pace approaching the woods near the "creek." Reaching "the bank of a stream, rather wide and too deep to be forded," the ambassador was ready for a well-earned rest. Imagine his shock when the president of the United States began to take off his clothes. "We had better strip," Roosevelt commanded, "so as not to wet our things in the Creek." Jusserand meekly took off his fine clothes, everything but his silk gloves. Roosevelt looked skeptically at the lavender kid gloves. "With your permission, Mr. President," he said, "I will keep these on, otherwise it would be embarrassing if we should meet ladies." They plunged into the water and swam to the other side. Touché.[7]

In October 1908 military aide Archie Butt rode with the president to Boulder Bridge in Rock Creek Valley and witnessed yet another feat of endurance. The president's leg was acting up again, and thinking ahead to his African safari when he left office, he wanted to test his limb. "He pushed through the brush like an Indian scout," Butt wrote, "and when he got to the water's edge he began to clamber out on the ridges and overhanging rocks. . . . I did not tell him how each time I thought it would be my last," he recalled, "nor did I show the real fear I had of falling." The president was full of compliments encouraging him with "bully" or "bullier" each time Butt made a death-defying step.[8]

Butt admitted later that, although he was terrified for his own safety, he still had it in him to worry about the president, too. He was just as terrified as he watched the overweight president climbing the jagged rocks as he was angry at him for taking such foolish risks. As Roosevelt reached the top, he slipped and went tumbling down the craggy cliff. He pushed himself away from the rocks as he fell and very fortunately missed all the jagged projections that would certainly have seriously injured him. He fell straight into the water, and looking down, Butt saw him bobbing in the water, ready to continue the adventure. "We trudged on for about an hour more," Butt wrote, "sometimes crawling, sometimes climbing." Just at dark, they reached a point where the creek bank narrowed and they had to swim across.[9]

The gloomy chill of Rock Creek numbed their bodies. It was a struggle, but they both made it across. Shivering from the water and now from the rain, they came to a forty-foot ledge. Roosevelt doubted that they could make the treacherous climb, but up they went. Halfway to the top, Butt found, try as he might, that he couldn't go any further. The footing was too slippery to go up or to go back down. Roosevelt, after he had reached the top, shouted to Butt that it would be "fatal" to fall. Risking his demise, Butt did manage to climb back down. Yet no sooner did he regain his footing than the president suddenly appeared, "coming out of the precipitous jungle like a bear, but laughing and evidently buoyed up over his prowess."[10]

Presidents for the remainder of the century would relax by golfing, sailing, jogging, swimming—or simply going to Camp David on the spur of the moment. Paradoxically Roosevelt seemed to relax by ratcheting up the degree of danger. It was a little like Dwight Eisenhower or Bill Clinton pushing themselves to break 80 on the links, only the physical demands—and dangers— were far greater. Never again, in the post-TR era, would a twentieth-century president be allowed to risk his life so deliberately while in office—or would he be so inclined. With a national press corps watching the president's every move, scrambles up rocky ledges and plunges into murky waters would have elicited a barrage of scathing newspaper editorials or derisive television features.

★

The First Camp David

In May 1905, while Teddy was completing one of his bear-hunting trips, Edith Roosevelt went to investigate what turned out to be a presidential retreat closer to Washington than Sagamore Hill on Long Island—it was just south of Charlottesville, Virginia, less than three hours by rail from the nation's capital. Edith was charmed by what she saw, a plain, two-story clapboard house with brown trim and green blinds. Immediately, Edith saw through the lack of conveniences—no stove or indoor plumbing. The name, Pine Knot, seemed just right, for the house was indeed nestled in the pines. Roosevelt often used the phrase "tough as a pine knot." She bought the house and fifteen acres for $280.

Roosevelt was delighted by his wife's venture into real estate. He liked the house, but best of all Roosevelt liked the sweeping front porch where they could sit in the daytime and listen to the birds—two years later Roosevelt and the visiting John Burroughs identified seventy-five avian species.

Pine Knot was light years from Camp David and far simpler than Herbert Hoover's Virginia lodge in the Blue Ridge Mountains. The Roosevelts seldom brought friends to Pine Knot, and the president never tried to do official business there. An occasional reporter from Charlottesville happened by, but Roosevelt was free to use his time as he pleased. Not surprisingly, he hunted when he came in the fall and winter, but instead of bear and bobcat his quarry was wild turkey and rabbit. He also spent time cataloging the birds of the area.

The Roosevelts spent the days following Christmas 1907 at Pine Knot, even with its lack of central heating and creature comforts—their bedroom even had a nest of flying squirrels. The president and his sons went hunting, occasionally for the elusive turkeys. Though he always hunted, in a lifetime of hunting Roosevelt only bagged a single turkey, this after an all-day hunt at Pine Knot. According to Roosevelt, he got up at between three and five o'clock "under a cold brilliant moon." The turkey kill took almost as long as the first bear he shot in the Bighorn Mountains of Wyoming. "The turkey came out of the cover not too far off and sprang into the air, heading across the valley and offering me a side shot at forty yards as it sailed by," he wrote. "It was an easy shot." He was as happy as that boy on the Nile shooting his first bird.[11]

According to historian William Harbaugh, one story of Roosevelt at Pine Knot has him fox hunting on the slopes of a not-distant mountain near Thomas Jefferson's home at Monticello. Roosevelt heard the baying of hounds owned by a local African American farmer, George Monroe, whom his guide—Dick McDaniel, also black—knew. "When he refused Dick's request to rent the hounds," Harbaugh writes, "Roosevelt either went to Monroe's house himself or, more likely, sent Dick to explain that he was president of the United States. Whereupon, Monroe retorted: 'I don't give a damn if youre Booker T. Washington, you can't borrow my dogs.'" So Roosevelt had to content himself with the hounds from Plain Dealing, the estate next to Pine Knot.[12]

John Burroughs, staying with the family at the cabin, noted Roosevelt's real isolation out there in the woods, and he mentioned the possibility of assassination—not a paranoid notion since Roosevelt had arrived in the presidency as a result of an assassin's bullet, and he would himself be shot in the chest while giving a speech in 1912. "Oh," the president replied patting his side, "they would have to be mighty quick to get the drop on me."[13]

Later that evening, Burroughs thought he heard some rustling in the leaves. Slightly unnerved, he asked Edith about this, and she revealed that they were not alone; she had instructed two secret service agents to patrol the grounds at night. She discreetly kept her decision from the president. It would only "irritate him."[14]

Pine Knot might have evolved into a more permanent retreat for the Roosevelt family, but when Roosevelt failed to win the 1912 election he never again visited Pine Knot. His love of the outdoors and outdoor sport would take him first on his post-presidential African safari and later to Brazil on a near-fatal journey of exploration, but the little house in the woods remained merely a footnote to his love of the outdoors.

Nevertheless, Pine Knot is the ancestor of Herbert Hoover's Rapidan Camp and Franklin Roosevelt's "Shangri-La," which we now know as Camp David.

There, presidents have tried to retain the emphasis on the rustic simplicity while transferring the nerve center of the imperial presidency to a mountain in Maryland.

★
The Strenuous Life: Its Cost

Yet the sporting presidency had a downside that may have contributed to Roosevelt's physical decline. This deterioration went largely unnoticed, except by members of his family and close friends. Not that the president could not pump himself up for big events, especially when his ego was on the line. Yet, since he took office in 1901, a series of accidents had befallen the president, who had heretofore been remarkably fortunate in dozens of brushes with danger. Now the damage to his resilient body came from unexpected and barely visible sources. The president's serious leg injury sustained in the trolley accident never ceased giving him problems, and he kept reinjuring it while pursuing the "strenuous life."

Teddy had always needed to test his limits with contact sports. In Albany he hired his own personal trainer, a champion wrestler who worked out with him at the Governor's Mansion several times a week. He also sparred with a professional boxer, Mike Donovan, a lightweight champion. After a dull first encounter, the governor told Donovan not to baby him. "You're not hitting me. I'd like you to hit out," he told the champ. Roosevelt more than held his own, throwing a right toward the ear that jarred his adversary. "I realized from that moment that Governor was no ordinary amateur," Donovan later wrote. "If I took chances with him, I was endangering my reputation." Donovan was one of the several boxers and wrestlers who visited Roosevelt at the White House.[15]

In the winter of 1904, the president imported two Japanese jujitsu wrestlers to the Executive Mansion for a workout every other day. "I am not the age or the build to be whirled lightly over an opponent's head and battered down on a mattress," he wrote his son Kermit. Nevertheless, these skillful athletes managed to handle the president with such dexterity that he suffered few jolts. He only complained of a sore throat as a result of one wrestler catching him in a stranglehold. In boxing and singlestick at the White House, he was not so lucky. In 1904, "I strained one leg; and on Thanksgiving I strained it again in jumping a fence on Rusty [his horse]." In December he wrenched his thigh again and, worse yet, ruptured a blood vessel in his eye while boxing with a naval aide, Lieutenant Dan Tyler Moore. According to Edmund Morris, "his vision immediately began to blur, degenerating into spotted half-blindness." Though the injury remained a secret, the eye condition did not improve.[16]

In August 1906 he wrote repentantly to his old friend Senator Henry Cabot Lodge: "I have been having a real rest this summer, and incidentally have grown to realize that I have reached a time in life when too violent exercise does not rest a man when he has had an exhausting mental career."[17]

His left eye—he was nearsighted from childhood—was deteriorating even before the boxing accident. This condition, in turn, made reading difficult. By the time he left the presidency, he was virtually blind in that eye. He also suffered from rheumatism, though he persisted in the strenuous sports that were his trademark. The rugged exercise, meant to alleviate the aching joints, may have done just the opposite.

Worse yet, his cardiovascular system was wearing down. For a man with a weak heart, Roosevelt's eating habits were deadly. Roosevelt had ballooned to 230 pounds on a five foot eight inch frame It is true that he didn't smoke and drank very little, but he made up for it when he sat down to eat. He relished heaping mounds of fried foods. Once his son Ted saw him eat a dozen fried eggs, topped off by two glasses of milk and four oranges. By his later years in the White House, he was suffering from high blood pressure and probably from hardening of the arteries. He also had contracted malaria when he tramped through the jungles and tropical savannahs of Cuba in the Spanish-American War, and the recurring fevers were nursed with drugs. In January 1919 Teddy Roosevelt died of a cardiovascular embolism at the age of sixty.

★

The Sporting Presidency: A Roosevelt Legacy

Roosevelt set the sporting standard for future presidencies—and the bar was set high. Not that his successors cared to embrace his dynamic approach to presidential sports, at least not until the first George Bush entered the presidency in 1989. Yet he showed that sports and the presidency do mix—just as Edith Roosevelt who rode horseback with her Theodore demonstrated that first ladies could share their husband's outdoor interests and actually find new outlets for physical activity. Roosevelt used his sports to publicize his commitment to conservation. His tramps in the wild helped to forge a bond with diplomats, military officers, and members of his official family—and to show others who was in control. He used his hunting trips to renew old political ties and to create new ones.

Not the least, sports served to release the energies bottled up inside him and no doubt made him more effective in his official duties. According to William Bayard Hale, "Mr. Roosevelt is the first President who has had time for exercise and play—and one reason he has time for a hundred features of work indoors which no other President ever did is because he takes time for recreation out of doors." Sports allowed this youthful, physically active chief executive to relax, to engage in theatrics, to assert control over himself and those around him. His successors—and, often, their first ladies—would employ bits and pieces of his sporting pursuits.[18]

Sports enabled Roosevelt to keep himself front and center, a veritable Barnum of a three-ring governmental circus. His successor, William Howard Taft, would fail the presidential test because he was unable to project his personality and activities with a Rooseveltian flair. It would be a hard—maybe impossible—act to follow.

If one considers his overall participation in and use of sport, to date none has matched Roosevelt as a sporting man.

Sports: Acceptable but Not Required

*William Howard Taft, possibly looking for a ball, before awestruck children.
His friend and predecessor, Theodore Roosevelt, cautioned Taft that "golf is fatal."
Taft disregarded his advice and spent his most enjoyable moments on the links, often
neglecting urgent business. His passivity in pushing the progressive agenda led to a break
with TR and a split in the Republican Party, pitting the remnants of Roosevelt's "tennis
cabinet" against the president's often plutocratic "golf cabinet." Courtesy of William
Howard Taft National Historic Site, Cincinnati, Ohio.*

William Howard Taft
A Large Legacy

Standing six feet, William Howard Taft weighed well over three hundred pounds. When he moved into the White House, a Taft-sized bathtub had to be installed. Like Roosevelt, he rode horseback—when told of a long horseback ride by Taft in the Philippines, Roosevelt's secretary of state, Elihu Root, asked, "How is the horse?" Unlike Roosevelt, he did not fish, hunt, or hike in Rock Creek Valley. Unsuited by size to tennis, Taft instead played golf enthusiastically and often. Roosevelt, who had refused to be photographed in his tennis attire, warned Taft not to be photographed playing golf, but Taft disregarded Roosevelt's advice. He allowed the press to see and photograph him playing what was regarded as a "rich man's game"—and, in fact, he played with some very rich men.[1]

William Howard Taft, always a reluctant president, preferred a judicial career to the presidency. While his wife Helen (known as Nellie) wanted her husband to become president, Taft himself longed for a seat on the Supreme Court. Before becoming governor general of the Philippines, he was a federal judge in Ohio and solicitor general in Washington. Nellie and her husband both got their wishes; Taft served as both president and chief justice.

★

Reluctant President, Ardent Golfer

Before he was nominated for president, Taft was an ardent golfer. In 1908, vacationing at Hot Springs, Virginia, before the upcoming election, he disregarded Roosevelt's advice to avoid golfing. Roosevelt, who believed that golf was an elite game not played by the common man, virtually insisted that Taft cease playing golf—at least until the nominating convention and election campaign were over. According to Nellie's biographer, Carl Sferrazza Anthony, "ten reporters and one photographer chronicled the Tafts in Hot Springs, especially Will's endless rounds of golf."[2]

In the winter of 1909, soon after he was elected (but before he was inaugurated), Taft left Washington for Hot Springs to play more golf and to choose his cabinet at his leisure. But Hot Springs proved to be too close to home, and the president-elect was besieged with visitors. After returning to Washington, he decided to go to the less traveled, more remote site of Augusta, Georgia, not yet the home of the Augusta National or the Masters Golf Tournament. There he ran into the retired billionaire John D. Rockefeller, at that time possibly the most despised man in America. Taft persuaded Rockefeller to let him use his quarters, but on his wife Nellie's advice, he refused the oil magnate's invitation to play golf. Nellie argued that Rockefeller's unpopularity might rub off on him.

Nellie Taft was the president's closest adviser and confidante. Bright and ambitious, Nellie had a lively interest in games that dated from her childhood. She rejoiced with her husband when he broke 100 in golf. She herself smoked, drank (but not to excess), and played poker for money. Her gambling itself was a potential issue in the presidential campaign, but the story did not come out until after Taft had won the election—or, as Carl Anthony puts it, the "period of rosiness toward the President-elect and his family that usually follows Election Day." Taft's golf stirred far more interest and controversy than her card playing. And, as it turned out, Nellie herself was soon to become the first misfortune in Taft's ill-fated presidency.[3]

Almost from the beginning, storm clouds seemed to hover over the Taft presidency. In early May, two months after taking office, Nellie suffered a stroke that left her bedridden and speechless. Though she would begin walking and going on short excursions in the White House automobile within a few months, the president worried constantly about her health. Deprived of her advice and companionship, he turned more to Archie Butt, Roosevelt's military aide, who now became not only his aide but also his constant companion. Soon after Nellie's stroke, Taft and Butt were riding their horses near the Potomac River, when the president's horse became frightened by the swiftly flowing water. He wheeled and threw the massive president onto the ground. With the president lying on his back, Butt vaulted off his own horse only to find the president convulsed with laughter. He looked up at Butt and asked him what he was thinking. "My only thought was, Mr. President," Butt responded, "that the devil was working overtime to see what next he could do to the Taft family."[4]

The relationship between Taft and Butt has no precise counterpart in recent presidencies. As military aide, Butt was responsible for escorting and assisting the president. In fact, Butt accompanied the president on horseback rides, golf outings, excursions in the White House autos, and even on political junkets. He heard more, saw more, and wrote more about Taft than anyone. In letters to his sister-in-law, Clara Butt, the forty-year-old bachelor conveyed his view of the president's moods, conflicts, humor, and companions more thoroughly than any of Taft's contemporaries. Because he regarded Taft as complacent and inert, Butt tried to keep him on his feet and moving. "To keep him up to the mark, to make him break engagements, and ride, even when I do not feel like it, to prevent him from yielding to lethargy, which is natural to one of his size, and to scheme to get him to the ball park and the golf links, and to buoy him up in many ways becomes in time, by constant performance, an interesting duty."[5]

Butt confessed to Clara that this job was far more challenging than serving under Roosevelt, who did "the thinking, the planning, the scheming for all his playmates." Never was it necessary for Archie to encourage the Colonel (as Roosevelt titled himself after the presidency). "It was he [Roosevelt] who swept one off one's feet in a sort of whirlwind motion," Butt observed, "and, when it was all over, left one exhausted, glad to yield to another playmate the place in the saddle, by his side, or to scale cliffs, or swim creeks." The difference between the two men could be seen through the lens of sport. Whenever Butt wanted to get Taft off the more traveled, familiar path when they were riding, he galloped ahead and led the way. "I find that nine times out of ten he will follow."[6]

Golf was clearly Taft's favorite sport. By the time he became president, the fifty-one-year-old played solid, if unspectacular, golf. He enjoyed the slow pace, the companionship, and low-keyed competition. He always—almost always—took his bad shots and high scores philosophically. On a good day, his score might range from the mid-90s to more than 100. When he first played the Myopia Club in 1909, club members made bets, some as high as $1,000, that he wouldn't break 100. Taft astounded them by shooting a 98.

According to one account, he played his best golf ever while in Georgia on a political tour. When he spoke to a local audience, he half-jokingly informed them that he did not know whether he would rather have shot that round or have been elected president. Later, while speaking in North Dakota, he used such unfamiliar golfing terms that he had to explain what "out of bounds" and "bunkered" meant to his golf-illiterate, farming audience.[7]

It wasn't often that he lost his temper on the golf course. Once, while playing near the "summer White House," he took nineteen shots to get out of a diabolic sand trap known as the "elbow." A caddy consoled Taft by recalling that a German nobleman had taken sixty-three strokes to get out of the same trap. In the summer of 1910, as political pressures mounted and Taft was becoming estranged from his old friend Theodore (Roosevelt), frustrations on the golf course finally got to him. According to Butt, the president "swore a terrible oath and threw his club twenty-five yards." Even the caddies were stunned by his outburst.[8]

Taft's physical and mental health would deteriorate during his presidency. Already hefty, his weight ballooned to well over 300 pounds. According to Archie Butt, he often fell asleep while he was writing or playing cards. His physical regimen, prescribed by his physician in Washington, required the dangerously overweight Taft to exercise in a stressful manner, running and throwing the large-sized medicine ball as well as rolling and bending. A doctor in Boston confided to Butt that the exercise had weakened the president's heart. Golf even when it was painful for Taft to walk was a far friendlier form of exercise. Though the president's physical regimen was halted, his political problems only grew worse.

In the summer of 1909, Taft, who avoided confrontations when he could, faced a battle between those Republicans who wanted a high tariff and fellow Republicans and reformers who did not. Increasingly, Taft found himself losing ground to high-tariff advocates. He threatened to call Congress into special extended session if the two houses of Congress could not reconcile their differences.

Despite his determination to get a tariff bill passed, Taft didn't often interrupt his four-hour golfing routine. Rather than ride herd on members of Congress, he spent his afternoons doing what he liked best. On July 30, Taft was besieged by Senate and House conferees who wanted him to endorse a higher duty on lumber and gloves. "They have my last word," he declared, as he and Butt were leaving for Chevy Chase, "and now I want to show my scorn for further mediation by spending the afternoon on the golf links." With this, the high-tariff interests in Congress passed the Payne-Aldrich tariff, which nudged many of the existing rates even higher. Contrary to his campaign pledge, Taft signed the bill and immediately left for his summer White House in Massachusetts to join his recuperating wife—and play golf.[9]

In late September, Taft embarked on an ambitious speaking tour that would carry him across much of the country to calm the political storm that had grown out of the tariff bill. "If it were not for the speeches," he confessed, "I should look forward with the greatest pleasure to this trip." Instead of preparing for the trip, he spent as much time as possible with Nellie—and on the golf course.[10]

★
Taft and TR: From Horseback to Horseless Carriage

While Roosevelt was in Africa shooting game, a feud broke out between the remnants of Roosevelt's tennis cabinet and Taft's golf cabinet (the press used "tennis" and "golf" freely, and the "playmates" of the president didn't necessarily have to be actual cabinet members). Not only had tensions erupted between the Roosevelt and Taft forces as a result of the tariff battle but a bitter dispute developed between Chief Forester Gifford Pinchot and Interior Secretary Richard Ballinger. By the time the latter dispute became public, Taft and Roosevelt were no longer speaking to each other, and the Republican Party was split into two hostile wings.

Roosevelt, upon leaving the White House, clearly expected that Taft would follow his policies and retain his cabinet members. When Taft made his appointments, he did indeed keep some of Roosevelt's cabinet members, including Gifford Pinchot as chief forester, but not Secretary of Interior James Garfield, one of the most progressive Republicans and one dedicated to conservation—and a TR tennis partner. Both Garfield and Pinchot worshiped Roosevelt, who had done so much to conserve the western forests and to reclaim government control of untapped minerals, especially timber and coal. Taft replaced Garfield with a little-known former government official from Seattle, Richard Ballinger. Ballinger had no interest in preserving valuable mineral deposits on government lands.

Almost from the beginning, Pinchot and Ballinger were at loggerheads. What became known as the Pinchot-Ballinger dispute originated with the discovery that Ballinger had turned over some valuable Alaskan coal lands to a syndicate of business barons. Because the syndicate included close friends of Ballinger from Seattle, the interior secretary was accused of fraud, and Pinchot demanded that the president deal with this.

While Taft was on vacation at the presidential retreat at Beverly near Boston, Ballinger came to Beverly to call on the president. Typically, the president was playing golf when Ballinger arrived, but he spent that evening with him and his attorney. Soon afterward, Taft sent a letter exonerating Ballinger.

Taking the matter public, *Collier's Weekly,* the favorite outlet of muckraking journalists, ran the story in November, just after Taft had returned from his two-month tour of the Midwest and West—a failed effort, it turned out, to calm the furor over the tariff. In the months that followed, Congress held committee hearings at which Pinchot, with his flair for high drama, bran-

William Howard Taft sitting regally in the back seat of a Pierce Arrow with Captain Archie Butt, his military aide, riding shotgun in front. Taft was the first president to use automobiles at the White House—he was interested in this new form of transportation and, given his size, the automobile was better suited to his needs than horse-drawn vehicles. Archie Butt became his closest companion until the spring of 1912 when, returning from a vacation in Europe, Butt went down on the Titanic. *Library of Congress, Washington, D.C.*

dished his charges against the Taft administration. In January 1910, Taft fired Pinchot, the last remaining member of Roosevelt's tennis cabinet.

But Pinchot then brought the leading player, Roosevelt, off the bench and into the contest. He sent a lengthy telegram delivered by native runners to the former president deep in the African bush. A few months later, when Roosevelt emerged from Africa, he summoned Pinchot to meet him in Greece and to discuss his statement that Taft had shown "a most surprising weakness and indecision."[11]

The conflict of the tennis and golf cabinets had far broader implications for the country—and for the president. To be precise, the two approaches were Roosevelt's commitment to the wilderness crusade and Taft's preference for tamed environments such as golf courses and well-trodden riding paths. Taft might have nipped the conflict in the bud by firing both Pinchot and Ballinger, but he didn't. He allowed the conflict to fester while he traveled on his speaking tour. Already Taft revealed his distaste for politics—and especially for being "politician in chief." Those hours spent so enjoyably on the golf course contributed to the declining confidence in his presidency.

One way to get Taft's ear was to approach him when he was riding horseback. He and Archie Butt particularly enjoyed riding in the late afternoons on a popular route known as the "speedway," where members of Congress might go to get a few minutes with the president. Senator Boies Penrose of Pennsylvania happened to be on the speedway just as Taft approached. Joining the president, Penrose brought up his agenda for political appointees. Taft responded by describing a plan for beautifying nearby Potomac Park. The government would purchase the land between the Capitol and Union Station (now the site of the Senate Office Building). Lobbying while exercising worked for Taft and for those who accompanied him—as it would for Bill Clinton, who jogged with congressmen and political donors eighty-five years later.

Although Taft enjoyed horseback riding, he came to appreciate the advantages of the automobile, which appealed to his interest in technology and new-fangled gadgets. Soon the entire Taft family incorporated motoring into their daily routines. These outings led Taft to remark prophetically to his son Bob (the future senator from Ohio and three-time presidential aspirant) and his daughter Helen: "Well, children, enjoy this all you can, for in four years more you may have to begin to walk [all] over again."[12]

The horse-and-buggy age for American presidents ended with the three-hundred-pound William Howard Taft riding in the rear seat of his limousine to Manassas, Virginia. The president decided to use his steam-powered car to journey to the site of the Civil War Battle of Bull Run to speak to Civil War veterans. Not that the transition was an easy one. Taft would soon find that the roads for jaunts and junkets by car on the Virginia side of the Potomac were sorely lacking. No doubt he soon realized that he was following many of the same roads traversed by President Roosevelt's midwinter horseback expedition in 1909. He would soon hear more than he wanted about the legendary Roosevelt ride of 1909. Despite the unexpected storms encountered by both presidents, the inert, jovial, affable—and comfortable—Taft would hardly compare with the grim, snow-caked, nearly blind TR.

Both Taft and Roosevelt encountered savage and erratic weather on their journeys. After starting out on a sunny July morning, the Taft party ran into downpours near Fairfax. It forded "torrents" near Centerville. Then, almost in sight of Manassas, the caravan was forced to turn aside and take a far more circuitous route.

The muddy, nearly impassable roads played havoc with the trip. Taking a break, the party stopped at Fairfax for a typically southern midday meal of fried chicken and Virginia ham before they resumed their difficult ride toward Manassas. But, approaching a swollen creek, one of the cars in their convoy packed with U.S. senators became stuck in the middle of the water. Wading into the torrent, Archie Butt gauged the depth and bed of the stream and concluded that Taft's steam-powered vehicle could make the crossing. The chauffeur gathered up a head of steam and then roared into the river.

Butt then trudged back into the water to help push the disabled senatorial car in the right direction. Then he found a team of horses to rescue the marooned vehicle. Once they were safely on dry land, the president took the relieved senators into his two automobiles.

Two miles farther Taft's vehicle halted at a once-small creek, now a raging torrent. Again Archie removed his military boots, rolled up the trousers of his uniform, and waded into the swiftly running water—this time almost chest high. The party would have to take a ten-mile detour. Haltingly, the chauffeur maneuvered the car toward a suitable crossing. Twice more, the long-suffering Butt had to get out in order to lead frightened horses past the huffing automobile. After a scary interlude of thunder and lightning, Taft and his entourage finally reached their destination.

Once mercifully in Manassas, the president made, in Butt's words, a "flubdub speech" about the blue and the gray, which brought tears to the eyes of veterans and sardonic smiles to the faces of the senators and local politicians. "Every politician has a canned speech up his sleeve for these reunions," Archie reflected cynically. While Taft flubdubbed before the veterans, aides tried to find a way back by railroad. Luckily, they succeeded.[13]

In contrast to Taft's comfortable ride back to Union Station in Washington in a well-appointed private passenger car, the determined Roosevelt had refused even a carriage ride from the shores of the Potomac to the executive mansion.

★

He Stood Up for Baseball

Taft's most enduring contribution to the sporting presidency was his association with major league baseball. Taft was certainly not the first president to follow baseball, but he was the one who began throwing out the first ball at the home opener of the Washington Senators, a tradition honored by every president until the Senators no longer played in Washington. So seamlessly was this tradition continued by later presidents that it might have begun with George Washington himself.

Though they rarely went to games, three of Taft's predecessors—Andrew Johnson, Ulysses Grant, and William McKinley—entertained baseball teams at the White House. Workaholic Grover Cleveland passed up the chance to watch the champion Chicago White Stockings in 1885, asking rhetorically, "What do you imagine the American public would think of me if I wasted my time going to the ball game?" His successor, Benjamin Harrison, became the first president to attend a major league game. Theodore Roosevelt, not a baseball fan, became interested in the Detroit Tigers' Ty Cobb because Cobb (like Roosevelt) did not drink or smoke. While McKinley entertained the Washington Senators, Roosevelt invited the recently formed New York Highlanders and the Cleveland Naps to make brief visits at the White House. The Highlanders would soon be called the New York Yankees, so the native New Yorker Teddy Roosevelt wound up entertaining the soon-to-be most successful and storied team of the twentieth century.[14]

Roosevelt was too active a man to spend much time watching sports—and he also was too politically astute to publicize his interest in such a time-consuming activity. And, except for Benjamin Harrison, no president had attended a big league game. Presidents correctly hesitated, as Grover Cleveland had, to spend their afternoons in such a frivolous pastime.

On top of this, presidents undoubtedly knew of baseball's dreadful reputation, especially in the 1890s. Gambling by spectators—and players—was rife. Vendors sold beer and liquor under the stands, and inebriated fans and combative players abused umpires and frequently got into brawls. Baseball historian Charles Alexander has described two encounters between the noisome fans of the Cleveland Spiders and the equally rabid followers of the Baltimore Orioles. "After the Orioles were showered with vegetables, beer bottles, seat cushions, and a variety of other objects during three games at the Cleveland park, hoodlums in Baltimore attacked the Cleveland Spiders' horse-drawn bus with rocks, bricks, and dirt clods." No wonder Amos Alonzo Stagg, an aspiring minister at Yale and also the best pitcher in college baseball, spurned an offer by the Boston Red Sox in 1889. Because of baseball's tawdry reputation, he became instead one of the most successful college football coaches of all time.[15]

By the early 1900s, however, professional baseball had improved its reputation. In large part, this change stemmed from the standards introduced by the American League's Ban Johnson, who refused to allow baiting of umpires and unruly behavior by players and fans. From 1903 to 1953, with the exception of the Chicago Black Sox scandal in 1919, major league baseball would prove the most stable of enterprises. In spite of Ty Cobb's vicious and unpleasant reputation among the players, the Georgian was a hero to Archie Butt. It was no accident that Cobb's Detroit Tigers made periodic visits to Taft's White House. With this enthusiasm for baseball and a need to get the president off his duff, Butt persuaded his boss to go the ballpark.

William Howard Taft was ready-made for an afternoon at the ball yard. He enjoyed baseball, and if he had the right size seat, he was not averse to sitting for long periods. The Senators not only gave him a free pass, but they also found a chair that was big enough

On April 14, 1910, Taft attended the opening game of the Washington Senators. Ban Johnson, the president of the American League and the force behind the merger of the American and National leagues, invited the president to throw out the first ball. According to historians William Mead and Paul Dickson, Nellie Taft held the ball while the president removed his kid gloves. Then Big Will Taft heaved the ball to Walter Johnson, the opening-day pitcher. Johnson proceeded to pitch a gem, shutting out the Philadelphia Athletics on one hit, 3-0. The Washington newspapers carried pictures and accounts of Taft's precedent-setting appearance. Johnson was so moved by catching the first presidential pitch that he asked a friend to take the ball to the White House in the hope that the president would sign it. Taft willingly obliged with one of the longest tributes ever to grace a baseball. "To Walter Johnson," the inscription read, "with the hope that he may continue to be as formidable as in yesterday's game. William H. Taft."[16]

Baseball became associated with Taft both in fact and in myth. The fact is that he established a presidential record still unbroken of seeing a game in both leagues on the same day. On May 4, 1910, he happened to be in St. Louis, where the Cardinals were playing his hometown Cincinnati Reds. When the Reds fell behind 12-0 after two innings, Taft headed for Sportsmans's Park where Cy Young was pitching for Cleveland against the other St. Louis team, the Browns.

But presidential myths have proved as hard to puncture as other tall tales. One story has it that the seventh-inning stretch began when Taft stood up to stretch at a game in Pittsburgh and everyone in the park leapt to their feet as a sign of respect. Actually, the seventh-inning ritual goes back at least as far as the 1870s. And, then there is a yarn about Taft's own baseball career. According to this tale, young Will Taft was so promising as a semiprofessional catcher that he was invited to play for the Cincinnati team. But he broke his arm, so the story goes, playing in the final game for an unknown minor league team before signing a pre-contract. So he attended Yale instead, never played baseball there, and from Yale went on to a distinguished career on the bench (judicial rather than baseball).

In baseball, just as with tariffs, Taft's political friends—and Archie Butt—tried to manipulate the president. Once Taft visited Pittsburgh for a day of social and political functions: to speak at the unveiling of a fountain; to attend a formal luncheon, where he would mix with the socially elite; and, finally, to end the day at a Yale alumni banquet—the equivalent of contemporary fund raisers. None of these activities would burnish the president's popularity, though he was willing to go through the motions. In the meantime, Archie Butt learned that the Pittsburgh Pirates were taking on the Chicago Cubs that very afternoon. Butt decided that attending the game would do just as much for Taft's political career as going to all those different social functions. Taft happily agreed, so Butt went to the local GOP committee to tell them. The committee was furious.

"It will break the entire program," the chairman protested.

"That is what a president is for," Butt responded, "to break programs."[17]

The committee wanted to see the president, but Butt said that he was writing a speech on the anniversary of Gettysburg and could not be disturbed. ("A pure fabrication," Butt confessed to his sister-in-law.) "He not only wants to see the game," Archie insisted to the committee, "but he wants to see it from the seats, so you had better get together and get them to rope off twenty seats just to the left of the catcher and order the railroad to bring him in on a special train from the Country Club no later than 3:30."

"Of course, they were all mad. I would have been angry myself," Butt admitted.[18]

At first, the delighted baseball magnates decided that the president should have four boxes, above the grandstand and out of sight of the crowd. Why should he have to sit with the common folk? Butt conspired with the Secret Service, however, to purchase both boxes and grandstand seats. "Archie," the president said, "I am on to your little game. You don't care whether I see the game or not. What you want is for me to be seen, and I will tell you frankly I don't care whether I am seen or not, but what I really want is to see."[19]

Afterward Butt told the press that the president had been set to occupy the boxes, and just before the game he had "refused to do so, preferring to see the game where all the lovers of sport saw it and where he could see the crowd and hear the comment of the fans." This early example of "spin," according to Archie, proved highly successful. The press made more of Taft's attendance at the baseball game than his speech commemorating Gettysburg or the events that he attended before and after the game. Archie boasted to Clara that it was Taft's most popular public appearance since his inauguration.[20]

★

Hobnobbing with the Plutocrats

Just as Taft refused to disguise his golf outings, he allowed himself—as in Pittsburgh—to mix with the plutocrats whom Roosevelt had publicly spurned. In 1910 Henry Frick, the steel baron, the very symbol of the exploitative capitalist, invited Taft to play golf and to have dinner at his lavish estate. An associate of Andrew Carnegie, Frick had amassed wealth and notoriety in his meteoric rise in the steel business. In 1894, during the Homestead steel strike near Pittsburgh, he had ruthlessly suppressed the steelworkers. His reputation led a young anarchist, Alexander Berkman, to burst into his office in an attempt to assassinate him. Unfortunately for Berkman, Frick received only superficial wounds while the assailant was imprisoned and later deported to his native Russia. In 1905 Frick, who had since left Pittsburgh for New York, bought a palatial estate within a few miles of the presidential retreat at Beverly, Massachusetts. There he surrounded himself with his beloved and rare paintings, for the flinty Frick also had an unlikely passion for art and music, especially paintings by the great masters.

Taft had shown discretion when he rejected John D. Rockefeller's invitation to play golf. Archie Butt and Nellie Taft now tried to steer the president clear of Frick, but to no avail. In September 1909 Taft's secretary of state, Philander Knox, arranged a golf game and a dinner between the steel magnate and the president. Luckily for Taft, the newspapers only reported that the president played with the secretary of state. There is no evidence that Frick asked Taft for favors, but he wanted to draw Taft into his orbit. Taft, like Roosevelt, showed discretion when he met quietly with the financier J. P. Morgan, whose name epitomized big business. But he allowed himself to be led by Knox, a former corporate attorney, who could play on either team, big business or antitrust.

After playing golf in the presidential foursome, Archie Butt accompanied Taft and Knox to the Frick mansion. "I felt I had done all I could do to keep him away from the Fricks," Butt acknowledged, "so I was rather glad to get a whiff of the outside world for one night." And what a whiff it was! Later becoming a part of the Frick Collection, the paintings included Gainsboroughs, Turners, and Van Dycks. The house, set in the midst of tall trees, was, Butt remarked, "a perfect palace." As he entered the house, Archie "felt as Aladdin must have felt after he rubbed the lamp." Frick, the farm boy from Pennsylvania, had reached the pinnacle of society, hobnobbing with the president and the secretary of state in a mansion that resembled a world-class museum, all part of an elaborate setting that he owned and orchestrated.[21]

While the president was there, Frick conveyed still another invitation to Taft through Knox. He wanted to give a reception for the president so that Taft could meet the social elite of north shore Massachusetts. When they were alone, the president asked Butt what he thought. In a letter to Clara, Archie told her what he thought rather than what he told Taft. "The President was to be bought," he cynically observed, "just as the portraits of men's ancestors had been bought except that Knox was doing the buying rather than a collector in New York." The president agreed with Archie's straightforward reply and declined the invitation.[22]

A year later Butt reported that the president was in a similar situation, but the outcome was different. On July 11, 1910, Taft again played golf with Frick and trounced the steel baron. Evidently Frick's own "pro," who instructed the plutocrat in golf, had convinced him that he could easily defeat the president. Archie Butt was far more cynical than he had been in 1909. "These millionaires buy ready-made hedges, ready-made sod, and ready-made everything else when they want it," he observed. "They think that because they take a professional with them everywhere they go, as Frick did this last winter, they can get ready-made golf along with everything else they want to buy."[23]

One evening in August, the president and Butt went to Frick's mansion for a poker game, outwitting Nellie Taft, who expected them to stay home and play bridge, and the secret service agents, who failed to notice them as they left. Like schoolboys, they surreptitiously stole into the Frick estate. Inside the house, the steel baron, who also loved music, had a large organ manned by an organist who was on call at all times. As the organ pealed, Frick showed the president a well-known Rembrandt for which he had paid $300,000. He also revealed that he was having his chauffeur trained as an aviator so that he could fly from his mansion to the Myopia Club in nearby Marblehead for a round of golf. Taft who had attended flying demonstrations by the Wright brothers was fascinated.

And so the game began, with the president being given the first opportunity to deal. Butt won a pot shortly, the first of several he won that night. Not so with the president. Taft occasionally tried to bluff, but all to no avail. Once he tried to fool Archie, while he was holding a straight:

> "How did you know I did not have four aces," he [the president] asked me.
> "By your face sir," I answered.

"Confound that face," he said. "I wish I had yours, Knox."

"If you had, you might have more money," laughed the secretary, "but you wouldn't be president."

"The President," Butt concluded, "does not hold very good hands, and when he happens to get one, his face lights up with a smile which proclaims the secret to the whole table."[24]

Hardly the face of a scheming politician.

While the president frolicked with Frick, he refused to be bothered with official duties. When the Ecuadorian ambassador arrived at Bar Harbor, he asked to see Taft on a pleasant "golfing" Sunday afternoon. A conflict was brewing between Ecuador and Peru, and the matter was crucial. Even the secretary of state felt that Taft needed to see the ambassador before conferring with the president of Chile, who was trying to settle the dispute. Taft greeted the news with typical reluctance. Why should he cancel his golf game because of disputes between banana republics? Taft's advisers had not reckoned with the obstinate streak in Taft, or, more precisely, his preference for a sunny afternoon of golf. "I'll be damned if I'll give up my game of golf to see this fellow," said the sulky president. He would only see him on Friday evening after nine or, possibly if he had to, on Sunday.[25]

Diplomacy be damned if it interfered with golf!

A Sinking Presidency

By early 1912, the presidential demands on Archie Butt's time were wearing him down. He had emotional ties with both Roosevelt and Taft, and was genuinely fond of both of them. He had swam, hiked, ridden in new fangled automobiles, played tennis, forded swollen rivers, ridden horseback, played golf and poker, and climbed slippery peaks with both Roosevelt in his day and Taft in his. As Taft's companion and confidante, Butt was at the storm center of the Taft-Roosevelt political feud and was privy to the distrust and disdain generated by Roosevelt's assault on the Taft presidency. On February 25 Roosevelt did what everyone anticipated—he announced his candidacy for the Republican nomination.

Finding Butt on the verge of a physical breakdown, his doctor advised a trip abroad. Archie knew that he was enormously tired and needed a break. But with all that was going on, he canceled his reservations. When he told the president, Taft insisted that he go ahead with his plans.

Butt sailed with a friend to Naples. Before he left, he wrote his soul mate, Clara Butt. "Don't forget that all my papers are in storage warehouse, and if the old ship goes down," he reminded her, "you will find my affairs in ship-shape condition." A glimpse of depression, born of the Taft-Roosevelt feud and sheer exhaustion? Possibly, but Butt's farewell note proved uncannily prophetic.[26]

On the evening of April 15, 1912, Taft was attending the theater when he heard the news that the *Titanic* had hit an iceberg. He rushed back to the White House to listen for further reports. Archie Butt and his companion had decided to sail on the HMS *Titanic,* the White Star Line's new state-of-the-art steamship.

Later, details of Archie Butt's final hours filtered back to the White House. A friend from the TR years, Marie Young, later told Taft that Archie spoke to her calmly as he helped her into one of the lifeboats. "Goodbye Miss Young. Luck is with you. Will you please remember me to all the folks back home." She last glimpsed him standing at the rail as her lifeboat descended into the murky waters.[27]

On the same day as the *Titanic* sank, the Taft presidency hit its own iceberg. Roosevelt won an overwhelming victory in one of the recently established presidential primaries. Though the party regulars would ultimately deliver Taft the nomination in July, he foundered in the general election. Roosevelt collected more votes than Taft but not as many as the Democrat Woodrow Wilson. A year before, Archie Butt and the president heard Wilson speak in Atlanta. Academic though he was, Wilson held the attention of the crowd for forty minutes. "The President said it was the polished utterance of a politician," Archie wrote. "But he has got to be reckoned with. I can see that."[28]

Ironically, these were notes that Butt had carefully kept and put in storage to preserve, just in case "the old ship goes down." Archie Butt could only have watched with distress the unfolding of events in the remaining months of the Taft administration, including the president's need for sport and recreation. Though the president played golf in the summer of 1912, the "sports presidency" of William Howard Taft essentially sank with the death of Archibald Willingham Butt. The Taft administration, not nearly as watertight as the *Titanic* was said to be, would itself sink on election night in November 1912.

Although Taft's relaxed approach to sports pales by comparison to Roosevelt's famously active years in the White House, Taft's emphasis on sports was nonetheless vital to his well-being. Roosevelt's variety of strenuous sports was unmatched (and still is), and he astounded those who observed him. But

Taft was simply a far different—and far more conventional—sportsman. Like those who followed him, he engaged in a few recreational sports because they were relaxing or, once in a while, politically useful.

For the most part, Taft found pleasure in his sports. The presidents of the next two decades would settle comfortably into a sports routine similar to Taft's. The dynamic approach of Teddy Roosevelt of energetically combining sports and politics would only gradually reemerge. In the meantime, presidents would occasionally meet with sports celebrities, attend baseball and football games, and participate in a handful of sports for fun and relaxation.

Taft was able to enjoy both his personal and public lives far more after he left the White House. Nellie recovered, and eventually Taft was reconciled to his old friend, Theodore Roosevelt. Best of all, in 1923, he became chief justice of the United States Supreme Court, the job that he wanted far more than the presidency.

Woodrow Wilson

More than Just a Game

Commenting on rumors that Woodrow Wilson had had an affair with a married woman, Teddy Roosevelt once remarked: "You can't cast a man as a Romeo who looks and acts so much like an apothecary's clerk."[1]

No image better depicts the prim, bespectacled, and intellectual Professor Woodrow Wilson—at least the public Wilson. That he was a golf-aholic during his White House days and that he was a fierce and clever football strategist during his time at Princeton is—and was—far less known. But, despite his chronic health problems, personal tragedies, his naturally intellectual angle on things, and the stress of a major war, Wilson can be counted as one of our more sporting presidents. Not a jock to be sure, but an active man whose intellect was sometimes directly and, more often, indirectly associated with sports.

In his twenties and thirties, Wilson played billiards and soon became something of an expert. Wilson's brother-in-law, Stockton Axson, discovered Wilson's enthusiasm for billiards while the two were traveling in Georgia. "We stopped over in Atlanta between trains at the old Kimball House," he recalled, "and Mr. Wilson led me to the billiard room, where we watched the players for some time." Wilson could critique each error that the players made. Later, he astutely observed billiard players in England and at the Nassau Club in Princeton. Wilson, "with his fine coordination" and eagle eye, would occasionally defeat Pete Van Doren, a classmate and indisputably the best billiards player in Princeton. Professor Wilson had a purist's contempt for pool, which he considered "too easy." Later, he played pool as well as billiards.[2]

When he was a young professor at Wesleyan University and later at Princeton, he played tennis. By 1889 Wilson had become a tennis addict, playing every afternoon during the summer, sometimes with one of his colleagues on the faculty. He also played with Axson, who now saw an athletic side of Wilson denied to all but a few friends and family members. "I was nearly always

Woodrow Wilson displaying an unusual putting stance, which may have been the result of a short putter. Though Wilson played more golf than any other president, he was the worst of the serious White House duffers. His physician, Cary Grayson, who played with him, felt that outdoor exercise was the best prophylactic against the strokes Wilson suffered before he was president. The president is said to have painted a ball red with iodine so that he could play on Christmas day in the snow. Courtesy of Woodrow Wilson House, Washington, D.C.

beaten," Axson wrote in a memoir published after Wilson's death, "for he had a sure eye, a steady hand, and good coordination." Wilson took up tennis for health, exercise, and the pure enjoyment of it.[3]

★

He Could Have Been a Football Coach

College football also engaged Wilson's imagination, intellect, and emotions. In November 1892, for the first time ever, the Princeton football team lost to the University of Pennsylvania, and Wilson took it hard. He was a professor at Princeton, but his passion for the sport began when he was a student there in the 1870s. Though Wilson never played football, he soon had a better grasp of the game than the players themselves. As in billiards, he possessed a keen eye for the game's strategy and technique.

Wilson was elected to be one of five student directors of Princeton football, and he alone supplied much of the strategy, energy, publicity, and financial acumen. Indeed, Wilson occupied a position nearly as important as the team's captain. In team meetings, he sketched out plays, which he may have learned by observation or through reading British journals. "He had," said one contemporary, "clear-cut notions of how the game should be played and insisted on them."[4]

As a student, Wilson spent his energies on raising money to outfit and transport the team. Teams in these early years often went bankrupt, leaving them unable to pay for equipment, transportation, and rental of playing grounds. Wilson accomplished these Herculean tasks by appealing to the college for money and by drastically raising the cost of admission to fifty cents (closer to fifty dollars in early twenty-first-century money and virtually a week's allowance for the average student).

He also used his position as editor of the *Princetonian* to whip the team and its supporters into shape. He exhorted the players to obey the captain without question, defended the hefty gate fees, and called upon the undergraduates to support the team. The season of 1878 was a preview of Wilson's first year as president when he won all of his legislative battles. Princeton finished its six-game season undefeated, trouncing both Yale and Harvard. Even with the considerable expenses, the football association turned a tidy profit, so much, in fact, that it was able to contribute $100 to the baseball team (Wilson was head of the baseball association). "We played a much more scientific game than our opponents did," he wrote in the *Princetonian*.[5]

Wilson's devotion to football persisted through a decade of graduate school and teaching at Bryn Mawr, the women's college, where he didn't have any opportunity to coach. But once he became a professor at Wesleyan University in Middletown, Connecticut, his love affair with football immediately revived. The Wesleyan team began the season with three demoralizing defeats. Then, Professor Wilson hosted a brainstorming session in his classroom, where he did the planning on the blackboard. One story, probably apocryphal, has Wilson leaping from the stands to lead cheers for the team, as he really did later when he was president of Princeton. On Thanksgiving Day in New York, the team resoundingly beat the University of Pennsylvania, achieving perhaps the greatest upset in Wesleyan history. Working behind the scenes, Wilson brought the faculty and fraternities together in support of the team. Even after he left for Princeton, he continued to supply advice to the Wesleyan team and supporters. One contemporary who knew Wilson was sure that he could have coached football for a living.

In 1894, when football came under attack, Wilson agreed to debate the issue: "Ought the Game of Football Be Encouraged?" He was critical of educators who dismissed the game as inappropriate for higher education. Wilson reeled off a number of arguments often used to defend football. The gridiron game built character, encouraged cooperation, led to endurance, and developed practical intelligence and presence of mind. Colleges that opposed football, he believed—notably Harvard, with its high-toned gridiron critic, President Charles Eliot—failed to organize their teams effectively. "They have not succeeded not because they didn't have manly men," Wilson declared, "but because they did not have the sort of organization to produce a good plan which wins in foot ball."[6]

Through football, it's possible to follow Wilson's changes in political ideology. When Wilson was president of Princeton, college football underwent its worst crises ever when deaths and injuries on the field led to calls for reform and even suspension of football altogether. In 1909, amid the uproar over football's brutality, Wilson proposed a broad mandate for change in football, or, more precisely, abolishing the formations known as mass play—the pushing and pulling of the ball carrier that were the bread-and-butter plays of the Big Three. He called for sweeping changes to make football "more attractive." Within months, the football rules committee removed restrictions from the recently introduced forward pass, and the bone-crushing, head-jarring mass play was abolished, just as Wilson advocated. In a brief talk to the Princeton football team in 1910, governor-elect Wilson of New Jersey declared that "the new rules are doing much to bring football to a high level as a sport, for its brutal features are being done away with and better elements retained."

Wilson declared a rebirth of American ideals and a rejection of pure material success.[7]

This concept of a rebirth would be evident in his call for a "New Freedom" in 1913, as President Wilson set out to apply his talents for organization and strategy, so evident in football, to winning congressional approval for precedent-setting legislative proposals.

★

Different Strokes

In 1896 Wilson suffered the first of numerous strokes, which resulted in what he called euphemistically "neuritis," a weakness in his right hand and arm leaving him unable to write with his right hand and numbing nerve endings in several of his fingers. Within days of the 1896 episode, he learned to write with his left hand. Physical problems were hardly new to Wilson. Since adolescence, Wilson had been subject to indigestion and headaches, and these problems persisted into his teaching career. Early in middle age, Wilson was susceptible to arteries that filled with plaque, usually a condition associated with aging. Moreover, Wilson may have suffered minor strokes in his early thirties or even before.

After his second stroke in 1906, Wilson went to Philadelphia to consult with specialists. "I know now more exactly than I did then what is really threatening Woodrow," his wife, Ellen, wrote after she heard the doctor's report; "it is hardening of the arteries, due to prolonged high blood pressure on brain nerves." Ellen called it "dying by inches." Still she was relieved that his condition had been diagnosed so early. She would have been shocked to know that her husband suffered not only from hypertension and arteriosclerosis but also from disease of the carotid artery for which there would be no cure, only more crises.[8]

Wilson was enormously talented as a writer and speaker, and he could easily have earned a living solely from lecture tours and magazine articles. But by the mid-1890s, the ambitious young professor had piled one obligation on another. He also faced vexing financial problems. Not only did he have to support a wife and three children but also had to underwrite extended visits by relatives and friends, often swelling the Wilson household to eight or ten members. No wonder Wilson had a deep-seated desire to build his own house, still another expense that he might have to assume.

After this first major stroke, his wife Ellen urged him to go abroad for the summer, and so off to England he went, bicycling from town to town, and his health seemed greatly restored. Once he was back at home, however, he became singularly focused on his ambitions, giving up both bicycling and billiards.

In 1898, at the urging of his wife, he took up golf. Little did he, or she, imagine that he would one day latch on to this game and become a true golf fanatic, or that he would log far more hours as a golfer than any other president in American history.

Wilson's major stroke in 1906 when he was president of Princeton resulted in sudden blindness in his left eye, a condition that never really improved. Wilson's approach to this crisis, as with the earlier one, was to forge ahead. He had reached a takeoff point in his career, having become virtually the best-known college president in the country. Typical of Victorian religious and medical approaches to health was Wilson's belief in the efficacy of *the will*. Wilson virtually commanded his body to function. "Consistent with his belief that the body was the servant of the spirit," medical historian Edwin Weinstein has written, "he told his wife that he would train his eye to 'behave.'" Unfortunately neither his eye nor his personality—also affected by the strokes—would be easily tamed. His uncompromising behavior, aggravated by these strokes, would lead to disputes with his friends, boards of trustees, and ultimately with the leaders of his own political party.[9]

Given the precariousness of Wilson's health, it is remarkable that his career continued to move forward, but then he had a knack for turning his weaknesses into strengths. In 1910, after being forced to step down as president of Princeton, he became the nominee for governor of New Jersey and was elected. Like Theodore Roosevelt, he was able to use the governorship as a springboard to the presidency.

When Wilson became president, a prominent neurologist predicted that he would not live out his first term. But Wilson was fortunate to have as his personal physician and friend Dr. Cary T. Grayson, the Navy doctor, one of the four who rode with Roosevelt to Warrenton. Grayson made it his job to preserve the health of the president.

Grayson was a good storyteller and, like Wilson, a native of Virginia, and he believed in fresh air and exercise. According to *Hidden Illnesses in the White House* by Kenneth Crispell and Carlos Gomez, Grayson had little use for medication. He believed that Wilson's illnesses, including the neurological ones, were the result of overwork. The medical historians who have studied Wilson believe that many of his problems were psychosomatic, but by no means all of them.[10]

So Wilson played golf and took up motoring in his favorite of the six White House automobiles, a gleaming, partially open Pierce Arrow Landaulet. Not that he had to drive. His chauffeur took Wilson on prescribed routes around Washington. Though touring in an automobile is not exactly sport, Wilson's motoring provided him with an outdoor diversion.

Golf was Wilson's sport of choice as president. By July, when Congress was no longer in session, Wilson and his physician were playing as often as five times a week, though, like William Howard Taft, Wilson never played on Sundays. On Saturdays, Grayson also prevailed on Wilson to go motoring. In September and October 1914, he and Grayson played twenty-eight times and their play continued during the late fall and winter. Normally, the president spent two hours away from the White House playing twelve holes of golf, and on Saturdays he and Grayson splurged, playing eighteen holes. Golf historian Don Van Natta has estimated that Wilson played more than twelve hundred rounds of golf in the slightly more than seven years that he was healthy enough to swing a club and able to play.[11]

Wilson teed up in every season and under practically all weather conditions. He even had balls painted red so he could practice in the snow. Once, when he was in Europe negotiating the treaty that ended World War I, Grayson suggested that he and British Prime Minister David Lloyd-George settle the world's problems on a golf course in England, but it appears that the match was never played.

Not that he was as skilled in golf as he was in billiards or tennis. More precisely, he probably never broke 100 or 110. From the recollections of Edmund Starling of the Secret Service, it appears that his drives often might have gone no more than fifty yards. Even if some shots went a hundred yards, it would have taken Wilson far more strokes than his predecessor, William Howard Taft, to reach the green. Once he neared the green, Wilson was able to use his fine motor skills, so evident in billiards, in his approach shots and putts.

Lacking a fairway game, Wilson was probably not capable of becoming even an average duffer. Maybe it was because he began playing too late in life, but more likely he had a far worse handicap. Because of near blindness in his left eye, Wilson faced a physical obstacle that few golfers can overcome. Wilson's intermittent problems with his weak right arm, his so-called neuritis, possibly slowed—or unhinged—his swing. Remarkably, Wilson was not only able to teach himself to write left-handed but also to play golf from the left side. History has not recorded where he obtained the left-handed golf clubs. Once, during World War I, he burned his right hand severely climbing out of a British tank and proceeded to play golf not just with one good eye but one-handed.

Luckily for Wilson, he didn't particularly care about his scores. In fact, he

A smiling, healthy Woodrow Wilson throwing out the first ball in 1916 with his second wife Edith (to his left) just as radiant. As a student at Princeton, Wilson managed the baseball and football teams, and wrote editorials in the student newspaper, urging fellow students to attend games. An invalid after he left the presidency, he watched the Washington Senators from a limousine that entered Griffith Stadium through a special gate and parked beside the bullpen. Library of Congress, Washington, D.C.

and Grayson seldom kept track. Because they were equally inept at golf, it was the exercise and fresh air that kept them on the links.

Wilson thrived on routine. Though he played the same golf courses and seldom let a round go more than two hours, he developed a genuine fondness for the game. He took pleasure in his good shots. "Lately I have been trying to master the brassy [a fairway wood]," he told an interviewer in 1915, "and on one links I made a wonderful shot one day. Every time I walk over that spot, I have a thrill of pleasure, of pride of accomplishment." However, his good shots were so rare as to find unexpected targets. Once he hit a ball around a dogleg and onto a green, nearly beaning one of the players in front of him. The player came charging back ready to do battle with the jerk who had played into him, only to draw up suddenly when he recognized the president. Whenever friends or acquaintances saw that golfer after his near mishap, they jovially yelled "fore."[12]

Some accounts suggest that Wilson lacked the urge to compete that most golfers relish. "If he played a few holes, nine, eighteen, it was all the same to him," the chief White House usher Ike Hoover wrote. Wilson "seldom kept score and paid little attention to it when he did. He would play at all hours, sometimes as early as five in the morning and sometimes late in the afternoon."[13]

Yet Wilson sometimes showed his competitive side on the links. On June 8, 1915, less than a year after the outbreak of World War I in Europe, Wilson was in the throes of a diplomatic crisis. Germany had sunk the passenger liner *Lusitania*, resulting in the death of hundreds of Americans. Wilson threatened to bring the United States into the war, and Secretary of State William Jennings Bryan, who insisted on strict neutrality, resigned. The crisis was both stressful for Wilson and a setback to Democratic Party unity.

On the day of Bryan's resignation, Wilson played eighteen holes of golf with an old friend, Colonel Edward Brown of Georgia. Wilson started out poorly, losing the first four holes to Brown. Then the president confided to Brown: "I will tell you what's the matter with my golf." And Wilson unloaded his worries on Brown.

"And then a curious thing happened to our game. Play as hard as I could, the President won the next four holes straight making us even."

Discussing the game at dinner, Brown jokingly accused Wilson of divulging Bryan's resignation to throw him off his game. Wilson slyly replied that there might be some truth in what Brown said. Again, as in football, Wilson proved himself a master of the brainy—even crafty and calculating—side of sport.[14]

★

The Games He Couldn't—or Wouldn't—Win

In the summer of 1914, abruptly and unexpectedly, Ellen Wilson's chronic kidney problems took a turn for the worse, and by July her incurable Bright's disease confined her to her sickbed. Even then, Wilson persisted in his routine, playing golf three times in the final week of July, just before she died on August 2. And when she died, his grief knew no bounds. He stayed with her two nights in the East Room of the White House and, in the words of presidential historian C. Brian Kelly, "he rode the special train to her hometown of Rome, Georgia, staying all the while in the compartment with her casket."[15]

After returning from the burial in Rome, Wilson was devastated; and the vacuum left in his life by Ellen's death led to his most intense period on the golf course.

The fact is that Grayson was planning a radically new form of therapy in which golf would play a part. In spite of golf, motoring, detective novels, and visits from his daughters, Wilson was desperately lonely, unable to forget his loss by immersing himself in work or recreation—not to mention trying to negotiate treacherous and unfamiliar terrain in dealing with the warring European powers.

"I have never seen a man more dependent on a woman's companionship," his adviser and friend Colonel Edward House wrote. Grayson too recognized that Wilson needed a romantic interest. To arrange a "chance" meeting between the president and Edith Bolling Galt, he invited the attractive Washington widow, a friend of Wilson's secretary (and his first wife's cousin) to the White House. Covered with mud and wearing their frayed golf knickers, Wilson and Grayson entered the room where the ladies were. Wilson rounding the corner nearly ran into the woman who would very soon be his new wife. Immediately the flame in Wilson's life was reignited.[16]

Wilson, who became like a moonstruck teenager almost on the spot, used outdoor recreations in the spring and summer of 1915 to court Edith Galt. At first, the two took walks and went for motoring trips in the Pierce Arrow around Washington. By the end of the summer, however, Edith and Woodrow were frequently playing golf together. "How jolly, my sweetheart," he wrote from Cornish, New Hampshire, where the Wilsons usually had gone on vacation, "that you are taking golf lessons (and how I envy the teacher—you will be adorable as a pupil!). Of course, we shall have many a game together—as many as I can persuade you to play." On December 18, 1915, Edith Bolling Galt became the first lady and helpmate of the president. Henceforth she and Dr. Grayson together would manage the president's regimen and arrange his schedule to allow for recreation. A wife, exercise, and vacations—Grayson's formula for Wilson's health—worked for three years.[17]

Edmund Starling, the flamboyant secret service agent who guarded four presidents, had an opportunity to observe the president and his lady playing golf, after they were married, while accompanying them at a discreet distance and remaining behind trees or hedges. "Neither of them really cared about the game," he observed. While the president and First Lady played their desultory game, Wilson—an accomplished storyteller—regaled Edith with impersonations in dialect. "The President and Mrs. Wilson were inexpert golfers," Starling wrote, "he averaging about 115 and she about 200." But they had fun even if they didn't take their golf rounds seriously. "They laughed at anything and everything in those days," Starling recalled. "They were completely happy, and the increasing burden of his job rested lightly on the President's shoulders."[18]

In February 1917 the Germans renewed their unrestricted submarine warfare, forcing Wilson to prepare for war. After several German attacks on passenger liners carrying Americans, Wilson gave the government and the country his war message on April 2, 1917. In the weeks before his speech to Congress, he played golf regularly, and on the day he delivered his message, he played golf in the morning. Colonel House advised him that it would be inappropriate for him to play in a period of grave emergency, but Wilson made no attempt to cut back on his golf. In spite of the advice, he played twelve times in April, the month that the United States marched off to war.

Did Wilson's daily excursions to the golf course cause criticism? Not in the least. Wilson's refusal to play with political or corporate magnates, insisting on keeping his golf private, and playing at unpretentious clubs all kept publicity to a minimum. On April 10 the Wilsons played golf in the morning and played host to Theodore Roosevelt in the afternoon. Roosevelt had come to request command of a volunteer regiment. In spite of Wilson's initial formality—and coolness—Wilson warmed to the effusive Roosevelt. Nevertheless, he rejected Roosevelt's request, unwilling to allow him to become a "loose cannon" on the battlefield.

During the war years, Wilson was relatively healthy, suffering few of the neurological symptoms that had marred his years at Princeton. All of that would change after November 11, 1918, when the armistice based on Wilson's Fourteen Points ended the fighting. On December 4 the president and Edith Wilson embarked for France aboard the *George Washington*. In his first few days in Paris, Wilson played golf twice at St. Cloud, outside of Paris—the only times he played golf in the next six months. His fellow heads of state, especially David Lloyd-George of England and Georges Clemenceau of France, who resisted his efforts to make a "just" peace, made his life excruciatingly stressful. In addition, he had to consult frequently with the staff members of the American peace delegation and insisted on writing state papers by himself, hunting and pecking on his typewriter. He worked for ten hours—sometimes twelve—and on Sundays only allowed himself to go motoring.

On February 15, 1919, Wilson left for the United States, a brief trip home to catch up on presidential business. Aboard ship, Wilson exercised as best he could, mainly by walking brisk laps around the ship's deck. He also attempted to play shuffleboard once with Doctor Grayson, but he could not seem to put his shots in the squares and barely scored. Back in Washington for a month, he was too busy to play golf. He did occasionally walk. Wilson, while a professor at Bryn Mawr, had sometimes walked to Philadelphia and back with Stockton Axson, a distance of about ten miles. In the Lake District of England with his family in 1906, after his second major stroke, he had walked fourteen miles across the rugged countryside. On this walk through the nation's capital, Dr. Grayson recorded that "he was recognized and cheered by many of the pedestrians, traffic finally becoming so congested that it became necessary for the police reserves to clear the sidewalks."[19]

Once again back in Paris, he was saddled with a heavy schedule. The chaos in war-torn Europe, especially with revolutions threatening in Germany and Hungary, made it urgent to conclude the peace treaty, but the deadlock between Wilson and Clemenceau persisted. The antagonism between the two world leaders over treatment of the defeated Germans put Wilson under incredible stress. In early April, his luck ran out. The president came down with influenza, perhaps causing neurological symptoms and possibly aggravated by a slight stroke.

His health never entirely recovered. When he returned to the Big Four sessions, he became easily fatigued and irritable. His memory failed him periodically. He drastically altered his positions on major issues, such as the Germans acknowledging their "war guilt"—or, simply put, that they alone were responsible for starting the war. He was worn out but labored on. Ray Stannard Baker, a staff member of the peace commission and his future biographer, testified to his precarious state of health. "Sometimes there in Paris when I went up to see him in the evening after the meeting of the Four, he looked utterly beaten, worn out, his face quite haggard and one side of it and the eye twitching painfully, but the next morning he would appear refreshed and eager to go on with the fight."[20]

After Wilson's illness, Dr. Grayson insisted that Wilson spend more time exercising . . . at least in outdoor activities such as automobile rides or brief walks. In the evenings, Wilson and Edith played cards, which seemed to relax the president. Once, in May, Grayson persuaded Wilson to attend the races at the Longchamps Course near Paris. Finally, in July, the president left for home in apparent triumph, the Versailles Treaty in his pocket. Edmund Starling, the secret service agent, recorded Wilson's deteriorating condition. Starling accompanied the Wilsons on their walks around the deck of the ship. "The President stumbled against one of the rings set into the deck and used for lashing the lifeboats in heavy weather," Starling recalled as they circled the deck. Then it happened twice more when they next approached it. Edith looked at Starling in alarm. Next time around, Starling stood in front of the ring so that the president would have to step aside. "He was pale and haggard, a tired man, and it seemed to me that since his illness in Paris he lacked the coordination of both mind and body which always before had been his outstanding characteristic."[21]

That summer, Wilson resumed his golf games with Grayson, but the pressure had taken its toll. Against the advice of Grayson and Edith, Wilson decided to embark on a speaking tour on behalf of the Treaty of Versailles and his cherished League of Nations. Late in September, the trip was interrupted when Wilson broke down physically and emotionally—during a speech in Pueblo, Colorado, he was incoherent and at one point burst into tears. After the speech, as the train headed for Wichita, Kansas, the doctor had it stopped so that Wilson could go out for a short walk. Only five speeches remained early the next morning but he was close to a physical and nervous breakdown. Grayson and Edith got Wilson's permission to return directly to Washington. With tears in his eyes, Wilson confessed that "this is the greatest disappointment of my life."[22]

The train sped back to Washington. During the first few days in the White House, as if to demonstrate his ability to function, Wilson took short walks and went motoring. He appeared normal and even played a game of billiards on October 1. Early the next morning, however, Wilson suffered a massive stroke. This final episode of his personal campaign to outrun neurological disaster nearly killed him. Though he eventually recovered partially from the paralysis of his right side, he was too weak to keep up the fight for his treaty. The Senate refused to ratify the Versailles peace treaty, and the United States never joined the League of Nations.

As Wilson hovered between life and death and then after his condition stabilized, Edith acted as the White House gatekeeper and the American public never realized how ill Wilson was and how rudderless the government had become.

In 1922, not quite a year after he left the White House, he wrote to a friend in Lyme, Connecticut, where he had played golf in 1910. Although there was now a new course, he dreamed of playing the old "pasture" course again. "It was one of the most interesting courses I have ever known," he wrote. "I often think of the pleasures of play and companionship which you and I had on it."[23]

In February 1924, Wilson died at his house on S Street in Washington. He was sixty-seven.

★

The Gridiron Battlefield

Wilson as war president would leave an unexpected legacy to the sport he loved, college football. On April 2, 1917, the same day that the United States entered World War I, Wilson's secretary of war, Newton D. Baker, came to talk to Wilson about the subject of using athletics at military bases. He specifically referred to the collegiate approach to athletics, and to football especially. The conditions in and around existing military camps shocked many, what with the bars and brothels existing near military facilities.

"I have the feeling that as our young soldiers are substantially men of college age," Baker wrote to the president, "the experience of our colleges in recreation will go a long way by analogy to help us." Put simply, the military determined to use the model of college athletics for both recreation and training. The "father of American football," Walter Camp, was enlisted to devise a training system. Although the Army authorities preferred to use boxing for training, football took over in the fall of 1917.[24]

Woodrow Wilson, the professor who once played godfather to football at Princeton and Wesleyan, had inadvertently encouraged it as a preparation for war in his "war to end all wars." His passion for football was finding new life in the military's use of the sport that he once coached.

Football was used to boost morale and to keep the troops occupied as well as to shape military training. A visitor to a military camp reported forty-seven different games of football taking place while he visited that single base. In addition, the military bases fielded all-star teams that played against college elevens or, more often, other Army or Navy teams.

The collegiate advisers to the military introduced collegiate rituals such as organized cheering and lusty military marches delivered by marching bands at halftime. Military training felt the effects of football in other ways. At Camp Upton in upstate New York, a military drill called Over the Top resembled gridiron line play. Each platoon, organized in opposing lines, went on offense in order to break through the static defense. Thousands of young men, who had never been exposed to college football, played according to the prevailing rules, discovering an exciting new pastime.

After World War I, college football flourished as never before. The sleek new game of football, which had won Wilson's blessing in 1909 and 1910, gained universal approval. Football attendance immediately set new records, a trend that continued until the Great Depression. Stadiums such as Soldier's Field in Chicago and the University of Michigan stadium at Ann Arbor held as many as 85,000 to 100,000 football fans. The spillover from college football led in 1920 to the formation of the National Football League, a development that would *not* have appealed to the amateur-oriented Wilson. In October 1924, only months after Wilson's death, Illinois's Red Grange became the first national football celebrity when he scored four touchdowns in the first twelve minutes against the University of Michigan, including a 95-yard run after receiving the kickoff.

Both football and golf, the two sports that Wilson either managed or played, took off in the 1920s, a decade often called the "golden age of sports." The thought again conjures up the picture of the slim, intelligent, and intense figure of Woodrow Wilson leading cheers for Princeton and hacking his way down snowy or muddy fairways toward elusive greens. Indeed knowing of his reputation as the apostle of progressive democracy and the architect of the League of Nations, it's hard not to smile a little at the secret sporting life of Woodrow Wilson.

The question arises whether Wilson could have postponed his "dying by inches" by following his regimen of golf and walking when he was in Paris. And if so, could he have won his struggle to get the United States to embrace his beloved League of Nations?

Possibly, then, he could have played the old course in Lyme, Connecticut, one more time.

Warren Harding showing the form of a serious golfer. He had slightly more success on the links than as president. His golf was on a collision course with his deteriorating health and floundering presidency. Occasionally, he took his Airedale Laddie to shag balls on the South Lawn of the White House. On the way home from Alaska in 1923, he became the first president to play golf in Canada. After stopping to play in Vancouver, he died in a San Francisco hotel room a few days later. Library of Congress, Washington, D.C.

Warren Harding
The Wager He Didn't Win

When Congress passed the joint resolution to formally end World War I, all it lacked was President Warren G. Harding's signature. The young government aide who brought the treaty from Washington to New Jersey, where Harding was playing golf, had to wait nearly two hours until Harding could be summoned from the golf course. Nattily dressed in a Palm Beach suit, a red-and-green bow tie, and white shoes, the handsome president carefully read the bound document, signed it, and returned to the golf course.

It had taken Woodrow Wilson six months in Paris to negotiate a peace treaty that Congress never ratified. It took Warren Harding ten minutes between rounds of golf in New Jersey to end the war.

After World War I, the American public and the news media were hungry for anything other than war-related stories. In addition to news stories about strikes, the high cost of living, and the wild changes in women's fashion, the public was caught up in sports and sports celebrities.

Historians generally agree that Harding was a failure as president. Though he ranks dead last in most presidential polls, he was far from the worst presidential athlete or sportsman. His interest in sports reflected a male sporting culture of golf and poker. To put it bluntly, Harding probably would have been happier—and healthier—if he could have focused entirely on sports and left the presidential business to others. Indeed, much of his time was spent on the links and in smoke-filled rooms playing poker. "The president was really a fan," recalled Dr. Joel Boone, a White House physician. "He loved sports: golf, baseball, football, and playing cards."[1]

Harding—and his successor Calvin Coolidge—occupied the White House in the Periclean age of American sports. The 1920s saw the rise of a celebrity culture, and nowhere was this truer than in sports. Sportswriters had more to write about because of the inexhaustible public interest in big-name stars as well as high-profile sporting events. Whatever the sport, a mega-celebrity emerged: Babe Ruth in baseball, Jack Dempsey in boxing, Red Grange in football, Bill Tilden in tennis, Bobby Jones in golf, not to mention women tennis players, swimmers, and golfers. Thanks to radio and movies, sports events became available to a far larger public than ever before. Millions of listeners heard announcers describe the dramatic fights of Jack Dempsey and Gene Tunney. Later in the decade, the golden tones of Graham McNamee carried the Rose Bowl across the country on New Year's Day. Dempsey, Ruth, and Grange even went to Hollywood to make films.

In contrast to these athletes, Harding's rise to the presidency was as unspectacular as it was unlikely. A small-town newspaper owner who went into politics, he might easily have crowned his career with his single term as Ohio's lieutenant governor and retired to his hometown of Marion, Ohio. But because of his good looks and agreeable personality, he moved from the Ohio state senate to the United States Senate. Compared with the senatorial stars, he was not brilliant, but he compensated by being loyal and congenial. In 1920 an electorate exhausted by wars and foreign entanglements handed the election to Harding, who said he would return the country to "normalcy." Instead, he ushered the country into a new era of photogenic statesmen and political thievery on an epic scale.

A great president he was not, but he did preside over a sports-friendly presidency. Because of his informal and gregarious manner, the president looked as if he belonged on a golf course. He played three times a week and, far more than his predecessors, was at ease in the company of big-time athletes. Even before he was inaugurated, Harding gave notice that he would not follow Wilson's discreet example of playing anonymously on unknown golf courses. In the two months before he was sworn in, he fished, golfed, and gambled with friends at Point Isabel, Texas, on the Gulf of Mexico. He played golf in Florida while cruising the rivers and canals in a houseboat owned by his wealthy friends. He even played golf on a pre-inauguration visit to the Panama Canal—on a course known as the $8 million links because of its proximity to the Gatun Locks built at that price. Brief newspaper articles followed the golfing tour of the president-elect. The American public had shown uneasiness when Taft took up this amusement, but now hardly noticed. After two decades of reform, war, and the quarrel over the League of Nations, the people breathed a collective sigh of relief at the return to "normalcy."[2]

One story has Harding taking up golf, as a senator, when he picked up a club and hit a picture-perfect shot. Though he had played before, golf now became a passion. Never as good as that initial shot might suggest, Harding was strictly mediocre, averaging 101 and never shooting lower than 92. Such was his obsession, however, that he became the first president to practice his short game on the South Lawn (setting a precedent for Dwight Eisenhower and Bill Clinton). Often he took the "first canine," his Airedale Laddie, with him to practice and, so it has been claimed, to the golf course itself. His favorite golfing retreat was the eighteen-hole course at Friendship, the lush estate of his wealthy friends Ned and Evalyn McLean. According to Evalyn McLean, "Harding loved it, naturally, because its eighty enclosed acres were the single area in the world where he could take a drink, play golf or cards or sing and still be sure that what he did would not be written up."[3]

On the golf course and at the poker table, Harding loved to place bets and side bets. In fact, he placed a bet on every swing. His betting became so complicated that he used Edmund Starling, the secret service operative, to total up and keep track of the various wagers.

Sports or "sporting" existed on a less visible level. Harding was described as a "sporting man," which, in the early 1900s, meant a man with a roving eye, a man who had an eye for women who were pretty and available. To be sure, he was certainly not the first—or last—president to stray from the marriage contract. But he would soon (after his death) become the best-known presidential philanderer up to that time. After carrying on an affair with a friend's wife, Harding settled on a teenaged admirer, Nan Britton, who later wrote what she claimed was a tell-all account of their relationship. And, if the rumors of flings and flirtations are accurate, there were many more. If sexual dalliances could ever be considered a sport, Harding might rank in the upper echelon of White House athletes.

Toward men, he was a loyal friend (with the exception perhaps of the friend whose wife became his mistress). When he became president, he appointed his cronies and friends from Ohio to cabinet, subcabinet, and even shadowy unofficial positions. Some, as it turned out, enriched themselves at the government's expense. Theodore Roosevelt's daughter, Alice, delivered the most damning portrayal of Harding. "He was not a bad man," she wrote. "He was just a slob." In contrast, Evalyn McLean regarded Harding as "warm-hearted"; unlike most men who gained influence, he never changed from being "sweet and considerate into being an egomaniac." But she added: "He really could not bear to make anyone feel badly; that was his greatest weakness."[4]

Harding's administration has been judged harshly, perhaps too harshly. This is not to suggest that he was in the same league as Alice's father or that he would ever look down from Mount Rushmore. Often overlooked are the achievements of his cabinet members who were responsible for a major naval disarmament treaty, tax cuts that injected life into the economy, and improvements in business efficiency. The policies initiated during his years in the White House persisted through a generally prosperous and productive decade. Unfortunately, Harding is remembered for the corrupt and unlawful side of his administration, for which he was also responsible.

★

He Couldn't Say No

In the early 1920s, "the golden age of sport," Harding was like a kid awed by the big names in the sports pages and hung around sports celebrities as often as possible. He invited Babe Ruth to the White House several times. Once his bodyguard Edmund Starling found him watching Bill Tilden, the greatest tennis player of his era, playing a match on the White House courts (Harding's wife Florence also presided over a women's match at the White House). In addition, Harding played golf with the top professionals, Walter Hagen and Gene Sarazen. The president so admired Sarazen's golf clubs, especially his driver, that he boldly asked if he could have the club. What could Sarazen say? He handed it over.

Harding also liked newspapermen, especially sportswriters. Once he played golf with big-name sportswriters Grantland Rice and Ring Lardner. Lardner sliced a drive on the first hole that hit a tree and beaned the president. The sardonic Lardner told Harding that he was just trying to make Vice-President Calvin Coolidge president. The president laughed heartily, and they continued their play, though Lardner's quip proved to be uncannily prophetic.

The president also enjoyed a snort of whiskey every few holes. Unfortunately, the Twentieth Amendment tacked onto the Constitution after the war made it illegal to manufacture or sell alcohol. Not that Prohibition crimped the president's style. Put simply, Harding acted as if the Volstead Act didn't exist. He paused every few holes for a booster shot of the illegal substance. When he and the newspapermen finished their round, they went to the president's cottage at the Chevy Chase Club where a servant brought a tray of setups—Edmund Starling unlocked a cupboard and pulled out the bootleg bottle of Scotch. Presidential drinking, barely out of sight, had become a means of escape for Harding, both on and off the links.

It was the same at his twice weekly poker games. Harding and his "poker cabinet" played and drank, though Harding normally had only one drink at these parties. Even those who were opposed to prohibition felt that "it was rather shocking to see the way Harding disregarded the Constitution he was sworn to uphold." Alice Longworth, attending a White House function, went upstairs to the president's study to check out the rumors of drinking and gambling in the Harding White House. "No rumor could have exceeded the reality," she wrote; "the study was filled with cronies . . . the air heavy with tobacco smoke, trays with bottles containing every imaginable brand of whisky stood about, cards and poker chips ready at hand—a general atmosphere of waistcoat unbuttoned, feet on the desk, and the spittoon alongside."[5]

Harding's love of betting was legendary, and his friends shared his passion. Despite Alice Roosevelt Longworth's distaste for the Hardings, her husband Nick and brother Ted Roosevelt both attended the poker sessions (Alice herself had a reputation as an enthusiastic poker player). Nearly every government official or friend of Harding (the two were almost interchangeable) attended these biweekly sessions, including out-of-town visitors. Once, Harding played at the beautiful and wealthy Louise Cromwell Brooks's home. He had met her while stuck in a Senate elevator. During the poker session at the Brooks's mansion, he bet a cold hand—in which the winner gets to name the stakes. Louise, soon to be the first wife of Douglas MacArthur, won the hand and summarily demanded a set of White House dishes. Harding anted-up the next day by delivering a set of inscribed Benjamin Harrison china. The poker games, the bottles of bootleg whiskey, and the casual handing over of presidential china reveal the same carefree approach that Harding had toward presidential appointments and, for that matter, toward government property.

One story has it that Harding's father once remarked to his son, "Warren, it's a lucky thing you were not born a girl, because you can't say no." Harding seldom said no to his friends. A paragon of generosity except when there were bets on the table, the president rarely checked on his associates' and appointees' thieving ways. To be sure, several of his appointees were capable men and not corruptible, such as Secretary of State Charles Evans Hughes and Secretary of Commerce Herbert Hoover. Others, such as his political manager, Edward Daugherty, who had become attorney general and Charles Forbes, director of veterans' affairs, lustily pursued their crooked schemes, lining their pockets or those of subordinates at the government's expense. Albert Fall, the secretary of the interior, a former senator from New Mexico, was later convicted of leasing valuable government oil lands to private interests in exchange for bribes. Daugherty's factotum, Jess Smith, pocketed the profits from the sale of pardons—and possibly Daugherty did too. Of course, all of these chums belonged to the poker or golfing cabinets, including the enormously wealthy secretary of the treasury Andrew Mellon.[6]

In contrast, Hoover and Hughes, capable and honest members of his cabinet, regarded the gambling as improper. When secretary of commerce and future president Herbert Hoover attended, he was so outraged by the tawdry atmosphere that he never played—or returned to the poker sessions again. But these few men were exceptional in an administration of locker room camaraderie and outright thievery.

Equally opposed to gambling, Secretary of State Hughes played golf once with the president but was embarrassed when they ended up at the president's cottage at Chevy Chase. The bets were totaled, the drinks were poured. "Charlie," the president said to budget director Charles Dawes, "fork over the money." When Dawes proffered the money to Hughes, the secretary's face reddened, and he stammered:

> "I cannot accept this," he said. "I have never gambled in my life."
>
> "Take it!" Harding boomed. "You won it."[7]

According to Starling, the secretary of state took the money—reluctantly.

In the early 1920s, professional boxing had a sleazy reputation, and no president would risk public censure by actually attending a fight. But Harding was a boxing enthusiast and watched films of prizefights at the home of his millionaire friend, Ned McLean (Harding's wife Florence was a confidante of McLean's wife, Evalyn, best known as the ill-fated owner of the Hope Diamond). In 1921 Jack Dempsey scored a knockout over the French war hero Georges Carpentier at a fight held in New Jersey. Even by watching the films of the fights, Harding was violating a law prohibiting fight films from being transported across state lines.

The law had been passed in response to the inflammatory and explosive reaction to the Great White Hope era in boxing (1908–15) when an African American, Jack Johnson, held the heavyweight title. A highly publicized attempt was made to find a white challenger. Reluctantly Jim Jeffries, who had retired from the ring, agreed to fight Johnson. Johnson demolished his opponent in a fight that was filmed and shown in movie theaters.

Predictably, the African American population in the South happily celebrated Johnson's triumph, one of the few black sports figures who had crossed the color line. Infuriated by this threat to white supremacy, racist whites in the South retaliated with violence that set off bloody race riots. Hoping to squelch Johnson's notoriety and prevent future racial strife, Congress placed a ban on trafficking in boxing films across state lines. At the same time, the Justice Department set out to remove Johnson from boxing. Using a law designed to outlaw prostitution, they convicted Johnson on a morals charge. The fighter fled the country, and when he returned in 1919, he was imprisoned. A few years later, and though Johnson's career had ended, Harding remitted a fine that Johnson owed so that the once great fighter could be released from prison.

At the McLeans, Harding enthusiastically watched the film of the Dempsey-Carpentier fight—a relatively short film since the Manassa Mauler, as Dempsey was called, knocked out Carpentier, the dainty Frenchman, in the fourth round. Because the law against transporting fight films remained on the books, Harding was technically breaking the law. In truth, though, this particular law had outlived its usefulness, if it had any to start with.

In fact, Harding's gesture toward Johnson is far more remarkable than his unlawful action of watching the fight film. When Harding paid the debt for the former champ, he was displaying a sensitivity that transcended his scandalous presidency. Perhaps, he was sympathetic to Johnson because of rumors that he himself had African American ancestors—he had certainly heard the rumors. The story was probably kept alive by political opponents, but it may have been responsible for a rare statement of support for black Americans (and the gesture on behalf of Jack Johnson). While speaking at Capitol Park in Atlanta, Harding delivered an impassioned plea on behalf of equal rights to an audience of 20,000 whites and 10,000 blacks. "We cannot go on, as we have gone on for more than half a century," he urged, "with one great section of our population, numbering as many people as the entire populations of some significant countries of Europe, set off from real contribution to solving national issues, because of a division on race lines."[8]

Though hardly committed to saving the wildlife and forests of America, Harding became the first president since Roosevelt to go camping. To be fair, Harding had done some bird hunting while he was in the Senate (usually followed by a poker game) and fished for tarpon in the Gulf of Mexico while president-elect, but a TR he was not. As with so much that happened in the Harding presidency, what you thought you saw was not exactly what really happened. In short, Harding motored out to western Maryland where he joined Harvey Firestone, Thomas Edison, and Henry Ford for the annual campout, first organized by Teddy Roosevelt's friend John Burroughs, to get away from "fictitious civilization." By 1922, when Harding joined the group, Burroughs had died, and the outing had grown far more unwieldy. Far from fleeing "fictitious civilization," the celebrity campers created havoc in the woods. Accompanied by fifty automobiles, Harding, the press, and the numerous gawkers arrived at Firestone's farm. Edmund Starling, as he swatted mosquitoes, reflected on the shabby campsite as well as his own civilized priorities.

The place was located along the road, which took away its privacy. The ground was low and looked like a small island. The river was sluggish, with mud banks. The tents were badly arranged and the flies were terrible. The eating tent had been up all day and when we sat down to lunch all the heat in that part of the country had succeeded in getting into it. There was only cold water for shaving, no arrangements for a bath, and a player piano for entertainment. With a jack knife and ten dollars I could have built a better camp.[9]

★

A Timely Exit

Fortunately, Harding did not try to emulate Roosevelt's rugged outdoor hikes and plunges into frigid rivers. Once, on his comfy excursion, the president chopped wood briefly and then turned the ax over to Henry Ford. Enough was enough. Only in his mid-fifties, Harding was hardly the robust specimen that this camping trip or his handsome face suggested. A smoker (he also chewed tobacco occasionally), he exercised only lightly when he wasn't walking the golf course, and occasionally he drank excessively, perhaps to dull the burdens of the presidency (normally he was a light to moderate drinker). Moreover, he had a paunchy midsection that suggested the potential for heart problems. Starling related that he learned that Harding was having trouble sleeping at night, because of his "high stomach." Harding had to be propped up with pillows in order to sleep. According to historian Robert Ferrell, he was probably suffering from cardiac asthma, a condition relieved only when the sufferer assumes a sitting position. Soon afterward, the president asked Starling "why after playing eleven or twelve holes do I drag my feet and feel so tired?"[10]

After recovering from a severe and prolonged cold in January 1923, Harding left in March for a month-long trip to Florida. Harding and the "Duchess," as he called his wife Florence, were once again (as in the winter of 1922) the guests of Ned and Evalyn McLean on their houseboat, the *Pioneer*. During their cruise of the intercoastal waterway, the president and McLean spent the days ashore playing golf. After the presidential party arrived at St. Augustine, Harding was reported to have played an all-day marathon of thirty-six holes. "A president who can play thirty-six holes of golf is physically fit" editorialized the *New York Times*. "From St. Augustine comes assurance that the little wrinkles in Mr. Harding's face wrought by the strain of his labors . . . have been ironed out on the links."[11]

In truth, the wrinkles in Harding's health had not been ironed out. Indeed, his stress level rose precipitously one afternoon after a golf game. Edmund

Starling delivered a letter handed to him on the course, a letter that described a scandal "brewing" over oil leases made by the secretary of the interior, Albert Fall, or what became known as the Teapot Dome scandal. "He seemed so tired and listless, so suddenly old," Starling recalled. Things got worse—there was that dirty linen in the Veterans Bureau where director Charles Forbes was engaged in massive thievery. After profiting to the tune of $250,000, Forbes was caught in the act. The president, who could "not say no," allowed Forbes to travel to France where he could announce his resignation from long distance.[12]

Though Harding flouted the law by watching boxing films in 1921, this was merely the tip of another scandal. Unknown to the president, his corrupt associates in the Justice Department, later dubbed the Ohio Gang, were reaping huge rewards by violating the same law. Jess Smith, who worked for Attorney General Edward Daugherty, took a bribe of $18,000 for allowing national screenings of the fight films. Two years later, as the schemes and scams were coming undone, Jess Smith put a pistol to his head and pulled the trigger. As we have seen, the scandals involving oil leases by Interior Secretary Albert Fall had just come to Harding's attention. These scandals, known and suspected, were oozing to the surface and moving inexorably toward the White House.

Wracked with worry, Harding traveled that summer to Alaska, on a trip that Daugherty designed as a warm-up for the campaign of 1924. Daugherty planned for Harding to run for a second term. His party assumed that he would, but secretly he knew that the job of president was more than Jefferson's "splendid misery." The weight of it was killing him. He had always wondered if he was up to the job. If he could compile two solid terms, well, that was about all he had initially hoped for. As the plans for the Alaskan trip matured, Harding was aware the misdeeds of his cronies were threatening to engulf him. The trip to Alaska had all the earmarks of a president fleeing from Washington where the presidency was suffocating him. To Evalyn McLean, he said, "I wish to God I could walk out and slam the door [to the White House] and never go in it again."[13]

Not that he minded the opportunity to travel. Harding had long talked of this trip to Alaska, designed as a western political trip, which would allow for political appearances—and golf—as the presidential train meandered across the country. With a population of only 60,000 hardy souls, Alaska had never been visited by other major political figures, let alone by an American president. Because of Harding's recent sickness and general feeling of fatigue and malaise, and because First Lady Florence was suffering from kidney disease,

Dr. Charles Sawyer, his personal physician, and Dr. Joel Boone, a young Navy doctor, came along. Family members and Dr. Boone may have suspected that Harding was suffering from heart disease.

True to form, Harding took his golf clubs, and he appeared fit when he played in Salt Lake City. Indeed, it may have been his finest moment on the first golf tee before a curious and friendly gallery.

There, playing with Hebron Grant, president of the Mormon Church, the two men stepped onto the first tee. When Grant insisted that Harding hit the first ball, Harding politely but firmly responded: "I do not play golf that way."

"But you are the President of the United States," Grant objected. "It is right and proper that you should tee off first."[14]

Harding pointed out that Grant was president of the Mormon Church and Salt Lake City was its headquarters. The matter was finally settled with typical Harding panache by a coin toss which the president won.

According to Dr. Boone, Harding made a "terrific" first drive "which brought wild cheers and great acclaim from the crowd, and I heard voices say, 'That's the kind of President to have!'" Harding's achievements as president were largely confined to public appearances such as this very visible golfing triumph in Salt Lake City.[15]

The trip to Alaska, though relatively leisurely, did nothing to stabilize Harding's deteriorating health. His heart condition even may have grown worse as his anxiety increased. While Harding was playing golf in Vancouver, British Columbia, on his return trip, Dr. Boone came upon the president as he was looking for a lost ball on the seventeenth hole. Harding insisted on searching for his own balls rather than using the secret service agents as ball retrievers.

"How are things going today, Mr. President," the doctor asked.

"Not at all well today, Boone," Harding responded. "I can't get on my game. I don't feel too well."[16]

There was every reason for Harding to feel tired. Though a veteran speechmaker, he was scheduled for more appearances in Seattle. Dr. Boone pointed out to him that he had already made two speeches that day and was scheduled to make another that evening, too much for an ailing president.

By the end of his brief stay in Seattle, he was clearly a sick man. Instead of stopping at Portland, the doctors decided that the president's train should go directly to San Francisco. As a result of taking his blood pressure, Dr. Boone soon discovered that the president had a dilated heart. Although Boone wanted to have Harding taken from the train on a stretcher, the president insisted on greeting the political dignitaries when he arrived. Only then did he go to the Palace Hotel, where he was said to be recovering from "ptomaine poisoning."

As Dr. Boone may have divined, President Harding's presidential game was almost over. On August 2, 1923, as his wife Florence was reading to him, Harding suddenly had a fatal coronary thrombosis. Whether he was the victim of bad genes, an unhealthy life-style, rapacious appointees, or all three, Harding would be the third president in the last four to die or to suffer a debilitating illness before the age of sixty-five.

Although Harding was only fifty-seven when he died, and although as president he ranks very near the bottom, there is something real and approachable, something we can understand about a man who can sit down comfortably with his buddies, play poker into the night, even have an occasional cigar, and hang around all the great sports celebrities and sportswriters. In short, he was a regular guy who enjoyed sports, just not presidential material. Shortly before his death, he is said to have asked how his team, the Cincinnati Reds, had fared the day before.

Yet the photo-ops with sports celebrities sum up much of the Harding presidency—robust outside and rotting inside.

But Harding had wire photos, radio, and movies to enhance his own popularity. Nowhere was this more evident than when the news of his death reached the American public. The president's sudden and unexpected demise saddened the country who mourned the man defined by his glad hand and handsome face. Fortunately for Harding, he died near the top of his game, or at least before his presidential foibles became public. The media that helped to create his popularity would chip away at his image for the rest of the decade.

His love of sports was one of the few Harding weaknesses that no one bothered to criticize. He was a president who would be similar to the later twentieth-century presidents in his addiction to golf and his schmoozing with sports personalities. For all his weaknesses as president, Harding helped to usher the presidency into an era of sports celebrities.

*Calvin Coolidge fishing for votes as president. Here the president dressed
in coat and tie practices his fishing technique for the cameras—one of the few
sports that he enjoyed. Later, when he left the presidency and retired to Vermont,
he relived his boyhood fishing and hunting in rural Vermont. Courtesy of
Vermont Historical Society Library, Barre.*

Calvin Coolidge

Grace, under Pressure

Among twentieth-century presidents, none was less athletic than Calvin Coolidge. In spite of his lack of interest and ability, Coolidge was able to create the appearance of a sports-friendly president who enjoyed the outdoors. Much of this stemmed from the efforts of others, particularly his wife Grace Coolidge.

Why doesn't Grace Coolidge stand out among presidential first ladies? While her husband was the tight-lipped, nonathletic, parsimonious "silent Cal," Grace was gracious, attractive, and a sports enthusiast. Of all the sports, she loved major league baseball the most. When Coolidge was governor of Massachusetts, she followed the Boston Red Sox and was a friend of Red Sox slugger Joe Cronin. She attended the World Series when the series was played in Washington. In addition, she took long walks across the rugged countryside when the first couple summered in the Black Hills of South Dakota. For all her interest in sports, her husband usually reaped the lion's share of publicity, even though he lacked her knowledge of the national pastime. Once he told reporters that "Babe Ruth made a big mistake when he gave up pitching."[1]

Calvin Coolidge comes across in textbooks as insipid and uninspired, a presidential nobody who slumbered his way through the 1920s. "While Rome burned, Nero fiddled, Coolidge just snored," the Baltimore journalist and cynic H. L. Mencken quipped. He was referring to the president's inordinate daily quota of twelve hours of sleep. Coolidge's tight-lipped, nonathletic public persona seemed better suited for a cartoon character than a head of state. A society woman seated next to Coolidge at dinner told him she had made a bet that she could get more than two words out of him. His response: "You lose."[2]

The nation roared through the twenties on presidential remote. With his Vermont twang and country mannerisms, Coolidge embodied a rural, less complex, more tranquil America. As if playing to the gallery, he seemed to cultivate this country-boy image, and his eccentricities spawned all manner of stories. Once the college and professional football celebrity, Harold "Red" Grange, visited the White House. He was introduced as a member of the Chicago Bears. "Nice to meet you, young man," Coolidge supposedly responded. "I've always liked animal acts."[3]

Even if Coolidge knew who Grange was—and was playing the scene with deadpan humor—he was neither athlete nor sportsman. As a child, suffering from respiratory problems, he learned early to stay away from athletics. "Cal always hated exercise," a college friend recalled, "and never took an inch of it if he could help it. Walk? O, he'd walk to classes, but that would be about enough to last him for a week." He occasionally exhibited some interest in the outdoors by trying out sedentary sports such as fishing or horseback riding.[4]

The youthful Coolidge was plainly unsuited to athletics. In physical endurance tests as a college student, Coolidge was normally dead last in weight, lung capacity, push-ups, and pull-ups. In February 1894, his junior year at Amherst College, he won a remarkable victory in a debating contest. His topic in one of the semifinal debates: "Resolved that the influence of football on college life is more harmful than beneficial." How did Coolidge know? Possibly because he roomed with the captain of the football team at Amherst, one sign that his lack of athletic ability would not hinder his career in politics.[5]

In contrast, Coolidge's attractive wife, Grace, not only exercised but also enjoyed watching sports. Calvin Coolidge was president in September 1924 when the Washington Senators beat out Babe Ruth and the New York Yankees for the American League pennant, their first title ever. An inveterate baseball fan, Grace kept score whenever she went to the ball park and was friends with the Senators' youthful manager Bucky Harris. She even dragged Coolidge to the young manager's wedding. Later, she wrote to Jack Level, a historian of presidential sports, putting an end to the rumor that her husband was a frustrated baseball enthusiast. "Mr. Coolidge never played baseball," she declared. "I know of no sport in which he took part. He did not share my enthusiasm for baseball." Even if she exaggerated slightly, she was not far from the mark.[6]

Still Cal knew a winning issue. Energized by the Senators' miracle season, Coolidge, a candidate for reelection in the fall of 1924, capitalized on Washington's Cinderella Senators by addressing a huge crowd at the bunting-draped speaker's stand on the Ellipse after a parade down Pennsylvania Avenue. He gave one of his most animated speeches, even proposing that Congress adjourn for the forthcoming World Series with the New York Giants.

Several days later, Coolidge attended the first game of the series. Then, with the game knotted 3-3 in the ninth inning, Coolidge got up to leave. "Where do you think you're going," Grace admonished him. "You sit down."[7]

He did just that, but the Senators lost. After five games, with the Giants ahead 3-2, it appeared that the Senators would lose the Series, but they clawed their way back. In the seventh and final game, the score was again tied 3-3 in the ninth inning. Thoroughly caught up in the drama of the game, Coolidge made no move to leave. He sat on the edge of his seat as Walter Johnson, pitching in relief, stifled several Giant rallies. In the bottom of the twelfth, the Senators' Earl McNeely grounded a ball to third that hit a pebble and hopped over the head of the Giants' third baseman. The Senators' runner on second base raced home. Improbably, in the decade of Babe Ruth, the Senators won the World Championship. Grace was wild with excitement, waving her arms, cheering, jumping up and down, crying out to Walter Johnson.

Reports of the Coolidges' interest in the Series played well in the newspapers and presumably with the electorate. The athletic wimp, just like the Senators, had been transformed, at least for the moment, into an enthusiastic sports spectator. It wouldn't have been the same if he had walked out of that first game—Grace's enthusiasm saved him from embarrassment.

He seldom gave his wife credit for her efforts to inject enthusiasm and color into his presidency, especially when she violated traditional norms. His physician, Dr. Joel Boone, recalled an incident when Grace told him that she would like to do some horseback riding. Boone had taught the young Coolidge boys to ride on the trails in Rock Creek Park and was prepared to accompany her. In fact, the story had already reached the newspapers, causing her husband some embarrassment.

With her usual enthusiasm, Grace purchased a complete riding outfit: leather boots, a riding jacket, and a hat that completed her costume. Proudly she "sauntered up the hall in the second floor of the White House," Boone wrote in his memoir, "strutted for the President to gaze upon his very attractive looking wife attired in this new riding habit." Boone recalled that she "really looked cute."[8]

Perhaps too cute for a 1920s first lady. The traditional Coolidge took one look at her and went into a fury. According to Boone, he yelled at her and ordered her to remove the outfit. He never wanted to see it again. Needless to say, Grace never wore the clothes again—and she never rode.

★

The Battle Creek Steed and Other Amusements

Edmund Starling, on the Secret Service detail with yet another president, was appalled by the new president's lack of athletic interests. "I was distressed to find that he took no other exercise than walking," Starling wrote. "He didn't play golf, ride horseback, fish, hunt, swim, bowl or even play billiards."[9]

Starling was close but not completely on the mark. Prodded by Grace, Coolidge did play at golf even if he didn't hit the ball very far. While Coolidge was vice-president, the McLeans set up a game on their private course at Friendship, where President Warren Harding was also golfing. According to Shepherd Campbell and Peter Landau in *Presidential Lies*, the vice-president "showed up wearing a suit jacket and high-waisted trousers that were held up by suspenders." He had just come from the Capitol where as vice-president he presided over the Senate. He did not like to change his clothes just for a game of golf. According to Evalyn McLean, the president and his foursome were decked out in plus fours, Scottish stockings with intricate designs, and elaborate caps that "contained so much cloth that on windy days there was a constant hazard that some guest or other would be wafted into the branches of a tree."[10]

So as not to embarrass Coolidge, his foursome began on a short 130-yard par three. Using an iron, Coolidge took eleven strokes to reach the green. Given his infrequent play as president, the "little fellow," as the Secret Service called him, suffered no public ridicule. Some even said that he hit short safe shots down the middle of the fairway so that he would not lose a ball—he was notorious for his parsimony. Despite this round of awful golf (possibly his first outing), he enjoyed posing with the young celebrity of 1920s golf, Bobby Jones, who would dominate tournament golf, retire at the advanced age of twenty-nine, and go on to found the Augusta National Golf Club.

Both Grace Coolidge and Edmund Starling may have forgotten Coolidge's low-keyed efforts to play golf when he was vice-president. Evalyn McLean recalled that the vice-president persisted in learning to play. "Eventually Mr. Coolidge became," she wrote, "through his practice out at Friendship, quite a fair golfer." Often he and Grace would stay for dinner after he finished his round of golf. His reputation as a golfer never extended beyond Friendship or those carefully closeted rounds.[11]

Early in his presidency, Coolidge did warm to one form of recreation that he may have regarded as sport—cruising aboard the *Mayflower*, the presidential yacht. A onetime naval ship used in the Spanish-American War, it also served for a brief time as Admiral George Dewey's flagship. Teddy Roosevelt used it to entertain and to take his family to Oyster Bay, and when Roosevelt was mediating the Russo-Japanese War in Portsmouth, New Hampshire, he housed the Russian delegation on board. Woodrow Wilson courted his second wife, Edith, on the *Mayflower,* and once married, they went for weekend getaways aboard the vessel. After serving on patrols in World War I, the *Mayflower* once again became a presidential yacht for presidents Harding and Coolidge.

Coolidge, the landlubber from rural Vermont, enjoyed the pomp of naval command. He donned white flannel pants and a navy blue blazer topped off by a yachting hat. Grace Coolidge, who could be expected to go in style, wore navy jackets and berets along with her white skirt. Even Colonel John Coolidge, the president's elderly father, who had spent his seventy years in the hills of Vermont, tested his wobbly sea legs.

Not that the presidential party had to go without diversion or dignity. When church services were required, as Mrs. Coolidge's biographer Ishbel Ross tells, "a stringed orchestra from the Navy band played processionals and hymns." Sometimes the president watched movies on the fantail of the boat. Seaplanes brought the Sunday morning newspapers, and Grace Coolidge listened to baseball games on a new sports-friendly device, the radio.[12]

In truth, the *Mayflower's* jaunts were just as much political as recreational. Coolidge often invited guests without informing his wife and then neglected them when they were on shipboard. The press reported that the presidential yacht was a floating White House. "A list of *Mayflower* guests would be like a roster of the people of the hour in American life," the *New York Times* wrote. "Generals and senators, labor leaders and returned Ambassadors, people whose views he needs to consider in his large job of steering the ship of state. They are invited for a purpose beyond that of providing him with companionship in his hours of ease." That was the view of the press. In truth, the tight-lipped, shy president, in the words of the Kansas newspaperman and Republican stalwart William Allen White, "avoided them and enjoyed them to the limit."[13]

Dr. Boone felt that Coolidge derived strength from his outings on the *Mayflower* and believed that the "President found release from cares and concerns, I think, with himself; as he walked the deck, he communed with nature and with his God with few distractions." The doctor believed that the president always "seemed improved in health and spirits after a few hours or an overnight or weekend aboard the *Mayflower.*"[14]

Calvin Coolidge liked to portray himself as the healthiest chief executive in

White House history. And with the number of hours he slept and the absence of national crises, he enjoyed one of the least stressful presidencies. Even while exercising, "silent Cal" could be a rather solitary figure: when he strolled through downtown Washington in the early morning hours, he was barely recognized. According to Dr. Boone, he enjoyed looking at displays of women's clothing in store windows—he often accompanied Grace Coolidge when she shopped. Why? Cynthia Bittinger believes he wanted her to buy clothes that brought out her good looks, though Bittinger acknowledges that he was also a controlling personality. Luckily for Coolidge, who preferred to remain anonymous, he did not have a particularly memorable face as, say, President Harding, or the stature to compare with William Howard Taft. Alice Roosevelt Longworth more than once said he looked like "he was weaned on a pickle."[15]

His physicians feared that the president did not get enough outdoor exercise. And though Coolidge loved the outdoors, he settled for an indoor electrical device known as the Battlecreek Health Horse. Like exercise machines of later eras, the president could press a button to change speeds. One button made his steed trot, another button for cantering, and still another turned the horse into a "raging monster, giving the President the experience such as he might undergo if he were astride a bucking mustang." Once, as he was mounting his nag, he caught his buttons in the machine and had to leap from the saddle. "The White House veterinarian was not consulted," the *New York Times* reported. "Instead an electrician was sent for."[16]

★

White House Sports Tragedy

The Republican convention had enthusiastically nominated Coolidge who had quickly and convincingly cleaned up the Harding scandals. In June 1924 the Democratic National Convention was taking place in New York, featuring a dramatic struggle between Governor Al Smith of New York and William McAdoo, the son-in-law of the recently deceased Woodrow Wilson, for the nomination. For the first time, the political conventions were being broadcast on the radio, and many of the White House aides, physicians, and staff were listening avidly to the political drama.

In the meantime, another drama was unfolding. The president's sons John and Calvin Coolidge were home from school and slightly bored with life at the White House. The younger son, Calvin, a sixteen-year-old, at five foot eleven, towered over his father. He was outgoing, like his mother, and loved sports— in fact, he had even taught his mother to swim. On Monday, June 30, a new doctor, James Coupal, had joined Dr. Boone, on the White House staff. To

*Calvin Coolidge getting ready to make a catch. Did Grace Coolidge
send her husband outside to play ball with his two teenaged sons, Calvin
and John? Calvin Coolidge Jr., shown in foreground throwing the ball, scraped his
foot playing tennis at the White House courts in the summer of 1924 and died
of a staph infection a week later. His father vowed that he would never run
for office after the election that year. Courtesy of Special Collections,
University of Notre Dame, South Bend, Indiana.*

amuse the boys and initiate the new arrival, a tennis match was arranged between the two boys and the two doctors. They played doubles in the morning and again in the afternoon.

During one of these games, Calvin, who had not found his favorite socks, had gone sockless, scraping the top of his foot on the tennis shoe. "It was a mere rubbing of the foot," wrote White House usher Ike Hoover, "just over and above the foot." On Tuesday, Calvin played tennis again, but complained of lameness in his leg. That evening his leg stiffened up, and he had to hobble to the White House elevator to go upstairs. "He remarked that he had a queer feeling," Hoover recalled, "and did not understand what the trouble was." Dr. Boone gave him an antiseptic tablet and some iodine, and, as it later turned out, he did not take the tablet.[17]

Preoccupied with the Democratic convention, the doctors and the staff barely noticed. Because Calvin needed to be examined for the Army cadet program, the doctors decided to use the opportunity to check on his ailments. It was here that they discovered that he was seriously ill. A blood test, three days after his tennis wound, established that he was suffering from an advanced case of blood poisoning or, more precisely, a staphylococcus infection.

Hoover believed Calvin should never have died of such a trifling wound. No doubt more attention should have been paid to Calvin's symptoms, but would that have saved his life? Not necessarily. Before the advent of sulfa drugs during World War II, a staph infection caused by the most trivial wound could easily prove fatal.

Soon after his condition was diagnosed, Calvin was rushed to Walter Reed Hospital where surgeons tried to drain the poison. Ishbel Ross, the Coolidge biographer, writes: "Artificial respiration, saline injections, blood transfusions, all manner of measures were tried." Seven physicians feverishly worked to save the boy. The anguished parents stood helplessly outside the room. Coolidge later wrote: "In his suffering he was asking me to save him. I could not." One week after the barely visible injury on the White House court, young Calvin died.[18]

The death of Calvin—only a year after Coolidge became president—profoundly affected the president and first lady. Both bore up stoically in public, but Coolidge did no campaigning that fall. In the aftermath of his son's death, he complained of ailments such as asthma and indigestion, and he worried about heart problems. Most compelling is the passage in his autobiography published soon after he left the presidency: "When he [Calvin] went, the power and glory of the presidency went with him. I don't know why such a price was exacted for occupying the White House." He vowed never again to run for public office (he was already the Republican candidate in 1924). His depth of emotion may be understood in a story related by secret service agent Edmund Starling.[19]

> Very early one morning when I came to the White House I saw a small boy standing at the fence, his face pressed against the iron railings. I asked him what he was doing up so early. He looked up at me, his eyes large and round and sad.
>
> "I thought I might see the President," he said. "I heard he gets up early and takes a walk. I wanted to tell him how sorry I am that his little boy died.
>
> "Come with me, I'll take you to the President," I said.
>
> He took my hand and we walked into the grounds. In a few minutes the President came out and I presented the boy to him. The youngster was

overwhelmed with awe and could not deliver his message, so I did it for him.

The President had a difficult time controlling his emotions.[20]

At the Democratic convention, Franklin Roosevelt, who was himself recovering his physical and political strength three years after his bout with polio, read a statement of sympathy to the Coolidges. (Failing to nominate either Al Smith or William McAdoo, the Democrats settled on a dark horse, John W. Davis of West Virginia, a former ambassador to the Court of St. James and a prosperous corporate lawyer.)

As the family took Calvin's body to Vermont for burial, the nation also grieved for the first family. High office, Coolidge believed, came at a high cost. Calvin's death served to bond the nation to the unpretentious Coolidge family and undoubtedly played a role in Coolidge winning the election.

★

Fishing for Votes

Edmund Starling hoped from the beginning to interest the president in sports, or at least in a sport other than his electric horse or strolling the *Mayflower*'s decks in his white flannel pants. To be fair to Coolidge, the reports of his disinterest in sports of every stripe may have been exaggerated. It would have been difficult to grow up in rural Vermont without taking part in some outdoor sport. As a thirteen-year-old, Coolidge went bird hunting with a shotgun. Evidently he learned to fish because when he was home from Amherst College, he persuaded a friend to go fishing with him. When Coolidge chose to vacation at White Pines Camp on Lake Osgood in the Adirondacks in 1926, Starling merely had to lure him into the boat and update him on casting and trolling on the lake.

Not that this was easy. Starling took the president out on the lake and demonstrated how to troll for pike. The time dragged on. Just when Starling was ready to give up on Coolidge, the president took the bait, so to speak, and asked Starling to let him try. Starling chose a lure and seated the president in the middle of the boat. They coasted along the shore for about thirty minutes with no result.

Then Coolidge's spinner began to move and the line tightened.

"What'll I do with it?" the president yelled at me [Starling].

"Keep a taut line with the rod tip up and let him stay in the water," I said.

Starling let the president battle his adversary. Coolidge was "wild" with excitement as he reeled the fish close to the boat.

"Get him in the boat! Get him in the boat!" the president shouted. . . .

"He's still your fish," I said, handing him the gaffe. "Lift him into the boat with this."[21]

Coolidge gaffed the fish, but not very skillfully. When the fish stopped fighting, Starling saw that the president had caught a "handsome" northern pike, weighing about six pounds.

As the boat neared shore, Coolidge called excitedly to Grace, to see what he had caught.

From then on, he fished every day rain or shine. He was even able to exploit his initial enthusiasm and success politically. Agent Starling had done his job well.

Governor Al Smith of New York happened to be vacationing nearby and came to have lunch with the Coolidges. The garrulous Smith, who had failed to capture the Democratic nomination in 1924, was the polar opposite of Coolidge. Smith relished the cameras and press corps that surrounded him. Always jealous of politicians who stole his limelight, Coolidge was initially reluctant to see the governor or pay anything more than perfunctory respects. Nevertheless, the two men and their wives had a friendly lunch.

Afterward, at Grace's prompting, Coolidge showed Smith around White Pine camp and took him on a boat ride around the lake. Proudly, he pointed to the spot where he had caught most of his fish—he had only been fishing for a week. He invited Smith to try his hand at trolling, but the New York City native declined. After all, Smith was known for his trademark song, "The Sidewalks of New York."

As Smith was leaving, the president gave him a six-pound northern pike, very possibly the same fish he had caught with Starling. In the afterglow of their meeting, Smith reportedly had it stuffed and mounted as a souvenir— or, more likely, ate it for dinner.

Coolidge reached the height of his popularity just as he was being eclipsed by a youthful phenomenon. He played a willing second fiddle to America's most celebrated hero of the 1920s, Charles A. Lindbergh, who had just flown nonstop from New York to Paris. The tousled-haired twenty-five-year-old aviator started out from Long Island in a drizzle with a single sandwich and managed to stay awake and on course for twenty-nine hours until he landed at Le Bourget outside Paris.

On his return trip, he and his plane sailed from Europe to Washington.

When Lindy reached Washington, he and his mother were guests at the Coolidges' temporary residence at Dupont Circle (the White House was undergoing repairs).

On the next day, more than 250,000 people gathered at a makeshift podium in Potomac Park to see and hear their new hero. When the president presented the fatigued and slightly overwhelmed aviator with the Distinguished Flying Cross, the overflow crowd cheered and then listened in silent awe as Lindbergh delivered a brief and humble speech.

Grace Coolidge took a maternal liking to the young hero, and Lindbergh reciprocated. Lindy invited her to accompany him on a short flight, but she politely refused. "I promised my husband I would never fly," she responded, though the prospect must have excited her.[22]

Lindbergh would not yet meet Anne Morrow, his wife-to-be, for several months. Thanks to Grace's introduction, he did meet the man who would become his father-in-law, Dwight Morrow, a classmate of the president's from Amherst College. Morrow was a banker with J.P. Morgan in New York, as well as Coolidge's ambassador-designate to Mexico. His talented daughter, Anne, would marry the handsome aviator two years later.

Some might contend that "Lucky Lindy" did not qualify as a sports celebrity in the same way as did baseball and football players, boxers and golfers. Strictly speaking, his feat was a technical one, a triumph by a skilled flyer and navigator in a machine designed for a marathon flight. Viewed from a different perspective, however, Lindbergh's feat was an early example of what we call extreme sport. Before his marathon flight, he had worked as a daredevil in a flying circus where he would stand on the edge of an airplane's wing to drum up business as the plane would circle over small towns in rural America.

When he stretched the limits of his small biplane, it was like the records broken by long-distance balloonists and mountain climbers of the late twentieth century. The French Academy of Sport put his name at the top of its list for the Grand Prix of Sports. Viewed from this perspective, Lindbergh might easily rank as the most popular sporting celebrity ever to be entertained by a president and first lady.

Once Lindbergh left for a ticker tape parade in New York, the Coolidges departed for their summer vacation. Without consulting his wife, Coolidge decided to locate his summer White House in the Black Hills of South Dakota. Hasty plans were made to use a high school for the summer White House. The rattlesnakes were cleared from the high grass and woods surrounding the game lodge in Custer State Park—the Coolidges might want to take walks, and state authorities quickly paved a road to Rapid City where the president could periodically devote himself to presidential business. Of course, the advance team also made sure that the streams were stocked with trout so Coolidge could pursue his newly revived zest for fishing.

The president spent time outdoors fishing and taking short walks. But this was *not* your ordinary angler. To begin with, a thousand trout were released in a nearby stream by a local fish hatchery. Coolidge fished wearing white gloves; he merely held the rod while the hook was baited and his catches were removed. "The secret service men complained bitterly when it fell to their lot to perform this most unusual function," Ike Hoover declared, "which they did not consider a part of their duty of protecting the President." In fairness to Coolidge, Ike Hoover, who did not like the president, may have exaggerated the president's use (or abuse) of the Secret Service. Coolidge did enjoy fishing and a year later, while vacationing on the Brule River in Wisconsin, he learned to cast. Even when Coolidge fished with worms that summer, he "baited his own hook."[23]

While he was vacationing in South Dakota, Coolidge was presented with a small horse, a real one, a substitute for the electric steed at the White House. But here too the president's athletic feats fell short of his wife's, which may have caused some resentment, or perhaps he was simply jealous. Grace and her secret service agent, Jim Haley, took long walks, tramping as far as eight miles each day. One day in August, Grace and Haley walked further than usual and missed lunch. Coolidge became frenzied with worry, certain that an accident, perhaps a rattlesnake bite, had befallen them. The search parties sent to scour the countryside soon discovered the pair—they had gotten lost.

Coolidge immediately demoted Haley, sent him back to Washington, and curtailed Grace's walks in the woods. "The newspapers came out with headlines picturing him in the role of jealous husband," Ishbel Ross writes. "The assumption was misleading, but the damage had been done and for the only time in her career as First Lady Mrs. Coolidge was seriously embarrassed by unwelcome publicity."[24]

Why did Calvin Coolidge react so angrily to his wife's tardiness for lunch? Or, more to the point, why did he relieve the agent Jim Haley and banish him to Washington? After all, Haley had managed to guide Grace back toward the lodge after briefly losing their way in the myriad of trails. The answer has to do with the president's resentment of Haley, whom Grace Coolidge liked and depended upon. Both enjoyed the arts and, in his company, she attended art galleries and concerts. Perhaps because the president gave her so little emotional support, she turned to Haley.

Unfortunately, the president had deeply wounded Grace Coolidge, who was just as much a victim of the incident as Haley. "This disgraceful act of the President caused a mental scar on Mrs. Coolidge," wrote Dr. Boone, "which, I believe, was never erased. It was one of the most deplorable instances of which I have ever known in my life." No wonder there were rumors that Grace Coolidge would ask her husband for a divorce as soon as his term was over.[25]

In 1927 the press and public assumed that Coolidge would be a candidate for a third term. The country, except for the farm states, was prosperous, and no foreign threats loomed on the horizon. Some politicians and commentators regarded his trip to South Dakota as an attempt to shore up his political support in the plains states where farmers were suffering from depressed prices. "[Robert] LaFollette Sees Third-Term Fishing," the New York Times headline, tongue in cheek, read. And another: "Senator Says Coolidge's Vacation in West Is Bait for Farmer Vote."[26]

So it came as a shock when Coolidge abruptly announced that he would not run for another term. On August 7, while still in the Black Hills, and without informing his wife, the president declared in a brief press conference: "I do not choose to run for president in 1928." Typically, Coolidge had an ability to get the most publicity with the fewest words and to leave everyone slightly befuddled.

Republican politicians reacted with stunned disbelief: "Coolidge Statement Surprises Wall Street," "Coolidge Amazes Party Leaders."[27]

Yet Coolidge was an experienced and adept politician whose decisions and statements were usually carefully thought out. The president had a number of reasons to spurn a third term: the toll the presidency had taken on his own health; the mounting strain on Grace and her declining energy level; the shrill protests over the executions of Sacco and Vanzetti, two anarchists convicted—possibly because of their politics—of bank robbery and murder in Coolidge's home state of Massachusetts; and, above all, the stress and distress caused by young Calvin's tragic death. The "glory" had gone out of the game of presidential politics, as Coolidge himself wrote.

After the trauma of the Depression and Franklin Roosevelt's twelve years in office, Coolidge (who died in 1933) became an object of derision, a quaint relic of the 1920s best consigned to the dustbin of history—an apathetic chief executive who happened to be in the right place at the right time. His wife, Grace, whose style and personality were reflected in her name, was soon overshadowed by the hyperactive Eleanor Roosevelt. Not until Ronald Reagan became president in 1981 would portraits of Coolidge be placed in the Oval

Office. And, long after Coolidge died in 1933, Grace Coolidge would be following baseball—in the 1950s when Dwight Eisenhower was president and she was watching the games on television.

Just as he played golf and fished, Calvin Coolidge played politics passively—and slyly. He seldom initiated anything, but instead reacted to events and questions in his characteristically frugal and folksy manner. "If you don't say anything," he once said, "you can't be called on to repeat it."[28]

As Cynthia Bittinger has written, Coolidge never learned to relax—or to play. "Life was always a serious matter with him," Grace later reflected. "He never felt the need of 'play'—wouldn't have known how to satisfy the need if he had recognized it." Grace noted that early in their courtship she had tried to teach him, and he tried at first to follow her counsel, but to no avail. He was more intent on teaching her "to face life in a serious manner."[29]

Yet, Coolidge learned how to use sports to his political advantage. He entertained athletic celebrities and attended baseball games. He managed to make his awkward fishing into a badge of his folksy, rural origins.

His successor would not be as cagey—or as lucky.

Herbert Hoover
No Place to Hide

Herbert Hoover was not a college athlete, but he had close ties with college athletics. A member of the first class at Stanford, he spent considerable energy managing the fledgling Stanford football team. When Stanford played the University of California on Thanksgiving Day in 1893, Hoover was the organizer who made the event possible. He rented a fifteen-thousand-seat baseball field in San Francisco and purchased uniforms for the team from anticipated receipts. All he needed were bodies to fill the seats.

To his astonishment, the crowd kept coming, swelling to unanticipated numbers. Twenty thousand spectators showed up for the game, and he had only printed ten thousand tickets. Most of the fans paid in gold and silver rather than in scarce paper currency, and so the two team managers rented a wash-boiler and a dishpan where they tossed the gold and silver coins.

Everything was perfect, except for one thing. The normally efficient Hoover and the team captain had forgotten to bring a football. The game had to be delayed half an hour while "we sent downtown for two pig skins." After the game (which Stanford won), Hoover and the California manager sat up until the early hours of the morning counting what turned out to be a king's ransom of $30,000.[1]

It was this reputation as an administrative genius that enabled Hoover to become a millionaire mining engineer, provide food for hungry Belgians, act as food administrator for his own government in World War I, and serve as secretary of commerce under Harding and Coolidge. When Coolidge announced that he wouldn't run, Hoover easily won the Republican nomination, and the "great humanitarian" trounced Al Smith. Four months later, Hoover began his term at the raging crest of the roaring twenties.

No president ever began his term under more favorable signs, at least if consumer confidence is an index. The economy was soaring on the wings of a surging stock market. Much of the country was flush with prosperity and

*A healthy and confident Herbert Hoover indulging in his favorite sport,
fly fishing, probably before he became president. Rather than fish so publicly,
President Hoover and his wife Lou had a retreat constructed in the Blue Ridge
Mountains, three hours by auto from Washington. A weary chief retreated to Camp
Rapidan (now Camp Hoover) to fish in specially constructed trout pools and to
supervise the building of stone dams—and to get away (but not too far away)
from the pressures of the Great Depression. Courtesy of Herbert Hoover
Presidential Library, West Branch, Iowa.*

consuming wildly as if there were no tomorrow. Just under nine months into
Hoover's administration, the stock market crash on October 29, 1929, ended
the party, and the country plunged into the worst depression in its history.

During the next three years, Hoover tried desperately to instill confidence
into a country that was rapidly losing its direction. He employed cautious
methods to restore public confidence, quietly predicting that prosperity was
"around the corner." But, because of his shy and aloof personality—and an
uncooperative economy—he failed to reassure the American public. Despite
his best efforts, he proved unable to arrest the downward spiral and unwilling to provide direct assistance to the unemployed. Glued to his desk, he gave
the impression of virtually sealing himself off in his presidential cocoon.

Even when he was engaged in presidential sports, he remained out of public view. To be sure, Hoover thought that the public wanted to know that he was in his office working, but increasingly he lost touch with the pulse of the nation. A desperate nation wanted to know that he understood its plight and was willing to assist its suffering and its demoralized citizens in any way that he could.

As the economy spun to a virtual standstill, the bubble of Hoover's popularity burst, leaving only a groundswell of hostility. How unpopular did Hoover become? In 1931 he showed up at a World Series game between the Philadelphia Athletics and the St. Louis Cardinals in Philadelphia. He later wrote: "I felt my presence at a sporting event might be a gesture of reassurance to a country suffering from a severe case of the 'jitters.'" But his appearance at the ball park was enough to leave the president with the jitters. Hoover smiled and waved his hat as he and his wife Lou walked onto the field headed toward their box seats. First, there was a ripple of polite applause, followed by booing, then from deep inside the stands a rhythmic cadence erupted, "we want beer." The Hoover administration had consistently opposed a repeal of the Prohibition amendment.[2]

Hoover went through the motions of throwing out the first ball, and then he and the first lady settled back to watch the game. In the seventh inning, the Hoovers unexpectedly got up, left their box, and retraced their steps across the playing field. Once again, there were boos and the ugly chant, "we want beer." What the crowd didn't know was that he had just received a telegram telling him that Senator Dwight Morrow, a prominent Republican and Charles Lindbergh's father-in-law, had died.

Earlier, in 1929, Hoover had attended a World Series game, also in Philadelphia, but this was before the stock market crash. Then, he had received loud applause when he threw out the first pitch. By 1931, with the Depression demoralizing and impoverishing the nation, he could go nowhere without risking sullen crowds or shouts of derision.

When Babe Ruth was asked if he should be making more money than the president of the United States, he famously responded: "Why not? I had a better year than he did." The Babe's clever rejoinder was a bit premature. In 1929, when Babe made this statement, Hoover had completed his first and best year in his presidency. In contrast, Ruth's Yankees had failed to win the pennant. Ruth hit forty-six home runs, down from his record number of sixty in 1927. But a good quote will stand the test of time. The quip by this rowdy, barely literate athlete has served well as a metaphor for the ill-fated Hoover administration.[3]

★

Medicine Ball—No Cure for Depression

How did this private man who walled himself off from the public cope with the sharp downturn? A number of words might describe Hoover in the early 1930s: clumsy, cautious, cutoff, miscalculating, misreading, unable, unwilling. But consider what Hoover faced. At the height of the Depression, 25 percent of the workforce was unemployed. The auto industry had cut back from 4.5 million units in 1929 to 1.1 million in 1932 (Henry Ford closed his Detroit plants, throwing seventy-five thousand workers out of jobs). More than a thousand banks failed in 1930, and nearly four thousand in the next two years. Stocks fell to a fraction of their value during the stock market frenzy of 1929. Farmers who had suffered in the 1920s saw prices hit rock bottom. Better to slaughter their farm animals than to sell them at market prices. In cities and towns, often on dumps or along railroad tracks, shanty towns that sprung up were known as Hoovervilles, newspapers as Hoover blankets, and empty pockets turned inside out as Hoover flags.

The Great Humanitarian, as Hoover was known in World War I, became the presidential curmudgeon who refused to help a nation on the brink of economic and spiritual starvation. Mainly he retreated from public view, relying on packaged statements released to the press. Unlike Harding, Coolidge, and Franklin Roosevelt, Hoover disliked being interviewed or photographed. Once when Thomas Edison and Hoover were talking, the popping flashbulbs unnerved the aged Edison, who complained vehemently.

"Why did you invent the dam [sic] things?" Hoover responded.[4]

Even though Edison had invented the movie camera, he had nothing to do with the flashbulbs that disturbed both men that day. But to Hoover, they were all the same—invaders of his valued privacy.

In short, Hoover's highly structured and very private approach to sports mirrored his presidency. By nature, he was not a public man or, strictly speaking, a politician. But he might have succeeded if the worst economic cataclysm had not descended upon him in his first year in the presidency.

As with Harding and Coolidge, the presidential doctor, Joel Boone, was disturbed by Hoover's lack of sporting interests, lack of exercise, and his burgeoning weight, 190 pounds, on a frame that should have been carrying 175. (The doctor already was unusually attentive because he had seen both President Harding and young Calvin Coolidge sicken and die suddenly.) Boone urged Hoover to devise some form of outdoor exercise that would be both stimulating and interesting, something that he would enjoy. Hoover objected that he was busy man, and his day was too full to exercise.

Dr. Boone had been on shipboard when the battleship *Utah* was sent to bring president-elect Hoover back from Brazil. Herbert and Lou Hoover had taken an extensive tour of Central and South American capitals to promote what was to be known as America's Good Neighbor Policy. Traditionally, presidents didn't leave the United States (Woodrow Wilson's peacemaking trips to Paris were an exception). On board the *Utah*, Boone and possibly Hoover participated in medicine ball, a game played with an oversized six-to eight-pound ball. Two teams of three or more tried to keep the ball alive by tossing it over the net.

Boone suggested a daily game of medicine ball and asked Hoover to give him a list of people with whom he would be willing to play. Boone contacted the initial group of nine who agreed to meet on the South Lawn of the White House every morning at seven. In Boone's words, "it was truly a very select group of the President's close friends and official associates." The newspapers dubbed the group the "medicine ball cabinet," in keeping with the tennis, golf, and poker cabinets of past presidents. For four years, the president joined with his medicine ball cabinet from Monday through Saturday, through rain, snow, sleet, and summer heat—competitive games for which Hoover devised the rules and a scoring system. Only twice in four years, when an absolute emergency occurred, were the morning sessions called off.[5]

Though playing time was brief, the games could be active. Occasionally Hoover "got socked with the ball." One of the participants, Justice Harlan Stone, a former All-American guard at Columbia University, could hurl the ball "with terrific force." After the game, the players would joke and chat while drinking juice and coffee.[6]

Boone found the sessions useful for checking on the president's health and his state of mind. If time permitted before breakfast, Hoover would scan the New York papers. "He was always interested in baseball and football," Boone recalled in his memoirs. Hoover scanned the sporting pages to see "what scores had been made and who had won the previous day and evening."[7]

While keeping Hoover fit, the medicine ball workouts proved to be another barrier between president and the outside world. As the Depression grew worse, Hoover's morale also deteriorated. He seldom smiled and disliked facing the public. He rarely talked with newspaper reporters and never held spontaneous sessions with the press. As much as the exercise kept his weight in check, medicine ball did not relieve Hoover's own state of depression.

Hoover preparing to serve the heavy, oversized medicine ball on the South Lawn of the White House. Every morning at seven o'clock (except Sundays), the president gathered with the "medicine ball cabinet," to get his daily twenty minutes of exercise. As with his trips to his hideaway in the Blue Ridge, the shy president preferred to exercise away from press and public. Courtesy of Herbert Hoover Presidential Library, West Branch, Iowa.

★

Lou Hoover: Natural Athlete

Luckily, the president had a wife whose enthusiasm for sports surpassed his own and who created a retreat for him that would cater to his love of fishing. It would also allow the Hoovers to flee Washington for weekends during the summer doldrums and to entertain in a rustic setting. These outings were not exactly vacations, but they reflected Lou Hoover's lifelong enthusiasm for both sports and the outdoors.

The proportion in her life lent balance to his own.

Lou Henry Hoover grew up with sports. By the age of six, her father had introduced her to "fishing, hiking, and overnight camping." When she was sixteen and a schoolgirl in Whittier, California, Lou thrived on a diet of physical education and botanical expeditions. She spent the summers hiking, camping, and riding bareback on her pony.

In fact, there were few sports that Lou didn't enjoy. As a child, when roller skates had only recently been introduced, she tore around a rink set up so that the girls could blow out candles that were set up on tables along the course. Lou defeated a field of older girls. At Stanford, she joined the vanguard of women who took up bicycling when the new "safeties," the modern-style bicycle, came on the market. She rarely met a sport that failed to interest her. Once she organized two baseball teams and set out to construct a playing field. She devised an ingenious, cost-free plan: the two teams would compete pulling at weeds; the losers would treat the winners to a meal, and both teams would have a place to play.[8]

Not surprisingly, the girl who was raised to do whatever men did and loved the outdoors became the first female geology major at Stanford. It was in the geology lab, as a freshman, that she met the shy senior, Bert Hoover. Bert would, like her father, encourage her to develop her talents in ways that women seldom were able to do at the turn of the century. When she graduated from Stanford, she wanted to go on outdoor geologic expeditions, which Bert had undertaken when he graduated. She was definitely ahead of her time, but she got her wish. She married Herbert Hoover and accompanied him to distant mining camps in Australia and China. The Hoovers didn't return to America except for occasional visits until Herbert became food administrator under Woodrow Wilson in World War I.

With Hoover's ascent to public prominence during the war, Lou's opportunities for organizing grew apace. Not long after her husband joined Warren Harding's cabinet as secretary of commerce in 1921, she became president of the national Girl Scouts. Extraordinarily capable and energetic, she transformed the Girl Scouts into a well-oiled, national organization. In 1926 she organized a national convention in St. Louis where the delegates slept outdoors in tents and cooked over campfires. In the same year, she presided over the international conference of the Girl Guides and Girl Scouts in Briarcliff Manor, New York. Among the guests were Lord and Lady Baden-Powell, who had introduced the scouting movement.

Because of her enthusiasm for sports and her vital role in the Girl Scouts, Lou Hoover became a major figure in a new sports organization, the National Amateur Athletic Federation. The federation was organized to protest big-time athletics, especially spectator sports that emphasized participation by only a few. Lou founded the federation's women's division, which she headed from 1923 to 1927. Her motto: "a team for everyone and every one on a team." She believed strongly that women should have their own sports programs adjusted to their capacities and abilities.[9]

One way to bring women to athletics was to hold "play days," in which all women would participate in a variety of sports. Women physical educators enthusiastically adopted this form of recreation on college campuses. Play days were on the cutting edge of women's athletics in the early decades of the twentieth century—a way to combine physical education with a less-masculine approach to athletics. Lou Hoover subscribed to a doctrine, later to become a sporting heresy, that women were inherently different than men and that their sports should be conducted in a more genteel, less competitive manner. Ironically, Lou Hoover was more competitive at sports than her husband.

When Herbert Hoover took office in March 1929, Lou Hoover transferred her sporting interests to a new project: Rapidan Camp located in the Blue Ridge Mountains about ninety miles, or three hours, from Washington. Not surprisingly, as the first presidential wife to drive an automobile, she sometimes made the trip in less than three hours, outdistancing the secret service agents.

★

Hoover's Camp David

Even before her husband's inauguration, Lou Hoover had begun to scout rural Virginia for convenient sites for a presidential retreat. She had to find a spot where he could fish, preferably on a site between two rivers—he loved to hear the sound of flowing water. An official of the Virginia State Conservation and Development Commission, William Carlson, took the initiative in helping Lou find the perfect spot. Using a veteran fisherman, he located fishing sites on the headwaters and tributaries of the Rapidan River and bought options to the fishing rights. Carlson also purchased 274 acres in the Blue Ridge Mountains on his own account.

Barely a month after Hoover's inauguration, Hoover and Lou made the challenging three-hour drive from Washington to the little town of Criglersville. They then changed their clothes and transferred to smaller Model Ts that could negotiate the narrow, twisting, rutty roads. Reaching an impassable stream, the party went by horseback for the remainder of the trip. Hoover then picked out the site where he would build his camp and negotiated to buy 164 acres from the enterprising Carlson.

Though Hoover would privately acquire the property, he called upon a sizable contingent of Marines to build and landscape his getaway. Not surprisingly, the architect was the husband of a Girl Scout official, and Lou Hoover drew up the elaborate plans for landscaping. When completed, the Hoover retreat could house up to twenty-five guests. Located in such an inaccessible spot, the camp was far from easy to construct. Major Earl C. Long, who directed building the retreat, declared that this was nearly the hardest task in all his years as an engineer. "It would have been easier to have moved an army of 10,000 men across the Blue Ridge than to have built this camp," he wrote. "I have been amazed to find so wild an area existing here so close to the eastern cities."[10]

In the fall of 1931, Lou Hoover finally insisted that Ike Hoover, the irascible chief White House usher, visit the camp. He reluctantly made the trip. The road up the mountain unnerved him as the county road disappeared and the car began the torturous two-mile drive up the mountain. "The thought came to me as we ascended," he recalled, "suppose this car starts backward and the brakes fail to hold! There would be nothing left but a crumbling mass of machinery and human remains to tell the tale."[11]

When he reached the camp, he was dumbfounded.

My first impression was one of bewilderment and, after inspection, of completeness. Even with all the money I knew had been spent and all the planning that had been done, I had no idea such a place could exist up in those wilds. . . . As a camp it is just as complete as the White House is as a place of residence. There is not a detail lacking. I do not know what more money could do, except enlarge it. It is like a small village in itself, built on the side of the mountain near the top, bathed by the cool waters of two streams. Two hundred or more Marines must have been on the job to attain such results.[12]

Just below today's Skyline Drive, the Hoovers got the site that they coveted, and their plan was Hoover-like in its precision. The three-hour drive suited

Hoover just fine. He used the time to hold discussions with cabinet officials or political figures who accompanied him. Upon his arrival, Hoover was ensconced in a thoroughly secluded, wild, and uncultivated pocket of the mountains, and in spite of its proximity to Washington, remarkably unchanged from the eighteenth and nineteenth centuries. The president was in touch with the capital; phone and electrical lines were extended through the mountains to the camp. And a military airplane would make mail drops at nearby Criglersville.

The president was quite happy to fish either by himself or in friendly company. Simply put, he lusted for trout streams, and trout streams he got. The pools were stocked with trout, and often restocked because of ravenous eels. Near the buildings, Hoover, who had previously fished in western waters, had a special pool for his pets, rainbow trout, which were not indigenous to the east and tended to cannibalize the local fish.

Human cannibals were sometimes just as ravenous. Unfortunately the president's prize rainbow trout Toby, who was also the favorite of the Hoovers' granddaughter Peggy, became the victim of an overzealous angler. The culprit, Hoover's ambassador to Belgium, accidentally snagged the fish, and Toby was consumed that evening at the presidential table.

The photos of the president fly fishing in high boots and a business suit with hat and tie have an aura of post-Victorian formality. Presumably, the president was a bit less formal when the press and photographers were absent. Hoover's commitment to fishing at Rapidan Camp—and his two deep-sea fishing excursions to Florida—testify to the recuperative powers of his time spent in and on the water. This workaholic president was able to banish an imperfect world and retreat into his inner self.

One example of a Hoover personality trait was his keen interest in dam building. A former mining engineer, Hoover enjoyed building small dams for trout pools along the streams or, more precisely, directing others in constructing his dams. The guests who chose to play at dam building with Hoover often found themselves donning high rubber boots and wading into the Rapidan. Unlike Teddy Roosevelt, who would have been hefting large stones with his guests, Hoover directed the building of dams from dry land. When a dam was leaking, several men had to engage in dam repair, which meant finding the right stones to seal the leaks. Charles Lindbergh was one of the most enthusiastic dam builders when he and his wife Anne Morrow Lindbergh visited the camp.

Dam building and repair might easily serve as the epitaph for the Hoover administration. Faced with an inexorable economic descent, Hoover tried to repair the many leaks in the economy or to build small dams to stanch the seepage. Unlike the Hoover Dam or Boulder Dam in Nevada begun when Hoover was in office, the economic dam building proved to be too little and too late. In the trout pools created at the headwaters of the Rapidan, Hoover achieved more success and satisfaction than ninety miles away in Washington.

At Rapidan Camp, the Hoovers worked independently and yet as a team. Lou often led hikes through the woods where she collected specimens of local flora to fill out the elaborate landscaping at the camp. Occasionally, Lou and the president might hike to the top of Fort Mountain, a moderately challenging climb that took nearly an hour. They also hiked to the site of Hoover School, a one-room schoolhouse that the Hoovers, primarily Lou, had set up at their own expense to educate the many illiterate mountain people.

Lou also led guests on horseback rides. The more than one hundred Marines who tended the camp saddled the horses, accompanied the parties through the various gates, and were on hand to provide first aid in case a guest fell from a horse or suffered a snakebite (there were practically no accidents or medical emergencies—the copperheads and rattlers, as well as wild razorback hogs had been killed by the Marines). The Hoovers also had a corps of Filipino servants from the *Mayflower*, the jettisoned presidential yacht, who now became his mountaintop servants.

The Hoovers made a variety of sports available to their guests and aides. A Ping Pong table in the "Town Hall" became a popular sport, with both men and women participating (though not the Hoovers). In August 1930 a former governor of Indiana was crowned Ping Pong champion.

Occasionally the guests played medicine ball, and in spite of sloping terrain, they were able to play baseball and croquet as well as emptying a quiver of arrows into a target.

Horseshoes also became a big hit. The enterprising Dr. Boone introduced the sport, and it caught on quickly. Charles Lindbergh went at it with Boone, and the doctor evidently won. But, according to his memoirs, Dr. Boone asked that the newspapers proclaim Lindbergh the champ to whet public interest.

The most illustrious convert to horseshoes proved to be Prime Minister Ramsay MacDonald of Great Britain and his daughter, Ishbel. The meetings between the president and the prime minister were the first summit talks and a precursor to the later Camp David talks during the Eisenhower, Carter, and Clinton administrations. To create a good story line for the press, MacDonald and Hoover were said to have conducted their discussions seated on a log beside the Rapidan River. "Decisions, of course, were made indoors," Doctor Boone noted. Diplomacy, by its nature, was secret. In time, the log was washed away, and the story faded into myth and legend where it rightfully belonged.[13]

In 1933, at the end of his term, Hoover donated Rapidan Camp to the state of Virginia; it later became part of the Shenandoah National Park. President Franklin Roosevelt visited it soon after his inauguration, but the sloping, uneven terrain was too hazardous for a president in a wheelchair. Eventually it fell into disrepair before the Park Service restored the remaining buildings and opened the camp to visitors.

Because of Hoover's workaholic personality and the black hole of the Great Depression, Rapidan Camp or Camp Hoover did not revolutionize the approach to presidential getaways. To the contrary, Rapidan Camp demonstrated the shortcomings of the Hoover administration. These brief vacations created still another barrier between the president and the public. In his private recreations as in his public appearances, Hoover was sometimes his own worst enemy.

★

Olympian Tasks

The grim months of 1930 and 1931 weighed heavily on the president. In spite of the long weekends at Rapidan Camp, the president had not permitted himself a vacation since February 1930 when he went deep-sea fishing in Florida. Increasingly he showed signs of fatigue and stress. He rarely talked or laughed freely with friends, and people noticed that his hands trembled visibly. Medicine ball each morning kept his body fit but did little to relax him. He needed to get away.

In April 1931 he decided to visit the Virgin Islands and Puerto Rico to inspect those outlying possessions. The naval vessel chosen for his trip was the ill-fated *Arizona* that was destroyed in the Japanese attack at Pearl Harbor with the loss of eleven hundred naval personnel. On this trip, the president surrounded himself with his friends, many but not all of them members of his administration. A *Washington Star* reporter wrote:

> He did not go leaping around the deck of the ship slapping his friends on their backs, yelling the while, "Hurrah! Hurrah! I'm on a vacation." He is not the yelling, back-slapping kind. He showed his change of mood and heart without any such collegiate manifestations of glee. He showed it in his face and voice and in his very manner. He dug out his old pipe, which substitutes for cigars, and the very way in which he bit down on it, as he either strolled the deck or sat looking out at the sea, suggested the vacationist [*sic*] rather than the busy business man.[14]

Even on his vacation, however, Hoover could not entirely unbend. "Mr. Hoover who is genuinely modest," the reporter wrote, "and really bashful, did not care to have such a large audience. He seemed to have no desire to go leaping about the deck in a competitive sport, with so many eyes upon him."[15]

Cruising to the eastern perimeter of America's Caribbean possessions did not help Hoover politically. Neither Puerto Rico, governed by Colonel Theodore Roosevelt Jr., nor the Virgin Islands had electoral votes or cities where he could reach out to the public. In short, Hoover was sailing away from his problems—appropriate for a vacation but not advisable for becoming a two-term president.

Hoover failed the litmus test set by other presidents such as Ted Roosevelt's father, the first TR. Hoover disliked trips in which he had to read speeches to large crowds. He lacked the common touch possessed by presidents schooled in electoral politics such as Harding and Coolidge.

To give Hoover some credit, he did set a precedent for future presidential cruises, especially by his seafaring successor, Franklin Roosevelt. As with the Latin American Good Neighbor Policy, originated by the Hoover administration but publicized by Franklin Roosevelt, Hoover received little credit for his pre-presidential tour of South America and his lone presidential trip to the Caribbean.

Still another opportunity to combine politics and travel came to his attention in 1932. In spite of the Depression, the Olympic Games were scheduled to take place that summer in Los Angeles. The Olympics had reached a certain maturity; Los Angeles had built facilities for crowds of more than 100,000. The organizers had also introduced the Olympic village for housing the athletes, at least the male athletes (the women were to stay in a downtown hotel). Because the Hoovers both graduated from Stanford and Lou had grown up in Whittier and later became an important sports figure, the Olympic committee hoped that the first couple would attend. In response to a formal invitation, there was an oblique but discouraging answer: a definite maybe.

If the organizers had known the president better, they might have realized that they had embarked on a fool's errand. There is no indication that Hoover ever seriously considered a trip to California for the opening of the Olympics. To shore up his political base, he did consider a western speaking trip, which might have been combined with a brief appearance at the Olympics.

After the Republican convention in early July, the Olympic committee not only reissued its invitation but also blitzed the White House with appeals. The committee members resorted to flattery, informing the president that he had more admirers in Los Angeles than anywhere else in the United States—a farfetched statement because Hoover failed to carry California in 1932. "They naturally have been led to believe that you were coming," the committee wrote. "The foreign visitors, too, anticipate that the Games will be opened in the traditional way by the Chief Executive of this great Republic"—another stretch since only one other Olympics had been held in the United States, the St. Louis Olympics in 1904, and Theodore Roosevelt did not attend but sent his daughter Alice instead.[16]

Presidential aide Lawrence Richey chastised the Los Angeles committee in a long telegram. He cited a laundry list of urgent demands on the president. He insisted that the health of the nation and of its chief executive were at stake: "For him to be away from Washington for three weeks would be a national disaster." By way of hindsight, of course, it wouldn't have changed the outcome of the election or Hoover's efforts to stem the economic epidemic.[17]

Hoover passed the ceremonial torch to Vice-President Charles Curtis. Since CBS radio was broadcasting the Olympics, presumably the president, First Lady, or the staff could have heard the highlights. Instead of attending, Hoover sent a written message welcoming the thirty-nine nations. Presumably, he could also have given his message on the radio, static and all, but there is no indication that anyone considered such a radical step. Instead, Hoover engaged in a presidential ritual—on July 29 he had the same bread as served on the training tables at the Olympic village. That was as far as he would go.

The Olympics were a huge success. More than 100,000 people jammed the new Los Angeles Coliseum for the opening ceremonies. Athletes established new records, and the estimate of a million in paid attendance at the games was also proclaimed an Olympic record.

Was there a way in which Hoover could have made his presence felt at the Olympics? His best move, it seems, would have been to send Lou Hoover.

Ironically, Lou Hoover's Women's Federation of the IAAF opposed women's participation, preferring to confine the women to low-stress archery or equestrian events. But the athlete who received the most publicity was not the favored genteel prototype but a loud, competitive Texan named Mildred "Babe" Didrikson. She won two gold medals in the 80-meter hurdles and the javelin, setting a world's record, and she won the silver in the high jump.

In fairness to the president, he had his hands full during the days before the Olympics. World War I veterans known as the bonus marchers descended on the capital during the summer demanding that Congress pay them the bonus that was to be given in 1945. When Congress only agreed to appropriate enough money to get them home, most of the bonus army drifted away from Washington. The hard core camped out in Anacostia Flats in Washington and picketed the White House.

Because of fears that his motorcade would be endangered, Hoover had taken a detour from Rapidan Camp on the previous weekend. Typical of Hoover's maladroit handling of affairs, he didn't meet with members of the bonus army, though he did meet with heavyweight wrestling champions and members of the Eta Epsilon Gamma sorority.

On July 27 Hoover directed that the marchers be cleared from their campsite and "all humanity consistent with the due execution of the law" be used in dispersing the marchers—and, especially, he called for "every kindness and consideration" to be shown toward the women and children.[18]

Instead, Chief of Staff Douglas MacArthur assisted by George S. Patton and Dwight Eisenhower used midget tanks, gas, machine guns, and mounted cavalry with sabers drawn to expel the remnant of the bonus marchers. Luckily, no one was killed, but the Army's ruthless tactics gave ammunition to Hoover's critics.

While Hoover played no golf or tennis, his passion for fishing and his daily medicine ball workouts with his close associates contributed in some way to the heritage of sports and the presidency. Like Harry Truman's swimming or George W. Bush's daily workouts in the White House gym, they helped to keep the first athlete trim and marginally reduced his stress level.

Hoover's input into the evolution of a presidential retreat is tangible and enduring. Both in its conception and inspiration, Rapidan Camp became the precursor to Franklin Roosevelt's Shangri-La, the original name of Camp David. Hoover was the first president to entertain heads of state at a country retreat and to use this informal setting for discussions—and a game of horseshoes.

Lou Hoover's contribution to sports for women—and to Rapidan Camp— must be included in any discussion of presidential sports. Except for the periodic sporting activities of Edith Wilson and Grace Coolidge, Lou was the "first" first lady to possess a sports resume.

Fortunately for Hoover, he had many years of fishing after his single term in the presidency, opportunities to relax and to remain out of the limelight. Indeed, he wrote his own presidential epitaph as a kernel of fishing wisdom, much later when he was in his late eighties and John F. Kennedy was in the White House.

Next to prayer, fishing is the most personal relationship of man; and of more importance, everyone concedes that the fish will not bite in the presence of the public, including newspapermen.[19]

Never again did Hoover have to hide from the public or the press.

Franklin Roosevelt as a youthful golfer.
FDR learned to play golf as a teenager and
designed the course at Campobello Island,
where he was also the manager. When he was
assistant secretary of the Navy, he often played
in senatorial foursomes. Once, so the story goes,
he played fifty-four holes in a single day.
Courtesy of Franklin Roosevelt Presidential
Library, Hyde Park, New York.

Franklin Delano Roosevelt
Politically and Physically Challenged

Franklin Delano Roosevelt was born too late to have his face on Mount Rushmore—his cousin Teddy received that accolade. Instead, in 1997, the nation honored FDR with a memorial on the Washington, D.C., mall, placing him on a par with Thomas Jefferson and Abraham Lincoln. The imposing memorial to Roosevelt differs from the other portraits and sculptures of FDR because it shows him seated in a wheelchair. To be sure, this monument reflects our acceptance of the handicapped, which came of age in the 1990s. The sculpture also seeks to bring us an enlightened image of the handicapped, certainly a change to which FDR contributed. But is the story of this remarkable president more complex than the sculpture suggests?

Stricken by polio at the age of thirty-nine, Roosevelt spent twenty-four years of his life in wheelchairs and other types of chairs. Because of society's irrational fear of polio victims, Roosevelt was compelled to suffer the painful discomfort and the enormous difficulties of appearing to stand and to walk unattended.

FDR labored and intrigued tirelessly to hide his frailties from the public. His goal was to present to the world a robust man whom they could admire, not one of those cripples whom society normally shunned. That said, the sculpture may do a disservice to a president whose finest athletic performances took place while giving the illusion of walking and standing. This political giant, who worked so assiduously to hide his wheelchair-bound prison—would he have wanted this image of himself cast in bronze for all posterity to view?

Athletes come in many shapes and forms. Like a circus high-wire artist or an Olympic gymnast, Franklin Roosevelt learned to defy the forces of gravity as he stood and moved on his totally paralyzed and useless legs. Moreover, he learned to do it gracefully, laughing and talking, and giving his jaunty, uplifted, infectious smile. None of these movements came naturally. They demanded athleticism and determination. If we define athletics as embodying strength, agility, and endurance, FDR displayed all of the qualities of a trained athlete. And it was not sheer vanity. Given the temper of the times, his athletics were based on political and personal need.

The Roosevelt portrayed at the Roosevelt Memorial hardly conjures up images of an athletic president. But FDR's presidency was, more than most, a presidency marked by extreme athleticism and one that will not likely be repeated. Franklin Roosevelt, a victim of polio, lived before the handicapped participated in traditional sports; before there were mobile paraplegics participating in the Special Olympics; before the handicapped cycled, skied, ran, and played team sports. He lived before society was mature enough to accept a handicapped person as, first of all, a person.

His greatness lies not in his ability to hike, box, or ride horseback, or in conventional sports such as tennis and golf, though he was a fine golfer before he was disabled by polio. Franklin Roosevelt excelled in an arena into which no president before or after has entered—or is likely to. He competed as a handicapped president at a time when the physically challenged were also challenged by society's norms.

In 1921, while vacationing at Campobello Island in New Brunswick, Roosevelt suffered a severe case of poliomyelitis that would leave his lower body paralyzed. Without the use of wheelchairs and burly helpers, this large man was rendered immobile. Only when he was in the water, preferably at Warm Springs, Georgia, could he achieve the buoyancy to exercise his legs and move about at will. Because of the stigma attached to polio, he had to overcompensate.

Not that the public expected that a governor and, in the 1930s, the president to excel as an athlete. Al Smith, presidential candidate in 1928, who supported FDR's run for New York governor, argued that the candidate's lack of mobility posed no problem: "A Governor does not have to be an acrobat," Smith insisted. "We do not elect him for his ability to do a double back-flip or a handspring." Four years later, the American people, suffocating under the weight of the worst depression in American history, wanted a president who exuded confidence and promised to lend them a helping hand.[1]

Would the Democratic Party have nominated a candidate with visibly heavy steel braces and withered legs? Probably not in 1932. Party leaders feared that voters might repudiate a man in a wheelchair. In an age when the effects of polio were not understood, and polio victims caused as much fear as the disease itself, the public recoiled at their withered and weakened limbs. Even worse, the public believed that polio could eventually enter the brain and cause insanity. Franklin Roosevelt, with his family's wealth, could have led a reasonably pleasant, if inactive, life by retiring to the family estate at Hyde Park and could have lived as a country squire as his overbearing mother wished. Instead, FDR chose to rebuild his body and attempt total recovery, and to set his sights on returning to politics—and, once again, to learn to walk.

Before he contracted polio, he was a well-known political figure and was on a fast track leading to the presidency. He married Eleanor Roosevelt, a niece of his distant cousin Teddy. A Democrat, he served as undersecretary of the Navy under Woodrow Wilson; he ran for vice-president on the Democratic ticket; and he possessed a charming personality to go along with the magic Roosevelt name. Less well known was his ability as an athlete that would later enable him to develop his upper body strength and create the appearance of a recovery.

Following his attack, FDR's doctors were optimistic about a full recovery. Sadly they—and Franklin—were wrong. Nevertheless, Roosevelt set out to rehabilitate his lower limbs so that he could walk. To reenter politics, he had to convince the public that he was cured. Incurably optimistic, he undertook the grim task of building his body, or, more precisely, rebuilding his legs and strengthening his arms, neck, and chest. Laboriously, this Hudson River aristocrat used his parallel bars, crutches, water, and even the floor in a body-building program involving the most extreme discipline and pain.

In time, FDR did reeducate his body. He developed a bag of tricks—a broad smile, a devil-may-care tilt of the head, charming banter—all designed to direct attention away from his disability. Unfortunately, he never came even close to recovering the strength in the muscles of his legs.

In the meantime, he enjoyed the benefits of a moratorium from public life—seven years of rehabilitating mind and spirit. When he reentered politics in 1928, he possessed a powerful and commanding presence unequaled by any political figure since his cousin Theodore.

★

When He Was Young and Healthy

Franklin and Theodore Roosevelt were a generation apart in age, yet, in some ways, similar in intellect and temperament. That their early lives bear some striking similarities is not simply due to the Roosevelt wealth. Both of their fathers gave them guns and taught them to shoot. Like TR, Franklin as a boy was a dedicated ornithologist. He learned the lore of the woods; he became familiar with birds and bird calls; and he carefully stuffed and mounted the birds that he shot. In the winter, he ice-sailed on the Hudson River near the family estate of Springwood at Hyde Park. He swam in the Hudson and roamed the woods along the river. His elderly father, James Roosevelt, taught him to stand at the helm of his yacht at an early age, imparting a lifelong love of the sea and fishing. FDR would delight in his proximity to salt water—and in commanding his own crafts, both yachts and fleets.

In the summers, the family escaped to Campobello Island off the coast of New Brunswick. Here, Roosevelt fished, sailed, and also golfed. One story has FDR learning to play golf on his father's nine-hole course at Springwood. According to another story, while sailing by himself to Campobello, he stopped at a friend's house in New Brunswick where he was introduced to golf. Either way, he took to golf enthusiastically. He helped to design a nine-hole golf course at Campobello, and at the age of twenty-two he won the club championship. At fourteen, while a student at Groton School, he had already shot a 41 for nine holes.

Later, when he served as assistant secretary of the Navy, he was a frequent golfer and a good one, playing at Chevy Chase in the "senatorial foursome." Once he played with Senator Warren Harding of Ohio, two future presidents in the same foursome (he is said to have played as many as fifty-four holes in a single day).

Sent to Groton School when he was fourteen, Roosevelt didn't stand out as an athlete. Headmaster Endicott Peabody who trained generations of future leaders and Roosevelts, emphasized team sports, especially football. Though FDR would grow to be a big man, six foot three and close to two hundred pounds, as a young man he was too light for varsity football at Groton—and, anyway, he had grown up with individual sports. Eventually, he earned his letter as manager of the baseball team. His sole athletic triumph occurred in a Groton event known as the high kick, where he managed to outkick the school, raising his foot to seven feet three inches, two feet over his head. Those long legs that enabled him to win the high kick would become virtually helpless after his bout with polio at the age thirty-nine.

As a college student at Harvard, Franklin led cheers and ushered at football games, and was named editor of the *Harvard Crimson*. At Harvard, his diary indicates, he played a variety of sports with the girls that he courted—tennis, croquet, tobogganing. On June 22, 1903, he made one of his first references to his future wife: "Eleanor, Mary, LB [Lathrop Brown] & I played tennis." Just before he graduated, he took Eleanor, now his fiancée, canoeing. In spite of an occasional horseback ride and a single attempt to play golf, Eleanor at first showed little interest in athletics. Only in midlife did she develop her latent athletic interests—and talents.[2]

In his early political career, Franklin modeled his image on the other Roosevelt, TR. He wore the same pince-nez glasses and began his career like Teddy in the New York legislature. To have the Roosevelt name was to have a running start in politics, and FDR capitalized on it. Despite his charm and skill as a campaigner and administrator, it is doubtful that Franklin could have achieved political success so quickly and effortlessly if he were not a Roosevelt.

If we look at FDR in his thirties, we gain a clearer view of the presidential sports that a pre-polio FDR might have embraced. Like John F. Kennedy, he would have sailed and played golf; his sporting pursuits would have been elitist and conventional. In this, he would not have differed from Kennedy or, for that matter, Dwight Eisenhower.

Not that the presidency was a sure bet either before or after polio. Yet one thing is certain: after emerging from his Olympian program of therapy, he possessed a powerful presence born of sheer strength of body and will. As Theo Lippmann has observed, polio became his "log cabin," making him far more than just another wealthy aristocrat.[3]

★

Sunset at Campobello

On August 5, 1921, Franklin sailed for Campobello, fatigued by a congressional investigation of a Navy morals scandal at the Newport naval base. Aboard a friend's yacht, he did some deep-sea fishing in the Bay of Fundy. On the day before he came ashore, the normally sure-footed Roosevelt slipped and fell into frigid waters, in itself a temporarily paralyzing experience.

Once at Campobello, he began his usual vacation routine in what proved to be a hyperactive day. On August 9, his last day scheduled on the island, he played a round of golf and then took his children aboard his yacht, the *Vireo*, for a fishing lesson. In sight of land, they spotted a forest fire and hurried ashore to beat back the flames with evergreen mats. After grueling hours of fire fighting, they all hiked to a landlocked lake across the island, swam for an hour and jogged home. FDR capped off the day with a brief plunge into the Bay of Fundy.

After dinner, Franklin Roosevelt felt tired and climbed into bed. The next morning he could barely get his left leg out of bed. His temperature climbed well over a hundred degrees, and then his right leg refused to work at all. Eleanor sent for a doctor who was vacationing on the island and whose diagnosis proved to be wide of the mark. Soon afterward, FDR's uncle, Frederic

Delano, deeply disturbed by his nephew's condition, rushed to Boston to consult with doctors at Harvard. Here a young internist guessed correctly that Franklin had infantile paralysis. The eminent Dr. Robert Lovett, a polio specialist, hurried to Campobello and diagnosed FDR's sickness as polio.

The pain suffered by Roosevelt in the initial days is hard to fathom because the patient kept a cheerful exterior and never complained. Not only had the disease ravaged his legs, it also attacked his upper body, causing pain in his back and making it impossible for him to hold a pen. After a month at Campobello, he was moved laboriously—and secretly—from the house and ferried by motorboat to the mainland where a specially rigged railway car took him to New York. Here he spent six months in a hospital.

Every attempt was made by his political mentor, Louis Howe, a former newspaperman, to mislead the press so that they would not know the severity of Roosevelt's illness. Howe and Eleanor were fighting for his political future even then. If the public had learned how sick he was, his political future would have been halted in its tracks—or so they thought.

The prognosis hardly boded well for his health or for his career in politics or for his personal life. Everything had come easily for Roosevelt before 1921, and now he was faced with the first challenge that would not yield to cleverness and charm. After six weeks in the hospital, much of the time feverish and in pain, he returned to the Roosevelt townhouse on East 65th Street in Manhattan. Here, in his bedroom, during the longest, bleakest winter of his life, he started his remarkable seven-year campaign to rebuild his body. He had already begun with a strap and a ring above his head in the hospital. Gradually, he would begin working out on the parallel bars, dragging his withered legs back and forth. He even practiced crawling across the floor using the muscles of his stomach, eventually mounting the stairs in an act of exertion that left him bathed in sweat.

He became an expert on the muscles of his lower body, learning the precise location and function of his atrophied muscles. In an era when information was far more difficult to obtain, Roosevelt summoned up an array of possibilities—massage, saltwater baths, ultraviolet light, electric currents, braces, an electric tricycle. Everyone, including his children, became partners in his visible efforts to regain mobility.

Stiff upper lip hardly describes his sunny disposition. He convinced himself and those around him that he would recover the use of his legs. By talking cheerfully as he performed these excruciatingly painful and groveling movements, he put his family and visitors at ease.

His upper body responded. The muscles of his arms and his chest became more powerful. According to Kenneth Davis in *The Beckoning of Destiny,* "the stern physical regimen he imposed upon himself broadened and deepened his chest." Davis describes the transformation of the tall, lithe Roosevelt into the bull-necked, broad-chested FDR, an image imprinted on the memory of millions of Americans. According to Davis, Roosevelt developed the arms and shoulders of a blacksmith, the neck of a professional wrestler, and a crushing grip.[4]

Unhappily, the lower body did not keep pace. FDR was certain that he could and that he must restore the use of his legs. Unlike a later generation of polio victims, people afflicted with polio in the 1920s, referred to as "polios," were the victims of a cruel stigma. For the most part, they were hidden from view because healthy people didn't want to see them. That meant lives spent in drab hospitals or, more likely, in out-of-the-way back rooms. Roosevelt was luckier than most because his fortune enabled him to have the best of care and the latest in treatments. For three winters, FDR pursued his obsession with recovery, spending his time on a houseboat off the coast of Georgia and Florida. He learned that swimming allowed him to use his legs, lightening their weight and enabling him to exercise them. He could also fish and socialize with companions, including his attractive young secretary, Missy Lehand, who hopelessly worshiped him.

In 1924 FDR decided to investigate reports of Warm Springs, Georgia, which was said to have brought full recovery to a polio victim. Mesmerized by the setting and helped by the buoyant waters, he spent months at Warm Springs, eventually purchasing the run-down spa and converting it into a convalescent center for polios. FDR derived renewed strength, not just from the warm sulfuric waters, but also from the company of his fellow sufferers and from the pine-scented countryside. At Warm Springs, he became "Dr. Roosevelt," giving highly informed advice and cheerful encouragement to the others. Here, he could frolic in the pool playing water polo. Aside from the polio itself, his health and spirits had never been better. Would he ever return to politics?

Eleanor and Louis Howe kept the political fires burning in New York, and in 1924 they convinced Governor Al Smith to let FDR make the nominating speech for Smith at the Democratic National Convention at Madison Square Garden. Here, FDR faced his first and most crucial test. Though his legs were still virtually useless, he had learned to walk using leg braces and crutches. Preparing for the convention, he enlisted the enthusiastic help of his oldest son, James or "Jimmy." To avoid using a wheelchair, the symbol of a cripple, he would have to hobble on crutches to the podium. After locking his braces in place, he would lean one arm on Jimmy and the other on the crutch.

In *Sunrise at Campobello,* the playwright Dore Schary has Roosevelt considering taking the ten steps to the lectern.

> FDR *(Thinking):* Ten steps. I can do that. I'll take Jimmy with me—he's the biggest. *(Rolls his chair and seems to be measuring)* Ten steps—about twenty feet?
>
> HOWE [Louis Howe, FDR's alter ego]: About.
>
> FDR: I'll work on that. We have got to get the exact measurement.
>
> HOWE: Work hard, Franklin. *(A pause)* They are liable to be the ten biggest steps you ever took in your life.
>
> *(FDR looks up questioningly. MISSY eyes them both)*
>
> FDR *(Eager to break the solemn mood):* Perhaps—or, to be clinical, I may fall on my gluteus maximus.[5]

He did not fall. He walked those ten paces, one agonizing step at a time, assisted by Jimmy who was ready to catch him if he fell. By the time he reached the lectern, bathed in sweat, "he threw back his head in that exaggerated gesture that was to become his hallmark, and across his face there flashed a vast, world-encompassing smile, and the audience went wild." He handed his crutches to Jimmy and, gripping the lectern with his left hand, he waved to the crowd. After he nominated Smith—the speech was the easy part—he had James bring his wheelchair and was wheeled from the Garden to a thunderous ovation.[6]

This act of athleticism achieved its immediate purpose. It thrust FDR back, however briefly, into the political arena. The walk across the stage was no less athletic than a gymnast on parallel bars or a weight lifter hefting half a ton. He had relentlessly prepared his body for it and had practiced the movements over and over with James. It was his first attempt to demonstrate to the political world that he was on the road to complete recovery, though it proved to be more a political comeback than a physical one. Not that he gave up his dream of a full physical recovery. For the next four years, he spent months on end at Warm Springs, leaving his political career in the capable hands of Eleanor and Louis Howe. Just a little more time and he would restore his lower body!

Once again, in 1928, he nominated Al Smith at the Democratic convention in Houston. In the four years since his appearance at the Garden, he had learned to walk, using his son Elliott and a cane. His legs still had not recovered, though certain muscles were slightly stronger. Instead, he used his powerful arms, one tightly clasping Elliott and the other on the cane, to support the weight of his body.

Because of his height, the trip across the stage was fraught with peril—a smaller man with a lower center of gravity could have moved more surely. One fall, he knew, could bring an end to his political career. As he walked, he swung his legs in a wide arc. At the same time, he demonstrated a remarkable acting ability, a smiling man, apparently relaxed. And once again, he succeeded in a virtuoso athletic performance.

The immortal Walter Camp, father of American football, had once called FDR a superb athlete. In his performances before the Democratic conventions, he proved it.

When he ran for governor of New York later that year, he was determined to demonstrate to the voters that he was not a "sick man." His plan was to campaign vigorously in Republican upstate New York, where Al Smith's Tammany Machine could not turn out Democratic votes. To support himself upright, he devised a steel rod across the back seat of the touring car from which he campaigned. This version of a modern walking or standing device for the handicapped allowed him to stand and deliver speeches from his automobile. When he got out of the car, the movements were more complicated. He perfected an athletic pivot whereby he grabbed the jump seat, used it while he turned, and was supported by members of his bodyguard. Occasionally, he had to be carried to the rostrum, but several of his bodyguards clustered about him disguising the movements.

In his 1928 campaign for governor, FDR demonstrated that he was healthy enough to hold high office. In truth, the public rarely glimpsed his legs or heavy braces below his pants. Instead, they saw an extremely healthy and vigorous campaigner. "Too bad about this unfortunate sick man," laughed Roosevelt after he reeled off the numerous appearances he had made or was to make. The crowds applauded, as Roosevelt intended them to, at the stories that he was a victim. He wanted them to believe that he was cured or nearly restored to pre-polio self—and he succeeded.[7]

Why didn't the press or, more specifically, the photographers reveal the precise nature of his disability? Among those of us conditioned to the probing post-Watergate media or the titillating details of presidential liaisons, the Roosevelt cover-up seems a quaint, overly respectful approach to reporting the news. To be sure, a photo of those withered legs or a fall in which the president foundered helplessly in public was a constant source of worry. Roosevelt and his advisers discouraged the press from taking photos while he was alighting from cars or locking his braces before walking. On top of this, Roosevelt's robust health above the waist defused the rumors of his disability. A code among newspaper reporters and photographers, encouraged by the Roosevelt campaign, kept the media from being entirely candid. It would not happen today, but today Roosevelt could have campaigned in a wheelchair.

Vigor and vitality became the trademark of FDR. He had recharged his political batteries. He had spent seven years recuperating. He had shed the aristocratic persona. He had practiced his craft in Warm Springs, discussing muscle movements with polios and crop prices with Georgia farmers. In short, he was far better equipped to run for high office than when he was a vice-presidential candidate in 1920. Then he had good looks, charm, and the Roosevelt name. Now he had much more.

In 1932, when Roosevelt ran for the presidency, he would draw strength from politics itself. Once he had perfected the mechanics of campaigning, he relished the roar of the crowds and watching the countryside moving past the window of his train compartment. His buoyancy in the midst of a frightening period in American history added to his appeal. Recovery from polio, as he presented it to the public, became a metaphor for his ability to cure the country, or "Dr. New Deal," as he referred to himself. Of course, he himself was not cured nor would he succeed, at least in the 1930s, in pulling the country out of the Depression. What he did for the country, however, was a variation of his own brand of therapy and optimism. How did Roosevelt, the polio victim, and Roosevelt, the leader of a nation in depression, intersect? Grimly determined, he had managed to reach a point where his own disability did not prevent him from functioning. By the same token, President Franklin Delano Roosevelt brought to a still ailing nation a degree of health that enabled it to operate, though not at full throttle.

Only once, in a politically charged situation, did FDR actually face a situation when his disability might have been splashed across the newspapers. How he handled himself says much about how he viewed his carefully crafted image—and how he functioned under pressure. In 1936, as he was poised to deliver his acceptance speech at the Philadelphia convention, he spotted John Markham, an aged and well-known poet. As Roosevelt neared the platform, he reached out to greet Markham. Just as his arm extended, someone jostled his son James who walked behind him and who fell against his father. The lock on the president's right leg brace came undone, and, unable to brace himself, he began to fall. His bodyguards barely caught him, then straightened him and relocked the leg brace. "He was white and worried," Mike Reilly of the Secret Service recalled, "because he had little enough confidence in braces, at best. He was soon in complete command, of course, and snapped, 'Okay let's go.'" The six pages of his speech fluttered to the ground. Retrieving the pages (one page was out of order, but FDR brilliantly ad-libbed until he had his speech together), he carried off his appearance as if nothing had happened.[8]

Besides possessing strength, agility, and endurance, outstanding athletes have to possess presence of mind. When he fell at Philadelphia in 1936, Franklin Roosevelt showed that he had that rare quality that Ernest Hemingway called "grace under pressure."

★

FDR's Sporting Presidency

Despite his handicap, FDR could still enjoy swimming, fishing, and sailing. Once he reentered politics, his opportunities to spend time at Warm Springs were limited, but he managed to vacation there for two or three weeks at a time. His Spartan cottage became the "Little White House." He often brought a New Deal administrator or member of Congress to join him for several days. Every year he spent Thanksgiving at the spa where he shared his dinner with his fellow polios and presided as the "turkey carver in chief." Because of his responsibilities and the timing of his visits, mostly in November, he never again swam in the resort pool.

Recognizing his need to swim, FDR's supporters wanted a pool built in the White House. In the midst of the Depression, the president would have invited criticism if he had employed public funds. Herbert Hoover had been criticized for using government funds to provide the materials and labor for his Camp Rapidan. To avoid this problem, the publisher of the *New York Post*, Joseph Patterson, began a campaign to raise $15,000 to install a pool in the White House. As Theo Lippmann relates in *The Squire of Warm Springs*, Patterson pointed out that this was his only sport. "He can't ride horseback, as have so many of his predecessors. He cannot, actually, go outdoors for any distance, except in an automobile." The *Post* milked the story for its publicity and circulation value, acknowledging gifts as small as ten cents. Bernard Heigh, aged nine, wrote from New York, "I hope you will soon get your swimming pool built ready for a splash. I, too, saved my pennies and sent them to the News for the pool." The children's campaign overshadowed the more lucrative benefit put on by prominent show business supporters of the president.[9]

The pool was ready for the president in June—a small pool, to be sure, but one suited to his special needs. He swam regularly at 5:30 p.m. and accompanied the swim with exercises and a massage.

*Governor Franklin Roosevelt of New York offering a healthy and
hearty smile for the cameras at Warm Springs, Georgia, where he lived much
of the year during the 1920s. What you don't see in this photo are his withered legs
conveniently hidden beneath the water. FDR's exercises to rebuild his body after
polio gave him a rugged upper torso to go with a winning smile. Courtesy
of Franklin Roosevelt Presidential Library, Hyde Park, New York.*

Throughout his presidency, Roosevelt seized upon any opportunity to sail, cruise, and deep-sea fish. Strapped to a chair, he could give battle with his powerful frame to haul in sailfish and barracuda. Robert Cross in *Sailor in the White House* points out that Roosevelt had remarkable patience; he could wait for hours trolling, "waiting to hook the big one." In fact, he often did not need the leather harness used by deep-sea fishermen. His powerful shoulders and chest supplied the leverage.[10]

In the summer of 1933, only months after taking office, he showed his remarkable seamanship by captaining a sailing trip with his sons along the coast of New England aboard a small yacht, the *Amberjack II*. Setting sail from Marion, Massachusetts, they headed north along the treacherous coast toward their destination, Campobello, returning for the first time to the scene of his bout with polio. The president had just completed one of the most productive legislative sessions in American history, known as the Hundred Days. Congress had passed a flurry of acts designed to calm the fears of the nation, feed the destitute, assist farmers, and restart the industrial engine. He was also orchestrating the American position at the London Economic Conference meeting convened to stabilize world currency. In short, he was navigating the *Amberjack* through the shoals of coastal New England as he set the country on a new course.

Zigzagging along the coast, he tried to outfox the naval escorts that were sent to protect him. For a time, he was able to outmaneuver the escorts. He steered the *Amberjack* from one port to another, welcoming aboard friends and family, greeting the well-wishers who came to see the sailor-president. Ultimately his luck nearly ran out. The *Amberjack* sailed into an impenetrable fog one fateful day, and the yacht and the naval vessels that made up the presidential armada ground to a halt. What would later turn out to be a story that could provoke some laughter was no laughing matter when FDR was fishing at the stern of the boat. The fog was dense, and he found he needed to use the toilet. Instead of calling for his sons who had to heft him below deck to the head, he decided to use the cover of the fog and the stern of the boat as his toilet. But then suddenly the shroud of fog began to lift, threatening to display the president, in all his un-glory, to the fleet of nearby vessels. "They can't see the President like this," he snapped. Quickly, his two sons hoisted him, pants down, and conveyed him to the privacy of the companionway—no harm done, but a close call.[11]

Nevertheless, the president enjoyed fishing and conferring with government officials on board. Just as TR had used the railroads to mix politicking and outdoor sports, FDR cruised beyond the limits of previous presidents. In 1935 he boarded the cruiser *Houston*. He fished and picnicked in the Cocos Islands before meeting the presidents of Costa Rica and Panama. Crossing the isthmus through TR's Panama Canal, he headed north to Charleston, South Carolina, where he gave a speech at the Citadel.

In the spring of 1936, FDR once again sailed into international waters, this time from Miami. "Roosevelt to Mix Fishing and Work," the headline in the *New York Times* proclaimed. Using an automatic lift, the president was precariously lowered from the *Potomac* to the presidential yacht. Visiting the Bahamas, he dined with the British governor and his wife, Sir Bede and Lady Alice Clifford. It was one of the rare times that a president while in office had broken the tradition of not going beyond the nation's boundaries. Only TR when he visited the Panama Canal, Woodrow Wilson when he had gone to the Paris Peace Conference, and Warren Harding on his brief visit to Vancouver had traveled internationally (though President Chester Arthur had accidentally strayed into Canadian waters in the 1880s).[12]

Later in 1936, after the congressional elections had increased his majorities in Congress, FDR embarked on his most ambitious trip. Leaving the American lake, as the Caribbean was sometimes known, he cruised to Buenos Aires for the Pan-American Peace Conference. Arriving in the Argentinean capital, he received ringing cheers from throngs of well-wishers. Two days later, as he departed, thousands turned out in a downpour, tossing flowers at the presidential limousine.

On Sunday, December 13, after "Divine Services," the USS *Indianapolis* stopped its engines near the West Caicos Islands. "The President embarked in his fishing boats with Colonel Roosevelt and Colonel Watson [honorary titles for his son James and military aide, Edwin "Pa" Watson]," the ship's log read. Three hours later, the fishing party returned with the presidential party having landed fourteen fish, including red snappers, groupers, and barracudas.[13]

As war approached in 1939 and 1940, Roosevelt had more opportunities for inspection trips. After FDR traded vintage American destroyers to Britain for bases in the British colonies, the president took a cruise to inspect the bases. Later, he watched training exercises in the Caribbean and once inspected the defenses of the Panama Canal. On one of these trips, an errant torpedo approached the presidential ship but luckily missed. Pleasure cruises on the high seas had acquired new perils.

FDR used fishing trips to disguise high-level conferences. In August 1941 the White House announced that the president was planning to fish off Canada. Actually he intended to meet with Winston Churchill aboard a British warship, the *Prince of Wales*. The British had been at war with Adolf Hitler's Germany for nearly two years, and England had taken horrible punishment at the hands of Hitler's Luftwaffe. Packs of U-boats roamed the Atlantic attacking British freighters and military vessels, attempting to starve the island nation into submission. In Asia, the Japanese were waging a war of conquest against China, a potential threat to American and British interests in Asia.

His son Elliott, who was in the Marines, accompanied his father to the conference. Elliott recalled that his father delighted in throwing the press off his

*FDR caught in an unguarded moment as he fished at Warm Springs.
Fishing—freshwater and deep-sea—was one of the outdoor sports that he could
still do after his bout with the polio that devastated his lower body in 1921. Because
Franklin Roosevelt insisted that photos never show his legs atrophied by polio, the public
was unaware of his leg braces, ten pounds of hardware, which had to be laboriously
snapped into place each morning. The president never complained about anything
having to do with his disability. Courtesy of Franklin Roosevelt Presidential
Library, Hyde Park, New York.*

scent "much as a twelve-year boy playing cops-and-robbers will enjoy shaking a playmate who is trying to follow him." Elliott added that his father had gone fishing once on this trip and caught a "What-Is-It, unidentifiable by anyone on board." FDR suggested sending it to the Smithsonian and put away his fishing tackle for the rest of the trip.[14]

Roosevelt and Churchill, meeting off the coast of Newfoundland, drew up a list of war goals known as the Atlantic Charter, an abbreviated version of Woodrow Wilson's Fourteen Points. Less than four months later, the Japanese attacked Pearl Harbor, changing the nature of Roosevelt's presidency and of world politics. Roosevelt would take only one more fishing trip.

In August 1943, fatigued by war, Roosevelt traveled to Manitoulin Island in Lake Huron for six days of fishing. He wrote to his daughter, Anna: "We got a lot of black bass, several wall-eyed pike and pickerel. I am rested and browned and all ready for the next bout which you will read about by the time you get this." The "next bout" proved to be one of the most crucial wartime meetings with Winston Churchill, the Quebec Conference later in August. At Quebec, the decision was made to schedule Overlord, the cross-channel invasion, for 1944. Churchill and Roosevelt took time out of their work to spend a day fishing at a site that they christened as "One Lake," because Churchill caught nothing and FDR had only one trout to show for the day's outing.[15]

Except for these brief fishing expeditions, Roosevelt's sports and exercises came to an abrupt end in 1944. Because of his tremendous workload and the danger of German U-boats lurking offshore, he could no longer safely go deep-sea fishing. Perplexing as it is to our modern ears, FDR gave up swimming and exercising—on the advice of his doctors. Occasionally, he took a much-needed vacation as he did at the estate of Bernard Baruch, a wealthy Wall Street speculator and wartime administrator, at his plantation, Hobcaw, in South Carolina. His trips took him to North Africa and the Middle East by boat and plane, but there was no room in his schedule for recreation. His need for public appearances involving the virtuoso athletic performances of the 1920s and 1930s also came to a virtual standstill. In the presidential campaign of 1944, he made only one carefully staged appearance, and that to head off rumors of ill health.

The rumors had a basis in fact; his health was rapidly deteriorating. The heart condition that led to his fatal coronary has been well documented. Yet he also suffered from post-polio syndrome, when the muscles developed following his bout with polio began to atrophy. In his final year, FDR had trouble writing and holding a coffee cup. After his trip to Yalta in February 1945, he appeared before Congress sitting in a wheelchair. For once, he was candid about his handicap, surprising members of Congress who had barely known of what Hugh Gallagher has called his "splendid deception."[16]

He hoped that Congress would forgive him for sitting, but "I know you will realize it makes it a lot easier for me in not having to carry ten pounds of steel around the bottom of my legs [laughter] and also because of the fact I have just completed a fourteen-thousand-mile trip [applause]."[17]

Six weeks later on April 12, he died at Warm Springs of a massive cerebral hemorrhage. He was only sixty-three.

★
Eleanor Roosevelt: Coming on Strong

During the time her husband was paralyzed by polio, Eleanor Roosevelt was a far cry from the politically savvy and publicly active woman that she became later in the 1920s and 1930s. Orphaned at nine, she was shuttled from one relative to another, an upper-class foster child. In spite of her poor self-image, she was wooed by the handsome Franklin Roosevelt and married one year after he graduated from Harvard. Teddy Roosevelt appeared briefly to give away his niece (Eleanor was the daughter of his late brother Elliott), and congratulated the groom with the words: "Well, Franklin, there's nothing like keeping the name in the family."[18]

Eleanor's poor self-esteem extended to athletics and exercise. She had ridden horseback as a girl (a practice now discarded because of the opposition of her husband and mother-in-law), played tennis with Franklin (who was a decidedly poor player), and played field hockey at Allenwood, the boarding school in England where she found a temporary home. On their honeymoon, Franklin aroused her jealousy and rekindled her self-doubt when he went hiking with a brash and flirtatious older woman—it never occurred to Eleanor that she herself could make a four-mile hike.

In fact, Franklin never encouraged her to participate in tennis, sailing, golf, or mountain climbing; they were his interests and, perhaps, his way of asserting his superiority as a husband. Once she secretly took golf lessons so that she could participate in one of her husband's favorite sports. When they tried playing together, Franklin told her that it wasn't worth the effort. "My old sensitiveness about my inability to play games made me give it up then and there!" she recalled. "I never attempted anything but walking with my husband for many years to come."[19]

The mother of four boys and one girl, she left the athletics to her husband. Terrified of water, she did not know how to swim or sail. Once having given up riding, she did not resume it. She was never precisely barefoot, pregnant, or in the kitchen, but much of her early married life resembled an upper-class version of that scenario.

In the summer of 1921, all that abruptly changed. After the crisis had subsided, Eleanor realized that much had changed.

> I became conscious of the fact that I had two young boys who had to learn to do the things that boys must do—swim and ride and camp. I had never done any of these things. I had ridden when I was a child, and up to the

age of twenty, but that was far behind me. I had no confidence in my ability to do physical things at this time. I could go into the water with the boys but I could not swim.[20]

In truth, it was not until her late thirties and forties that she blossomed athletically. With her energy and long legs, she took up hiking—with a vengeance. She climbed mountains and outwalked her companions. She became a skilled—and fast—driver. She even took flying lessons, going up with Amelia Earhart. Although she passed her physical exams, she deferred to her husband when he asked her not to fly. Her driving was enough of a worry, especially when she took off by herself.

When Franklin Roosevelt became governor of New York, he assigned a bodyguard, Earl Miller, to protect his wife. She had become politically and personally active, heading up committees of Democratic women, commuting to New York to teach at Todhunter School, and championing numerous causes. Handsome and charming, Miller was also athletically talented—a former circus acrobat, amateur boxing champ, swimmer, equestrian, marksman, and gymnast. Miller encouraged Eleanor to take up the sports she had learned as a young women, riding and tennis. "Earl not only gave her a chestnut mare named Dot," writes her biographer Blanche Wiesen Cook, "but he regularly coached her tennis game, and later built her a deck tennis court at Valkill [her cottage on the grounds of the Hyde Park estate] for daily practice." He taught her to shoot so that she enjoyed target practice and learned to shoot from the hip. One might have said that she adopted Uncle Theodore's athletic passions.[21]

Remarkably, Eleanor, who had finally learned to swim, became obsessed with diving. For years, she labored at diving under Miller's tutelage, much to the amusement of her sons. "After countless belly-flops and much messy splashing," Cook writes, "ER learned to dive." She also learned to smile for the cameras, sometimes with Miller standing behind the photographer, clowning so that she would relax and break out in a laugh or a grin. Her years with Earl Miller represented the greening of Eleanor's personality and the emergence of a plucky, late-blooming athlete.[22]

As first lady, she rode horseback with Elinor Morgenthau, wife of FDR's treasury secretary, for an hour each morning and sometimes more. In the summer of 1934, she and her friend Lorena Hickok took a driving trip through the mountains of Nevada and California. They stopped at Yosemite, where she rode every day across rough terrain and hiked up the high Sierras to thirteen thousand feet. As Cook relates, she dashed into the frigid mountain lake each morning and swam vigorously. She was following the trail of her Uncle

Theodore, who had ridden and hiked with John Burroughs and John Muir in 1905.[23]

When she visited Earl Miller's camp in the Adirondacks, she showed how far she had progressed. With her friends, she began her day at half past seven with calisthenics in her bathing suit, then hiked up mountains, and practiced the skillful shooting that Miller had taught her. The once fearful young woman had blossomed into a skilled and confident middle-aged athlete who knew how to use her long legs and draw upon her unflagging energy. The athletic Eleanor paralleled the political Eleanor who would become the eyes and ears for her husband, breaking ground where first ladies had rarely trodden.

As her husband had lost the use of his legs, she had found hers. If polio had made FDR more patient and persistent, the liberation of Eleanor had enabled her to stride into history.

★

The Heroic and Not So Heroic

Historians have also claimed that polio made Roosevelt more sympathetic to the underdog. If it gave him humanity, the loss of his mobility may also have made him tougher, meaner, and more vengeful. Just as he learned determination and persistence from polio, it reinforced a latent tendency toward bullying and deceit. To be sure, he had always had this tendency as demonstrated by his love affair with Eleanor's secretary, Lucy Rutherford, when he was Woodrow Wilson's undersecretary of the Navy. As president, he virtually invented the imperial presidency later identified with Lyndon Johnson and Richard Nixon. He could use his office to hound opponents or those he disliked, individuals ranging from Herbert Hoover to Charles Lindbergh. He began the practice of secretly recording conversations and used the Internal Revenue Service to undermine opponents. He constantly misled members of his administration, making promises that he didn't keep and creating rivalries between functionaries who were charged with similar tasks.

Still, he excelled as a political leader who learned from his own and Woodrow Wilson's mistakes. In spite of his handicap, he attended sporting events such as baseball games—and lent his contagious self-confidence to whomever he touched. In 1933, when he attended the opening game of the season, the owner of the Washington Senators, Clark Griffith, remarked to FDR that he hoped that the New Deal would extend to the Senators. "Why not," the president responded, and, sure enough, the Senators won the American League pennant in 1933, their final championship of any kind.

He also buried his dislike for Judge Kenesaw Mountain Landis, the commissioner of baseball, agreeing to allow the major league baseball clubs to stay in business during World War II. He wrote Landis a "My Dear Judge" letter, suggesting that Americans needed recreation in wartime. "Baseball provides a recreation which does not last over two hours or two hours and a half," he wrote, "which can be got for very little cost." He pointed out that 300 teams—which included the minor leagues—using 5,000 to 6,000 players could help to entertain 20 million Americans. The numbers made sense.[24]

Though the militarily fit ballplayers enlisted, the continuation of play by major league teams did not lead to charges of draft dodging as in World War I. It would also create some fascinating anomalies, such as the physically challenged one-armed outfielder, Pete Gray, who helped the St. Louis Browns to their last pennant in 1944.

★

In Memoriam

If FDR were president today, he could safely address the public from his wheelchair; he could refer to his disability, as he finally did with Congress in 1945. Unlike the intolerant critics of his own time, a more enlightened public would give him the opportunity to display his leadership seated, and their sympathy would be balanced by acceptance. A physically challenged candidate would win or lose votes on the merits of his or her politics and not on whether the candidate could "do a back-flip," as Al Smith memorably remarked.

Does the Franklin Delano Roosevelt Memorial on the Mall in Washington aptly portray the heroic Roosevelt? Not if one judges him by the standard of the times in which he lived—the prejudices that the memorial wants us to forget. Nor does it remind us sufficiently of the solo acts of "walking" and "standing" that enabled FDR to reenter public life and be elected to the presidency. Roosevelt's political career was heroic precisely because his times required him to dissemble and deceive. In his case, the times indeed made the man as much as he made the times. Public prejudice dictated that he suffer with heavy leg braces and that he train himself in the deft use of crutches; it demanded that he use his powerful build to compensate for his helpless lower body. That he did it needs to be celebrated. If we are to ignore the prejudices against the handicapped, then we take something very important away from FDR and all the other polios of his day, who not only had to surmount the ravages of the disease but also the stigma it carried with it.

The designers of the memorial might well have taken into account FDR's remarkable public performances—these athletic performances—when he refused to admit to being a paraplegic. Or it might have made reference to the everyday difficulty of putting on his metal leg braces, locking them in place, and covering this heavy hardware with his trousers. Or simply getting his clothes on in the morning to face another day, which he did with self-confidence, optimism, and good humor.

Of course, we cannot expect a monument to capture all facets of FDR. As we view the man in the wheelchair, we should not forget the other FDR, determined to shed the stigma of polio, to walk and stand in public, to exude the same will to win in depression and wartime that he brought to his own affliction.

Flight from Washington

Oarsman Harry Truman in tie and shirtsleeves and fiancée Bess Wallace pausing to smile for the camera, probably in the summer of 1913. Harry baited the hooks and rowed the boat on their Sunday outings while Bess fished. Highly athletic (unlike Harry), Bess also played basketball and tennis, and enjoyed fishing and long walks. After an eight-year courtship, Bess and Harry were married in Independence, Missouri, after his discharge from the Missouri National Guard in 1919 following combat duty in France during World War I. Courtesy of Truman Presidential Library, Independence, Missouri.

Harry S Truman
Striding—and Flying—into History

Not only was Harry Truman one of the least athletic presidents; he was also one of the least prepared for the enormous tasks that greeted him when he took the oath of office. He had met with FDR only once before taking office and was wholly ignorant of the wartime military and diplomatic planning, including the project to build an atomic bomb. At his first press conference on April 13, he told reporters: "I don't know whether you fellows ever had a load of hay fall on you, but when they told me yesterday what had happened, I felt like the moon, the stars, and all the planets had fallen on me."[1]

Truman certainly knew about bales of hay. While other young men finished college, began careers, and spent time playing tennis or golf or relaxing on hunting and fishing trips, Truman devoted himself to making a go of the family farm. Even if he had been athletic, he still just wouldn't have had the time to linger on golf courses or watch football games.

His poor eyesight was another reason for Truman's lack of athletic interests. Those thick lenses kept him from participating in games with other boys. Recalled a friend: "Harry didn't do that much. Those glasses bothered him, but he couldn't do without them, so he just didn't." Instead, he read omnivorously and went into town to take piano lessons.[2]

Actually, Truman was probably as physically fit as any twentieth-century president. His early morning walks proved to be healthful physically and politically. He also regularly used the White House swimming pool installed for Franklin Roosevelt. At five foot eight inches, Truman's weight of 165 was precisely what his doctor prescribed. And, on weekends, he cruised aboard the presidential yacht, the *Williamsburg*, where he played poker with his cronies and often swam off the side of the boat. He also enjoyed the presidential retreat in the Catoctin Mountains, still known by its original name of Shangri-La.

Like other presidents, Truman escaped Washington for weeks at a time. But unlike his predecessors, he didn't set up a summer White House or reside at a family estate. By the time Truman came to office, air travel was becoming more efficient—and fairly common. He usually flew in one of his presidential aircrafts to his favorite place for relaxation, his Little White House on a submarine base at Key West. With a presidential plane available, he could fly to Florida in November or March. Though Truman didn't fly to golf tournaments or football games, his presidency set the stage for a new era of mobile chief executives.

It wasn't just Truman's flights to Key West that defined his travel. Truman used the *Williamsburg* to get to Key West several times, and the president who inaugurated the "flying White House" also launched his whistle-stop political campaign in the 1948 presidential campaign. Aboard a campaign train, Truman created an enduring presidential image by giving "hell" to the Republicans in unscripted speeches from the platform of the last coach—and winning a come-from-behind upset over the highly favored Republican, Thomas Dewey. Truman didn't find great delight in watching the countryside fly by from a Pullman compartment as his predecessor Franklin Roosevelt had. In travel as in exercise, he put a premium on efficiency. Hence, he enjoyed his early morning walks that often began at half past six because then the rest of the world was just waking up.

★

Sporting and Courting

Harry's penchant for walking began during his long courtship of Bess Wallace. Because of Harry's shaky finances and uncertain future, Bess delayed saying yes to her persistent suitor—and so the courtship took place over eight years. In 1911 Truman moved from Kansas City to work with his father and uncle on the family farm in Grandview, Missouri. On weekends, he went into Independence to see Bess; he had known her since elementary school. To escape the sharp scrutiny of Bess's mother, the couple began taking long walks and having picnics.

Bess also liked to fish, so Harry frequently took her in a canoe to fishing holes. But she didn't like the dirty job of baiting the hook, so Harry was put in charge of that messy task. And since Harry was not an ardent fisherman, he would guide the canoe while Bess did the fishing. Years later, when he was president, Harry and Bess went to a presidential fishing hole stocked with trout where Bess could catch her limit. Once, Bess wandered off and a photographer appeared. Harry, never at a loss to seize the moment, grabbed the string of fish and held them up for the photo. Why waste a good photo-op?

Unlike Harry, Bess loved sports and excelled at them. As a schoolgirl, she rode a velocipede (an early bicycle); ice skated; played tennis, basketball, and baseball; and rode horses. She also played basketball with the first women's basketball team in Independence. The women wore bloomers and white blouses. "We considered ourselves quite daring because we refused to wear over our bloomers the skirts that were considered by gym teachers as essential to modesty," one team member recalled.[3]

Now farming full time, Harry Truman set his sights on Bess Wallace. No longer living in Independence or working in a white-collar job, Harry faced uphill odds. Though he was well read and familiar with art and classical music, he was two or three steps down the social ladder from the once well-to-do Gates (Bess's maternal family) and Wallace families. Perhaps Bess hesitated to encourage Harry because her own family was barely solvent. Beset by debts and alcoholism, her father had committed suicide when Bess was eighteen. The family retained its house in a fashionable section of town and its foothold in the upper middle class, but little else.

Of course, try as he might, Harry never shared Bess's interest in athletics. He tried to equate his farm work with athletics. He wrote Bess that after carrying oats and hauling six tons of hay in a fierce wind, his face was wind burned. He looked like "raw beef or a confirmed booze fighter." He described wrestling hogs to the ground in an effort to vaccinate them. "A 200 pound hog can almost jerk the ribs loose from your backbone when you get him by the hind leg," he wrote. "It is far and away the best exercise in the list. It beats Jack Johnson's [the African American heavyweight champion] whole training camp as a muscle toughener."[4]

Possibly he was right, but hog wrestling would never quite make it as a gentlemanly sport.

To get Bess to visit the farm, he planned a Labor Day party for her and her friends and decided to build, for her pleasure and amusement, a grass tennis court. "Will you please send me the plan of a tennis court," he asked her. "We have a dandy place for it." He bought a heavy roller and consulted her tennis guide for tips on building the court. His mother was planning to cook a chicken, and Harry sketched out the directions to the farm.[5]

Unfortunately for Harry, Bess and her friends canceled the trip because it looked liked rain—Harry commented *without sarcasm* that "the weather was fine out here." He had really worked hard all day Sunday putting the finishing touches on the court and stocking up on watermelons. "It was quite a disappointment when you couldn't come yesterday," he wrote, and no doubt he meant every word of it.[6]

By the time she did make a visit, the court had deteriorated and Bess dismissed Harry's handiwork as "unusable." Never having played tennis, Harry had no way to know whether it was usable or not. And the court merely went to seed. Remarkably, Harry continued, against all odds, to pursue Bess Wallace. Less than two months before his struggle to build the tennis court, she rejected his first proposal. After fishing trips in the summer of 1913, Bess decided that Harry might make a good husband after all. When she told him of her change of heart, Harry was speechless. The unathletic Baptist farmer without prospects had finally won the grudging consent of the refined Episcopal college graduate. They were engaged in 1913 but would not be married for another six years, not until Captain Harry Truman had been discharged from Battery A of the Missouri National Guard after returning from combat duty in France during World War I.

Harry Truman's ambitious plan to build a tennis court, not to mention his tenacious pursuit of Bess Wallace, may have been forerunners of his challenging and turbulent presidency. Often facing problems without precedents, he made the right decisions. And, as with the threat of Soviet expansion and the election of 1948 (not to mention courting Bess), he usually faced stiff odds.

★

Physically and Mentally Fit

When he became president, Truman popularized the early morning walk. Accompanied by secret service agents and reporters, the president covered a mile or two in downtown Washington before most people were up and out. Sometimes his walks had to be rerouted to avoid the "cherry blossom" tourists. Yet he persisted in his routine, once walking two miles in a snowstorm in January 1947.

One of his most famous early morning walks took place in New York just before the 1948 elections. The president left the Biltmore Hotel at 7:15 a.m. with two secret service agents, walked briskly up Madison Avenue to 51st Street, gazed up at St. Patrick's Cathedral, went over to Broadway, and back to his hotel. By his surprise foray, he managed to avoid photographers, only posing with a passing taxi driver who had his own camera.

As the walks became his personal trademark, they became his own ambulatory press conferences. "Harry Truman was a walker, in and out of the White House," wrote one newsman after Truman's death. "His early morning walks on Pennsylvania Avenue became a ritual and a gold mine for reporters who went along throwing questions at him."[7]

The only other active sport that Truman did regularly was swimming. He swam in the White House pool after work, usually wearing his thick spectacles. He swam off the *Williamsburg* and at Key West. He even used the concrete pool at Shangri-La installed by Franklin Roosevelt. When he flew to Guam to meet General Douglas MacArthur in 1951, he stopped to tour Hawaii on his return trip—and swam.

Many people assumed that he also played horseshoes because he had a horseshoe pit placed on the White House lawn for his staff—he didn't; or that he bowled because friends gave him a bowling alley inside the White House. Again, he merely picked up the ball a few times. One form of exercise that he enjoyed was horseback riding, but again he did not ride while president because of the distance. His military aide, General Harry Vaughan, compared his careful approach to exercising to frugality in money matters. "He must get about ninety-eight cents on the dollar of the time he spends for recreation and exercise," General Vaughan aptly commented. "He likes very much to ride horseback, but the time wasted driving to Fort Myer and back again makes that sport inadvisable." So he didn't ride. Put simply, Truman exercised only when it would not interfere with his work.[8]

Truman truly enjoyed poker. Probably he began playing seriously when he was an artillery captain in Battery A in World War I. His games as president usually included his closest Missouri cronies and Washington political friends, including Chief Justice Fred Vinson. "He invites only the most intimate friends to sit at his poker table, usually eight at a time," wrote columnist Drew Pearson. "There they see Truman's most sociable side." Pearson reported that the president loved to taunt his fellow players when they called for a new card, and he would glance at the card before he put it down if he were dealing. He sometimes asked his table mates what game they wanted to play and then chose an entirely different game.

Truman had his various types or games of poker, sometimes named for his friends, such as "Papa Vinson," to honor the chief justice (who also visited at Key West). So much for separation of powers!

The stakes rarely got too high or the atmosphere too tense. Bets were limited, and to keep the losers in play, Truman levied an assessment on each pot or player to lend to perennial losers. When a player lost all his chips, he was allowed to borrow from the fund, and if he continued to lose, he could even get a second stake or loan. Truman played regularly at Key West and aboard the *Williamsburg*—even though the games seldom lasted past midnight and the president drank only moderately. "When the poker chips are flying," Pearson wrote, "and the presidential bourbon is flowing, the President forgets his burdens and for a few hours becomes just plain Harry again."[9]

President Harry Truman getting "ninety-eight cents on the dollar"
when he exercised. Since he didn't play golf or tennis, he took brisk early morning
walks, often giving impromptu press conferences to the reporters who trailed him. Bedecked
in his gaudy (for 1946) Florida sport shirt, Truman walks with House Speaker Sam
Rayburn near his favorite vacation spot, the Little White House at Key West.
UPI-Corbis.

Colorful as these games were, none exceeded the drama of the poker game played aboard a train headed for Missouri in March 1946. Great Britain's wartime prime minister, Winston Churchill, agreed to speak at tiny Westminster College in Fulton, Missouri, the alma mater of Truman's military aide, General Harry Vaughan. Truman had inherited a deteriorating relationship with the Soviet Union and its ruthless leader, Joseph Stalin. Already the Soviets had installed Communist governments in Eastern Europe and were proving uncooperative in the postwar administration of Germany. Churchill, who had long entertained suspicions of the Soviets, planned to give a speech summing up his view of the postwar world. After working on his speech and nursing a scotch and water, Churchill turned to Truman during dinner.

"Harry, I understand from the press that you like to play poker."

"That's correct, Winston, I have played a great deal of poker in my life."

"I am delighted to hear it. You know I played my first poker during the Boer War. I like poker—a fine game. Do you think there is any possibility that we might play during this trip?"

"Winston, the fellows around you are all poker players, serious poker players, and we would be delighted to provide you with a game."

After dinner, Truman confided to his associates, including presidential counsel, Clark Clifford, who recorded this episode: "Men, we have an important task ahead of us. This man has been playing poker for more than forty years. He is cagey, he loves cards, and is probably an excellent player. The reputation of American poker is at stake, and I expect every man to do his duty."

Once the game began, it became clear that Churchill was a poor player. "He was, so to speak," Clifford explained, "a lamb among wolves." In addition, he used British terminology for cards and hands which constantly had to be clarified. After an hour of poker, when Churchill left the room, the president turned to his fellow wolves: "Now look here men—you are not treating our guest very well. I fear that he may already have lost close to three hundred dollars."

General Vaughan laughed. Play for the nation's honor, and they'd have his pants. "If you want us to give it our best," he quipped, "we'll have his underwear."

The commander in chief gave a muted order.

"I don't want him to think we are pushovers, but at the same time, let's not treat him badly."[10]

As a result, Churchill occasionally won big, but nearly as often he lost, though not so much that he came close to losing his pants—or his underwear.

By the end of the evening, the Americans stepped up the pressure. When the chips were tallied, Churchill had lost only $250, according to Clifford, a small price for what the eloquent old man considered an enjoyable evening.

The next day, Churchill delivered one of the most memorable speeches of the Cold War. He used the phrase "Iron Curtain" to describe the growing Soviet threat to Western Europe. Deeply embedded in Cold War symbolism, the Iron Curtain epitomized the deep divisions between East and West.

Unlike his predecessors, Truman did not greet many athletes at the White House. He regarded photo-ops and schmoozing with athletes as relics of the 1920s. In 1948 the Olympic Committee wanted Truman to lend his support to the summer Olympics in London. They asked him to say a few words to kick off an Olympic fund raiser starring Bing Crosby and Bob Hope. He didn't do that, but he proclaimed a national Olympics week. That was as far as he would go. His rule: only go on the radio or television to raise money for a major charity like the Red Cross or Community Chest (predecessor to the United Way).

The American athletes did extremely well in London, winning the lion's share of medals. No doubt the fact that the Soviet Union would not participate until 1952 and that the recently conquered Germans were barred from competition contributed to the American sweep. Of the American athletes, a seventeen-year-old high school student from California, Bob Mathias, probably garnered the most publicity when he won the decathlon. Truman wired congratulations to Mathias and, against his photo-op beliefs, posed for pictures with him and an Olympic rifle champ at the White House.

His most newsworthy athletic reception, however, came just before the 1948 election. On October 22, Truman made history when he entertained seven African American Olympians at the White House—one male and six females. In 1947 Truman had issued historic executive orders desegregating the armed forces and the civil service. His support of civil rights had led to the formation of a splinter political party, the Dixiecrats, which nominated Governor Strom Thurmond of South Carolina. Though blacks traditionally lived in the South, tens of thousands had migrated during World War II to northern cities. In the states of the old Confederacy, literacy tests, poll taxes, and intimidation effectively kept blacks away from the polls. The southern states had relatively few electoral votes; those states that did *not* vote for Thurmond and the Dixiecrats would almost certainly vote for the Democrats, so Truman's gesture to the black athletes would make no difference. Not so in the North where black voters would help to decide the election's outcome. With African

Americans free to vote in the North, Truman was reaching out to this normally ignored bloc of voters by entertaining black athletes.

The reception at the White House, held months after the Olympics, was shrewdly timed to appeal to black voters. The opportunity arose because the "Negro" athletes were in Washington to appear at a football game between Tennessee State and Wilberforce University, two African American institutions. Besides congratulating the athletes, the president signed two footballs to be used at the game. Because the proceeds of the game would go to the United Negro College Fund, the president seemed to be stepping outside his ground rules for assisting only major charities. Was the opportunity simply too good to pass up? Certainly the results of the election suggest that Truman's advisers were covering all bases (there were no photo-ops as with Mathias). Truman's whistle-stop campaign may be better remembered, but this unprecedented meeting with black athletes was both bold and calculated.

★

Up, Up, and Away

The Truman presidency saw a revival of the summer White House, only in different form. Now the aircraft, the *Sacred Cow,* followed by the *Independence,* enabled the president to go from the chill of Washington to summer weather in Florida after several hours of flying. He began his long-distance flying in 1947 when he and Bess flew to Rio de Janeiro for the Pan American Conference. After six days in Brazil, the Trumans boarded the battleship *Missouri* and sailed across the equator, nearly passing in the path of a hurricane. Nevertheless, it was a leisurely trip aboard the very ship on which General Douglas MacArthur had accepted the surrender of the Japanese two years earlier. The landlubber was being transformed into a lover of sand and water.

But neither the presidential yacht nor trips home to Missouri answered Truman's need for a presidential getaway. In November 1946, after nineteen months in office, Truman needed a rest, and Chester Nimitz, chief of naval operations, suggested the submarine base at Key West as a presidential retreat. While he was president, Truman made ten trips to Key West, spending 175 days in the Florida sunshine. His shortest stay was 5 days in 1947, and his longest 31 days in the spring of 1951 (just before he took the courageous if unpopular step of firing General Douglas MacArthur). While the president visited Key West for relaxation, these visits were the closest he came to sporting vacations.

When the president arrived at the Little White House, he immediately changed into his Florida attire, his trademark open-collar Florida sport shirt with its gaudy colors and palm trees on the back. He expected members of his staff who accompanied him to don the same attire, even making a grab bag of these colorful clothes available for them to choose from.

At Key West the presidential press corps now consisted of between forty and fifty reporters and photographers. A number of them flew on a separate plane. Unlike other presidents, the outgoing Missourian had excellent relations with the press. Once Truman turned the tables on the press and strode into the press room. Instead of taking questions, he played the role of cub reporter firing questions *at them*—what they had to eat the night before, when they went to bed, and how many had written to their wives since they arrived.

Truman's work-play routine was far more relaxed than the life he led in Washington. He began with his morning constitutional, walking through the base and occasionally venturing out onto the streets of Key West. Later in the morning, he walked to the beach where he sat in the sun and swam. He often went fishing with visitors or members of his staff in the *Big Wheel*, a sixty-five-foot torpedo-retriever converted into a fishing boat. In Florida as in Washington, Truman was a lukewarm fisherman and sportsman, but he liked being out on the water. While at the beach, he also enjoyed watching members of his staff such as Clark Clifford and Stanley Woodward play volleyball on the beach (once his daughter Margaret played when she visited). Occasionally he tried his hand at the beach sports such as shuffleboard and pitching horseshoes.

Sometimes the president listened to sports events or classical music on the radio, including Margaret's operatic debut in Detroit in 1947. This would lead to one of Truman's most memorable fits of anger when he wrote a sizzling letter in response to a review of Margaret's singing by music critic Paul Hume of the *Washington Post*. "You sound like a frustrated old man [Hume was only thirty-four], an eight-ulcer man on a four-ulcer job and all four ulcers working. I never met you, but if I do, you'll need a new nose and a supporter below." Or, in another version: "When that [when Truman meets him] happens, you'll need a new nose, a lot of beefsteak for black eyes, and perhaps a supporter below." Years later, Hume paid a "courtesy" call in Independence after Truman's retirement, but the two music lovers never came to blows—and, in fact, had a cordial visit.[11]

In 1951, as the Truman administration began to sag in the opinion polls, the president was criticized for spending too much time away from Washington, especially when crucial issues were being debated. On November 13,

1951, with Truman in Key West and the Democrats plagued by Senator Joseph McCarthy and a Republican Congress, a barracuda alarm was sounded as the president swam off Truman Beach. The secret service agents had spotted a school of sharp-toothed sharks headed for shore. Immediately, the cartoonists went to work. One cartoon showed a perplexed president, fishing rod in hand, surveying menacing sharks labeled "foreign issues," "inflation," "budget troubles," and "political questions."[12]

★

Bess and Harry: Sports Spectators

For a president who had never participated in athletics or even attended college, Truman showed a surprising interest in sporting events. A World War I veteran, Truman followed the military teams, especially the powerful, postwar Army football squads; as commander in chief, he attended the Army-Navy games when he was not in Key West. In September 1946 he made a special trip to West Point to watch Army defeat Oklahoma, 21-6.

In 1951 practically the entire Army football team was expelled in a cheating scandal, including the coach's son. Newspaper articles indicated that the president was deeply troubled by the episode. On August 9 he ordered a probe of the scandal and refused to attend the Army-Navy game that fall.

Truman's nadir as a sports spectator came in the spring of 1951 when he threw out the first pitch at Griffith Stadium in Washington. A week earlier, Truman had sacked General Douglas MacArthur, a former chief of staff and Far East commander. MacArthur had orchestrated the campaign against the Japanese in the southern Pacific and then served brilliantly as head of the American occupation in Japan. The general's reputation, in some ways, exceeded the president's, or so MacArthur believed. When the two met at Wake Island the previous November, MacArthur all too obviously failed to salute the commander in chief. After the Chinese entered the Korean War in December, relations between the two began to erode. When MacArthur leaked his criticisms of the president's war strategy to Congress, Truman fired "the SOB."

MacArthur returned to the United States as a hero, at least in many quarters. On the day before the Washington Senators' opening game, the general addressed a joint session of Congress, climaxing his speech with the memorable phrase, "old soldiers never die, they just fade away." When Truman appeared at the ball park the next day, he was booed by the crowd. No president had been treated with such disrespect since Herbert Hoover attended the World Series twenty years before. In the eighth inning, the crowd again booed when the public address announcer requested all spectators to remain in their seats until President Truman and his official party left the stadium. Surprisingly, the ball game turned out better for the Senators than for Truman. The lowly Washington team defeated the world champion New York Yankees, 5-3, in spite of a dramatic triple by the future superstar, Mickey Mantle.

Once the Trumans returned to Independence after his presidency, Bess Truman continued to be an enthusiastic baseball fan. In 1955 the former Philadelphia Athletics became the Kansas City Athletics, and Harry attended games with Bess. On one outing, the president of the Athletics, Charles Finley, presented the former president of the United States with a green and gold ten-gallon hat with the team's logo. Truman graciously agreed to wear it for three innings. When the three innings elapsed, he asked Bess if he could remove it. No, the "boss" said, it looked good on him—so he was stuck with it for the rest of the game.

At the time Harry Truman died, in December 1972, the reputation of the thirty-third president had risen like a phoenix from the ashes. Once criticized for his handling of foreign affairs, he was now admired for his decisiveness, even for his firing of MacArthur. Critics who had once joked that "to err is Truman" now found his outspoken manner refreshing. He had become for many Americans "the uncommon common man," a rarity in public life.

Now living as a widow, Bess continued to follow the Kansas City teams. The Athletics had moved to Oakland, and Kansas City now had a new start-up team, the Royals. Even in her eighties, Bess Truman listened to Royals' games on radio and watched them on her antiquated black-and-white television. Bess had long since given up tennis and basketball and her velocipede, but her interest in sports stayed vibrantly alive.

Truman's belief in getting "ninety-eight cents on the dollar" from exercise and his free-wheeling poker games in the White House with his cronies reflect an older, almost quaint time in presidential history. On the other hand, Harry Truman's presidency came at a moment of big changes in media, technology, and mobility. The airplanes that zipped him to Key West and the large and hungry press corps that followed his every move both served as harbingers.

Immediately after Truman's death, Woody Hayes, the popular and volatile Ohio State football coach, eulogized the former president at a pre–Rose Bowl luncheon. "He had guts," Hayes said. "When I see a great man, I ask myself what kind of a football coach he would make." Predictably Hayes believed that Truman would have made "a great one." He cited the Truman axiom, "if you can't take the heat, stay out of the kitchen." Hayes concluded: "He could take it."[13]

14

Dwight D. Eisenhower
Hero under Assault

On September 23, 1955, President Dwight Eisenhower had the worst twenty-four hours of his presidency.

He was vacationing in Colorado as he had done for three consecutive summers. It was a great place for fly-fishing, for spending time with old friends or his four brothers, and especially for playing golf. But on this sunny morning, Ike's golf was, as he put it, "badly broken up." When the president began his round of golf, he was interrupted by one call after another from Secretary of State John Foster Dulles, who was back in Washington. Dulles was not on the line but left a message that he would call back in an hour. When Ike returned to the phone an hour later, the circuits were not working. With more time off the course than on, Ike struggled with mounting irritation and a rapidly deteriorating golf game. Finally, Dulles and Eisenhower spoke but, when it was all over, Ike was aggravated by the call. It was inconsequential, he thought.[1]

Because of this exasperating morning on the links, Ike decided to play another round of nine holes. He wolfed down a massive hamburger topped with onions and headed back to the course. On the first hole, there was yet another call from Dulles. "At this point," his doctor recorded, "his anger became so real that the veins stood out on his forehead like whipcords." Ike tried to resume his golf, but his stomach was now bothering him. On the eighth hole, complaining of indigestion, he quit the round. He had played twenty-five holes but had spent a good part of the day going to and from the telephone alternating between anger and frustration. That night, the president had a heart attack.[2]

He was rushed to a military hospital in critical condition and placed in an oxygen tent. He spent nearly four months recuperating in Florida and at his farm near Gettysburg, Pennsylvania. "For five weeks I was not allowed to see a newspaper or listen to a radio," he wrote a friend.[3]

Cadet Dwight Eisenhower shown kicking the ball as a promising
sophomore halfback at West Point. After he injured his knee, he never
again was able to play varsity football, although he coached military teams.
As a result, he devoted his time and energy to poker, a game that became a virtual
business pursuit when he was a young lieutenant trying to make ends meet.
Ike invariably went home with money in his pockets. Courtesy of
Dwight D. Eisenhower Presidential Library, Abilene, Kansas.

Ike was a problem solver. He had faced daunting challenges as supreme commander in Europe during World War II, including the complex logistics of launching Overlord, the invasion of Normandy on June 5, 1944. Now, as the first Republican president since Herbert Hoover, he had to decide whether he could recover his health sufficiently to run for a second term in 1956.

★

Sporting Assaults: From the Gridiron to the Links

Years before, Ike suffered another assault to his body. In 1912, as a talented sophomore halfback at West Point, he sustained a knee injury that abruptly ended his football—and intercollegiate athletic—career. Ike was crushed; his world was turned upside down. He had played semi-pro baseball before he came to West Point, even disguising his amateur status by using another name, possibly Wilson. He was a boxer who planned to compete on the Army team. Above all, he loved football, and the newspapers were already calling him one of the most promising halfbacks in the East. At five foot ten and 170 pounds, he used his work ethic, athletic ability, and gritty determination to make up for his lack of bulk.

When he realized that he could not play football, the bottom dropped out of his life as a cadet. "Life seemed to have little meaning," he recalled, "a need to excel was almost gone." He continued to eat as if he were on the team and gained twenty pounds. He also took up smoking cigarettes, an activity that was banned at the Point (he would eventually smoke four to five packs a day during World War II). His studies suffered. He passed his time in bull sessions and playing poker.[4]

Before the next season, the Army football coach asked Cadet Eisenhower to coach the junior varsity. As a coach of the JV, Ike made an instant reputation. "Because we used all the formations and signals of the varsity, I was able to send on to the [varsity] squad a few performers who made the grade," he recalled. The second stringers were so good, in fact, that crowds of cadets began flocking to the games. He had always had a love affair with athletics, and, as coach, Ike moved to a higher level, one that required brains as well as experience and grit.[5]

In 1916, while stationed at San Antonio, he was asked to coach St. Louis College, a Catholic preparatory school that had gone winless for five years. Under Eisenhower, the team did so well that it wound up in the San Antonio city tournament and nearly won the city championship. After his success with the Army junior varsity and other teams, word circulated among the base commanders. If a team needed a coach—and competition among the base commanders was intense—Eisenhower was their man.

In the fall of 1924, nearly a decade after his graduation from West Point, he returned for a second tour at Fort Meade, Maryland, and was immediately assigned to coach the football team. The season proved to be a disaster, but Ike's reputation as a coach remained intact. Again, two years later he reluctantly agreed to coach the football team at Fort Benning. "Even 1924's dismal record did not weaken the adhesive on the label I wore," he later wrote. "It still said *Football Coach*."[6]

By this time, the ambitious young soldier had already completed the command course at Fort Leavenworth, Kansas. Though he never coached another game, he had learned through football to organize, work hard, train, manage, and get the best out of those he coached—and now those who were his subordinates. Both as the commanding general in Europe during World War II and as president, Ike relied strongly on teamwork. As his biographer Stephen Ambrose has pointed out, he excelled at getting men of different backgrounds to work together. So thoroughly wedded to team play in football, he was able to act as coach—and then athletic director—when he led the allied armies and then served two terms in the White House.

Much later, he put in his own words why he felt so strongly about the gridiron game. "I believe that football, perhaps more than any other sport, tends to instill in men the feeling that victory comes through hard—almost slavish—work, team play, self-confidence, and an enthusiasm that amounts to dedication."[7]

Ironically, the injury suffered in his favorite team sport caused Eisenhower problems for the rest of his life. "To this day," he wrote in 1967, "I have to be careful in my movements." Unhappily for Ike, it may have impaired his golf. For a right-handed golfer, the left side—especially the left knee—is critical. The golfer pivots largely on the left leg, which needs to stay anchored while the knee absorbs the thrust. Ike was capable of driving the ball well over two hundred yards, even in the era of wood-headed drivers. For all of that, the weakest link in his golf game, his putting, could never be blamed on his bad left knee.[8]

Golf became the game that consumed his excess energies. He took it up in his thirties, probably while assigned to Fort Leavenworth. Starting later than many, the game didn't come easily to him. Because he hated to be defeated by any sport, the highly competitive young officer set out to tame the beast. He became a good golfer, but the road to a respectable game was littered with three decades of frustration, fits of anger, mood swings, and a fierce devotion to the game. His son John remembered his father on the golf course in 1929.

The nearly forty-year-old soldier had, he said, "a powerful swing but a horrendous slice to go with it. He seemed to wind up in the alfalfa an inordinate amount of time, the air punctuated with certain expletives that I had thought were unknown to adults—only to kids."[9]

Mamie Eisenhower also played golf while the Eisenhowers were stationed in the Philippines. A marital row erupted when Ike started playing golf with the wife of a naval officer—a friend of the Eisenhowers. No one regarded it as anything more than a golfing twosome, except for Mamie. She was furious. She tried to learn the game and went so far as to pronounce it a "swell" game, but not swell enough to pursue after they left the Philippines.[10]

Following World War II, Ike played golf more frequently and with better results. When he was president of Columbia University from 1948 to 1950, he played the best courses in the New York area and belonged to the exclusive Blind Brook Country Club in Westchester. His friend William Robinson of the *New York Tribune* invited him to play Augusta National in 1948, and soon afterward he became a member. Augusta and Ike would be joined at the hip during his presidential years. When he returned to Washington and New York after World War II, Ike mixed with a group of wealthy and influential friends whom he referred to as the "gang." To a man, these friends were successful businessmen and lawyers who liked to play golf and bridge with Ike. They admired the general, and he, in turn, respected their business acumen.

Most of the gang were members of Augusta, including Clifford Roberts, an investment banker, who had founded the club with Robert Tyre (Bobby) Jones in the 1930s. Ike's wealthy friends didn't, strictly speaking, make monetary gifts to the general. Instead, they found ways to entertain him, to help him travel to golfing spas like Augusta, or to advise him on his investments. Above all, Ike enjoyed his buddies; he could relax with them, and he depended on their conviviality when he was president.

Several of them—most notably Bill Robinson—used their influence to lure Eisenhower into politics and made major contributions to his campaign. Once Ike reluctantly threw his hat in the political ring, as well as when he became president, he often talked politics with his friends (albeit not on the golf course). He used his gang as informal advisers, a twentieth-century version of Andrew Jackson's "Kitchen Cabinet."

★

Occasionally the Presidency Got in His Way

One of Ike's other passions was playing cards. Later known for his obsession with bridge, Ike actually began as a poker player. After his football injury, he played poker for small stakes at West Point. His fellow players might have guessed that the cadet who seemed to win consistently had played before— as, indeed, he had. As a boy in Abilene, Kansas, he had come to know an odd character named Bob Davis, a fisherman, hunter, trapper, guide, cook—and poker player. Unknown to Ike's devout parents, Davis taught the boy how to play winning poker by calculating the percentages and odds. The illiterate Davis educated his young protégé to play a patient, unspectacular brand of poker. The highly mathematical Eisenhower absorbed the lessons which proved to be invaluable for winning consistently and providing himself with a few extra dollars.

As a young officer, living on a pittance, he needed extra money to court Mamie Doud, who came from a moneyed, socially respectable background. The poker winnings enabled him to present Mamie with an engraved jewelry box as a Christmas present. Later, he was able to lift the young couple from their genteel, military poverty, at least periodically, by his skill at poker. The game that Ike played at the card table demonstrated the street smarts that enabled him to survive and inch forward professionally during those interwar and antiwar years when the United States Army barely ranked in the world's top twenty.

By World War II, Ike's card playing had morphed from poker into bridge. Friends spoke of his remarkable powers of concentration, nowhere more evident than in bridge. In bridge as in his other pursuits, Ike played to win. Clifford Roberts remarked that Ike considered it almost "sacrilegious" to play cards with less than total concentration. He rarely played with his wife Mamie, herself an enthusiastic card player, because he yelled at her when she made a mistake.[11]

Ike also fished and hunted, just as those other small-town boys who became president had done from the time of Rutherford Hayes and Grover Cleveland. He was adept at trout fishing, and as president he spent part of his late summer vacations fishing on the ranch of Axel Nielson in Colorado. In 1953 he invited his young vice-president, Richard Nixon, to try his luck. Typical of beginners, Nixon spent much of his time untangling his line (Ike had also challenged Nixon to become a golfer, a task he was undertaking with similar results). One year later, Ike invited Herbert Hoover, the dean of presidential fishermen, to join him in Colorado. He even made the presidential cottage available to Hoover, forcing Ike to bunk with his brother Edgar in lese majesty.

His cooking skills, honed as a boy in a household of five sons, were considerable. And so it was Ike who donned an apron and cooked the day's catch. In 1953 Priscilla Slater, one of Mamie's closest friends, recorded in her diary that Ike cooked breakfast that morning for the grandchildren. She reported that he was "active every minute, trying to crowd in as many games of golf, hours of fishing, fun with the children, and bridge with his friends as he can during his brief vacation."[12]

Not only was he the first president to cook (proficiently), he was also the first chief executive since Teddy Roosevelt who hunted while in office. Ike was an excellent shot who regularly bested the competition in the skeet shooting at Camp David. George Humphrey, secretary of the treasury under Eisenhower, had a lavish plantation in Thomasville, Georgia, where the president often went to shoot quail. Invariably Ike bagged his limit, and once he was able to shoot a wild turkey, the bird that had so frustrated TR in his turkey hunt at his Pine Knot retreat in Virginia. "Residents said the turkey," reported the *New York Times*, "a difficult game bird to down, was one of the largest shot in this South Georgia area."[13]

Occasionally, the gang went overboard in its efforts to please Ike. In 1955, when Ike visited Augusta, he happened to mention that he had heard that there were quail on the property. A good quail dog was found, and Ike went off with his gun in hand. To the chagrin of his Augusta cronies, the president and the dog failed to find any quail. Stealthily, two of the members went to a breeding farm, bought fifty quail, and planted them on the property. Not surprisingly, Ike caught on at once that he was not hunting wild quail. No matter, he still appreciated their efforts.

In 1962, at the age of seventy-two, Ike flew to California for the funeral of an old friend, Pete Jones. Afterward, he and what was left of his gang went to Baja California for fishing and shooting. The former president (John F. Kennedy was now in the White House) got up at five o'clock to station himself in the ravines where the white-winged doves flew past shortly after dawn. On successive days, he shot twelve, sixteen, and thirty, which won top honors. He also bested his buddies in saltwater fishing when they went fishing for marlin later in the morning.

Unlike TR or Herbert Hoover, Ike showed little interest in preserving the environment. Though he hunted with wealthy sportsmen, he never acquired the ethic of the early twentieth-century conservationists. He remained the farm boy who simply enjoyed hunting birds in the fields and hooking fish in the streams. On the large estates and ranches where he vacationed, the fish and game were always plentiful and the countryside unspoiled. What was there to worry about?

Ike agreed to become a Republican candidate for president in early 1952. Republicans were alarmed by the candidacy of the conservative senator Robert

Ike on the links in the Philippines, where he was assigned as an aide to General Douglas MacArthur in the 1930s. Eisenhower learned to play golf on bare-boned military courses when he was stationed in Washington after World War I. Later as president, Eisenhower's frequent rounds in Washington and at Augusta National made his pastime an easy mark for nongolfing critics. Courtesy of Dwight D. Eisenhower Presidential Library, Abilene, Kansas.

Taft (son of William Howard Taft). They were certain that Taft couldn't defeat the Democrats, the majority party since the 1930s, and were suspicious of Taft's isolationist views. Leaders in both parties realized that Ike could win, no matter whose banner he ran under. The general's popularity virtually locked up the nomination. He won on the first ballot.

In November, to no one's surprise, Ike triumphed handily over Governor Adlai Stevenson of Illinois. In a near landslide, he amassed 55 percent of the vote and practically all of the electoral votes. On January 11, 1953, he took the oath of office.

Although the country knew of Ike's military achievements, most Americans did not know that they had elected a sports fanatic. He was the first active and enthusiastic golfer in the White House since Warren Harding; the first trout fisherman since Herbert Hoover; the first serious hunter since Teddy Roosevelt; and the first president to have piloted planes before he became president. Like FDR and Truman, he enjoyed swimming, and, unlike his predecessors who played poker in the White House, he was a dedicated bridge player.

Soon after he became president, he scrapped the presidential yacht, the *Williamsburg*, and renamed Shangri-La Camp David (in honor of his six-year-old grandson David). He confided to a friend, "Shangri-La was just a little fancy for a Kansas farm boy." Still another pastime, suggested to him by none other than Winston Churchill, was painting in oil. He often relaxed with his brushes and easel before he went to bed.[14]

Early in his administration, he and Mamie flew to Augusta where he played golf and visited with his friends immediately after the Masters golf tournament. There, he stayed in Bobby Jones's cottage and played with Masters champ Ben Hogan—he later played rounds with Arnold Palmer (a periodic visitor to his Gettysburg farm). He also had Senator Robert Taft flown down in the *Columbine*, the presidential plane (named for Colorado's state flower), and engaged his former rival in a round of golf (Ike had an upset stomach and had to use a golf cart to get around the course). Not long afterward, his friends would build him a "cabin" on the Augusta golf course known as "Mamie's cabin." The rambling two-story house, appropriately painted white, was far more presidential than the cramped cottage suggested by the name.

Frequently during his presidency, he would gather with his friends at Augusta, and they were almost always available to meet at the White House, visit him at Camp David, or spend weekends at his Gettysburg farm. He enjoyed their unbridled good humor. When he became president, the gang kidded him that with his new job he could "afford to play $5 nassau [golf wager] and won't have to worry about his bridge losses." Not so, Ike responded. "Hell, this job is no easy touch. Truman says I'll be lucky if I don't use $25,000 of my own money." Ellis Slater recalled that at Augusta "when the boss [Ike] made a particularly good shot, we all blew our little [golf] cart horns."[15]

Eisenhower never concealed the extent of his golfing or the names of the people he played with. No wonder the president got the reputation of being friendly to big business. Not only did he pick cabinet members from the ranks of business, but he also played golf with them. He also played golf with men such as W. Alton ("Pete") Jones, the president of Cities Service, and Robert Woodruff, the head of Coca-Cola. When he hunted, it was usually at the Georgia plantation of George Humphrey, the treasury secretary who was former president of the M.A. Hanna Company of Cleveland. His friends included golfing legends such as Bobby Jones. Now immobilized because of a progressive and painful spinal disease, Jones once sent the president a new set of clubs as a mark of his affection.

In August 1953 Ike unveiled his version of the movable White House. He flew to Colorado where he spent three weeks trout fishing and playing golf at Cherry Hills near Fraser. Ike frequently brought several of his four brothers to Colorado, where they fished with him. In November, it was Augusta for Thanksgiving and a round of golf with his son Major John Eisenhower and his family. In February and April 1954, it was Augusta again. He nearly decided to forgo throwing out the first pitch of the opening game of the Washington Senators because it might interfere with his vacation in Georgia. On sober second thought, he stayed long enough to toss out the first ball and watch the Senators defeat the World Champion Yankees in extra innings. After the game, he promptly left to keep his golfing date in Augusta the next day.

Unaccustomed to partisan sniping, Ike grew irritated at criticism of his golfing and vacationing. He was certain that he could conduct business as efficiently in Georgia or Colorado as in Washington—and then relax on the golf course or on trout streams. Charles Yates, one of the gang, described his routine at Augusta. "Every morning, if you woke up about 7 o'clock and looked out the window, you could pretty well set your watch by the fact that shortly after 7 the President would be strolling from Mamie's Cabin down to the Pro Shop, which was a distance of 200, 300 yards, and he would be there with Ann [his secretary, Ann Whitman] working on his mail, reading his correspondence. And then about noontime, after he'd put in a pretty good day's work, then he would have lunch and go out and play golf." Ike may have believed that a workweek at Augusta was no different than what he accomplished at the White House, but articles and editorials commenting on his absenteeism from Washington and hours playing and practicing golf occupied more and more space in the newspapers.[16]

Take the squirrel controversy that erupted in 1954. An unsuspecting Ike found himself cast as a heartless sportsman who would run roughshod over anyone or anything that got in his way, even furry little inhabitants of the South Lawn—the White House squirrels. In some ways, it was TR's teddy bear story in reverse. It began with a putting green outside the oval office presented to the president by the United States Golf Association. The squirrels on the South Lawn, pampered by President Truman, boldly buried nuts and acorns on Ike's putting surface. Just as boldly the White House staff took the offensive, devising a plan to trap and remove the pesky critters. When news stories appeared, a small tempest erupted. Senator Richard Neuberger of Oregon, a Democrat, rushed to the squirrels' defense, and a "Save the Squirrels Fund" was established. Soon afterward, the White House called off its squirrel-removal campaign; Senator Neuberger declared his crusade at an end and donated the contributions to the Wildlife Management Institute. "Golfer Squirrels Victors in Match," the New York Times proclaimed.[17]

If Coolidge slept on the job, Ike golfed. He often swung an eight iron in his office for recreation. He also had a golf net installed in the White House gym for indoor practice. He left the office promptly at five o'clock on weekdays for an appointment with the squirrels on the White House green. At Camp David, he had a mini-course built around a single green, which he could approach from several different directions.

The president even employed golf in personal diplomacy. When heads of state visited Washington, they were likely to find themselves at Burning Tree or Chevy Chase. Ike golfed with the premier of Thailand and the prime minister of Japan. When the Japanese premier's interpreter muffed his first drive, Ike encouraged him to hit another (equally bad). "The President's own first drive curved into the rough but his second traveled 220 yards right down the middle," the New York Times recorded. "Mr. Matsumoto [the interpreter] smashed two into the rough, tried again at the President's urging, and lost his third one in the woods." The fourth player who cracked his drive down the center of the fairway was Senator Prescott Bush of Connecticut, the father and grandfather of two golfing Bush presidents.[18]

Ike's golfing in the big bang era of H-bombs and space satellites caused more controversy than Coolidge's naps in the snoring twenties. On the same day that his golfing supporters gave him the putting green, the French citadel of Dienbienphu fell, a major event that would lead to American involvement in Vietnam. Ike's golf became an easy target (one of the few) for his opponents. The controversial Senator Joseph McCarthy, a member of the president's own party, got into the act. He told an audience that Ike should spend less time with golf and more in freeing American citizens held by the Chinese Communists.

Ike's recovery from his heart attack proved rapid. He returned from Colorado and Florida to his Gettysburg farm, where he tried to change his habits, notably those identified with a type A personality. He took naps. He made an effort to control his temper and his eating habits (he had quit smoking cold-turkey in 1949). He announced that he would delegate more work to his capable cabinet and staff. Just as he had informed the public of his illness, he made no effort to disguise his hours on the job.

The press and the Republican Party wanted him to answer one question: would or could he run for a second term? In turn, Ike wanted to know how soon he could play golf again. Ike was probably more determined to play golf than he was to serve a second term—he had hoped to serve only four years.

By January 1956 he was swinging his club and practicing his putting. By the end of the February, Ike resumed golfing at Augusta, first nine holes and then eighteen the following day. After he returned to Washington, he announced that he would run again. As if to emphasize the point, he traveled in March to the Greenbriar resort at White Sulfur Springs, West Virginia, where he golfed with Sam Snead. On his way home, he spoke from the train at Covington, Virginia—a trial run to test his vocal cords and infectious smile. Operated on for ileitis (an intestinal inflammation) in early June, the president once again demonstrated his rapid recuperative powers and assured the public that he was ready for a second term.

On August 22, 1956, the Republican convention renominated Eisenhower and Nixon at San Francisco. After giving his acceptance speech, Ike with his gang hustled down to the Monterey Peninsula where they played golf at Cypress Point. His golfing and bridge-playing buddies accompanied him back to Washington on the *Columbine* where they played bridge for the whole eight-and-a-half hour trip.

The Democrats had precious few issues to run on in 1956. Peace and prosperity, usually only campaign verbiage, had returned in the mid-1950s. Ike's extraordinary popularity made it hard to criticize his performance, so the Democrats tried to link golf, vacations, and health. They portrayed Ike as an absentee president. His opponent Adlai Stevenson, an unathletic "egghead" (or so he was labeled), ridiculed Ike as the "'head coach' who seems to have missed the plays and not [to] be too sure of the score." Despite crises in the Middle East and Hungary in late October, Ike again trounced Adlai Stevenson. The voters evidently did not care what Ike did as long as he could flash that famous Eisenhower grin and the government hummed along as if on autopilot.[19]

When he returned to Augusta for the first time after his heart attack, the members pulled the genie out of the bottle and virtually offered him anything in their power. "Mr. President," Clifford Roberts said, "we're so glad to have you back at the club, the first time since your illness, and we're going to grant you any one request as regards the modifications of the golf course."

And the president said, "Cut down that big tree on 17."[20]

Ike had wrestled too many times with the large pine on the left side of the seventeenth fairway. He claimed that it attracted his balls like some kind of golfing magnet.

Alas, the tree remained. They just couldn't honor that particular request. But the tree grew in size and stature long after the president had departed; now viewers of the Masters and golfing aficionados know it as the "Eisenhower pine."

Sports and Ike's Presidency: Uppers and Downers

In 1954 the Supreme Court handed down a landmark decision in *Brown vs. Board of Education of Topeka,* in which they declared school segregation unconstitutional. Now the president could no longer sidestep the civil rights issue. That summer, a Chicago teenager, Emmett Till, visiting a small town in Mississippi, was murdered and mutilated for allegedly making a provocative remark about a white woman. In 1955 the refusal of Rosa Parks to sit in the back of a bus sparked the Montgomery bus boycott and brought Martin Luther King Jr. to national prominence. The Eisenhower administration could not avoid the growing conflict in the South. In 1957 a federal judge ordered Central High School in Little Rock, Arkansas, to admit black children. Governor Orval Faubus of Arkansas announced that he would not allow black children to attend—his unwillingness lighting a short fuse that would lead to an explosion in Little Rock.

In truth, Ike himself had grave doubts about the *Brown* decision. On top of this, he believed that African Americans would not be ready for an equal status with whites for fifty to a hundred years. The president himself had many southern friends and was appalled by the prospect of intervening in the Little Rock crisis. In spite of his far-ranging military career, he was a man of his times—the early 1900s.

In early September, Ike and Mamie, along with Ike's loyal gang, flew to Newport, Rhode Island, for a golfing, bridge-playing, and seaside vacation. He tried to relax, but the menacing clouds in Little Rock kept interfering. At the president's request, Governor Faubus flew up to Newport to talk, but Ike feared the worst. He was right—he lost at bridge—an omen of what was to come. He played golf, cooked steaks for the gang, and opined that matters in Little Rock would only get worse.

The crisis erupted sooner than he thought. A full-fledged mob turned out in Little Rock on Monday morning, threatening to "lynch the niggers" and rushing the police barricades around Central High. Reluctantly, Ike federalized the Arkansas National Guard, which had been called up by Faubus to prevent integration, and he sent a thousand paratroopers from the 101st Airborne. Southern white opinion erupted in anger. Having taken the oath of office to uphold the laws, Ike knew he had no choice. The chaos in Little Rock gave him little opportunity for compromise.

The president was "saddened" by the need to take such drastic action—and, golfwise, he wondered how "Little Rock" would play in Augusta. Would it keep him from enjoying his cherished golfing vacations? Most of the club members came from all parts of the country—hence the term "national"—but Augusta was a golfing community that had opened its arms and heart to the Eisenhowers. But it was, after all, deep in the segregated South.

The answer to golfing at Augusta came firsthand in December when Ike and Mamie found out for themselves. To be sure, the troops had brought a quick end to the riots in Little Rock, and the nine black children were attending classes without incident. But bad feelings persisted among white southerners. When Ike and Mamie made their trip to Augusta, the locals were still angry about the president's assault on their "states' rights," code words for the Jim Crow system of segregating the races.

The *Augusta Chronicle*, usually an ardent fan of Ike, now ran daily editorials personally attacking the president. The Augusta officials had to persuade local officials to greet him on his arrival. Along the route into town, there was a far smaller turnout of Augustans than usual. Instead of their normal cheers, they stared sullenly at the president's motorcade. Surveying the grim scene, Mamie promptly canceled her Christmas shopping plans. Cliff Roberts, Ike's golfing friend, noted the president's uneasiness. "During this stay, it didn't seem to me that the President ever did unwind. He seemed tense when he arrived and remained so. He looked all right and he played golf rather well, but his mind seemed to be elsewhere." His distraction and unease showed up at the bridge table too. For the first time since Roberts had known him, he felt that Ike was unable to concentrate.[21]

In 1957 Ike had a mild stroke. He recovered, though his golf deteriorated. Nevertheless, Ike stepped up his world travels in a quest for peace with the Soviet Union and closer relations with the Third World. In 1959 he made a world tour that took him from Spain to India. Soon afterward, he made a two-week trip to Latin American capitals in which he delivered thirty-seven speeches. In June 1960 he made a two-week trip to the new states, Alaska and Hawaii, and then on to Asia.

He would also play host to the irascible Soviet premier, Nikita Khrushchev, in 1959. Ike was to make a return trip to Moscow but was rebuffed in Paris at the hands of Khrushchev after the U-2 spy plane and its pilot Gary Francis Powers were shot down over Soviet territory. On the brink of Ike's departure for Moscow, Khrushchev withdrew the invitation. Closer to home, a new revolutionary thorn in the administration's side, Fidel Castro of Cuba, was verbally assaulting the United States and seizing American property.

The medical and political crises took their toll on his worsening golf game. In December 1958 he had twelve subpar golfing rounds out of thirteen. By April 11, 1959, the frustration proved too much. According to his personal physician, Howard Snyder, he played well on the front nine, but his game went to pieces on the final nine holes. Snyder recorded in his diary that the president made a particularly bad wedge shot out of a sand trap.

"Fine shot," Snyder said.

"Fine shot, hell, you son of a bitch," the president exploded.

He threw his sand wedge at Snyder. The metal shaft of the club wrapped around the doctor's legs, but the heavy iron club head missed him. "Otherwise, I would have had a fractured leg," Snyder wrote.[22]

Ike made a perfunctory "pardon me." But the good doctor felt that it was probably well for the president to blow off steam. He believed that he was doing his duty in maintaining the president's health. He didn't speculate that Ike's violent behavior might also have been the result of heart disease—in particular, arteriosclerosis or hardening of the arteries.

After he left office in January 1961, Ike was able to play a stress-free golf game for the first time in his life. In 1967, less than two years before he died, paired with his friend Freeman Gosden (a white actor who played an African American on the radio show *Amos and Andy*), he shot his first hole-in-one. Stephen Ambrose has written wryly of Ike's reaction. "'The thrill of a lifetime,' he [Ike] gloated, thereby putting Overlord and the Presidency in their proper perspective."[23]

Eisenhower's two terms in the presidency received mixed reviews. The 1950s were called the era of complacency, a "troubled feast," and the affluent age, presided over by a slightly bewildered chief executive who preferred golf to running the country. Contrary to this less than glowing report card, Ike proved that he could run the country and play more than two hundred rounds at Augusta, not to mention scores of rounds in Washington. Unlike other twentieth-century presidents, Ike refrained from playing partisan games with the American public. He seldom tried to disguise his sporting activities or his medical condition. Unlike the professional politicians who followed him, Ike was proudly a nonpolitician.[24]

Instead, he remained the hero from World War II, who, like George Washington, rode a crest of victory into the White House. Though few people knew of his bad temper or his fierce competitive spirit, they loved his smile and enthusiasm. Ellis "Slats" Slater wrote in 1957, "Really, it's remarkable how people feel when he waves or says hello—their whole countenance seems to light up."[25]

The campaign slogan, "I Like Ike," sums up the presidential appeal of Dwight Eisenhower. Despite the pressures of high office and assaults on his presidency, he played that game remarkably well.

John F. Kennedy
Swimming into Politics

In 1962 President John F. Kennedy published "The Vigor We Need," an article in *Sports Illustrated*. Vigor, or "vigah," as JFK pronounced it, might have summed up Kennedy's short life and brief presidency. Because he was seldom healthy, he had to feign the vigor and vitality that came naturally to other members of his family. Yet, when he sailed, golfed, or played football, he performed these sports with natural grace and gritty determination.

To be sure, John F. Kennedy exuded "vigah" and vitality. He was a war hero who had been awarded the Naval Star and Marine Medal for heroism after the sinking of his PT-109. He appeared youthful, tanned, and relaxed. He played an occasional round of golf, but not the interminable rounds of Dwight Eisenhower. He was a devoted family man, or so it appeared. He inspired young people to bestir themselves, to become a nation of doers rather than spectators, and to expect more from themselves than from their government.

Kennedy ushered in the age of presidential sports. Not that he appeared regularly on television at baseball or football games or at pro-am tournaments. JFK came to the presidency on the cusp of a boom in televised sports. In the fall of 1960, he forged ahead of Nixon on the strength of his showing in the first televised debate. He appeared healthy and animated, whereas Nixon looked pale and sweaty as the heat of the television lights transformed his appearance. Although Nixon actually was the healthier of the two (in spite of a knee injured getting out of the car), black-and-white television proved that it could transform reality.

What we did not know about Kennedy ran far deeper than the image that he projected in the debates and in his brief presidency. Many of us were barely aware that he was the son of Wall Street manipulator and pre–World War II appeaser, Joseph P. Kennedy. Nor did we know that Joe Kennedy had spent millions of dollars to further the political and presidential prospects of his son Jack. Nor that JFK's athletics had been curtailed because he had Addison's dis-

Lieutenant John F. Kennedy at the controls of his command, PT-109. Assigned to the Solomon Islands in 1943, Kennedy's craft was rammed by a Japanese destroyer, sinking his fragile ship and throwing the survivors into the shark-infested waters. Kennedy's remarkable four-hour swim to an unoccupied island, towing a wounded crewman by his teeth, stands as the most remarkable athletic performance in battle by any future president since George Washington's heroics in the Pennsylvania wilderness two centuries before. Courtesy of John F. Kennedy Presidential Library, Boston.

ease, a malfunction of the kidneys, and that more than once he had been administered the last rites of the Catholic Church, or even that his healthy tan was an attempt to cover up a sallow and sickly complexion.

When we looked at this slim, athletic specimen, most of us knew nothing of Jack Kennedy's struggle against countless ailments and disabilities that kept him from competing in sports. Of course, we knew of his chronic back problems, but not of the medications that enabled him to avoid disabling pain and chronic ailments. Indeed, the vigor he needed as president had to be supplied by a medicine chest of pharmaceutical remedies, including cortisone, adrenal extracts, tranquillizers, uppers, and downers.

That said, John Kennedy was a natural athlete, far more talented and accomplished than most Americans realized. While George Washington rode on horseback through Revolutionary War battles and ultimately to the presidency, Kennedy made a series of equally fateful swims.

★

Prelude to the Swim

"Great crises produce great men and great deeds of courage," John Kennedy wrote in *Profiles in Courage,* his best seller written during his long convalescence after surgery in the 1950s.[1]

John F. Kennedy's crises began when he was a teenager and continued for the rest of his life. Illness and ailments had kept him from regularly engaging in sports as a student at Choate School. When he was a sophomore, he was so sick that the school staff feared for his life. "Actually, he came very close to dying," his friend Lem Billings later recalled. Prayers were said for him in chapel. In addition to lying in the school infirmary, Jack Kennedy spent countless days and weeks at the Mayo Clinic in Rochester, Minnesota, and the Lahey Clinic in Boston. As mysterious as his illnesses were, so were his recoveries. In spite of illness, he never engaged in self-pity, and he always kept his sense of humor. But he was also able to engage in some forms of athletics—his yearbook photo shows Kennedy playing left end on the football team.[2]

Jack Kennedy also played freshman football at Harvard; he sustained a serious back injury when a family retainer hurled him to the ground with a flying tackle immediately after the game as an ill-considered practical joke. He went out for swimming and beat out the star backstroker. In fact, Kennedy's Harvard freshman team is generally acknowledged as Harvard's best ever. He also played golf. His friend Lem Billings was awed by his natural athletic ability. "He was beautifully coordinated and one of the best natural athletes I've ever seen. He was fantastic. He had this natural coordination. He could pick up a golf club, having never played golf before, and play pretty decent golf. Same with tennis. So he'd catch a football and do all the things that take coordination. But he had very delicate health there. He was lightweight. He played football but for health reasons he didn't do very well."[3]

Kennedy also ran with an athletic crowd. During his second year at Harvard, all of his roommates were athletes, including Torbert MacDonald, the star of the football team and a lifelong friend. Jack Kennedy was competitive, a quality encouraged by his father who heaped scorn on "losers." By associating with athletes, cultivating a macho image, and trying to take part in rugged sports, Kennedy sought the vitality that had been denied him by his frail constitution. When he vacationed with his family at Palm Beach or Hyannisport on Cape Cod, he participated in all the summer sports.

He especially competed with his older brother Joe, also a graduate of Choate and a student at Harvard two years ahead of Jack. At the end of his sophomore year, Jack raised himself from his sickbed to participate in the Intercollegiate Yacht Regatta to be held near Hyannisport. Jack and his crew were competing against ten colleges and twenty crews. Jack captained one of Harvard's boats, and Joe captained another. According to Nigel Hamilton in *JFK: Reckless Youth*, in the final race "Jack took second place, giving Harvard an overall seven-and-a-half point victory in the regatta over its nearest rival, Dartmouth. All in all, it was a thrilling finish to Jack's sophomore year." He had also nosed out his older brother.[4]

Both Kennedy brothers had remarkable opportunities to travel in Europe on the cusp of World War II. Jack and Lem Billings made a circuit around Europe, visiting Mussolini's Italy, Munich, and Paris, as well as attempting to get into Franco's Spain. His brother Joe also visited the fascist capitals, praising the Nazi police state. Eventually Jack's innate curiosity about world affairs would find expression in his honors thesis, later published under the title *Why England Slept*. That his father Joseph Kennedy was ambassador to the Court of St. James opened doors that for ordinary students would have been firmly padlocked.

After graduating and spending a desultory semester at Stanford University Business School, Jack Kennedy joined the Navy. Given his chronic back and abdominal pains, it is remarkable that Kennedy managed to pass his Navy physical. Ensign Kennedy wound up in South Carolina where his military duties left him plenty of time to carry on a torrid love affair with "Inga Binga," actually Inga Arvad, a Danish divorcee. Her earlier contacts with Goebbels and Hitler made her a prime target for FBI surveillance. During this exile in South Carolina, JFK played golf, and later at Newport he regularly played his favorite pickup game, touch football.

Bored by his work in South Carolina, Kennedy volunteered for service in the PT squadrons. Touted as America's secret naval weapon, the PT boats were rather puny boats built of plywood and armed only with torpedoes. Few had artillery or even radar. Exposed to enemy surveillance, bombing, and gunfire, they were expected to maintain radio silence as they cruised the waters looking for a reason to launch their torpedoes. PT trainees such as Kennedy were whisked through two months of training at Northwestern University in the Chicago area and then practiced gunboat runs at Newport, Rhode Island. Despite the PT's obvious flaws, the small boat fit with Kennedy's experience in sailing and captaining small sailing craft.

Jack Kennedy's assignment to the South Pacific where he got to captain

PT-109 showed both slipshod screening by the Navy and his own gritty determination to keep his disability under wraps. Or perhaps having an influential father in the right place and at the right time was also helpful.

Wracked by back pain at Newport, he found a board that he could put under his mattress. Kennedy's back pain was far more complicated than the injury that he suffered on the gridiron at Harvard. Actually, it may have gone back to his chronic stomach ailment at Choate, when he was treated with adrenal extracts. Robert Dallek in *An Unfinished Life: John F. Kennedy, 1917–1963* suggests that adrenal extracts "can have deleterious long-term chronic effects, including osteoporosis with vertebral deterioration and peptic ulcers. In addition, chronic use of corticosteroids can lead to the suppression of normal adrenal function and may have caused or contributed to Jack's Addison disease."[5]

To Jack Kennedy's credit, he endured back pain in Newport and in the South Pacific. In his finest moment, Captain Kennedy would rise above his disabilities, as if they never existed, and perform at a physical level that most athletes would have found impossible.

★

PT-109

If Teddy Roosevelt called San Juan Hill "the great day in my life," it is fair to call JFK's week in the waters and the atolls near the Solomon Islands his greatest week. It certainly ranks with that other week in October 1962 when Kennedy stared down the Soviet Union in the Cuban Missile Crisis. Once in the Solomon Islands, JFK took command of the eighty-foot boat with a crew of thirteen. Every night, the fleet of PTs made routine patrols but rarely got to use their torpedoes. In fact, the boats were ill-suited to offense or defense. Rather, the flimsy craft were juicy targets for Japanese aircraft and shore batteries. The PT commanders were literally in the dark. Even if they had known precisely where to launch their torpedoes, the PTs would have contributed next to nothing to the war effort.

On the night of August 1, 1943, the PTs took off on a night patrol to ambush what was known as the Tokyo Express, a line of supply barges convoyed by Japanese warships. The PT raid was a fiasco. Out of radio contact, lacking radar and artillery, and running at half speed to muffle their sound, the boats had to navigate by primitive methods. Most of the boats fired their torpedoes aimlessly and then scurried for home. A Japanese destroyer coming out of the inky blackness spotted Kennedy's craft and, possibly by design, headed directly at it. With fifteen seconds to react, PT-109 had little chance to maneuver. The destroyer sliced the craft in two killing two members of the crew and hurling the rest into the water.

Had the PT-109 crew been rescued, JFK might possibly have faced a court martial or certainly an inquiry. Colliding with an enemy destroyer would inevitably have raised questions about the captain's competence, in particular, his decisions that night. However, the PT higher-ups assumed that there were no survivors. All of the PT boats fled, and unbelievably none returned to investigate the scene of the accident.

The crew of PT-109 clung to the hull of the boat until daylight. When it became clear that they were marooned in enemy waters, they decided (JFK polled the men) to swim for a small island. The eldest member of the crew, thirty-seven-year-old Pat "Pappy" MacMahon, was badly burned, so that Kennedy was forced to tow him. Clenching MacMahon's life preserver in his teeth, Kennedy swam sidestroke for four hours, struggling and spitting out sea water. Once ashore, Kennedy made a nighttime swim into the shark-infested waters to Ferguson Passage, hoping to catch up with the nonexistent search parties.

On the third day, the survivors decided to move to a larger island. Kennedy again towed MacMahon. Two days later, Kennedy and Barney Ross swam to yet another island where they found water, crackers, and candy that the Japanese had cached. They also made brief contact with natives in a canoe who turned out to be British scouts. Although the natives were afraid to land, they eventually carried word of survivors to the British military authorities.

Kennedy's fearless (some called it foolhardy) marathon swims through treacherous waters would turn a near-death accident into an epic story of war heroism. When the survivors were rescued, they praised the skipper for his leadership. His never-say-die spirit, they declared, had kept up their morale (Pappy MacMahon readily acknowledged that he owed his life to Kennedy). Not only did he risk his life, but his tenacity and courage also led to the crew's rescue.

PT-109 was one of many heroic stories from World War II, but because JFK was former ambassador Joseph Kennedy's son, it received instant notoriety. Jack Kennedy's mishap in the Pacific turned him from the survivor of a minor naval disaster into a media hero. All the stories from the crew portrayed the ambassador's son as heroic. Headlines read: "Kennedy's Son Saves 10 in Pacific; K's Son Is Hero in Pacific." Even JFK himself, who refused to call his role heroic, sardonically remarked that he was now a "legitimate American hero." In December 1944 author John Hersy wrote a detailed article about PT-109 for the *New Yorker*. As a result of string-pulling by Jack's father, *Reader's*

Digest then condensed the story for its millions of readers. Once the story became public, the question of Kennedy's responsibility never came up. Taken together, the boat, the man, and the story represent one of the best outcomes from one of the worst naval experiments of the war. It created a war hero who was not reluctant to use bits and pieces of PT-109 in his climb to the presidency.[6]

In the postwar era, candidates for office invariably played the war card, and Jack Kennedy was no exception. JFK's certified heroism proved to be of incalculable value from his first congressional campaign in 1946 to the presidency when a movie, *PT-109*, immortalized—and romanticized—the episode. Joan and Clay Blair in their ground-breaking history, *The Search for JFK*, summed up the PT-109 legacy: "For the rest of his life, Jack Kennedy would be inordinately proud of, and would capitalize on, his war record. In the postwar years, he would hold offices in veterans' organizations and maintain close contact with many PT buddies from the Solomons." The Blairs also emphasize that Kennedy was "scornful" of politicians who did not serve in the war.[7]

Ambassador Joseph P. Kennedy manipulated, bribed, and finagled to get his son's story into the national press. Possibly Joseph Kennedy's eldest son, Joe Jr., may have undertaken his final hazardous mission because he had to outshine his younger brother whose exploits in the Pacific were now well known. If Joe was motivated by his brother's heroic story, PT-109 was indeed a mixed legacy.

On August 12, 1944, Joe Kennedy's aircraft left on a hazardous bombing mission in a Liberator crammed with TNT. The plane exploded twenty minutes after takeoff, obliterating the aircraft and its crew. With Joe's death, Jack Kennedy became the beneficiary of his father's ambitions. Hereafter, Joseph Kennedy used his immense wealth and media influence to promote Jack. Now that Joe was gone, the surviving second son became the crown prince anointed for the highest office in the land. It was he whom the powerful elder Kennedy wanted to put in the White House.

★

Physically Challenged

Running as a Democrat, Jack Kennedy was elected to Congress in 1946 and upset Senator Henry Cabot Lodge six years later in spite of the Eisenhower landslide. After being discharged from the Navy, Jack's health improved, at least temporarily, as a result of cortisone injections. Nevertheless, the glamorous young senator set his sights on the White House. Since he had few legislative achievements, Kennedy relied on his youthful glamour. In 1953 he

Senator John F. Kennedy strolling across a quiet street in Georgetown to play touch football in a nearby park. A natural athlete, JFK was also an outstanding golfer who played all sports with Kennedyesque competitiveness. This photo was taken by photographer Orlando Suero who in 1954 spent a week with Kennedy and his family (see Jackie, Ethel, and Bobby in foreground). Because of a bad back, Kennedy as president had little opportunity to play football or golf. Courtesy of Archives, Peabody Institute of the Johns Hopkins University, Baltimore.

married the young and fashionably attractive Jacqueline Bouvier. Despite his Roman Catholicism (still a negative in the 1950s), he came within a few votes of being nominated as vice-president in 1956.

His health remained a serious concern. In 1954, his physical condition worsened. He had contracted Addison's disease, a deficiency of the kidneys, which in turn contributed to a deteriorating spinal condition and the need thereafter to walk on crutches. As his naval experience indicated, Kennedy was willing to gamble his life in order to be in the thick of the political wars. In 1953 and 1954, he underwent life-threatening back surgery to insert a plate and then, when infection set in, another operation to remove the plate. While recovering, Kennedy—and others—put together the Pulitzer Prize–winning *Profiles in Courage*. Despite his athletic interests, after the surgery all sports activities would have to be greatly reduced.

JFK shifted his quest for vitality and vigor to the nation itself. In 1960, against steep odds, Kennedy became only the second Roman Catholic to be nominated by a major party and the first to be elected to the presidency. His televised debates with Richard Nixon in the presidential campaign were nothing less than a one-on-one competition between two determined opponents vying for the ultimate prize—a spectator event nonpareil. That Kennedy could appear on camera healthier and more relaxed than Nixon was a tribute to his ability to disguise his disabilities and project his charm and intelligence, not to mention the transforming effect of television itself.

In his inaugural address, he called for Americans to renew their commitment to winning the struggle with communism. He would follow it up with proposals to put a man on the moon and to harness the idealism of young Americans by initiating the Peace Corps. "And, so, my fellow Americans, ask not," he implored, "what your country can do for you—rather ask what you can do for your country." This statement reflected a bold shift in perspective that permeated Kennedy's foreign policy.

Even before he took the oath of office, Kennedy began a campaign to inject vigor and vitality into American youth. His article, "The Soft American," published in *Sports Illustrated* in late 1960, deplored the failure of children in America to measure up to their European counterparts. "We do not want our children to become a generation of spectators," he wrote. "Rather we want each of them to be a participant in the vigorous life." Kennedy's message echoed his own struggles to overcome his own disabilities—by participating in sports and by volunteering for combat in World War II.[8]

Not that the Kennedy administration introduced the President's Council on Physical Fitness. In 1954 President Eisenhower had called a conference of sports notables to discuss ways to improve the physical condition of American youth as well as to combat juvenile delinquency. Two years later, Vice-President Richard Nixon had presided over the first full-fledged Council on Physical Fitness and President's Advisory Council.

Despite efforts to exhort American youth, the Eisenhower administration's approach had been to crank out pamphlets and to display well-known former athletes or screen stars. A sweeping survey in 1960 indicated that more than half of American youth failed the fitness test, as opposed to less than 10 percent of Europeans. Ike, a former college athlete, was far from apathetic. In a press conference, he commented at length on American youth having become "affluent and soft." But, asked by a young visitor the best way to become athletic, Ike suggested that golf would be a "good game."[9]

The Kennedy administration took Eisenhower's Council on Physical Fitness and beefed it up. A high-profile college football coach, Charles "Bud" Wilkinson, replaced the little-known Shane MacCarthy as executive director. Programs were initiated at the grass roots to bring students up to acceptable standards. The Kennedy administration picked five states to initiate the programs, and 200,000 students took part. In 1962, in his article "The Vigor We Need," the president claimed promising results, though he emphasized the need for more programs, more participation, and more facilities. "It was physical hardihood that helped Americans in two great world wars," he wrote, "to defeat strong and tenacious foes and make this country history's mightiest defender of freedom." Now the war for freedom was being fought "in the jungles of Asia and on the borders of Europe."[10]

Sixty years after Teddy Roosevelt's presidency, Kennedy's words echoed the emphasis on the "strenuous life." TR had also worried about the softness of youth and the need to develop "hardihood" to defend ourselves and to play our rightful role in the world. In 1963 Kennedy came across one of the letters Roosevelt had written to the Marine commandant challenging the officers to make a fifty-mile walk in a single day. Now, as the Marines at Camp Lejeune agreed to do the same, JFK suggested that members of his own administration and even the press go along to prove their mettle.

As he faced the press, he eyed his pudgy and nonathletic press secretary Pierre Salinger, who often served as JFK's court jester. "John F. Kennedy, a natural athlete himself, had a passion for fitness that was almost the undoing of his chubby Press Secretary," Salinger recalled. Attorney General Robert Kennedy, among others, successfully completed the fifty-mile hike, but Salinger did not. After several hilarious false starts, he wrote a statement begging off and then held a press conference to explain his decision. Salinger, known more for his brain and wit than for his brawn, made a sound decision in sitting out that particular day's activities.[11]

Unlike TR, President Kennedy did not attempt to put words into action. It was enough for him to throw down the gauntlet.

Camelot: Games and Sport in That Most Romantic Spot

In March 1961, while visiting Palm Beach, JFK revealed a passion that he wished to downplay. Like Ike, whom the Democrats criticized for his golf, President Kennedy also played golf and was a better golfer than Eisenhower. On April 4, 1961, he posed on the first tee with his father and brothers-in-law, Stephen Smith and actor Peter Lawford. On the next day, the president earned the dubious distinction of hitting a secret service agent with his ball, the first president to bean an onlooker since Warren Harding hit writer Ring Lardner in 1921. Though the incident was reported, Kennedy's score was not. And no photos were permitted of the president swinging a club. Often the president played only three holes or hit iron shots to relieve tension such as in the hours leading up to the disastrous Bay of Pigs invasion in 1961, the failed attempt to topple Fidel Castro.

Castro, an unlikely golfer, taunted the president by boasting that he could easily defeat Kennedy on the links. Castro had already joined Khrushchev and Adlai Stevenson in criticizing Ike's golf playing, a bourgeois sport for the idle rich. But Castro was curious enough that he had recently played with Che Guevara in Havana, wearing his olive-green army uniform, boots, and beret, a far cry from the president's informal sports attire. Guevara, who won the match, said that he had worked as a caddy in his native Argentina and had played golf as a student. Castro had already proclaimed his prowess in baseball, basketball, fishing, shooting, swimming, and cutting sugarcane, so why not golf? The credibility gap was quickly turned to comedy at Castro's expense. A caddy who claimed to have walked the course with Castro and Guevara reported that their golf was awful. "They couldn't even beat you," he informed a reporter. According to the caddy, Castro shot over 150. Guevara waltzed in with a 127. This particular Cuban missile confrontation was clearly an American victory![12]

How did the president get around the course? Press secretary Pierre Salinger recalled that JFK was erratic with his long irons, which was perhaps why he hit the secret service agent. However, Salinger stressed that "his strong tee shots and deftness around the greens always kept him within range of par." Ben Bradlee of the *Washington Post* remembered Kennedy as fun to play with, a trademark of JFK since his youth in athletics. He kept up a constant chatter on the course. He would quip, "no profile needed here, just courage." According to Bradlee, he could become a TV commentator as he hit the ball, with the commentator's stage whisper that "with barely a glance at the packed gallery, he whips out his four iron and slaps it dead to the pin."[13]

Bradlee wrote that the president was a good golfer "with a natural swing, but erratic." Not only was he good at the game, but he also enjoyed himself. If he shanked a ball into the water, he would exclaim "bahstard," but he teed up his ball immediately. Like Warren Harding, he liked to make bets on the tee. Salinger said that he ran his "con" on the first tee, making so many complex bets that his opponents couldn't possibly win. Bets were made not only on who would win the hole, but also for the longest drive, first on the green, closest to the pin, and first in the hole. No wonder Bradlee called the president "competitive as hell."[14]

Jackie Kennedy, an accomplished rider, rented an estate, Glen Ora, in the horse country of Virginia, as a weekend getaway. Jackie loved fox hunting and, according to Sally Bedell Smith, believed that it was not (in her words) "a cruel sport of the idle rich" but brought out "the best in people—lover of animals, each other, nature, sport, happiness etc." Though she also enjoyed tennis at the White House courts and once took golf lessons at the Hyannisport Club, Jackie preferred riding and jumping or attending equestrian events, such as steeplechase races. A fearless rider, she once was thrown across a post and rail fence while on a fox hunt but arrived at the hunt breakfast so entirely intact that no one knew of her spill—until *Life* magazine published a two-page photo of her fall taken by a local photographer.[15]

To lure the president into spending weekends at Glen Ora, Jackie presented him with a rough-hewn, three-hole golf course. A throwback to the earliest days of golf, the course ran through pastures, and the holes were merely pins with Confederate flags protruding from the grass. The hazards were large rocks, hills, long grass, and a swamp, known as the "water hole." Instead of the usual pars of three, four, and five, the pasture course boasted a hole with a par of nine. According to Bradlee, the small green strips cleared by a friend doubled as both tees and greens.[16]

In June 1961, barely five months into his presidency, Kennedy's golf came to a screeching halt. During a tree-planting ceremony in Ottawa, he sprained his back—and then made it worse by playing golf immediately after. The result: he would not play golf for two years until his last summer in the presidency. In September, it was Jackie Kennedy who was pictured playing golf on a day that she also went water skiing.

Two years after his accident, the president resumed his golf, or so the newspapers reported. To be sure, Kennedy was playing, but not always at golf. On some of those golfing afternoons, he pursued another activity, extramarital sex. Golf provided a convenient cover for what was decidedly unpresidential, not to mention a politically hazardous pastime. Because of his back and lack of stamina, Kennedy could barely manage to play nine holes. Which could not be said of his numerous liaisons with youthful and attractive women.

Not surprisingly, Kennedy's daily exercise was oriented toward relaxing and rehabilitating his body. Swimming, especially in ninety degree water, relaxed his body and mind. Normally, he took a half-hour swim—in the buff—every afternoon and evening in the White House pool, often conversing with his pal Dave Powers (who often spouted sports statistics) while he swam leisurely in the company of reporters. According to Sally Bedell Smith, JFK "thought nothing of talking to reporters in his bedroom or while taking a swim in the nude."[17]

In spite of his back injury at Harvard, JFK never lost his interest in football. Before he took office on New Year's Day 1960, he attended the Orange Bowl. And he enjoyed the Army-Navy game in 1961 and 1962. While his brothers and sisters played touch football, Kennedy spent his vacations yachting at Hyannisport. Once again the president reactivated the presidential yacht, re-christened the *Honey Fitz,* after his grandfather, the onetime mayor of Boston—part of a small presidential flotilla. Like FDR, Kennedy preferred to vacation on or near the water.

In 1961, after running back Ernie Davis of Syracuse University won the Heisman Trophy, Kennedy greeted this first African American trophy winner at the White House. Davis told Kennedy that he dreamed of playing professional football. Indeed, a number of NFL teams were eager to draft and sign Davis, including the Washington Redskins and Cleveland Browns. By 1961 times were changing—the all-white Washington Redskins team was under pressure from Secretary of the Interior Stewart Udall to draft an African American player. George Preston Marshall, the longtime owner of the Redskins, had stubbornly refused to integrate his team. Kennedy, though he had won black votes when Robert Kennedy pushed for Martin Luther King's release from jail in Birmingham, had done little to advance civil rights since taking office. Udall learned from the Justice Department that the administration could deny Marshall the right to play at D.C. Stadium, part of the National Capital Parks System. Udall demanded that Marshall place a black player on his team if he wanted the Redskins to play in the stadium. According to

Charles K. Ross in *Outside the Lines,* "the President supported his position, as did his brother Attorney General Robert Kennedy and Secretary of Labor Arthur Goldberg."[18]

The Redskins had won only one game in 1961, the worst record in the National Football League, which entitled Marshall to draft the best player available. Udall made it clear that the Redskins owner had to follow through on his promise to draft a black player. The Redskins then chose Ernie Davis in the first round of the NFL draft as well as two other African Americans in subsequent rounds. Before drafting Davis, Marshall traded him to the Cleveland Browns for a standout black halfback, Bobby Mitchell, and a first-round draft pick, Leroy Jackson, also black.

When training camp began the next summer, the Redskins had five African American players. It was Bobby Mitchell who made both Marshall and the Kennedy administration look good. The Redskins compiled a respectable record of five wins, seven losses, and two ties. More important, Bobby Mitchell had a banner year. In the team's first game against the Dallas Cowboys, he ran back a kickoff ninety-two yards for a touchdown and also scored on two pass receptions. Mitchell's eleven touchdowns in 1962 led the NFL, and his seventy-two receptions led to a spot in the pro bowl.

Ernie Davis was not so fortunate. The Browns had traded for him, planning to use him in tandem with the great fullback Jim Brown, also a graduate of Syracuse University. Sadly, Davis was diagnosed with leukemia before the season began and never played a professional game. He died less than a year later, having played a minor role in the contest between Marshall and the Kennedy administration, a prelude to the racial conflicts in the summer of 1963 and Martin Luther King's march on Washington.

In the fall of 1962, as Mitchell was reviving the moribund Redskins, John F. Kennedy was facing his greatest challenge since PT-109. The Soviets had been sending missiles to Cuba, and American overflights photographed the missile emplacements. For a week, Kennedy pursued a struggle for survival, in this case, the survival of the world in the face of nuclear war.

As Kennedy entered into this game, he appeared as the weaker player. The earlier abortive attack on Cuba at the Bay of Pigs had made Kennedy appear ineffectual. Nikita Khrushchev, the Soviet premier, regarded him as young and inexperienced when they met at Vienna in 1961. Once again, when he challenged Khrushchev to remove the missiles, Kennedy responded with intelligence and pragmatism—as he had in the Solomon Islands nineteen years before. Once again, he was tough but not panicky in the face of potential disaster. And, again, he was able to triumph in a manner that if not heroic proved to be life saving. Though he made the decisions, he relied on the consensus of his crew—or, in this case, the crisis cabinet or "wise men" he had assembled.

While the Cuban Missile Crisis was not an athletic event, this particular confrontation involved gamesmanship of the highest order. Kennedy had spent his early life learning how to compete while not letting the other guy look bad. He was able to use his strength of will honed in sports and the flexibility that had allowed him to overcome so many physical adversities. As much as he wanted to infuse vigor into the American initiative in the Cold War, he was able to step back from his competitive instincts when the situation required.

Surely, this was one of the most crucial games ever played by an American president, a head-to-head conflict with Nikita Khrushchev, with the fate of the world at stake. As Secretary of State Dean Rusk famously said, "we're eyeball to eyeball, and I think the other fellow just blinked."[19]

And, indeed Khrushchev had blinked as events in the next few days would demonstrate. Just as the PT-109 crew made it to safety, John F. Kennedy, America, and the world also survived. Kennedy's courage and his ability to endure and overcome were indeed magnificent examples of athletic ability, determination, and an instinct for survival.

On November 22, 1963, the day of his assassination, the myth of Camelot became frozen in time. People who could barely remember the names of Washington and Lincoln placed JFK at the top of the presidential pantheon. Whether his short tenure as president deserved such high marks, JFK himself had many remarkable qualities, not the least being his sporting interests and talents.

The poet A. E. Housman might have written JFK's athletic epitaph in his poem "To an Athlete Dying Young."

> Now you will not swell the rout
> Of lads that wore their honours out,
> Runners whom renown outran
> And the name died before the man.[20]

When he died so tragically at forty-six, President John F. Kennedy may indeed have outrun his athletic renown. The story of his marathon swim, however, would not die before the man.

President Lyndon Johnson herding cattle on his LBJ ranch.
Dressed in western-style coat and tie, Johnson used the ranch, which
included the farmstead where he was born, to shape his image as a westerner
and to entertain colleagues and celebrities. He also built a swimming
pool after his heart attack in 1955, where he engaged in one of
the few sports that interested him—swimming laps.
AP Wide World.

Lyndon Johnson
The Games He Didn't Play

On November 22 the staff at the LBJ ranch in the hill country near Austin was preparing for the visit of President John F. Kennedy. Before coming to the ranch, JFK would travel to Houston, San Antonio, and then Dallas. Additional security arrangements were in place as well as the preparations for a lavish barbecue spread out under the live oaks and facing the Pedernales River.

When Kennedy visited the Johnson ranch in January 1961, Vice-President Johnson had taken him on the mandatory deer hunt, a new experience for the president. An easterner who grew up near the water, JFK was, in the words of Sally Bedell Smith, "a reluctant participant in blood sports." Even so, after some brief instructions with the deer rifle, he managed to shoot two bucks in three rounds (later JFK told Johnson he had seen the "rope burns" on his quarry's legs). But he was clearly impressed with Johnson's expertise with a rifle when Johnson downed a deer at what Kennedy estimated as six hundred yards.[1]

According to comedian Richard "Cactus" Pryor, who often served as master of ceremonies, the famous LBJ barbecues featured a typically Texas flavor—a sheepdog act, cutting horse demonstration, and a show of pistol marksmanship by a Texas Ranger. "And, ironically," Pryor reflected, "the Secret Service worked . . . for a couple of hours that morning to make sure that there was no danger of the president being hit by a ricochet." JFK never made it to that barbecue, his trip ending tragically in Dallas.[2]

★

Politics as Sport

Lyndon Johnson was born on his grandfather's ranch, which later became part of his own LBJ ranch, but he grew up in nearby Johnson City, Texas. The rangy boy with his father's oversized ears spent his early years playing baseball, hunting deer, and fishing. He participated in outdoor sports because that was what you did in rural Texas. After graduating from high school, he spent a year working on the Texas roads and then entered Southwest Texas State Teacher's College (now San Marcos State). A college friend recalled hunting with the future president. "Oh yes," he explained, "mostly deer. Oh, we had a few timber wolves. . . . But most of the hunting during that time was deer."[3]

In his freshman year at Southwest, he became friends with Boody Johnson (no relation), a star athlete. Boody got Lyndon to go out for the baseball team, but the gangly, nonathletic freshman failed to make the team. Boody also tried to get his friend into the Black Stars, the most influential student society, but Johnson was blackballed. After his sophomore year, Johnson dropped out of school and taught at Cotulla in a small school with a largely Mexican student body. When he returned, he took over the White Stars, an organization formed by bookish students who were shunned by the Black Stars. Under Johnson's leadership, the White Stars swept to victory in the elections for student government. As he would do so often in the future, Johnson used his influence with an older man, in this case the school president, to further his ambitions. Athletics played no part in his college career.

Out of college, Johnson landed his first job in a Houston high school teaching business math and coaching the debate team. He approached debate as if he were coaching a major sports team. Like a hard-nosed football coach, Johnson pushed and prodded his debaters, used imaginative techniques in training, and arranged for extensive coverage in the Houston newspapers. The team ran up victory after victory in the city and district competitions and went to the state finals in Austin determined to win (they lost in the first round). Johnson "got the rest of the school to treat his debaters like football heroes, with rallies and dances in their honor." By the time he left, one debater remembered, "we were more important than the football team."[4]

Even though Johnson never played football, years later Hubert Humphrey, his Senate colleague and then his vice-president, compared LBJ's style of politics to football. "He was not delicate. There was nothing delicate about him. He was not a ballet dancer. He was a downfield blocker and a running fullback *all the time*."[5]

Johnson left for Washington in 1931 to become secretary to Congressman Richard Kleberg. Just as he had organized the White Stars and the debate team, he took over the Little Congress, the assembly of congressional staff members and made it into a facsimile of Congress itself. When Kleberg was absent from Washington, Johnson transacted business and made decisions as if he were the congressman.

In 1935 the young wheeler-dealer became head of the Texas office of the National Youth Administration, an organization designed to help young people find jobs. In 1937 he won a seat in the House of Representatives vacated by the death of a congressman, and in 1948 he eked out a victory for the Senate in a controversial election that bestowed upon him the nickname "Landslide Lyndon."

As a congressman, Johnson played games and sports, but only occasionally. According to Congressman Sam Worley, he played golf (badly), went to the racetrack, and played poker. "Never caught him cheating," Worley recalled. "He'll try to bluff the devil out of you—like Harry Truman in that respect."[6]

Worley remembered once when they played golf that Johnson prevailed on him to give LBJ a stroke handicap on each hole. Johnson complained that he had been so busy that his game had grown rusty. At the seventeenth hole, down a stroke, Worley proposed a double or nothing on the final hole. Johnson's response: "'Hell, I didn't work seventeen holes to give it back to you on one hole.' And he didn't."[7]

Personally or politically, he never liked to lose. "As I say, whether it's golf or poker or what not . . . ," Worley concluded, "he takes it pretty hard when he loses." In both sports and politics, Johnson usually arranged to have things lined up so that he didn't find himself caught short.[8]

When Johnson took his Senate seat, he immediately set out to cultivate the power brokers among southern senators. He picked Richard Russell of Georgia, the de facto leader of the southern caucus and a bachelor. When Johnson learned that the older man loved baseball, Lyndon accompanied him to watch the Washington Senators. But he talked so much about politics during the games that Russell, who became his mentor, was relieved when Johnson lost his so-called enthusiasm for baseball and stopped going to the games.

Ironically, Johnson would be portrayed as a baseball fan in 1955 after a heart attack that nearly killed him. "He has seen virtually every televised home game played by the Washington Senators since he suffered his near-fatal attack last July," a *Sports Illustrated* columnist wrote. The columnist added that LBJ also rooted for the Boston Red Sox because a Texan, Michael "Pinky" Higgins, managed the club, and another Texan, Pete Runnels, played second base. "I'm going to give him [Higgins] a luncheon up on the Hill next year," Johnson said. "It'll be a big affair." Still further, he speculated that when he left the Senate, he might buy a baseball team in Texas. "We could stay there and run the team until we were old men," he reflected. But Johnson had left Texas precisely because the seat of power was in the East. When he attended the opening game as president, he still spent most of his time jawboning with his guests. Baseball clearly was the means to another end—politics—which had a much higher priority.[9]

★

Home on the Ranch

As a Texas senator, Johnson found that he could use not only his home state but also employ his boyhood sports to his advantage. To be sure, the games that Johnson played were almost always political. The Johnson ranch appeared an unlikely choice for the retreat of a powerful senator—far from Washington and distant from fashionable sporting venues. But Johnson, now majority leader of the Senate and vying for the presidency, had a political design to promote his western roots, even incorporating the deer hunting that he and his friends had once pursued.

In 1951 Johnson purchased his grandfather's run-down property that he would transform into the LBJ ranch. Lady Bird Johnson remodeled the ranch house, and Lyndon plowed money into making it a working ranch. Soon a network of roads crisscrossed the property, and Johnson added more property to the nucleus. He also made special arrangements with the owners of nearby ranches so that he could use their land for hunting. Eventually, the Johnson ranch was well enough stocked that Johnson could take his friends and visitors hunting from the back of his large white convertibles, mostly Lincoln Continentals. The back seat of one was equipped with a bar so that you could pour yourself a stiff Scotch before drawing a bead on a buck.

While the ranch was useful to Johnson as a retreat, it took on a more fundamental meaning—it became the image of Johnson himself. Most people regarded Lyndon Johnson as a southerner and for good reason. He had begun his climb to majority leader under the tutelage of Senator Richard Russell of Georgia and had a pro-southern voting record in the Senate. That meant voting against liberal measures such as the bill to outlaw lynching, introduced—and defeated by southern filibusters—in 1949. Actually he had not signed the southern manifesto after the *Brown* desegregation case in 1954, breaking ever-so-slightly with his southern colleagues. Ambitious for the presidency, Johnson had to escape the label of southern segregationist—and regional politician.

He began his ascent to power as a southerner, but now he planned to transform his image from southerner to a westerner. To be a westerner meant to belong to the popular culture of the frontier—to be rooted in the west of the endless panoramas and vast ranches, of singers and actors like Gene Autry and John Wayne, of classic films like *Giant* and *Gunfight at the OK Corral*, not to mention the popular westerns that flooded the TV airwaves in the late 1950s. That western culture was light years from William Faulkner's inbred and half-witted Snopes and the angry mobs threatening African American children (who were knocking at the doors of lily-white southern schools). It was America writ large and without the ugly and glaring stain of racism.

Johnson built a ranch that was also a set for his live performances. The ranch was carefully altered to enshrine Johnson in this virile and colorful culture. Not that western barbecues beside the Pedernales River would get him the Democratic nomination. He could, however, extend his political turf. LBJ invited dignitaries to the ranch, as in 1959 when he entertained President López Mateos of Mexico, an event attended by former president Harry Truman and Speaker of the House Sam Rayburn. As vice-president, he entertained President Ayub Khan of Pakistan and Konrad Adenauer of West Germany, as well as a camel driver named Ahmed, also from Pakistan, who unexpectedly accepted LBJ's offhanded invitation to visit America.

At home on LBJ's ranch was not always pleasant for the less prominent guests. Games that Johnson played on the ranch had the effect of humiliating the dudes and city slickers and underscoring the power of the ranch owner. The dudes were often easterners who had no experience deer hunting, which Johnson used as a rite of initiation. When Robert Kennedy visited the ranch in 1959, Johnson and the ranch manager showed him how to shoot. Kennedy, then a congressional aide, had never hunted. Despite the lesson on the use of firearms, the gun kicked and hit Kennedy in the face. Later, when Johnson became vice-president and then succeeded JFK as president, the two strong-willed rivals would come to despise each other. What part did this incident play? Perhaps this initial slap in the face began what was to become an increasingly contentious relationship.

While playing the role of a fatherly mentor, Johnson practically guaranteed that his eastern visitors would miss their target. After showing them how to use the rifle and preparing them to shoot, he did his utmost to distract them. "Such seemingly childish behavior," Hal Rothman writes in *LBJ's Texas White House*, "allowed Johnson to prove himself more accomplished and somehow more entitled to lead." Those who graduated to hunting from the back seat of a convertible while sipping Scotch may have also had trouble hitting the mark. To Johnson, the indulgent and bullying manipulator of the hunt, the whole charade was uproariously funny—and, no doubt, satisfying. Johnson's debating partner in college once recalled: "When he knew he had the advantage, why, he could become ruthless."[10]

When Johnson joined Kennedy on the Democratic ticket in 1960, he began three years of political eclipse. He no longer held the cards. The man who had run the Senate as majority leader had to live in Kennedy's shadow. But a fateful trip to Texas in November 1963 suddenly thrust Johnson into the position he had so long coveted. Like Theodore Roosevelt in 1901, he could at last play the political game on a stage measured to his lofty ambition.

While he was president, Johnson made more than forty trips to the LBJ ranch. More frequently than any of his predecessors, Johnson invited cabinet officers, advisers, political figures, and heads of state to his retreat. The setting and recreation had faint overtones of Teddy Roosevelt. When Walter Heller, his economic adviser, visited the ranch, LBJ took the Minnesotan on a ride in the Lincoln Continental with his daughter Lynda Bird and actor George Hamilton. While Lynda Bird and Hamilton hunted from the back seat, Heller struggled to discuss with the president "the question of whether he should reverse himself on excise taxes."[11]

The trauma of Kennedy's assassination surely worked to discourage Johnson from hunting. At the ranch in early December 1963, Johnson got up before dawn and shot a large buck—and the story was immediately relayed on the wire services. The Bambi-huggers were shocked. A letter from a woman in Pittsburgh, through its fractured punctuation, captured this outrage. "Only— 1 month—after Mourning Our Dear President John Fitzgerald Kennedy— with a Rifle—You would go out with a Rifle—President Johnson—you set a bad example to the World—those Deers—love life—and want to live—the same as you and Me." The writer suggested that Johnson get up before dawn and feed the "beautiful Deers" rather than gunning them down in the same way JFK was killed.[12]

Being in the motorcade with JFK at Dallas certainly could have made hunting repugnant to him. Or, perhaps as a practical politician, he understood its downside. During the election of 1964 and then during the bloody war in Vietnam, he may have realized that hunting could only interfere with his increasingly troubled presidency. So LBJ himself refrained.

Uninterested in playing or watching sports, Johnson managed to be the least athletic president since Calvin Coolidge. Occasionally, he bowled at Camp David or with a spurt of energy began a short-lived walking regimen around the grounds of the White House. After his heart attack in 1955, he began swimming and did laps in his pool at the LBJ ranch and later as president in the White House. He swam in the nude in the swimming pool built for FDR, as did everyone who used the pool when he did. It was as if he needed to shock and unnerve those around him, to use his earthiness and crudity as a means of control. Whatever his motives, he seemed to enjoy swimming as much as any physical activity—with the possible exception of his lobbying tactic in the Senate of hoisting smaller colleagues up by their lapels to threaten or cajole.

Like other presidents, Johnson understood the uses of sports and sporting celebrities. In 1965 he invited that year's Heisman winner, Mike Garrett of Southern California, to the White House. He continued JFK's President's Council on Physical Fitness. In place of Coach Bud Wilkinson of Oklahoma, he appointed the recently retired baseball standout, Stan Musial, a Democrat of Polish background from Pennsylvania, who had played his entire career for the St. Louis Cardinals. When Musial showed no administrative talent or political savvy, he was replaced by former astronaut James Lovell.

Nor did LBJ neglect physical fitness in his massive War on Poverty. In a campaign against flabbiness, he recommended $195 million for a youth development act for disadvantaged kids and $53 million for the School Health and Physical Education Act. His Civil Rights Act of 1968, designed to prevent discrimination in hiring, would lead to the Title IX amendments in 1972 which would contribute to the blossoming of women's sports.

Still it was difficult to portray Johnson in a sporting context. *Sports Illustrated* wanted to do an article on Johnson's outdoor sports, but the project died almost as soon as it was conceived.

★

A Secondhand President

Lyndon Johnson never escaped JFK's glamour, especially when it burst into full flower after his death. For all his attempts to add luster to his image, Johnson was a traditional politician who made his reputation passing legislation. Not that the president's legislative record lacked substance. In his first eighteen months in office, Johnson signed into law Kennedy's civil rights bill, a flurry of antipoverty programs, Medicare, and a tax cut. The war in Vietnam soon undercut Johnson's domestic policies and led to distrust among fellow Democrats. Still, Eisenhower, a popular World War II general, and Kennedy, a glamorous young politician, had created mystiques that Johnson simply could not match.

The physical differences between Kennedy and Johnson only made his problem more visible. Whereas JFK exuded athleticism, LBJ was jowly and inert, and moved with none of the natural grace of JFK. Kennedy carefully censored photos of himself in bathing trunks so that the public would not see what he called his "Fitzgerald breasts." Johnson bared his flabby stomach to reveal his scar from a gall bladder operation. A letter to *Life* magazine in response to a photo of Johnson in a swimsuit suggested that the president should see designer Rudi Gernreich, a swimsuit designer, to create a better one, "preferably one that was not topless."[13]

According to historian Paul Henggeler, Johnson "overate, frequently drank alcohol, sometimes smoked cigarettes, and had little patience for athletic recreation." That Kennedy functioned with powerful medications hardly mattered because the public knew next to nothing of his precarious health. In fact, people only knew that Johnson had recovered from a serious heart attack, not that Kennedy suffered from life-threatening Addison's disease. Only a psychic or a fool would regard LBJ as healthier than his predecessor.[14]

Writing to the president, a seventeen-year-old who said he planned to join the Navy regarded Johnson as second-rate, not because he governed poorly, but because he compared so unfavorably with Kennedy *athletically.*

> The late President Kennedy was a younger man than you and set an example for the people of America. Whenever you are shown on television, you are either relaxing or taking it easy. This does not make me get up and jump. I see the leader of the country lounging around and I don't see him engaged in any type of sports. I think you should engage in sports and try to set an example for the American people as the late President Kennedy did.[15]

In fairness to Johnson—and many people were patently unfair—governing the country and dealing with the ballooning war in Vietnam consumed most of his time and energies. Even if he had wished to play golf or watch football, he realized that he would have been criticized for frivolity in the midst of a bloody and controversial war. With protesters chanting "LBJ, LBJ, how many babies have you killed today?" the president could hardly afford to be cavorting on the links or shooting deer in Texas.

In 1968 Senator Eugene McCarthy of Minnesota challenged and nearly defeated Johnson in the New Hampshire primary. Senator Robert Kennedy of New York, who had been rudely clobbered by the butt of a deer rifle, declared his candidacy for the Democratic nomination. On March 31 Johnson declared that he would not run.

And, after the Republican victor Richard Nixon took office in January 1969, Johnson retired to his LBJ ranch. Much of his time in the next few years would be devoted to fund raising and construction of the LBJ Library on the University of Texas campus in Austin and to unexpected new sporting interests.

★
The Greening of LBJ

After returning to the ranch, Johnson showed more genuine interest in sports than at any time since he had left Johnson City for college. The ranch ceased to be the Texas White House, and the barbecues under the live oaks next to the Pedernales no longer featured visits by heads of state or cabinet members. With far too much time on his hands, Johnson referred to himself, half in jest, as "an old age pensioner."[16]

On trips to Kingsland, Texas, or to exotic Acapulco, where he once encountered Bob Hope on the links, Johnson played golf, though by his own rules. He never played a bad shot. Secret service agents would retrieve the errant shots, and Johnson would swing until one of his many shots proved satisfactory. He had cut corners in politics, and why should golf be an exception? According to Darrell Royal, coach of the Texas Longhorns, he and Johnson played an informal game. "I would just say, 'why don't we just drop it [the ball] up there somewhere where I am and we'll hit on in.' So that kept it moving and he wasn't just standing out there swinging and hitting at balls and trying to get the ball to advance."[17]

LBJ's growing friendship with Coach Royal led to an unanticipated interest in Texas Longhorn football. Royal won national championships in 1963 and again in 1969 and 1970. Johnson admired the iron-willed Royal, who treated his second-tier players, as one former player wrote, like "meat on the hoof." Johnson, the ruthless politician determined to win at any cost, had much in common with Royal.

So Johnson developed a passion for Texas Longhorn football. Oddly, he seldom attended Army-Navy games while president—even nonathletic chief executives such as Harry Truman honored that tradition. Just as the Texan LBJ had fought his way to the presidency, Coach Royal's Longhorns had won the Excalibur of college football. Johnson became a booster extraordinaire, attending both home and away games.

When he became aware of Johnson's interest, Royal tried to bond him to the team. He asked Johnson if he could bring several players to the ranch. Royal thought that LBJ would enjoy the games more if he had met the players. "He got to know those guys personally," Royal recalled. After Texas defeated Notre Dame, 21-17, in the Cotton Bowl in 1969, Johnson hurried to the locker room where he congratulated the players and coach. "I was proud of both teams but I was especially proud of Darrell Royal and every man on his team. Notre Dame fought to the last play and we just had a little luck. God bless you all."[18]

When Texas was trying to shed its racist image, Royal invited five African American football recruits to the campus. Because impressing these high school players was so crucial to Texas football, the coach asked Johnson if he would lend a hand. The best-known booster in college football agreed to fly by helicopter from his ranch to the LBJ Library in Austin where he would pitch Texas football to the young men. Johnson did his best, but none of the five players, in the end, attended the University of Texas. The political heavy-weight, who had twisted arms and hoisted colleagues by their lapels, proved remarkably unpersuasive.

Royal's efforts to interest Johnson in individual players led to one memorable experience. It happened unexpectedly when Royal and his wife were visiting the Johnsons at the LBJ ranch. The former president told the coach that he had an invitation to attend a special event honoring running back Jim Bertelsen in his home town of Hudson, Wisconsin. "I know that you don't want to be traveling around with an old-age pensioner," Johnson announced to Royal, "but I've been invited to come up to Jim Bertelsen day." The former president said he would travel to Wisconsin if Royal would accompany him— and if Royal could get someone to donate an airplane. Using Johnson's name, Royal had no trouble finding a donor.[19]

When they arrived in the small town of Hudson, Johnson instructed Royal to stay close to the secret service agents. "When we get ready to leave, we're outta here." In other words, Johnson made it clear that they would not linger after the event ended.[20]

"Well, after it was over, he got to visiting with those farmers and those old people up there and he was having such a time, we were one of the last ones to leave that place," Royal recalled. "He was standing there shaking hands and visiting with those people."[21]

Sports had taken a long time to catch up with Lyndon Johnson. It took a trip to a small town in Wisconsin, which perhaps reminded LBJ of the dusty crossroads he had visited early in his political career. Still one wonders whether politics really trumped football that night. Pumping the flesh with rural people still held a fascination for the former president. It was the contact sport that he excelled at.

On January 22, 1973, Lyndon Johnson suffered a fatal heart attack. Football and golf were simply not sufficient to stem the heart disease that accelerated once Johnson left Washington and abandoned his favorite sport of politics.

V

In the Public Eye

Richard Nixon with members of the Whittier College football team.
Nixon was too small, too light, and too unathletic to play football at the
college level. Still, he was a guard on the third team for three years, which
meant that he was "cannon fodder" for the first string and seldom appeared
in a game. Later, he used his football "career" as an icebreaker with
athletes, sportswriters, and NFL coaches. Courtesy of Richard M.
Nixon Library and Birthplace, Yorba Linda, California.

Richard Nixon

Show Me a Good Loser . . .

In 1952, at the Republican convention in Chicago, Senator Richard Nixon happened to see Jackie Robinson, the first African American major league baseball player, in the hotel lobby where the California delegation was staying. Upon being introduced to the ballplayer, Nixon said that he heard that Jackie had just hit another home run. "Yes, I had pretty good luck," Robinson replied, a sparkle in his eyes.

Nixon then recalled the first time that he had seen the Dodger ballplayer in 1940, when Robinson was playing football for UCLA. He described in detail what he referred to as a perfect play.

It was a long pass from Kenny Washington, also black, to Robinson. Catching the ball between three Oregon defenders, Jackie somehow eluded all of them. "When he got over the goal line," Nixon later recalled, "he just turned around and grinned at them. He had outsmarted all of them."[1]

While Eisenhower relaxed with western novels, bridge, and golf, Richard Nixon immersed himself in baseball and football. Ike chose Nixon as his vice-presidential candidate, and the Republican victory gave Nixon an entry into the national sporting arena. In his eight years as vice-president, he addressed sports groups, got to know high-profile sports figures, and even golfed and fished with Ike. In fact, Nixon's foray into big-time sports would be a prelude to his presidential play calling, crowning of national championship teams, and dreaming up all-star baseball teams. On top of this, he would use both *Air Force One* and the television camera to fashion an image of the sports "spectator in chief."

Jackie Robinson was the most notable of Nixon's early professional sports conquests—and a friendship took shape. In the late 1950s, as Nixon was planning his run for the presidency, the two men would frequently correspond. Though Robinson endorsed Nixon in 1960, he was deeply disillusioned when the Republican standard-bearer remained silent when Martin Luther King was jailed in Birmingham.

Given Nixon's reputation for winning at all costs, the question arises: was Nixon genuinely interested in sports figures like Jackie Robinson or did he only use them for his political advantage?

To answer that question, we need to look at the tension between Nixon the struggling athlete and Nixon the overachieving student. If Dick Nixon really cared about sports, his sporting career in high school and college is the place to begin.

★

Cannon Fodder

In high school and college, Nixon played scrub football—the C team—and rarely got into a game. What is remarkable is that he played at all.

Nixon may have first embraced sports because his volatile father, Frank, encouraged it. In high school, he played football, basketball, and track without winning a position on any of the starting teams. He put in long hours of practice. But all the while, he earned scholastic honors, participated in debate, and worked in the family store. Upon graduating from high school, he was awarded a scholarship by the local Harvard Club, based on his credentials as the best all-around student. Sadly for Nixon, he could not afford to attend Harvard even with a scholarship. Instead he enrolled at nearby Whittier College so he could live at home, commute to Whittier, and continue to work in the family store.

Once again, he took on a backbreaking schedule. He went out for football and, except for the barebones freshman team, failed to make first or second string. Nevertheless, he scrimmaged with the varsity for three years, serving as a "punching bag" for the starting team in practice and seldom getting into a game. As a 165-pound tackle, Nixon was small, slow, and awkward. His greatest strength was his tenacity. "He wasn't cut out to play the sport," a teammate said. "Nixon and I were cannon fodder. . . . I'll say that for Nixon. He had guts." Other teammates wondered why he played at all.[2]

Later, a high school teammate tried to explain it in a folksy aphorism. Football strengthened his tenaciousness, "like the old saying, 'stick to it, like a pup to a root.'" Nixon was temperamentally incapable of quitting, no matter how much punishment he took.[3]

Next to his father, Nixon most admired his college coach, Wallace Newman, and learned more from him than from his teachers and professors. A tall man who held himself "ramrod straight," Newman had won All-American honors playing at Southern California. Known as "chief" because of his Native American background, he was not afraid to schedule big-time teams like Southern California and Arizona. While he believed in keeping his temper, Newman told his team, "show me a good loser and I'll show you a loser." Nixon was an apt student. "There is no way I can adequately describe Chief Newman's influence on me," Nixon wrote in his memoirs. "He drilled into me a competitive spirit and the determination to come back after you have been knocked down or after you lose."[4]

Since Nixon got knocked down regularly, we can assume that these words came from his heart. Dick Nixon, the consistent loser at sports, had a complex relationship with college football—in many ways similar to his problematic political career.

Warming the bench, Nixon had lots of opportunity to absorb the cerebral side of football. "Dick could analyze and tell you what the tackle was doing and what the guard was doing or where the strengths of the opposition were after viewing it from the bench," a teammate recalled.[5]

One point seldom made by Nixon's biographers is that he liked football, even if it meant being "cannon fodder." In 1934, he made the traveling squad, which meant that he was with the team every game. He reveled in being at the nerve center of the team, cheering on the starters, and analyzing the plays. When a teammate was injured, Dick Nixon was at his side encouraging him, telling him that he would be back in action the following week. (Nixon was always more optimistic than the team physicians.) For nearly every minute of every game, he had to settle for sitting on the bench beside Chief Newman and occasionally giving his teammates a pep talk before they went out for the second half.

When he did finally get into the game, the Whittier students went wild. "I shall never forget the tremendous roar which went up from the rooting section when Dick got into the lineup for the last few minutes of a few games," a teammate recalled. For his few minutes of playing time, which may have entailed only embarrassing penalties (Nixon frequently jumped offsides), he paid dearly in practice.[6]

Nixon's passion for football at Whittier was so remarkable that it made him an oddity. Here was a Quaker youth at a Quaker institution who relentlessly pursued a violent contact sport. And, not only that, he was a gifted student, debater, and organizer whose weakest link was athletics. A serious student and "loner" with a backbreaking schedule, he never engaged in locker room banter. Still, he won the respect of the athletic elite. Soon after he entered Whittier, Nixon was invited to join the Orthogonians, a social club begun by athletes to compete with the existing Franklin Society (fraternities were banned at Whittier). Nixon not only became president of the Orthogonians, but he was also elected president of the student body.

The macho culture of college football became Nixon's link to a world denied him by his background and talents. In one sense, he was too unathletic, too talented in debate, and too busy with student activities and the family store to spend long autumn afternoons on the practice field. But losing had its upside. He was always able to use his losing seasons in football to project his awkward personality to audiences of sports fans and sports celebrities. Nixon's football, as he hinted in his memoirs, was a paradigm for the low points in his political career. There was always a new game and a new season.

★

Coach Nixon

Nixon served two uneventful years in the South Pacific in World War II and was discharged from the Navy in 1945. He had a law degree from Duke University, prewar legal experience in Whittier, and a resilient wife—Pat—who learned to live with her husband's ambition. Above all, he had a compelling desire to enter politics. While in the Navy, he had learned to play poker and to play it well. In fact, he saved enough money from poker to launch himself into a postwar political career. Just as important, poker taught him how to gauge his adversaries and to judge whether they were bluffing. An actor in amateur productions, Nixon knew how to keep a poker face . . . and how to use his acting ability to go for larger stakes. "Sometimes the stakes were pretty big," another officer recalled, "but Nick [Nixon] had daring and a flair for knowing what to do."[7]

When he ran for Congress in 1946, he held a strong hand. For the first time since 1928, the Republicans were poised to take control of Congress. The new Nixon, toughened by his military experience, portrayed his opponent as a Communist sympathizer. Two years later, Congressman Nixon used his poker-playing experience to call the bluff of a suspected Communist, Alger Hiss, whom Nixon pursued like a pit bull. In 1950, Nixon again played political poker when he ran for the Senate. Just as he bluffed in poker, he used Communist scare tactics to discredit his opponent, Helen Gahagan Douglas. Again he displayed the daring—and cunning—that he perfected as a poker player.

In the presidential contest of 1952, Nixon once again played an audacious game, pretending to be neutral between the presidential contenders—Robert Taft and Dwight Eisenhower—and loyal to the state's native son, Governor

Earl Warren. Behind the scenes, Nixon worked furiously to deliver California to Ike. His reward: the Republican vice-presidential nomination.

As vice-president from 1953 to 1961, Nixon had lots of opportunities to mix with sportswriters and sports figures. He got to know college coaches such as Woody Hayes. To show his uncanny grasp of sports, he once authored a sports column on the great plays that he had witnessed. He briefly headed the President's Council on Physical Fitness and addressed the council's meeting at West Point in September 1957.

Above all, he was able to use sportspeak to translate his political experiences to the public. Addressing the football writers in 1958, he described how he was almost "mousetrapped" by Nikita Khrushchev, the Soviet premier. When a defensive lineman goes through a hole deceptively created by the opposing line and is blocked to the side so that the ball carrier can go through that opening, he's been mousetrapped. A mousetrap play was set into motion when Nixon and Khrushchev attended a reception where champagne was being served.

Nixon, preparing to toast the Soviet premier, was shrewd enough not to raise his glass before he asked for a translation of the toast. The crafty Khrushchev had proposed the end of American bases and withdrawal of American troops from Europe. Instead, Nixon told him that he would only drink to peace, and when the Soviet premier refused, the vice-president proposed that they drink to talking because if they persisted in talking, they would not go to war.

"So, as a former tackle with some small experience in what it can do to you," Nixon told the football writers, "I kept on guard."[8]

He had walked into the trap, but he avoided being caught by the wily Soviet premier. He had learned well from those long practice sessions and Chief Newman, who knew all about gridiron "mousetrapping."

In the same speech, Nixon went on to use the sports phrase, "a strong offense is the best defense," to explain why America should continue to maintain military bases abroad.

After serving eight years as vice-president, Nixon ran and lost in the 1960 presidential election to Senator John F. Kennedy. Then, hoping to position himself for the 1964 Republican nomination, Nixon ran for governor of California and lost. In his postelection press conference, he uttered the famous cynical line to the press, "you won't have Nixon to kick around anymore because . . . this is my last press conference." It was as if he were quitting the C team at Whittier (which he never did). In other words, the press would have no one to serve as cannon fodder.[9]

In both college football and politics, Nixon was simply unable to quit. He had fired up the Whittier team with his pep talks, and now Nixon played a similar role after the Republican nominee, Barry Goldwater, was overwhelmed by Lyndon Johnson and the Democrats. In 1966 he tirelessly campaigned for Republican candidates for Congress. Just as his team effort inspired respect at Whittier, his work on behalf of the underdog Republicans regained him his leadership of the party. Richard Nixon was again nominated in 1968, and this time he defeated Hubert Humphrey in a close election. Just like his experiences in college football, he never really lost; he merely found ways to make lemons into lemonade.

In 1969 Nixon received the sporting respect denied him in high school and college. On January 1 the president-elect watched the Ohio State Buckeyes, coached by his friend Woody Hayes, overcome a ten-point lead and defeat the University of Southern California to win the national championship (despite a brilliant, eighty-yard run by Heisman trophy winner O. J. Simpson). Four years later, the president wrote to Hayes after he lost in the Rose Bowl: "Dear Woody: I have always liked your statement—'show me a good loser and I'll show you a loser.'" It was the phrase that Coach Wallace Newman used—only Newman was a far better loser than Hayes or Nixon. The Whittier coach believed that the losers should focus their anger on what they did wrong.[10]

On the following day, the president-elect did actually see his old coach. Art Linkletter, a well-known TV personality, hosted a testimonial at which he produced thirteen people who played important roles in Nixon's life. Wallace Newman presented the other team members with the bench that Nixon supposedly warmed—and, best of all, he presented Nixon with his varsity letter. Asked why he had not let Nixon play, Newman responded: "Well, a sportswriter friend of mine says I wasn't a very good judge of talent."[11]

He never said what kind of talent.

Once inaugurated, Richard Nixon became the most active sports fan of any president. The number of calls to winning—and losing—coaches and managers, big games attended, and letters to sports figures would dwarf those of his predecessors. Throughout his presidency, he contrived new ways to rub elbows with sports celebrities.

In November 1969, the war in Vietnam, for which Nixon was to find a solution, continued to rage. He had recently delivered his "silent majority" speech, which he fatuously believed had changed "the course of history." He had a plan for peace in Vietnam, Nixon insisted, though he refused to spell out the details. On November 14–16, antiwar protesters poured into Washington, a preview of what would happen in May 1970 after the Cambodian invasion (when he would wander among student protesters at the Lincoln Memorial talking football). On November 17, the story of the My Lai massacre by American troops in Vietnam hit the newspapers.

Faced with problems which might spin out of control, Nixon turned to football.

On December 4, 1969, the University of Texas Longhorns were playing the University of Arkansas Razorbacks in Fayetteville, Arkansas. Both teams were undefeated and ranked first and second nationally. Nixon planned to attend the game and present the national champion's plaque to the winner. The president required extra security at the stadium, and even so his appearance was risky. Inevitably, there would be anti-Vietnam demonstrations, possibly escalating into violence between overzealous police and jeering students. Happily, the demonstrators agreed to station themselves on a hill outside the stadium, in full view of Nixon but out of harm's way. Landing at Fayetteville on a drizzly Saturday, Nixon entered the stadium after the game had started. As the president watched, Texas overcame a 14-0 deficit and rallied to win a dramatic 15-14 victory.

Nixon went to the Texas locker room where he congratulated Coach Darrell Royal and the Longhorn players, and using television (the first time a president had appeared on TV before a national sports audience) presented the Longhorns with a plaque.

"What convinced me that Texas deserves that [the number one plaque] is the fact that you won the tough one," Nixon said. "For a team to be behind 14-0 and then not to lose its cool and go on to win, that proves you deserve to be No. 1 and that's what you are!"[12]

Nixon also went to the Arkansas locker room to console the losers, just as he had talked with injured players at Whittier. "It's good for people to be for somebody, for a team," he pronounced. "You can learn something about losing as well as winning—I've had some experience with that."[13]

But Penn State, with the longest winning streak in the country, protested that it was being shortchanged. Why couldn't the president honor the Nittany Lions, who were undefeated and in the running for the national championship?

Nixon's attempt to make amends to Penn State got nowhere. The Penn State coach, Joe Paterno, rebuffed Nixon. "It would seem a waste of his very valuable time," Paterno remarked, "to present a plaque for something we already have undisputed possession of—the nation's longest winning streak."[14]

Nixon's passion for college football persisted into the postseason. A few days after returning to Washington, he attended the annual banquet of the National Football Foundation in New York. Again, protests erupted, this time in front of the Waldorf Astoria Hotel where the dinner was being held. The violent confrontations between protesters and police resulted in sixty-three arrests and eight injured police. "The policemen formed a wedge," the *New York Times* reported of one face-off, "and, nightsticks at the ready, tore into the demonstrators, bowling over several youths and arresting one."[15]

Inside the hotel, Nixon shared the stage with poet and playwright Archibald MacLeish who had played for Yale in 1914 and 1915. Nixon was awarded the foundation's gold medal award, which his predecessors, Hoover, Eisenhower, and Kennedy, had also received. Now the winner, President Richard Nixon, speaking for anyone who had ever tried to play the game, could poke fun at Dick Nixon, the onetime bench warmer. "One reason he [Coach Newman] didn't put me in," he joked, "was because I didn't know the plays. I knew all the enemy's plays though. I practiced them all week [against the starting lineup]." Unfortunately, Nixon would pursue his passion for obtaining the "enemy's" plays in 1972 when members of his administration, possibly with Nixon's consent, sanctioned the Watergate break-in.[16]

Nixon had won the laurels denied him as a college football player. Now he was ready to move up to the National Football League.

★

Down and In

By the fall of 1971, Nixon had almost completed a productive, if controversial, first term. He had begun his withdrawal of troops from Vietnam. Somehow, he had survived the uproar following the American invasion of Cambodia, accompanied by the tragic deaths of students at Kent State and Jackson State universities. He confounded the diplomatic establishment by announcing a trip to visit Communist China; the politician who had made his reputation pursuing Communists and opposing the Reds in China, would visit Beijing in February 1972. After signing the first SALT disarmament treaty with the Soviet Union, he would initiate a second round of talks.

All of these presidential actions, as notable as they appeared, were no more astonishing than his journey into the magic kingdom of professional football. By the early 1970s, professional football had become a national mania. Color television, increasingly affordable in the 1960s, transformed many sports, but none more than professional football. In 1970 ABC kicked off its Monday night football which became one of the weeknight rituals. The Washington Redskins, a team that had languished for more than two decades (despite integration during the Kennedy era), suddenly became a contender for the playoffs under Coach George Allen, a Republican and a onetime coach at Whittier.

On November 24, 1971, at Coach George Allen's request, the president paid a visit to the Washington Redskins training camp located near Dulles Airport. Allen, who had traded draft choices for veteran players, had astounded the football world by leading the Redskins to six straight victories. On the Sunday before Nixon's visit, the "Skins" had lost 13-0 to Tom Landry's Dallas Cowboys, their second loss in a row. Still, they were in hot pursuit of the NFL playoffs. Approaching the field unnoticed, Nixon greeted his friend, George Allen. The president had known the onetime Whittier coach since the 1950s. During practice, Allen let the gold-medal winner call a play and give one of his patented pep talks.

In his fifteen-minute talk, Nixon told the players that he understood the boos they had received that past Sunday—he had experienced a few himself. Then, stretching the metaphor, he compared a football team losing a game to a country keeping its pride. "When it's lost one," he said, "it doesn't lose its spirit." Not unlike the Vietnam War, he might have been saying, "not won, but far from lost." He assured the Skins that they would get into the playoffs by winning at least three out of their last four games.[17]

A month later, the Redskins had made the playoffs and now had a chance to get into the National Conference title game if they could beat the San Francisco Forty-niners. Late in the second quarter, leading 10-3, the Redskins had the ball on the eight-yard line. Coach Allen sent in a risky flanker-reverse play suggested by none other than Richard Nixon, or so the newspapers would report. A flanker reverse involves a fake to the running back and a handoff to the wide receiver. It requires speed, precise blocking, and a large measure of surprise. The play lost three yards, and the Skins did not score.

The president's team lost the game in the second half, 24-20. Nixon was blamed for calling a harebrained play, even though Allen had actually sent in the play. After all, he was not on the phone with the president when he called it.

One of the Redskins coaches, Marv Levy, later head coach of the Buffalo Bills, cast doubt on Nixon's role. According to Levy, Allen suggested the play to Nixon so that the president could call it. Normally, the conservative Allen would have called a more conventional play—as he had indicated in the press that he would. "[George] wanted the president to look very sage," Levy recalled. "Afterwards I remember chuckling among ourselves about it. George gave the play to the president, and then it didn't work."[18]

If so, both Nixon and Allen had been willing to gamble on a dangerous play—and they both looked bad.

The president called Allen and encouraged the Redskins "not to look back." All of Washington was proud of a team that had made it to the playoffs after twenty-five years.[19]

In January, Nixon followed up his play calling from Washington to suggest a play to Don Shula, the Miami Dolphins' coach. The Dolphins were coming out of a strong season and a conference championship and would be playing two weeks later in the Super Bowl against the formidable Dallas Cowboys. Paul Warfield, the speedy wide receiver, had enjoyed success with the "down and in" pass play against the Baltimore Colts. "He wanted to talk technical football," Shula said of the president's telephone call.[20]

Unfortunately for Shula and Nixon, the Cowboys were primed for the "down-and-in" and proved the better team, winning 24-3. "They had two weeks to prepare," Warfield said. "And they made sure that under any circumstances we wouldn't be able to catch that pass."[21]

But Nixon's play calling was only a suggestion, not an executive order. As with the Redskins, he had not commanded the coach to use the "down and in." Just the same, Nixon haters and baiters, especially in the press, had plenty of opportunity to lampoon the president.

Nevertheless, Nixon continued to congratulate the winners, especially the University of Nebraska Cornhuskers who won the national championship twice in succession. On January 14, 1971, the day before the Super Bowl, he spoke at the University of Nebraska. "Mr. Nixon warmed his audience by talking at length about Nebraska's team before he launched into his prepared remarks," the *New York Times* reported, "and he presented Bob Devaney, the Nebraska coach, with a plaque honoring the Cornhuskers for their ranking." Nebraska's football team had been ranked number one in the country after defeating Louisiana State in the Orange Bowl.[22]

A year later, on February 1, ten days before his memorable trip to China, he met with Nebraska's football team, once again the national champions. "He is an avid fan," the *New York Times* reported, "and though he apologized for not being able to see the team in person, he knew each of the players by position." The team received a blue leather folder with a parchment certifying their national ranking. In turn, the Nebraska team presented Nixon with an oversized Styrofoam model of their state bedecked with carnations and topped with a football. It was the high point of the president's gridiron presidency. His enthusiasm for spectator sports never ended, but was gradually crowded out of the news.[23]

On January 14, 1973, just before Nixon's second inauguration, George Allen's Redskins lost to Don Shula's Dolphins, 14-7, in the Super Bowl. The president sent telegrams to each of the coaches. But, in deference to his friend George Allen, he didn't call.

Nixon attempted to call neither the "down and in" nor any other play, except when he visited the Redskins' training camp. Yet sportswriters treated it as still another ill-conceived play that he was responsible for. Ironically, the president himself would be "down and out" in 1974.

★

A Sportswriter's Downfall

Stephen Ambrose, Richard Nixon's biographer, has written that Nixon, a driven man with scarcely any interests or hobbies outside politics, relaxed only with sports. He relished the calls to locker rooms, the visits of coaches and athletes to the White House, and his appearances at sporting events.

Earlier as vice-president, Nixon confided that he might one day want to be a sportswriter—to a convention of sportswriters. "When I finish my term as Vice President, I might go to work as a lawyer. But if I had my choice—and the ability—there is nothing I'd rather do than write sports."[24]

Was this a brief glimpse into the murky Nixon personality? Or was he simply boasting that his grasp of sports rivaled those who made it a profession? Possibly this was Nixon as Walter Mitty, but more likely it was one of his more pleasurable political gambits. Nixon who lacked the common touch used sports to communicate with the public. He enjoyed being the ultimate sports spectator—the most analytical since Woodrow Wilson.

Given the highly statistical nature of baseball, Nixon's encyclopedic memory and analytical mind made him a natural. Hence, his compelling interest in major league baseball. During the fall of 1971, rumors surfaced that Bob Short, owner of the Washington Senators, planned to move his team to Dallas. Like most Washingtonians, Nixon mourned the loss of the Senators—he would now have to travel to Baltimore to throw out the first presidential pitch. Nixon vowed that he would now root for his hometown California Angels. Nevertheless, he left a conference of governors in Louisville the following season to catch the major league All-Star Game in nearby Cincinnati, taking his daughter Julie and son-in-law David Eisenhower, also a baseball fanatic. In the spring of 1972, he advised Charlie Finley, owner of the Oakland A's, that he should pay his star pitcher, Vida Blue, the amount that Blue demanded. Nixon had met Blue and Finley at the White House when he told Blue that "you must be the most underpaid pitcher in the game." The A's pitcher was making only $13,000.[25]

In 1972 Nixon probably was not spending much time thinking of baseball.

He was busy facing reelection in the fall. Already a potentially perilous event had occurred. On June 17, 1972, four employees of the Committee to Re-elect the President, or CREEP, were arrested for illegal entry at the headquarters of the Democratic Party inside the Watergate apartments. Barely on the political radar at the time, the break-in did not affect the outcome of the election, a landslide victory for Nixon-Agnew. Nevertheless, the incident was a political time bomb that led to Nixon's resignation two years later.

Still it was surprising that Nixon turned to what might be called "fantasy baseball" or, more precisely, choosing an all-time, all-star team. Actually, Cliff Evans of RKO General Broadcasting came up with the idea when he asked Nixon to name his favorite ballplayers. Then Evans challenged Nixon to draw up an all-time baseball team. According to the president's collaborator David Eisenhower, Nixon was so well versed in pre–World War II baseball that Eisenhower said that he "handled it off the top of his head." Aware that his son-in-law knew more about postwar baseball, he assigned him the task of drawing up the post–World War II team. David had worked as special assistant to the Washington Senators in 1970 after graduating from college.[26]

Soon afterward, Nixon presented his prewar and, with David's help, his post–World War II all-star teams. Red Smith, the *New York Times* sportswriter, savaged the president's invasion of the sportswriters' world, charging that Nixon put players on the list for personal and political reasons, such as Nixon friends slugger Harmon Killebrew and the nimble second baseman Nellie Fox. More damning were Smith's charges that Nixon was playing political baseball because of the fall election. "He has, therefore, saluted young and old, white and black, Latin and Nordic, left-hander and right-hander, Catholic and Wasp, Jew and the American Indian (Early Wynn). He has chosen fastball pitchers, curveball pitchers, a master of the knuckleball (Hoyt Wilhelm), and even a specialist in a politically unappetizing spitball (Burleigh Grimes)."[27]

Red was overreacting to the "New, Slow Boy on the Baseball Beat." In an election year, candidate Nixon understandably was trying to touch all the political bases. Indeed, many of the players and the children of the old-timers expressed pleasure over the president's line-up. Casey Stengel, once the clown prince of baseball and more recently a highly successful Yankees manager, was ungrammatically grateful. "Well, for heaven's sake, it's very nice the President is so well versed in sports with so many things he has to do in his sojourn as President and being international and all he has to take care of so many countries it's an honor he chose me."[28]

Nixon had once compared political elections to the big game. "You know, in politics we work for two months—that is the average length of a political campaign," he reflected, "and we work our heads off, and then there comes just one day when our fate is decided."[29]

He had always dreaded losing, though in 1972 he won a landslide victory against George McGovern. Like a championship coach cashiered for cheating, Nixon had won his final national title. The secret political campaign to undermine a weak opponent ended Nixon's reign as the nation's number-one sports fan. In August 1974, after his attempted cover-up of Watergate unraveled, Nixon resigned and left for San Clemente. His public career—and health—were in shambles.

Now, dropped to the C team, he would resort to the tactics of a third-string lineman (one of the first people to be invited to San Clemente was his old coach, Wallace Newman). Reverting to his years on the Whittier team, he took the innumerable hits and then began a dialogue with the starting team in Washington. As with football at Whittier, he regained a measure of respect.

Never again would he play on the first string, but then he never had at Whittier.

★

Golf and Bowling: Nixon as Everyman

Other than politics, Nixon had few interests. In 1952, after Nixon was nominated for vice-president, Eisenhower gave him a lesson in trout fishing. "After hooking a limb the first three times," Nixon wrote, "I caught his shirt on my fourth try. The lesson ended abruptly." Later, fishing in the Florida Everglades, Nixon fell overboard twice. His photo, clinging to the side of the boat, appeared in the national press with the caption, "Fish Catch Nixon." That ended his fishing career.[30]

Nevertheless, he managed to bowl and play golf. In 1971 Nixon revealed that he bowled occasionally in the lanes (donated by his friend Bebe Rebozo) under the Executive Office Building—and even posed once for photographers. "I usually bowl at about 10 o'clock at night," he explained. "When I'm here, I bowl alone. I bowl from seven to twelve games, one after another. That gives you a tremendous workout." His average was 152, he said, and his score topped out at 232. There is no evidence that he bowled after his first term.[31]

His golf was more public, if just as infrequent. Nixon, who had only played for two years, took up golf seriously at Eisenhower's suggestion in 1953. As in football, he was awkward, and once again he took some hits in the form of ridicule. Playing with Ike at Cherry Hills in Denver before a golfing gallery, Nixon smashed a drive that split the fairway and landed next to Eisenhower's ball. "Great guns!" the astonished president exclaimed. "What are you doing?

*Nixon teeing off as comedian Bob Hope and a gallery of spectators look on.
As vice-president, he wasn't much of a golfer, but he doggedly worked to make his game
respectable. After he resigned from the presidency, he resumed golf as post-Watergate
therapy and actually managed to break 80, after which he hung up his clubs
for good. AP Wide World.*

Driving the green?" On the second hole, the vice-president shot a par to Ike's 6. Unfortunately, his game then went rapidly downhill. According to golf historian Don Van Natta, he was in and out of trouble all day. The Ike-Dick partnership in golf looked like a burlesque of their success in the 1952 election. "Look here," said the president after their team lost the match, "you're young, you're strong and you can do a lot better than that."[32]

So Nixon took lessons at Burning Tree and ran up against the physical shortcomings that had handicapped him in all sports. Van Natta asserts that Nixon bent the rules in his vain effort to play the game. He "improved" his lies, hit several tee shots until he had the one he wanted, and pleaded with his golfing partners to give him non-gimme putts. Generally his political foursomes tried to make him look good.[33]

As president, he tried hard to clean up his act. He played in a foursome with Bob Hope, Jimmy Stewart, and Fred MacMurray (Hope made a point of playing with all the presidents) and sometimes with Billy Graham, who commended the president's newfound golfing integrity. Nixon's golfing friends, a group of Republican contributors, pitched in to build a three-hole course at the western White House in San Clemente. By the time the 1972 election approached, the president was shooting in the high 80s and low 90s. No longer was he a golfing joke.

But Nixon's golf required high maintenance. He didn't play in his second term and then, after he resigned, nearly died from phlebitis. Isolated at San Clemente, Nixon gradually expanded his athletic galaxy. He took up golf seriously. He was so out of practice and physically weak that he almost gave up. His chief of staff, Colonel Jack Brennan, a scratch golfer, worked tirelessly to help Nixon improve his score—and his self-image. For Nixon, who had never liked golf, the game suddenly became his therapy. "Golf became my lifesaver," he declared.[34]

Nevertheless, he did give it up. According to the former president, he finally broke 80 on a relatively easy course in San Clemente. For most people, breaking 80 would be incentive to play more frequently and enthusiastically, but not for Nixon. "I knew I could never get better." He had conquered "Mount Everest." So he gave up golf and took up walking four miles a day.[35]

Back in San Clemente, he once again became interested in baseball. According to David Eisenhower, he listened to the California Angels' games almost every evening. In time, he began to go to the ball park, which led to "friendships" with players such as Bobby Grich, Don Baylor, and Nolan Ryan. Later, when he moved to New Jersey, he adopted the New York Mets and befriended superstars Gary Carter, Rusty Staub, Keith Hernandez, and Davey Johnson. In 1986, when the Mets won the world championship, he predicted that New York's second team would supplant the Yankees as the Yanks had once done to the New York Giants. It never happened.[36]

In 1992 he and David Eisenhower drew up another dream team for the Richard Nixon Museum in Yorba Linda, California.

Nixon died in 1994, never having ceased trying to strip the tarnish left by Watergate. Though he never played games well, sports served as a metaphor for the highs and lows of his political career—as Nixon acknowledged after Watergate.

In September 1975 Kenneth Clawson, Nixon's communications director during his final months, visited a recovering but bitter Nixon at San Clemente.

"You were a good athlete," Nixon said to Clawson, "but I was not, and that was the very reason I tried and tried and tried. To get discipline for myself and to show others that here was a guy who could dish it out and take it. Mostly I took it."

Clawson said that this time there was a difference.

"Yes," Nixon added ruefully. "This time we had something to lose."

He had lost the contest to retain the presidency.[37]

Show him a good loser and he would show you a loser, Coach Newman had once said.

Richard Nixon learned that lesson well.

He was not a good loser—never was and never would be. Nixon did, however, know how to pick himself up and to show the world that he was a guy who could take it.

Gerald Ford
The Pigskin President

Gerald Ford, one of the greatest presidential athletes, stands alone as the only unelected president and, for that matter, the only unelected vice-president. Richard Nixon picked him to succeed Vice-President Spiro Agnew, who resigned in disgrace in 1973. Then, when Nixon himself resigned in 1974 over Watergate, Ford became the "accidental president."

To distance himself from Nixon's tawdry image, Ford had to demonstrate that his was an open and honest presidency. This became far more difficult when Ford, in one courageous—and politically disastrous—sweep of the pen, issued a blanket pardon for Richard Nixon. Ford had to struggle against the suspicion that he had made a deal with Nixon and that he was simply a party hack. Everything that Ford did in his twenty-eight months as president was scrutinized minutely by a zealous press corps. That scrutiny did not stop with the presidential pardon or the fall of Vietnam, but extended as well to Ford's golfing companions and his sporting vacations in Colorado and California.

One might expect that an athletic resume would enhance a president's image. Not so with Jerry Ford. This outstanding football star at the University of Michigan was stigmatized as a dumb jock. Lyndon Johnson commented that Ford played "too many games without a helmet"—and that he could not walk and chew gum at the same time. As vice-president, Ford hit a spectator with a tee shot at an invitational golf tourney, a mishap that saddled Ford with the reputation as a loose cannon on the links. After barely three months as president, a Ford staffer wrote: "Cartoonists delight in reminding us that the President is a former football player who still enjoys the game." The memo complained that Ford wrote too many congratulatory letters to sports figures. People might get the impression that the president "spends his days reading the sports pages and writing to coaches."[1]

One unspoken concern was that Ford might be seen as a sports dilettante like Nixon, who spent his time offering unwanted advice to coaches. Possibly

A handsome, determined Jerry Ford posing at practice in the mammoth University of Michigan "big house." After starring at center as a freshman, Ford sat on the bench because he was playing behind the best center in the country. In his senior year, Ford was not only voted All Big Ten, but he also played in the College All-Star Game in Chicago and was drafted by the Detroit Lions and Green Bay Packers. Instead, Ford went to Yale where he coached football. A year later he was admitted to Yale's law school. Courtesy of Gerald R. Ford Presidential Library, Ann Arbor, Michigan.

Ford's letters caused more concern among aides than the comic antics of Nixon because Ford was a genuine football hero who had come as close as any president to becoming a professional athlete.

★

A Towering Team Player

Soon after Gerald Ford was born, his mother fled her wife-beating husband, Leslie King, married ambitious, hardworking Jerry Ford, and moved to Grand Rapids, Michigan. Ignorant of his true identity until he was a teenager, Gerald Ford, though named at birth Leslie King Jr., never used his father's name. With his mother and new father, he absorbed solid, midwestern values. As a fifteen-year-old high school sophomore, he started at center on the city-champion South High School team. Two years later, he captained the South High team and led it to another city championship while winning all-state honors—and earning a B+ average. He also worked in his free time to help out his family, struggling to stay afloat in the early years of the Great Depression.

Like Richard Nixon, Ford's coach became his role model. His coach considered Ford the closest thing to the all-American kid as any player he'd ever coached. Ford learned to value teamwork, but on both offense and defense he often towered above his teammates and seemed to be everywhere—on defense making tackles and on offense almost flawlessly making the long passes from center. "Anyone who says he played without a helmet has rocks in his head," exclaimed a teammate, Silas McGhee. "Junie [Ford's nickname] was the mainstay of the team."[2]

Because Ford had no money for college, the principal of South High began a scholarship fund to send Jerry Ford to the University of Michigan in Ann Arbor. Once there, Michigan coach Harry Kipke got Ford a job waiting tables. Ford's biographer, James Cannon, emphasizes the crucial role football played in Jerry Ford's development. "He learned to listen to teaching and perform his assigned role, that a team is greater than the individual player, and that the best players may not get all the glory."[3]

Not getting all the glory sums up two of Ford's three years on the Michigan varsity. Having played first-string center on the junior varsity and been voted the most promising freshman player, Ford found himself as a sophomore playing second fiddle to the best center in the country, Chuck Bernard. The team went to the Rose Bowl in 1933, but Ford only warmed the bench. When he started at center in 1934, Michigan's team was exceptionally thin, and the team won only one game. Even so, Ford was named to the All Big Ten Team. Ford played in the postseason East-West Shrine Game and the College All-Star Game in Chicago against the Green Bay Packers—an indication that he was one of the best players in the country. Though offered professional contracts by both Green Bay and Detroit, Ford declined the offers. The NFL could barely pay its players a living wage in the 1930s. Ford's playing days were over.

Off the playing field, football taught him equally valuable lessons, notably in race relations. One of his teammates (and roommate on the road) was Willis Ward, a champion African American sprinter. "He was my best friend on the team," Ford declared. When Georgia Tech played Michigan at Ann Arbor, Ward was informed that he couldn't play due to a "gentlemen's agreement" with Tech to keep Ward out of the game. While such arrangements were typical of North-South games in the 1930s, Ford would have no part of it and decided to refuse to play in the game. "Still unsatisfied, I went to Willis himself. He urged me to play," Ford recalled in his memoirs. "'Look,' he said. 'the team is having a bad year. We've lost two games already and probably won't win another. You've got to play Saturday. You owe it to the team.'" As it turned out, Georgia Tech was the only game that Michigan won that season. Much later, Ford encouraged Ward to run for Congress as a Republican, but unfortunately he lost. Ford then had Governor George Romney of Michigan appoint Ward, a lawyer, as a state judge, where he served until he retired.[4]

After graduating, Ford wanted to attend law school at the University of Michigan. While playing football and working to pay expenses, Ford had compiled a B average as an economics major. Again Coach Kipke, though he had no coaching job for Ford, stepped in to help his star player. Raymond ("Ducky") Pond, football coach at Yale, was looking for an assistant football coach, and Kipke arranged an interview. Ford landed the job as assistant football and boxing coach. Because he had never boxed, he took lessons that summer at the YMCA in Grand Rapids while working in his father's paint factory.

But coaching was not Ford's ambition, but rather a way to pay off his college debts and attend Yale Law School. Initially, neither the athletic department nor the law school wanted someone who was not full-time. "My scholastic advisers were convinced that I couldn't handle law school and a full time job," Ford recalled. After a successful year of coaching, Ford spent the summer in Ann Arbor taking courses in the law school. With a salary of $3,600 for coaching the junior varsity and scouting Yale's opponents, Ford managed to convince the law school to admit him as a part-time student. Professor Myres McDougal, who interviewed Ford, was impressed. He predicted that Ford would finish in the top third of his class.[5]

A year later, Ford became a full-time student on top of his coaching job (after persuading Ducky Pond to let him go full time, he took a full load only in the spring and spent a summer at the University of North Carolina making up courses). At Yale, he and Professor McDougal shot baskets at noon in Payne-Whitney Gymnasium. "He could both chew gum and hit baskets," McDougal recalled, thereby refuting Lyndon Johnson's gibe. Just as McDougal predicted, he finished in the top third of a class that included a future Supreme Court justice, Potter Stewart, future secretary of state, Cyrus Vance, and the first head of the Peace Corps, Sargent Shriver. Ford also became one of five presidents who earned money from a sports-related activity (the others: Andrew Jackson, Theodore Roosevelt, Ronald Reagan, and George W. Bush).[6]

While he was at Yale, Ford was told to look up Phyllis Brown, a student at Connecticut College for Women. Tall, athletic, and stunningly beautiful, Brown appeared at the perfect time in Ford's life. She introduced him to skiing at Stowe, Vermont, and a brief "career." Brown soon quit school to become a model at J.D. Powers Agency in New York. In the March 12, 1940, issue of *Look* magazine, a story on skiing at Stowe featured Brown and her attractive blond boyfriend, Jerry Ford, modeling ski attire. Ford became the only president who could have included modeling on his resume. "Ford became so interested in modeling," write his biographers Edward and Frederick Schapsmeier, "he put up $1,000 of his hard-earned money to form a new agency with Harry Conover as his partner." The agency prospered, but Ford soon got out. He wanted to pursue a legal career, not to sell—or pose for—ads.[7]

Ford returned to Grand Rapids only to be called to active duty as a naval reservist after Pearl Harbor. Assigned as an athletic officer, he applied for sea duty and served aboard an aircraft carrier for nearly two years. Once, when his ship was foundering in a powerful typhoon, Ford was washed face-down along the flight deck toward the raging ocean. As he slid toward certain death, he caught his fingers on a ridge at the edge of the ship, then, twisting and rolling, thrust himself onto the catwalk below. Ford's athleticism surely helped to save his life.

After the war, Ford returned to Grand Rapids where he practiced law and set his sights on a political career. In 1948 he ran for Congress as a Republican and defeated the ten-year incumbent in the primary. He also married an athletic former dancer, Betty Warren, who had returned to Grand Rapids after training with the celebrated dance innovator Martha Graham. Not only did Betty become a wife and mother, she also played golf and skied with him. During his presidency and after, she became one of the most admired women in America.

As Ford advanced politically, he no longer had to rely on his athletic background. In 1965 he was elected as House minority leader because of the hard work that had made him into one of the most knowledgeable members of Congress. Only occasionally did his sports career emerge into public view. All of this changed when Nixon selected him to become vice-president. All at once, he returned to the spotlight as a former big-time football player. Powerfully built, Ford looked like a former jock. Unlike Nixon, who feverishly pursued sports and sporting celebrities, Ford used athletics far less artificially to highlight his presidential image.

While Ford occasionally mixed with sports personalities, he used sports—and his own sporting background—in a careful and even calculated manner. That said, Ford's administration had to tackle public issues related to sports as had few before him. In spite of his cautious approach toward sports, Ford held office at the precise moment when the government was faced with the most sensitive athletic issues in its history.

★

Wrestling with the Olympics

For decades before Ford became president, a jurisdictional dispute had simmered between the American Athletic Union (AAU) and the National Collegiate Athletic Association (NCAA). Each claimed the right to sanction certain events such as track meets. When the AAU did not get its way, it sometimes disqualified athletes or coaches. Not only did the NCAA do the same, but it also mounted a lobbying campaign against the AAU. In 1962 a flare-up threatened to cripple the American Olympic effort, and Congress held hearings in the late 1960s. Once again, before the Montreal Olympics in 1976, the long-standing conflict threatened to undermine the American Olympic effort.

Just after Gerald Ford took office as vice-president, bills were introduced into Congress to resolve the dispute. One bill sponsored by Senator John Tunney of California proposed creating a governmental agency to oversee sports. Normally, Congress and presidents were reluctant to intervene in sports, which were regarded as amateur and beyond regulation. Republicans particularly objected, on philosophical grounds, to federal intervention in an amateur activity. Moreover, they argued that the International Olympic Committee might regard a government agency as a violation of amateur sports and suspend the American Olympic Committee.

In addition, Congress had also grown uneasy about America's Olympic performance. The Soviet Union and East Germany had overtaken the United States in a host of lesser sports such as field hockey, volleyball, team handball, and fencing. In 1972, among these lesser sports, the United States had won a medal only in the low-profile sport of canoeing. It was clear to Republicans and Democrats alike that the government had to coordinate the Olympic movement. To do this, it was necessary to begin by disentangling the AAU and NCAA and giving some other agency the authority to make final decisions.

The Republicans brought Vice-President Ford into the contest over Tunney's bill. Ford wrote letters to members of Congress, recommending a sports commission that did not include a permanent government role. Undoubtedly, Ford helped to bring about an act providing for a commission to study the American Olympic structure. Whether Ford was simply a figurehead in the effort is difficult to say, but he continued to play a role in the commission's deliberations when he became president.

On June 19, 1975, President Ford created a five-man presidential commission and made sure that it was properly funded. Later in the year, he enlarged the commission to thirteen, including some members of Congress, and lengthened its tenure to January 1977, the end of his term in office. The recommendations of his commission became the basis of the Amateur Athletic Act of 1978. Congress delegated the ultimate sports authority to the American Olympic Committee, terminating the nearly sixty years of conflict between the AAU and NCAA. It also provided for the support of Olympic athletes through soliciting corporate donors. Undoubtedly, the third-place finish in the Olympic medal count by the United States at the Montreal Olympics fueled support for the bill, but the presidential commission deserves credit for making the recommendations adopted by Congress.

Ford was also involved with preparations for the winter Olympics, scheduled for Lake Placid, New York, in 1980. Though the organizers had no place to house the athletes, the use of a former state drug facility had been suggested. If the administration would plow $50 million into refurbishing the New York state property, the federal government could use the housing for a corrections facility when the Olympics ended. The cooperation of the Ford administration with the state of New York resulted in a remarkably successful winter Olympics. In 1980 a team of college players defeated the veteran, highly subsidized Soviet hockey team, a victory that not only led to a gold medal but also boosted American morale during the Iranian hostage crisis. It was a tribute to the former college athlete who had occupied the White House three years before.

Actually Ford and his secretary of state, Henry Kissinger, faced a more immediate Olympic problem in 1976. Canada, which was hosting the Olympics, was being pressured by the People's Republic of China to ban Taiwan. Although Nixon had improved relations with the People's Republic, the United States recognized the island nation of Taiwan as representing China, even though the government of Chiang Kai-shek's Nationalists, which governed the island, had fled the mainland almost thirty years before (Chiang died in 1975, but his son succeeded him). Not long before the opening of the Montreal Olympics, Canadian premier Pierre Trudeau decided to exclude Taiwan, a member of the International Olympic Committee and a participant in past Olympics.

Ford and Kissinger were sorely provoked. "That Trudeau is being a real bastard," Ford commented in an Oval Office meeting.

Looming in the foreground was the possibility that the American Olympic

Committee might withdraw from the games. In an election year, Kissinger foresaw domestic repercussions "from [Jimmy] Carter saying we screwed it up."[8]

The United States did not withdraw, but finished third behind the Soviet Union and the German Peoples' Republic (East Germany).

Later in the year, the Ford Administration sponsored a White House Conference on the Olympics. With the report of the Olympic commission in January, the Ford administration had done more than any of its predecessors to put the Olympics back on track. Like much else that happened during the Ford administration, these initiatives earned Ford and his advisers scant credit.

★

Betty, Gerald, and Title IX

Gerald Ford served as president when feminism was still new and controversial. Laws passed earlier to bring about equality for women in athletics landed squarely in Ford's lap. Ford himself was caught in a no-win situation. His wife, Betty, endorsed the Equal Rights Amendment, which would have prohibited discrimination against women in both jobs and pay. Many conservative Republicans resisted what they considered nontraditional gender roles. To be sure, the president never threw his weight behind the ERA. Yet his relatively conservative administration had its hands full trying to sort out the new regulations governing the role of women in athletics.

In 1972 Congress passed and Nixon signed the education amendments to the 1968 Civil Rights Act. Most famously, these amendments affected women's athletics at the college level, which had barely registered on the athletic radar before the late 1960s. By 1975 sixty thousand women participated in college athletics, a 100 percent gain in three years. The Title IX amendments prohibited discrimination on the basis of sex in education. Though it affected all facets of educational life, Title IX came to be identified with women's athletics. Any college that received aid from the federal government, not necessarily in athletics, had to ensure equality of opportunity—and most colleges did receive some form of aid.

It fell to the Ford administration, notably the Department of Health, Education, and Welfare, to establish guidelines for Title IX in athletics. As Caspar Weinberger, the HEW secretary, hammered out the guidelines, thorny problems arose. Did women have the inalienable right to participate on men's teams? Should women's teams receive the same funding as men's teams? Did equality of opportunity mean mere interest by women in intercollegiate athletics or participation by a number proportionate to the women on campus? As one aide pointed out, "Title IX is the most volatile issue in sports."[9]

The most sensitive issue pertained to revenue sports such as football and basketball. Football, in particular, required far more scholarships, equipment, coaches, and time spent in training. If college football were not excluded, coaches believed, the goose that laid the golden egg would be turned into just a barnyard hen. Football, they argued, helped to support the entire athletic program. Put slightly differently, big-time football might have to shrink the numbers of scholarships and coaches, very troubling prospects for coaches and athletic directors.

During 1974 and 1975, HEW worked to translate Title IX into clearly stated and workable regulations. Not surprisingly, opposition to Title IX centered in the NCAA. Walter Byers, the powerful executive director of the NCAA, had thrown his organization's lobbying efforts against Title IX. With a former football player in the White House, the chances of heading off a strict interpretation of Title IX regulations seemed promising. In June 1975, just before the HEW regulations were issued, Coach Glenn "Bo" Schembechler, head football coach at Michigan, visited his friend President Gerald Ford at the White House. He persuasively set forth his case for excluding revenue sports from Title IX. Evidently, Ford who looked at athletics from a former football player's point of view, agreed with Schembechler. Shortly afterward, Schembechler wrote a carefully crafted letter to the president. He had heard football would *not* be excluded from Title IX. "I earnestly hope and believe, Mr. President," Schembechler wrote, "that with your assistance a way can be found . . . to assure that strong athletic progress for both men and women will be permitted to survive and prosper."[10]

In all likelihood, Ford did not intervene with the officials at HEW. "Needless to say," wrote an aide, "this is a hot issue we are trying to stay on top of." Given his uphill struggle as an accidental president, Ford was willing to sacrifice revenue sports or at least to leave the framing of the guidelines to HEW. The National Organization for Women was against any compromise, and the administration believed that "NOW is the big problem." Rather than garner adverse publicity, Ford chose to steer the course of least resistance. It was also the course favored by most Americans, and the one that won out in the courts and on the playing fields. When the American women's soccer team won the 1999 World's Cup, much credit was given to Title IX for leveling the playing field. If Title IX was responsible, the Ford administration deserves at least a nodding glance of recognition.[11]

★

A Ford, Not a Lincoln

Just as he had warmed the bench at Michigan for two years, Jerry Ford served in the House of Representatives nearly twenty-six years and then, when he became leader of the Republicans in the House it was as minority rather than majority leader. When Nixon chose him to replace Agnew as vice-president, Ford sat on the bench as vice-president for what turned out to be less than a year.

Eight months before he became president, Vice-President Ford had uttered the memorable phrase: "I am a Ford, not a Lincoln." It was a clever phrase, especially coming from a former congressman from the automotive state of Michigan. To be sure, no one would confuse Ford's labored public speaking with Lincoln's brilliance and eloquence. Though both Ford and Lincoln were experienced politicians, both entered the White House without a strong national base of support. But there was a difference. Unlike Lincoln, who won decisively in the electoral college, Gerald Ford lacked any kind of mandate from the voters. For the first time in American history, a president had come to office who had neither been nominated by a major party nor won election as president or vice-president. When Ford pardoned former president Nixon on Sunday, September 8, 1974, his presidential honeymoon ended. After that, anything that Ford did or anywhere he went, he was considered fair game by the press corps, feeling its oats after the Watergate scandal.[12]

Sports proved no exception. Who did the president play golf with? Ford's staff drew up a list of presidential golf partners made up of those in and outside Washington because the president was being criticized for playing with too many lobbyists. Ford did play frequently with Rodney Markley, a vice-president of the Ford Motor Company. One might argue that Ford, a former congressman from Michigan, probably played golf with automotive officials more often than other members of Congress. Still Ford's golf playing was more balanced than the media made out. Among his golfing partners were Bob Hope (who made a point of playing with every president), movie producer Frank Capra (who directed the classic small-town drama, *It's a Wonderful Life*), and comedian Jackie Gleason, not to mention members of his administration such as economic adviser Alan Greenspan. Like Dwight Eisenhower, he played with golfing heavyweights such as Jack Nicklaus, and also with Lee Elder, the first African American golfer to play in the 1975 Masters at Augusta, Georgia.

The most scathing criticism of his golfing came from news anchor Dan

Rather. "What's going on here?" asked Rather on the CBS Morning News: "Millions of Americans are out of work, the stock market is going down again; looks like interest rates may be going up again—prices on just about everything are; Vietnam is going down the tube; American power and influence is on the wane all over the globe; and, the President has just wound up a nine-day golfing vacation."[13]

Actually Ford toiled diligently. In the White House, he got up at 5:15 a.m., read the *New York Times* and *Washington Post,* and scanned a news summary put together by his press secretaries. He admitted in a personal interview that he read the sports pages first. "I still read them first," he said, "because you have a fifty-fifty chance of being right on the sports pages. Your odds aren't that good on the front page." Then he exercised, showered, dressed, ate breakfast, and was at his desk by seven o'clock."[14]

In his memoirs, Ford proudly states that he thrived in the presidency. Neither was the White House a prison (Harding) nor the presidency a "splendid misery" (Jefferson). "I never felt better physically," he wrote. "I never had a clearer mind. I never enjoyed an experience more. The truth is that I couldn't wait to start the day."[15]

Ford particularly enjoyed swimming. His house in Alexandria had a pool, something that was lacking in the White House. Nixon had converted FDR's cramped swimming pool into a press pool (members of the press complained of being "thrown in the pool"). Predictably, nearly five hundred friends of Ford contributed $2,000 each to build a pool for the president. A far different story from the children in 1933 who contributed their nickels and dimes to fund FDR's pool. Ford's sporting vacations included winter excursions to Colorado where the Ford family skied (Ford became the first president to ski since Teddy Roosevelt). The Ford family—wife Betty, sons Michael, Jack, and Steven, and daughter Susan—were all athletic. Betty Ford, who had trained as a dancer with Martha Graham, enjoyed skiing and played golf occasionally. The reporters traveling with the president clamored to see Ford ski and were surprised to see a bold downhill skier who flew down the slopes and rarely fell (when he did, his falls made the national news). His ski instructor pronounced him an "advanced intermediate."[16]

The irony was that Ford—trim, coordinated, and powerful—could not shake the image of "dumb jock." Any president lacking the quick mind of Jack Kennedy, Lyndon Johnson, and even Richard Nixon appeared to be slow-witted. Admittedly, Ford had a deliberate manner and spoke sometimes in a monotone; speaking either off the cuff or from a script did not come easily to him. Late-night comics created a stereotype of a bumbling, uncoordinated chief executive. "Week after week, Chevy Chase [actor and comedian] portrayed Gerald Ford, a former college football star, as an irredeemable klutz," recalls Elizabeth Kolbert in *The New Yorker*. A klutz he was not, nor for that matter a dunce. The media and the voters were not only blind to his athletic ability, but also to his academic credentials. After all, he was a Yale law graduate who finished—Ford pointed out in his memoirs—in the top third of a class that included 98 Phi Beta Kappas in a class of 125.[17]

In a 1976 presidential debate with Jimmy Carter, Ford etched this unfortunate image in the public's mind. In one fatal lapse, he damaged his reelection prospects by insisting that the Soviets did not control Eastern Europe, a statement that he surely knew to be untrue. He compounded it by insisting that Poland, Rumania, and Yugoslavia were not Soviet satellites. In that second debate, Ford pursued his initial statement as if he had been sucked into a draw play by a retreating quarterback. Richard Nixon might have said that he had been "mousetrapped."[18]

Uncharacteristically, he also stumbled and fell while getting out of *Air Force One*. Once, he hit his head while exiting the presidential helicopter. Though he hit an onlooker with a golf shot once as vice-president, that duck hook became a source of gags on late-night talk shows long after the initial incident (his predecessor, Vice-President Spiro Agnew, had begun the Republican golfing "rain" of terror). Rarely noticed was the president's monster drive on the first hole at Pinehurst Country Club in 1974 when he outdrove well-known professionals Arnold Palmer and Gary Player, and came within ten yards of matching one of Jack Nicklaus's legendary drives.

The political planners in the Ford administration used the president's athletic reputation effectively. His contacts with sports celebrities were brief and carefully choreographed. The White House staff budgeted his time, planned his movements, and prepared his remarks, sprinkling them with humor about his own sports career.

He became close friends with Joe Garagiola, a onetime major leaguer, then sportscaster and TV host. They had met when Ford attended baseball's All-Star Game in Philadelphia. On the way back to Washington, they talked at length and formed a friendship that would be forged in campaign commercials and on the night following the 1976 election.

When Muhammad Ali defeated heavyweight Richard Dunn, aide (later vice-president) Richard Cheney prepared the script for a presidential call. Ali had already visited the White House, and he and daughter Susan struck up a friendship. When she appeared at an Ali practice session, Ali showed his delight. "Being the president's daughter, I thought you'd have on silks and capes," Ali joked. Susan Ford explained that she had been a fight fan since she was six because her brothers watched boxing and there was only one television in the house. On *Face the Nation*, Ali indicated that he might support the president in the upcoming election.[19]

Because Ali was a potential supporter, Cheney proposed three carefully crafted talking points. Ford would congratulate Ali, but his remarks would include a reference to the election: "I would like to have seen the fight but I have my own championship bout." He then would thank him for his "kind words" and tell him that he looked forward to seeing him soon. On July 6 Ford placed the call to Ali—the call required only three minutes of his busy schedule.[20]

When Ford attended a testimonial dinner for the black golfer Lee Elder, his staff prepared a brief speech for the president. Typically, it included a humorous, self-effacing reference to Ford's own sports. "I'm still looking forward to that round of golf, but I'm going to have to ask for more strokes than I had originally planned," he quipped. "Inflation has affected my game too." The president did play a round of golf with Lee Elder and African American comedian Flip Wilson on May 10, 1975.[21]

Three weeks before the election, the Fords went to New York to confer the presidential Medal of Freedom on dancing doyenne Martha Graham. No doubt, the close connection between First Lady Betty Ford and her former dance teacher prompted Ford to choose Graham. That he did it so close to the election points to the popularity of Betty whose candor had won her a wide following. Asked her reaction *if* her daughter Susan had an affair, her response was refreshing, candid, and shocking to some. Not only would it not bother her, she would also not be surprised if Susan was having an affair (Susan quickly informed the press that she was not). When Betty Ford had a mastectomy, she was unusually candid with the press and public. Likewise, she quieted feminist criticism of the administration with her support of the Equal Rights Amendment. Ford himself sometimes joked that he was "Betty Ford's husband." In 1976 there were buttons reading "Betty's Husband for President."

In fact, the First Lady almost matched her husband's pace on the campaign trail. Faced with questions by reporters, she answered them deftly. Defending her husband's choice of golf partners, she made it a family matter. "It [golf] was something between old friends," she said. "They [the president's golfing partners] were guests of ours many times." Nevertheless, she placated those who supported traditional roles of women by declaring that "I had a career at one time and then I gave it up for a marriage and a family."[22]

In spite of the dumb-jock jokes, Ford, for the most part, seamlessly incorporated athletics—and athletic issues—into his presidency. He carefully avoided emphasizing his career as a college football player, and he mentioned his time on the bench as much as his playing time. He joked about his golf scores and errant shots. He let the public know that he believed in physical fitness and practiced it himself. He cultivated athletes, but did not turn his sporting interests into a presidential carnival.

On election night in 1976, Ford invited his good friend and fellow campaigner, Joe Garagiola, to watch the returns with him. The former major league catcher had made campaign commercials in which he conducted half-hour interviews with the president. Ford began the campaign almost hopelessly behind. After almost losing the Republican nomination to Ronald Reagan, the president was thirty points down to former Georgia governor Jimmy Carter. Always at his best in competitive situations, Ford managed to overcome the deficit—or so it appeared. On the eve of the election, some polls showed him ahead of Carter.

Ford's campaigning helped turn the election into a real horse race, but his horse came up short. Carter managed to win the crucial toss-up states, and at eleven o'clock Ford telephoned Carter to offer his congratulations. Returning to the Oval Office to be with his family, he and Joe Garagiola threw their arms around each other.

"There we were, two has-been athletes, hugging each other in total silence," he wrote. "Then the mood broke and tears began to flow. 'Damn it, we shouda won. We shouda won,'" Garagiola said.

Ford tried to comfort Garagiola, remarking that "there are more important things to worry about than what is going to happen to Jerry Ford."

"Not today, damn it," Garagiola sobbed. "Not today."[23]

★

A Team Player—Always

After such a bruising election, Ford harbored some distaste for Carter. In the heat of battle, the challenger had made statements that Ford regarded as low blows. But he was not a player or politician who held grudges—never had been.

After Carter left the White House, he and Gerald Ford served on a commission together. Putting away the bitter memories from the 1976 campaign, they became close friends. When the Miller Center at the University of Virginia was dedicating a new wing, the presidential center asked Ford to dedicate the facility. But the eighty-nine-year-old Ford was ill, and he had to decline; he asked Jimmy Carter to make the dedication in his stead, and he agreed.

Once again Ford relied on teamwork that he learned as a high school and college athlete. It never bothered him that a former rival might get the spotlight.

*President Jimmy Carter dancing with the Georgia state square dancers,
who entertained at one of the congressional picnics held on the South Lawn of the
White House. A deceptively good athlete, Carter played varsity tennis and basketball in
high school and junior college, and at the Naval Academy he ran on the cross-country
team. As president, he continued his running, which led to a well-photographed crisis
when he had to withdraw from a road race because of heat exhaustion. USIA.*

Jimmy Carter
More than Meets the Eye

Jimmy Carter came to the White House without a conspicuous sports resume. Nothing about his persona or demeanor evoked anything close to the image of a sportsman. He had not played football in high school or college nor did he attend big-time sports events. He didn't even play golf, and only a few people knew that he was passionate about tennis.

The voters had rejected Ford, a onetime sports star, in favor of a religious and scrupulously honest southern governor who promised that he would never lie to the American people. Carter was content to keep his sports interests on the back burner.

Yet Carter was a sports maven. Unknown to most Americans, Carter had engaged in numerous outdoor sports as a boy, as a young man, and even as governor of Georgia. Very much like nineteenth-century presidents, he grew up in a rural setting where fishing and hunting came quite naturally. He competed on the clay court that his father built in the tiny farming community of Archery, Georgia. In high school, he played on the tennis and basketball teams, and at the Naval Academy he ran cross-country. In the presidency and afterward, he embraced cross-country skiing, jogging, and fly casting.

Carter was more like Teddy Roosevelt in his array of outdoor interests than any of TR's successors (with the exception of Dwight Eisenhower). On the plains of southwestern Georgia were swamps, ponds, and streams offering a wide variety of opportunities for fishing, even for exotic species such as the Atlantic eel. Unlike TR's hunting for trophies, the Carter philosophy, born of practicality in rural America, was to eat what you killed. As Carter himself points out, in the Depression years of his childhood, most of his neighbors relied on the game they killed to supplement their sparse incomes. Young Jimmy took pride in his skill in pursuing game. "I was a popular companion even when quite young," he writes, "because of my willingness and ability to climb high into trees." He was adept at shaking the limbs until the raccoon or possum fell from the tree.[1]

All of these sports laid the foundation for Carter's later sporting interests. Carter played tennis as governor and president, even going so far as to monitor the scheduling of tennis on the White House courts. He also learned to fly-cast, and with First Lady Rosalynn Carter, explored trout streams around Camp David and became an expert in tying flies. Back in Georgia for vacations, he hunted quail and hiked through the woods. After he left the White House in 1981, he fished and hunted for exotic species wherever he went, even authoring a book on his outdoor sporting experiences.

No first family before the Carters spent as much time in the woods, streams, and meadows surrounding Camp David. While other presidents relaxed with skeet shooting, bowling, or even golf, no presidential couple investigated the natural habitat as thoroughly as Jimmy and Rosalynn did. Ironically, for all his love of his "Shangri-La" and its surroundings, we identify Carter with Camp David almost entirely for brokering the Camp David Accords between Israel and Egypt.

While Carter engaged in sports as president, he generated far more sports headlines—and controversy—when he initiated the Moscow Olympic boycott in 1980. When the Soviet Union invaded Afghanistan in December 1979, Carter refused to allow an American team to participate in the Moscow Olympics. He also tried with far less success to put together an international boycott, thereby becoming the first president to convert the Olympics into diplomatic hardball—and, given the results, perhaps the last.

When Carter left the White House in 1981, he returned to Georgia. The sports of the Carter presidency, cut short by the election of Ronald Reagan, would resume in rural Georgia where they had begun in the 1930s.

★

The Acorn Falls Not Far from the Oak

"'Why do you hunt and fish?' I'm often asked," Carter once wrote.

"The easiest answer is: 'My father and all my ancestors did it before me. It's been part of my life, since childhood, and part of my identity, like being a southerner or a Baptist.'"[2]

The lure of hunting and fishing proved seductive to generations of boys growing up in the rural South. Carter had a friend, the son of the druggist, who lent hunting and fishing magazines to other boys. Just as other children might have played baseball all day, Carter's playmates honed their outdoor skills.

My friends and I would spend hours throwing up tin cans for one another to shoot at, varying the distance and direction to simulate as best we could the explosive rise of quail or the swift passing flight of doves. An open bucket in the yard was an excellent target for bait casting. I would vary the distance and my arm delivery to correspond with the circumstances we would face in the creeks and ponds.[3]

In describing the origins of Jimmy Carter's sporting life, it is sometimes difficult to relate the elite, all-white sports like tennis with the hunting and fishing that he and his friends so ardently pursued. Carter as a youngster lived in a rural setting where many families subsisted—barely—often by working farmland that was rented from larger landowners. He recalled fishing and hunting with his mostly black friends, who were—some of them—tenant farmers on his father's land. The medical problems such as hookworm so prevalent in the rural South still posed a danger. Water moccasins and rattlers were either lurking in the water or the woods, or, just as likely, in their youthful imaginations. Yet Jimmy Carter never had to endure the chronic medical problems suffered by his less fortunate neighbors. His mother Lillian had the skills to treat infections and rural maladies such as lice and ringworm.

One obvious reason for Carter's immersion in both down-home and elite sports was his mother Lillian, a professionally trained nurse and the daughter of a well-known politician, not to mention his father, the ambitious and disciplined Earl Carter. To call Earl Carter a simple farmer does him an injustice. In the 1930s, Earl Carter was a substantial landowner and peanut producer, fencing off parcels of his land and renting them out to poor blacks. He was also an influential figure in the community. He served on the school board and, when electricity came, on the Rural Electrification board. Not long before he died, he was elected to the Georgia legislature.

The sports interests of the tough and demanding Earl Carter became Jimmy's sports interests. But, as time would tell, Jimmy proved to be as fiercely competitive as his father. Though Earl never attended college, he played tennis and played it well. On his specially built clay court, Earl had one primary rule: the winner got to continue playing, and Earl dominated the courts. Jimmy Carter recalled when he and his father finally played: "Although I eventually became the top player in high school, I could never beat him—and he certainly never gave me a point." The competition between father and son became a part of Carter's personality—both a key to his strengths and shortcomings.[4]

Earl Carter also played baseball for American Legion teams and often brought his family to watch. Here, too, Earl was tough. "Once, when Daddy was catching," Carter recalled, "he blocked the plate as an opposing player slid in with spikes high; he had to spend several weeks on crutches with the resulting injury." When the St. Louis Cardinals played an exhibition game at nearby Americus, Earl encouraged Jimmy to get the players' autographs. One star player, Frankie Frisch, signed his name on Carter's peanut bag, but Pepper Martin—the Cardinal third baseman—spat tobacco at Carter and ordered him to "get your ass off the field, boy!" A high price for one treasured autograph.[5]

Miss Lillian, as she came to be known, happened to see the first game in which African American Jackie Robinson played as a Dodger. Though Earl Carter supported the existing segregated "Jim Crow" system of race relations, Miss Lillian was remarkably progressive for her generation. Not only did she cheer the Dodgers that day, but she also became a lifelong Dodger fan. When Carter became famous, she would sometimes call Dodger manager Tommy Lasorda and question his managing.

In short, Earl Carter introduced his son to a world of elite sports in which the black tenant farmers, not to mention many poor whites, would not have been welcome. "My daddy reserved only the bobwhite quail and mourning doves for himself," Carter remembered, "leaving rabbits and squirrels to be hunted by the others who lived or worked on our land." Though he fished and hunted with his father's tenants, Jimmy occasionally accompanied Earl on fishing trips to the Okefenokee Swamp in southeast Georgia or other places. "These were the times when I felt closest to my father," he writes, "and I appreciated deeply the fact that I was again the only child permitted to accompany the grown men."[6]

To be sure, Earl was a tough taskmaster. When Jimmy shot his first quail, he proudly raced to tell his father, who had taught him to hunt and to handle guns, only to be chastised for dropping his gun on the ground when he ran to retrieve the quail and then leaving it. It was different when he went with his father's tenants. When he hunted squirrels with his dog Bozo, the tenants who accompanied him were grateful for the game that Jimmy killed. As adept as Carter was as a youthful hunter, the tenants may also have deferred to him because of his race and status. Just as when Jimmy played baseball, he always insisted on pitching—and he did. Here too, Earl's black employees allowed him "to be the star."[7]

Rachel Clark, his nanny, taught him to fish, and his companions as a boy were generally black. But his father's presence always lurked in the youthful Jimmy's mind—and would for decades to come. Once, while fishing with Jimmy, Earl entrusted his son with the stringers on which the fish were secured to be later brought home, cleaned, and eaten. Jimmy strapped the stringers, his own and his father's, to his belt as he continued to fish. Suddenly, he hooked a large fish, and as he battled it, he forgot about the stringers, which slipped away. In tears, he went to his father and admitted that he had lost both stringers. Knowing well his father's high standards, Jimmy had good reason to fear the worst.

"Daddy was rarely patient with foolishness or mistakes, but after a long silence, he said, 'Let them go, Hot [Carter's nickname, short for "hotshot"]. There are a lot more fish in the river. We'll get them tomorrow."[8]

Earl later felt that he had been too hard on his elder son. But he planted his acorns in fertile soil. In sports, as in business and politics, Jimmy Carter became compassionate and competitive, audacious and introspective—an updated version of Earl Carter. Above all, he was stubbornly resolute once he made up his mind.

★

Underneath It All, a Sportsman

Many people still find it hard to conceive of the pious and dedicated Carter as a sportsman. Yet the number of sports that Carter embraced matches or exceeds those of most presidents. In high school, he played basketball and tennis, and he pole vaulted. After he graduated from high school in Plains, he played basketball at Georgia Southwestern College, a junior college in nearby Americus. After failing to get an appointment to the Naval Academy in 1942, he went to Georgia Tech for a year, boning up on engineering courses and becoming a lifelong Georgia Tech football fan, a sport that his small high school in Plains had not offered. At the Naval Academy, he was a pole vaulter and high jumper. He excelled at cross-country, a sport well suited to his slender build and solitary temperament.

When his father died in 1953, Carter resigned from the Navy and returned home to run the family peanut business. After his graduation from the Naval Academy, he had married Rosalynn Smith, also from Plains. Rosalynn became a lifelong partner in many of his outdoor sports. In a passage about hunting for Indian artifacts in his autobiography, *An Hour before Daylight*, Carter drops a casual reference to golf. In discussing his passion for Indian artifacts, he remarks, "Rosalynn and I played golf for a few years, and I found several nice points [arrowheads] along the heavily traveled paths between greens and tees, overlooked by thousands of golfers." He and Rosalynn belonged to a club nearby where they took their children for golf lessons. Soon after the *Brown* desegregation decision in 1954, Carter refused to join the White Citizens

Council formed to combat integration and was expelled from the club. Presumably, the Carter golfing experience ended there. Carter has never been included in books on golfing presidents, even though he did play the game on occasion.[9]

Carter developed an interest in stock-car racing while continuing to play tennis and engaging in outdoor sports. In 1962 Jimmy Carter was elected to the state legislature in an election that required the candidate to challenge the election returns, take his case to court, and defeat the local political boss who cheated him of victory on election day. Four years later, he ran unsuccessfully for governor of Georgia, but in 1970 was elected. While governor, he played tennis with Bert Lance, a banker and one of his political advisers and two members of his staff, including Hamilton Jordan, future White House chief of staff. His biographer, Peter G. Bourne, quotes one of his tennis playing partners who summed up the governor's approach to tennis—and politics: "Carter played to kill as he did in the campaign and as governor."[10]

Carter also continued to hunt quail, only now on a grander scale. He had hunted quail on farms near Plains but never on the large plantations cultivated specifically for that sport. "Only after I became governor and then President," he writes, "was I ever invited to enjoy the beautiful pageantry of the large plantations south of Plains around Albany and Thomasville, whose prime reason for existence was quail hunting." Like Dwight Eisenhower, Carter was invited to plantations owned by wealthy northerners and took part in highbrow hunting with horses, dog handlers, and groomed servants, followed by formal dinners in which the sportsmen dressed in coat and tie.[11]

As governor, he was introduced to fly fishing in the high country north of Atlanta where trout were plentiful. It was the beginning of a love affair that would continue into his presidency and would become a passion thereafter. Like so much that Carter did, he could not embrace a sport without attempting to master it. It comes as no surprise then that Carter set about learning to tie his own flies for trout fishing. In spite of one presidential mishap, when a hook became lodged in his cheek, Carter ranks with Chester Arthur, Herbert Hoover, and Dwight Eisenhower as a proficient flycaster.

In 1976 Jimmy Carter became the first southerner since the Civil War, other than Woodrow Wilson who was serving as governor of New Jersey and Lyndon Johnson who was already president, to be nominated for president. Unlike Nixon and Ford, Carter was not a national figure and had not served in Congress. Few voters would have known that he played tennis or was an outdoor enthusiast. Because he and Rosalynn valued their privacy, sports in the Carter White House took place with little fanfare.

According to his speechwriter James Fallows, Carter took it upon himself to schedule tennis on the White House courts or at least to approve of the schedule of his subordinates' time on the courts. Fallows recalled that he would send notes through Carter's secretary asking to use the courts while Carter was otherwise occupied. "I always provided spaces where he could check Yes or No," Fallows wrote. "Carter would make his decision and send the note back, initialed J." Operating the presidency as he ran the peanut warehouse in Plains proved to be a Carter trademark—and, some would say, a short-coming. This hands-on president could not keep his hands off the minutiae of governing. Bert Lance, now budget director, continued to be his most con-stant tennis partner and closest confidant. When Lance was forced to resign over allegations of financial irregularities in early 1978, Carter gave up tennis and took up the far more solitary sport of jogging.[12]

President Carter continued to pursue his newly minted interest in fly cast-ing. In July 1980, returning from Japan, he stopped in Alaska where he and Secretary of State Edmund Muskie flew to a choice lake and spent a few hours trout fishing. "We flew northward from Anchorage," Carter writes, "circled Mount McKinley, landed on one of the glaciers to see the slowly flowing ice at first hand, and flew close to some cliffs to observe a number of Dall sheep on the steep mountainsides." One of the flies that he had created in his first flush of enthusiasm, an imitation of a small yellow caterpillar, proved irre-sistible to the grayling (a species related to trout).[13]

While he flew at bird's-eye altitudes across the lakes, rivers, and forests that day, Carter made mental notes for his crusade to protect wilderness areas. A bill was pending that would greatly expand government-protected land, most of it in mainland Alaska. On December 2, 1980, in one of his final acts as president, he signed the conservation act. "We set aside for conservation an area larger than the state of California," Carter proudly relates, "doubled the size of our National Park and Wildlife Refuge System, designated twenty-five free-flowing Alaskan streams as wild and scenic rivers—and, as a result, in-stantly tripled our nation's wilderness system."[14]

Unfortunately for Carter, his bold stroke of the pen lacked Theodore Roo-sevelt's exquisite timing and flair for the dramatic. The signing of this impor-tant bill came one month after he lost the presidency to Ronald Reagan. One of the states to wind up in the Reagan column was Alaska. Did he wait to sign the bill until after the election? As it turned out, his timing did not matter since Alaska wound up in the Republican column.

Most of Carter's outdoor activities took place near Camp David. He and Rosalynn found a trout stream down the mountain from Camp David and

President Carter fishing leisurely at St. Simon's Island off the coast of Georgia. Of all his outdoor sports, Carter pursued fishing with the most gusto, learning not only to fly fish but also to tie his own flies. His most embarrassing moment came when a story made the rounds that he was nearly attacked by a giant banzai bunny while fishing at a pond in Georgia. His best fishing came after he left the White House when he stopped to fish on his visits to foreign countries. USIA.

explored streams in the headwaters of the Potomac. They fished successfully, ignorant of the fact that secret service agents were stocking the streams before they arrived. Unlike Calvin Coolidge, who had to have the most basic instruction from agent Ed Starling, the Carters were accomplished and committed fishermen who just happened to fish where the trout abounded. Herbert Hoover, who had the streams around Camp Rapidan stocked, would have understood.

Once, the Carters invited a dozen expert fly-fishermen to Camp David to discuss the technical side of fly fishing and to demonstrate casting and fly tying. Not long afterward, the Carters flew by White House helicopter to the Spruce Creek Hunting and Fishing Club north of Camp David to fish the club's streams. When the press got wind of the trip, Carter was forced to defend his use of a helicopter to go fishing. In the midst of an energy crisis, his critics found it tempting to criticize him for wasting fuel. It was one of the only times that the workaholic Carter mentioned his need for sports outings. "I really believe that it's good not only for me but for the country to be able to do that on occasion," he told a press conference. "I, like the average American, need some recreation at times." He added that he had enjoyed the outing except "I didn't catch as many fish as my wife." Meant to be humorous, the remark was all too close to the truth—he did *not* enjoy finishing second to anyone, even to the First Lady.[15]

Too often, it seemed, Carter's outdoor activities seemed to drive home a vision of Carter as indecisive—or even as weak and ineffectual. Carter took up cross-country skiing, but late in 1980 fell and broke his arm. On September 15, 1979, running in a six-mile road race, Carter showed signs of exhaustion. His physician, Dr. William Lukash, noted that he was "pale, wobbling and moaning, standard signs of exhaustion for runners." The president agreed reluctantly to drop out. According to his biographer Peter Bourne, "pictures of an ashen, collapsing Carter were flashed across the nation." Without a doubt, the photos exaggerated Carter's condition. "But the picture stuck irrevocably in people's minds," Bourne asserts, "shaping their overall perception of his leadership in a far more forceful way than any of the positive actions he was taking." If a picture is worth a thousand words, it takes two thousand words to try to dispel its image.[16]

The caricature of Carter that caused both guffaws and disbelief resulted from the "attack bunny." Vacationing in Georgia, he was fishing on a pond when a swamp rabbit, hissing and foaming at the mouth, swam toward his boat. The president easily deflected it with his oar, but made the mistake of relating his story to his press secretary Jody Powell. A few months later, Powell casually told a White House reporter, and the next day a story appeared in the *Washington Post*, "President Attacked by Rabbit." Out of control, the rabbit story grew into the "banzai bunny," a creature that morphed into a monster almost as large as the president. To defuse the issue, Carter even had a photo of an oversized rabbit created by the White House photo lab, but it was suppressed by his aides. Coinciding with the takeover of the U.S. embassy in Teheran by the strictly Islamic Ayatollah Khomeini, the banzai bunny became the cartoon counterpart of Khomeini, who was "holding America hostage."[17]

Once, earlier in his presidency, the Carters were walking a field in Georgia looking for arrowheads, their eyes fixed on the ground. As he reached the end of the field and turned, his foot stopped eighteen inches from a large rattlesnake, lurking in dead leaves, ready to spring. "Its rattles began to sing a deadly song and I leaped backward and fell down," Carter writes, "yelling for Rosalynn to be careful."[18]

Unlike the attack rabbit, this was not reported (Carter refers to it in his book on hunting and fishing, *An Outdoor Journal*). The rattler, like international dangers lying in wait, serves as a far more stark symbol than an oversized, overrated, and altogether fictitious killer bunny. Though he killed the rattler, Carter was unable to dispatch the Iranian hostage takers, or to intimidate the Soviets, whose military action provoked America's most serious use of Olympic sports as an international weapon.

★

Flexing His Olympic Muscle

On December 27, 1979, the Soviet Union invaded Afghanistan, deposed and killed the president, and installed its own government. The Carter administration reacted promptly and resolutely. Carter embargoed grain sales and technology transfers. He also threatened to boycott the 1980 summer Olympics in Moscow. Carter's threat brought an instant protest from Robert Kane, president of the United States Olympic Committee (USOC). He informed the president that boycotts ran counter to the principles of the Olympic ideal and that the Olympics must remain a nonpolitical world event.

Presidents had rarely concerned themselves with the Olympics, let alone threatened to make them into a global issue. Not that American presidents since Kennedy had *not* worried about the performance of Olympic teams. As we have seen, the Ford administration pursued legislation that would unify the nation's Olympic authority. American Olympic officials had always insisted that the "games must go on," as stated by Avery Brundage, the only American to serve as International Olympic Committee (IOC) president, immediately after the slaughter of the Israeli athletes at the 1972 Munich games. Yet, as Olympic historian Allen Guttmann has suggested, the idea of a presidential boycott "was attractively available and relatively inexpensive in political and economic terms."[19]

In his State of the Union speech, Carter broke with this tradition of Olympian detachment, formally proposing a boycott of the Moscow games and giving the Soviet Union until February 20 to withdraw its troops from Afghanistan. Carter set out to organize an international boycott and, in the hopes of softening the blow, began to explore the possibility of an international sports festival. Polls showed that Congress and the American public strongly supported Carter's boycott. Carter, who began his presidency promoting human rights and easing Cold War tensions, joined most of his predecessors in pursuing a hard line toward Soviet expansion and subversion.

Even with public support, the Carter administration lacked the statutory authority to proclaim a boycott. That resided with the U.S. Olympic Committee, an eighty-member group put in place by the Amateur Athletic Act of 1978. Carter immediately launched a campaign to persuade these Olympic officials. American corporations were asked to withhold Olympic contributions until the USOC had agreed to a boycott. The administration assured the USOC and the Olympic participants that the government would work with like-minded nations to set up a substitute site for summer games and suggested that the government might then help to make up shortfalls in Olympic revenues.

From the beginning, the administration was confident that it could persuade other countries to join in. The campaign proceeded on two levels: Carter approached U.S. friends in Europe and Asia, certain that friendly governments would comply. An effort was also made in Africa by a personal emissary, Muhammad Ali. But Ali, a former Olympic champ himself, did an embarrassing about-face and declared that he opposed the boycott.

Among our closest allies, intense lobbying was required. Other countries also had their Olympic committees and sports federations that held the decision-making power, and European Olympic committees and federations were reluctant to forgo the Olympics, as was the IOC, presided over by an Irishman, Lord Killanin, and Monique Berlioux, the executive director. An Olympic boycott appeared to be a political gesture by the beleaguered Jimmy Carter to win votes in the 1980 election. Because Carter never personally took his case to European governments or Olympic officials, the Europeans never took the boycott as seriously as they might have. To believe that the Soviets would withdraw their troops because of an Olympic boycott required a stretch of the imagination.

To complicate matters, the winter Olympics at Lake Placid unexpectedly made Carter's job even more difficult. With the American embassy officials still held hostage in Tehran and the Moscow Olympics under siege, the Carter officials did not anticipate the excitement generated by the incredible upset of the American hockey team over the Soviet team.

Made up of amateur college players, the American hockey team had little chance to defeat the veteran Soviets, who were professional in all but name. But win they did in a thrilling, semifinal game and then went on to win the gold medal. "From New York to Los Angeles," the *New York Times* reported, "at sport arenas, in theaters, and in barrooms, family rooms and other watering and television-watching spots, hockey fans and Americans who had never before seen a hockey game cheered wildly, hugged one another and groped for superlatives."[20]

This paroxysm of patriotic fervor got in the way of Carter's boycott. Interest in the Moscow Olympics burgeoned, as did the number of Americans who wanted to send a team to Moscow. Carter hastily phoned his congratulations to Herb Brooks, coach of the U.S. hockey team, and his aides made plans to receive the medal winners at the White House. Carter used the White House reception as an occasion to announce that the United States would definitely not send a team to the summer Olympics. Billed as an event to recognize the medal winners, the reception was hardly an appropriate venue for selling the boycott.

Carter, who had not met with IOC officials at Lake Placid, seemed to be substituting force for persuasion. While he praised the winter Olympians, he had yet to meet with the summer athletes. With the measurable rise in support for sending a team, American officials and athletes had reason to hope that Carter might back down. Opponents of the Carter policies complained that the Olympic athletes once destined for Moscow were "being held [as] political hostages" by the Carter administration, an obvious reference to the continuing embassy crisis in Tehran.[21]

The multilateral boycott did not go as Carter had hoped. Of the major U.S. allies, only the Germans, Canadians, and Israelis refused to send a team to Moscow. Even the USOC, though agreeing to the boycott, put off the final decision until May. A fragile hope remained among the athletes and USOC officials that the boycott might be called off.

But it was not. By summer, more than fifty countries joined the boycott. Unfortunately for Carter, many of those countries were Islamic or athletic nonentities such as Upper Volta, Niger, and Surinam, which might not have participated anyway. As a result, the alternate games never got off the ground. The American athletes paid the price for the Carter embargo as did American corporations, especially NBC. Contracted to televise the Olympics, NBC was making payments to the IOC. Carter used legislation already on the books to ban American Olympic exports or telecasts related to the Olympics.

Did the Olympic boycott succeed? Measured by numbers, the answer is a qualified "yes." By Carter's count, fifty-five nations joined the boycott. But the list did not include France and Great Britain, two of our closest allies who ended up participating. While the Soviets continued to bomb, gas, and murder Afghans, the Moscow Olympics took place as scheduled with eighty nations participating. A less robust version of the Olympics was celebrated without the United States, but it hardly lacked participants or medals for the

Soviets and their satellites. Carter's hope that the International Olympic committee would relocate or cancel the games altogether met with a cold reception when Carter's top officials—not Carter—broached it to Olympic officials at Lake Placid. Carter was forced to set more modest goals. Even the hope that the American boycott would send a message to the Soviet people seemed like an idealist's pipe dream. The partial boycott became still another sign of Carter's ineffectiveness. Even Carter himself admitted in his memoirs that many of his actions in 1980, among them the Olympic boycott, were "politically damaging."[22]

Boycotting the Olympics proved damaging to both his image and to his administration's scorecard. Once again, he failed to lobby personally for the international boycott and had not expended much effort to appeal to the American athletes or Olympic officials. In the words of speechwriter James Fallows, "Carter often seemed more concerned with taking the correct position than with learning how to turn that position into results."[23]

Carter was fifty-seven when he left office—young by presidential standards. In the years after he left office, he was able to reclaim his reputation—as a sportsman, as an author, as a nail-pounding, house-building humanitarian, and as a peacemaker. In sports, Carter hunted and fished wherever he went, in a style befitting a former head of state. The banzai bunny story and initialed memos on who was to use the tennis courts were merely consigned to presidential anecdotes, like the errant golf balls and calls to coaches of his predecessors.

Gradually the American public learned that Carter was more of a regular guy than they imagined, a man who rooted for the Atlanta Braves and Hawks, and who might even show up for a postseason baseball game. The private sports that he pursued during his presidency never projected the image of a man who had a lifelong love of the outdoors or who found pleasure in watching mainstream sports. Neither did it express the image of a man who really cared about the Olympic games in and of themselves and not as a political weapon.

Carter's presidency has been called the "unfinished presidency." Yet Carter's achievements and awards after leaving the White House, including his sporting life, writings, and the Nobel Peace Prize, place him among the most distinguished "retired" presidents. His enthusiasm for hunting, hiking, and fishing, virtually unknown and unappreciated in his presidential years, has been a constant throughout his childhood and adult life, pre-presidential to post-presidential. With more than two decades of vigorous activity, Carter's commitment to the outdoors continued to grow.[24]

Will our increasingly urbanized society produce another president with the enthusiasm for and commitment to hunting, hiking, and fishing demonstrated by Theodore Roosevelt and Dwight Eisenhower? Or will the outdoors president become an extinct species? If so, the president who grew up hunting and fishing in rural Georgia may represent the end of an era.

20

Ronald Reagan
Creating a Sports Legend

Ronald Reagan more than once described himself as an ordinary guy. "I like to swim, hike and sleep (eight hours a night)," he said in 1942. "I'm fairly good at every sport except tennis, which I just don't like."

He played bridge, liked steak covered with onions, and was interested in politics and government. "I love my wife, baby, and home," he declared.[1]

Yet this ordinary guy a half century later would be known as the Great Communicator, the initiator of the Reagan Revolution, the Teflon president—and the "Gipper." Or, to be more precise, "win one for the Gipper."

Winning one for the Gipper originated before World War II, when movie actor Ronald Reagan played a football player named George Gipp in *Knute Rockne, All American*. Gipp was an All-America fullback in 1920 on a Notre Dame team coached by the legendary Knute Rockne. Soon after the final game of the season, Gipp died from strep throat and pneumonia.

In the movie, as Gipp lies dying in a hospital, he tells Coach Rockne: "Someday, when the team's up against it, breaks are beating the boys, ask them to go in there with all they've got. Win that one for the Gipper. I don't know where I'll be. But I'll be happy."[2]

Eight years later, Knute Rockne used what he claimed were Gipp's dying words in a dramatic locker room speech. In the film, Rockne, played by famed actor Pat O'Brien, enters the locker room. In contrast to his usual rousing talks, Rockne quietly tells the story of the Gipper and then leaves the somber group of players. After a dramatic pause, the boys yell, "what are we waiting for?" and rush out of the locker room ready to do battle, and playing with fire in their bellies, overcome Army for a dramatic come-from-behind victory. To "win one for the Gipper" was firmly entrenched in gridiron folklore.

Actually, Reagan nearly missed getting the part of the immortal George Gipp. When he heard that Warner Brothers—his studio—was planning to do the movie, he rushed to director Hal Wallis to plead his case. Reagan knew

*A handsome Ronald Reagan striking a pose for a woman
friend when he was a lifeguard at Lowell Park on the Rock River near his
hometown of Dixon, Illinois. Gifted as a swimmer, Reagan rescued a reputed
seventy-seven victims during his seven summers as a lifeguard. It was his
first of many starring roles and helped to pay for his schooling at
Eureka College. Courtesy of Alvah C. Drew Jr., Dixon, Illinois.*

football—he had played, announced, and dreamed it. Wallis, who had another actor in mind, was skeptical. Not only had he played football, Reagan explained, but he was also almost the same size as the great Gipp. He retrieved photos of himself in uniform, and Wallis reluctantly allowed Reagan to try out for the part. The actor's friend, Pat O'Brien, already selected to play Rockne, generously agreed to read his part in the script for Reagan's tryout.

Reagan's role in *Knute Rockne* idealized—even canonized—an All-American reprobate. George Gipp was shady, tough, and irreverent. To be sure, a remarkable athlete, Gipp lived life on the edge—a pool shark and gambler who resided in a hotel in downtown South Bend. He seldom attended class or arrived on time for practice. Sometimes, he even failed to show up for the games. Losing at halftime against Army, Rockne yelled to an insouciant Gipp, leaning against the wall, a cigarette hanging out of his mouth, "I don't suppose you have any interest in this game." Gipp calmly replied: "Look Rock, I got four hundred dollars bet on this game, and I'm not about to blow it." His second-half heroics led Notre Dame to a 28-17 triumph.[3]

Not only did Reagan's portrayal sanctify Gipp, it also lifted the actor out of his stalled career as—in the actor's words—the "Errol Flynn of the B's. I was as brave as Errol, but in a low-budget fashion." Though Reagan was on screen only briefly, he had the juiciest scene. "When I read Gipp's death scene," he recalled, "I had a lump in my throat so big I couldn't talk." Wreathed in saintly white, Reagan's eyes light up in an other-worldly smile as he delivers his final words to Rockne—Rock's hand on his arm.[4]

What did playing Gipp mean to Reagan, the politician? A great deal. In 1986, a fan of long standing wrote to ask if Gipp was a forgotten part of Reagan's life. Not in the least, the president replied. "He has remained very much a part of my life, indeed playing him was the role that moved me into the star category. Curiously enough, at political rallies during my last campaign [1984] there would always be signs out in the crowd referring to me as 'the Gipper.' And believe me, I liked that very much."[5]

Knute Rockne, All American was one of Reagan's first celluloid triumphs. Later, the first actor in the White House would use the media—and his imagination—to become the most visible and entertaining president in history; he was seen and heard via television by more of his countrymen than his one-time hero, Franklin Roosevelt. The Reagan mystique, born of legend and electronic legerdemain, exceeded almost all of his twentieth-century predecessors, especially the presidents who served in the pre-newsreel, pre-television era.

★
Where Is the Rest of Me?

Reagan's best movie performance took place a year later in *King's Row*, where, waking up from surgery, he asked, "where is the rest of me?" A surgeon in an act of revenge against playboy Reagan for taking liberties with his daughter amputates his legs, at mid-thigh level. Years later, Reagan used this line as the title of his 1965 autobiography.

The "rest of him" began in the Midwest. Drearily poor but not that much different from his neighbors, Reagan grew up in Dixon, Illinois—the son of an alcoholic father, Jack, and a self-sacrificing, saintly mother, Nelle. He was a small, dreamy kid who liked to read and play football. He never liked baseball because he was hopelessly nearsighted—and didn't wear glasses until he was eleven. On a losing team in high school, he got his chance to play guard on the varsity, but he also starred in high school theater productions. He never spent much time on his studies because he had what his brother Neil (Moon) called "a photographic mind." Relying on his memory in high school and college, he simply opened a book before the test and absorbed the material. It was a mind well designed for sports and for memorizing his scripts, if not necessarily for analyzing complex issues.[6]

His mother belonged to the Disciples of Christ and the young Dutch, as he was known until he arrived in Hollywood, joined his mother's church, turning his back on his father's Roman Catholicism. Although the Reagans lived close to the poverty line (sometimes above and other times below), his mother wanted Dutch and Moon to attend college. In 1928 Reagan drove his girlfriend, Margaret Cleaver (daughter of the church pastor), to tiny Eureka College for her freshman year. While she was enrolling, he talked to the football coach, Ralph McKinzie, about getting a football scholarship. Although Reagan was not top college material, McKinzie arranged for a half scholarship and an introduction to the Tau Kappa Epsilon fraternity where he could pay for his room and board by washing dishes and where the sociable Reagan soon became a member.

Ready to jump into the starting lineup at Eureka, Reagan was humbled by spending—not unlike Richard Nixon and even Gerald Ford—much of his time on the bench. Yet he idolized his coach, Ralph McKinzie, or "Mac," and soldiered on. In 1930, the Eureka yearbook had this to say about Reagan after his second year: "Although 'Dutch' failed to get much competition this season, he has the determination and fight which will finally win out, if he sticks to football throughout his college career." He did, and for the next two years was starting guard on a losing team. Reagan always enjoyed the macho culture of football. Intensely competitive, the nearsighted lineman loved the one-on-one combat against the adversary on the other side of the line.[7]

As with Gerald Ford, football introduced Reagan to the problems of racial discrimination in the Midwest. Surprisingly, given President Reagan's lackluster record on civil rights, Dutch grew up in a family that found discrimination of any stripe intolerable. Among the members of the team, two African Americans stood as exceptions; one of them—William Burghardt—was recruited by Dutch. In his senior year, the Eureka team stopped at Aurora on its way to a game with Elmhurst College. Inside the hotel, Mac was told that no hotel in town would take blacks. Reagan volunteered to house Burgie and the other African American player with his parents in nearby Dixon. "Mac gave me a funny look; he'd just had a chance to observe first hand what the [local] people . . . thought of blacks," Reagan wrote in his memoirs, "and I'm sure he had his doubts my parents would think much of the idea."[8]

But take them Dutch did with the lame excuse that the hotel was overcrowded. His parents graciously welcomed both players. "She [Nelle] was absolutely color blind when it came to racial matters," Reagan later wrote, "these fellows were just two of my friends." His parents' tolerance may have lulled Reagan into believing that there were no serious racial problems in the Midwest of his youth—as he later stated—or perhaps he simply failed to put this, a typical experience, into a larger context.[9]

Football never paid the bills, but another sport did. Reagan was a gifted swimmer. As a boy, he learned to swim at Lowell Park on the Rock River outside Dixon—the "Hudson of the Midwest." Located upstream from a dam, the Rock River was wide and treacherous; the current flowed swiftly, creating an undertow. Swimmers who foundered in midstream might never reach either shore because the river broadened to 685 feet. After losing several swimmers, the town officials were ready to close the park. Having sprouted six inches to five foot ten (two inches from his adult height), the fourteen-year-old Reagan applied for the job of lifeguard. For the next seven years, he spent his summers in the lifeguard stand where he received seventeen dollars a week and all he could eat from the concession stand.[10]

Reagan was worth every cent that the city paid him. In seven years as lifeguard, he rescued, by his count, seventy-seven swimmers, the numbers notched on a log beside the lifeguard stand—although one local resident recalls the rumor that some of those "victims" were damsels in only modest distress who plotted to be rescued by the handsome lifeguard. Remarkably, no one drowned on Dutch's watch. In the photo of Reagan from his lifeguarding days, he stands confidently, tall and slim, wearing the standard 1920s swimsuit with Life Guard emblazoned across the chest. It was his first starring role. Anne Edwards quotes Reagan, who recalled how much "fun" he had. "I was the only one up there on the guard stand. It was like a stage," he recalled. "Everyone had to look at me." For twelve hours a day seven days a week, Reagan carved a niche in Dixon folklore. It was the drama he loved more than the swimming—the starring role.[11]

At Eureka, he *was* the swim team. "Ronald Reagan Wins Two Fourth Places in Swim Meet" reads the headline in the March 29, 1930, issue of the *Pegasus,* the student newspaper. Fourth place might seem unremarkable, except *nineteen* teams were competing in the meet. Reagan took fourth place in both the 50- and 200-yard freestyle. In his senior year, nicknamed "Little Mac," he coached as well as competed. As Coach McKinzie himself later suggested in his interview with Anne Edwards, Reagan could have been an outstanding swimmer if he had chosen to devote himself to this one sport; instead, he dreamed dreams of football glory and a professional football career.[12]

With Reagan, extracurricular activities rather than his classes prepared him for his multiple careers. He gave his first political speech as a freshman in a student strike against the school president—a movement strongly supported by his TKE (Tau Kappa Epsilon) fraternity and which resulted in the president's resignation. He was active in theater; Reagan and his girlfriend, Margaret Cleaver, finished third in a drama competition at Northwestern University—remarkable for coming from the only school without a full-time drama department. Cast as a shepherd in the antiwar drama *Aria de Capa,* he ends up dying from strangulation. "Death scenes are always pleasant for an actor," he wrote of the experience in the competition, "and I tried to play it to the hilt."[13]

And Dutch did imitations of sports announcers, which proved to be a more accurate predictor of his future career than what happened on the playing field.

He graduated in 1932 as the Depression had the country in a death grip. The plight of his family was desperate. Out-of-work Jack Reagan became an unpaid volunteer in FDR's presidential campaign. Nelle worked as a clerk-seamstress. Reagan returned to his job as lifeguard that summer and worked out a sketchy plan to become a radio announcer (he later claimed that he wanted to be an actor but was too shy to reveal this fanciful ambition). At the end of the summer, he hitchhiked to Chicago and made the rounds of the radio studios without success. Then, using his father's car, he drove to radio stations in nearby towns. In Davenport, Iowa, a sportscasting job had been open, but he arrived to find that the job had been filled.

Frustrated as he turned to walk out, he blurted out to the station manager, "how the hell can you get to be a sports announcer if you can't even get a job at a radio station?" Pete MacArthur, the arthritic station manager, hobbling on two canes, caught up with Reagan. "Wait up for me you big bastard," he barked in his Scottish brogue. He asked Dutch if he could describe a football game so he could visualize it as if he were listening to the radio. He parked Reagan in front of a microphone where Reagan recast the final quarter of a game that Eureka had won his senior year against Western Illinois in the closing seconds.[14]

When he played guard in that game, Dutch had missed his block, but Eureka scored anyway. "In the reenactment I want you to know," Reagan wrote to a friend in 1980, "I didn't miss that man in the secondary—I delivered an earth-shattering block that sprung Cole loose [the ball carrier who ran sixty-five yards for the touchdown]. Then, having announced the touchdown, I just grabbed the mike with both hands and said, 'That's all.'" Once again, his imagination had won in a way that his physical abilities could not—a pattern where art imitates and builds on life.[15]

Reagan had rehearsed for this moment—unknowingly—when he imitated a radio announcer while walking to and from football practice. That Pete MacArthur, the station manager, was impressed with this "walk-in" was hardly surprising. MacArthur gave Reagan spot assignments announcing a track meet, the Drake Relays, and then college football games. Several months later, once again out of work and back home in Dixon, Reagan got a call from MacArthur who had found him a full-time job with WHO clear channel radio in Des Moines, a station that reached much of the Midwest. Here he soon became the voice of the Chicago Cubs and Big Ten football, not to mention an all-purpose sports announcer, a script reader for commercials, and interviewer of celebrities passing through Des Moines.

However, he was best-known as the midwestern voice of the Cubs—his first intoxicating experience of being a celebrity. Not that he actually announced the Cubs games live from Wrigley Field. Rather, he re-created them from telegraphic reports wired from Chicago to the station in Des Moines. Because Reagan had never seen a major league game, his employer, WHO, paid for an overnight trip to Chicago before the season, where he got to see quirky Wrigley Field with its vine-laced outfield walls. There, he had the technique of re-creating explained to him by the man who had invented it. Reagan, who had never played varsity baseball—nor cared much for playing the game—suddenly became "Mr. Cub." Half a century later, he returned to Wrigley Field and to the press box where he had merely toured in 1933; there, he would broadcast a full inning of a game, live, from the booth.

The technique of re-creating baseball depended on the telegraph—and if the telegraph failed, the announcer was left hanging. Dutch Reagan's ability to ad-lib was tested several months later during a game between the Cubs and the St. Louis Cardinals. Normally, the telegraph operator in the next booth slipped him a piece of paper through the glass with a brief, coded description of what had just happened, say a strike, a foul ball, or even a home run. Dizzy Dean, the St. Louis Cardinals star right-hander, was facing the Cubs' Bill Jurges. As Reagan had Dean wind up and fire his pitch, he glanced down at the telegraph clerk's note—it read: *"The wire's gone dead."* Unable to rewind his narrative, Reagan had Jurges foul off the pitch. "I slowed Dean down," he recalled, "had him pick up the resin bag and take a sign, shake it off, get another sign, and let him pitch." Reagan invented more fouls, one just missing a home run, kids scrambling in the stands for the ball, and a red-headed boy holding up his trophy. "By then I was in much too deep to admit the wire was dead, so I continued to let Jurges foul Dean's pitches." After more than six minutes, the telegraph operator started typing again. Jurges had popped out on the first pitch.[16]

It was a virtuoso performance; the listeners simply thought that there had been a remarkable number of foul balls—a woefully long at bat for Jurges.

Reagan's first acting performance on the radio—without a script—had gone without a hitch. Actually, he could have ad-libbed football more comfortably, but working the Big Ten games he mainly broadcast live. "I only broadcast one football game in the same way via remote control and radio's 'theater of the mind,'" he wrote in his memoirs. That one game, Iowa versus Michigan, featured the center for the Wolverines, Gerald Ford, whom Reagan nearly edged out for the Republican nomination in 1976.[17]

Reagan's early biographers often neglect the impact of his midwestern sportscasting career in Davenport and Des Moines. Here it was that Dutch Reagan became a well-known media star, albeit by voice rather than image. Though he sent money to his parents and to his brother, he had enough to buy a car and begin dating (he had broken up with the pastor's daughter).

His lifelong passion for horseback riding began in earnest when he joined the Fourteenth Cavalry Regiment (he had first ridden in Dixon). On his way to becoming a reserve officer, he received expert instruction from experienced cavalrymen. Somewhat naively, this dyed-in-the-wool supporter of FDR (his father Jack was a lifelong Democrat) believed that there would never be another war.

Sometimes, after riding at Camp Dodge, he went swimming. According to Anne Edwards in *Early Reagan,* a friend, Richard Ulrich, a lifeguard and semipro football player, recalled: "We first met at a radio broadcast of a game I played with the Des Moines Comets [a semipro team]. He idolized athletes," Ulrich declared. "He was a terrific swimmer, but otherwise just fair. I think he once might have wanted to be a ball player. But now he just wanted to be a 'jock,' one of the boys. He liked to put on riding breeches and ride and make like the cavalry."[18]

Reagan got to do interviews with celebrities who happened to be in Des Moines, such as the boxer Max Baer and actor Jimmy Cagney. He also interviewed Joy Hodges from Des Moines, who had small parts in movies and who tantalized him with the suggestion that he might be suited for Hollywood. A group of cowboy singers who had performed on WHO had just been hired by Gene Autry to do a film. If these Iowans could be in the movies, well . . .

The Cubs spring training at Catalina Island, the Pacific playground of owner William Wrigley, is where Reagan finagled a paid vacation so that, he insisted, he could hang around and get to know the team. When he arrived in Los Angeles, Joy Hodges brought him to her agent. Once signed by the agent, he managed to get a screen test at Warner Brothers. His screen test conflicted with a Cubs game on Catalina, and the usually dependable Reagan chose to play hookey. For this, he was "taken to the woodshed" by Cubs manager Charlie Grimm.

He kept the announcing job—for the time being. In spite of the pleas of his agent, he left Los Angeles at the end of spring training, his movie career still hanging in limbo. Two days after he returned, he received a telegram: WARNERS OFFERS CONTRACT SEVEN YEARS STOP ONE YEAR OPTION STOP STARTING $200 A WEEK STOP WHAT SHALL I DO MEIKLEJOHN [the agent]. He signed.[19]

A month later, he was off to Hollywood. Sports helped to create "Ronald Reagan" in a way that horses, ranching, and coaching did for Jackson, TR, and Ford. Only it gave him far more than simply a means to support himself. It provided the tools that he needed to play larger roles. Sports had smoothed the way for Reagan, both the action of the games and the technique of the sound booth. Now he was ready for the spotlight that sports had made possible.

★
Ronald Reagan—New Name, New Roles

When Ronald Reagan arrived in Hollywood, he was "Dutch" Reagan and always had been—ever since his father took his first look at his newborn son and said he looked like a "fat Dutchman." Luckily for the young actor, the Warner Brothers Publicity Department liked the name Ronald Reagan and suddenly he was known by a name he had never used. What's in a name? Plenty. Reagan biographers would be intrigued by the conflicting identities conveyed by the various names, Dutch, Ronald, Ronnie, and the Gipper.

In Hollywood, Reagan expanded upon his sports interests. He had brought along with him from the Midwest his riding and swimming, but now he body surfed, skied, and even took up golf. Golf represented a giant leap from his midwestern roots. "You youngsters probably don't remember, but when I was young, golf was a sissy, rich man's game," he told an audience in 1970. By his standard, it was sissy in 1940, but Hollywood was bringing the onetime caddy, now a prospering movie star, into the company of rich men.[20]

In 1940 Reagan married Jane Wyman, a promising young actress, who was also a golfer—the newlyweds planned to play golf but were rained out on their honeymoon. Reagan, who caddied some in Dixon, now took up golf in earnest. Spurning the blatantly anti-Semitic Lakeside Club, the Reagans joined the Hillcrest Country Club in Beverly Hills. There, they played with Jack Benny and Mary Livingstone, George Burns and Gracie Allen. Later, in the 1950s, he got the chance to play frequently when he was host of television's *General Electric Theater* and when he traveled to visit General Electric plants. His handicap dropped to 12 before he left GE and gravitated into politics. Since his second wife, Nancy, didn't play, Reagan then drifted away from the game.

While he was president, he golfed so infrequently that he was reluctant to divulge his scores. In 1983 he made one memorable trip to Augusta to play in a foursome with Secretary of State George Shultz and Treasury Secretary Donald Regan. Approaching the sixteenth green, word came that a terrorist had taken over the golf shop after barreling his pickup through the gates. Holding seven people at gunpoint, the unemployed factory worker demanded to speak to the president. Hustled into a bullet-proof limousine, Reagan made six futile attempts by phone from the car to reach the gunman and never finished his golf round. The incident at Augusta proved a prelude to a far more serious—and deadly—act of terrorism the next day when a suicide bomber detonated a truck full of explosives in Beirut, killing 241 U.S. Marines.

Long after he lost interest in football, Reagan continued to ride. When he went to his ranch as both governor and president, he rode every day. In 1986, writing to the son of his secretary, Reagan extolled riding. "That's been my sport for many years now, and I would hate to ever have to give it up. It's a great, healthy exercise, in addition to being a lot of fun." In westerns and other movies, he often did his own stunts. One movie review did a brief profile on Reagan: "Best athlete: Ronald Reagan not only came to films from the field of sports broadcasting, but he knows whereof he speaks!"[21]

For someone as gregarious and extroverted as Reagan, his choice of sports and sports occupations was remarkably solitary. When he was a lifeguard, he sat atop his lifeguard stand or swam alone to the rescue of a distressed swimmer. When he rode horseback, it was by himself, except when he rode with his wife, Nancy. His golfing, it is true, was more sociable. But he played golf mainly when he was married to Jane Wyman or when he found that it fit into his job as spokesman for General Electric. To be sure, football was an exception, but Reagan never paid much attention to that sport after he left Des Moines and WHO. He lacked Richard Nixon's interest in being known as a sports spectator or for blatantly cultivating athletes. He rarely participated in celebrity golf tournaments.

Larry Speakes, press secretary for President Reagan, has commented on the difference between the public and private Reagan. Publicly he was "an outgoing, friendly, personable man." Not that the private Reagan was not "charming and affable, but almost in an impersonal way. Privately, he tends to be a loner, content to spend most of his time with his wife and no one else." Even his wife Nancy has written, "although he loves people, he often seems remote, and he doesn't let anybody get too close. There's a wall around him."[22]

And as Reagan's George Gipp says to Bonnie Rockne, "I guess I'm a private guy." He was right, in the script as in real life. Art or, in this case the movies, imitated life.[23]

There was a distinct difference even in the 1930s between the macho, locker-room Dutch Reagan and the Ronald Reagan who was offstage—between Reagan, the football player, and Reagan, the swimmer. Speaking of football, Reagan once said, "It is the last thing left in civilization where two men can literally fling themselves bodily at one another in combat and not be at war. It's kind of good, clean hatred . . . I know of no other game that gave me the same feeling that football did. That's why you can look at the bench when the TV camera comes along and see the fellows there crying. I've sat there [alone] crying." Reagan saw football as a combat between two individuals, one on each side of the line—a moment when he had an opportunity to rise above the ordinary, but to do it individually.[24]

His worst injury in sports came, not in football, but in a pick-up baseball game in Hollywood—and may well have provoked genuine dislike for the actor-comedian at first base who allegedly tripped him. In 1948, while playing in a charity game between leading male actors and comedians, Reagan either was tripped or slid into the first baseman, comedian Eddie Bracken, and fractured his leg in three places. Reagan was in the hospital for eight weeks, in traction afterward, and then in a cast. While in the hospital, he met a boy whose father, a World War II veteran, "came home on leave and killed himself and the boy's mother." He wrote a letter to Bob Feller, the strikeout king of the world champion Cleveland Indians, asking him to autograph a ball for the boy. He and a friend, in Reagan's account, "managed to break through the kid's shell on the subject of baseball."[25]

He is an ardent fan and it seems to be his real one interest. With his birthday coming up, he'd be in Heaven if he had a baseball bearing some Indians' names. If you'd do this, Bob, you'd contribute a lot toward pulling this little guy out of a dark world he's making for himself.

Ronald Reagan
("Dutch")

That Reagan was sympathetic to the boy's plight is to his credit. His sympathy for the boy coincided with a low point in his own career—his recent divorce from Jane Wyman, his sports injury, a near-fatal case of pneumonia, and a declining post–World War II movie career. Always, there was an element of idealism that permeated Reagan's sports—and politics—a sense of doing something that no one else could do, of being a hero.

Increasingly, politics became an adult version of football and lifesaving. Reagan's nostalgia for growing up in Dixon and attending Eureka turned those difficult years into an idyll. Reagan was constantly reshaping the significance of his sports life to reflect an optimistic and happy view of his childhood and young manhood. "Win one for the Gipper" took on a new meaning. It reaffirmed the pieties of his midwestern past, or perhaps became a denial of the realities of that time period when poverty hovered over the Reagan household.

In 1952 Ronald Reagan got his one and only chance to play the lead in a sports movie—portraying the troubled baseball superstar Grover Cleveland Alexander in The Winning Team. The good news for Reagan was that the studio hired "about a dozen" major leaguers as technical advisers. Reagan spent two hours a day with pitcher Bob Lemon of the Cleveland Indians learning the difference between "throwing from the mound and just throwing." Unfortunately, the film producers hesitated to explain that Alexander suffered from epilepsy as well as alcoholism. *The Winning Team,* unlike *Knute Rockne, All American,* did not win Reagan immortality. It only served to ease him out of his Warner Brothers contract. "I've always regretted that the studio insisted we not use the word [epilepsy], although we did try to get the idea across," he later wrote. This denial of the truth, confusing to moviegoers, merely led to bad reviews.[26]

According to Reagan, his bride Nancy was a baseball fan. "Nancy is a baseball buff: she comes by it honestly," he wrote. "Her birthday is July 6 only because her mother put off having her until after the Fourth of July doubleheader—at least that's her mother's story." That Nancy herself was a dedicated fan may have only been temporary. In her memoir, *My Turn,* she repeats the story of the July 4 doubleheader, but doesn't otherwise try to compete with baseball first ladies Grace Coolidge or Bess Truman.[27]

In the 1950s and 1960s, Reagan bought tracts of land north of Los Angeles. And by the 1970s, having horses that he regularly rode, he was ready to buy a ranch. The result was the purchase of a 688-acre mountaintop ranch near Santa Barbara, rechristened Rancho El Cielo. The ranch was supposed to seal Reagan off from the rest of the world, but unfortunately for President Reagan the press could get within camera distance. Still, he was able to shed his presidential shackles during his vacations (his advisers housed in a hotel in Santa Barbara complained that they lacked access to the president). Larry Speakes has written: "There were times when the president would look like an old man when he arrived, and would appear twenty years younger after a week or two at the ranch."[28]

Reagan chopped wood, rode, and worked at clean-up, fix-up projects—an extension of what he did when he acquired the ranch in 1974—when he threw himself into painting, roofing, and laying flagstones for the patio. He even had a lake bulldozed on the property named Lake Lucky. As president, Reagan spent 345 out of 2,682 days at his western retreat. Guarded by the Secret Service, he got a kick out of alarming the agents by wading into the water to catch blacksnakes—or by peppering them, the snakes that is, with shotgun pellets (his version of TR's varmint killing). Every day, he and Nancy started the morning by riding horseback on the trails he had created. Normally, the Reagans did not entertain there, but in 1983 they did host Queen Elizabeth and Prince Philip. "I'm sure that Nancy and I were as proud of our ranch as they were of Windsor Castle," he declared. For the Reagans, the White House and Washington were more like the Tower of London.[29]

After winning the election of 1984, the Reagans flew to the ranch for "three days of rides in the morning and cutting and splitting wood from downed oak

Ronald and Nancy Reagan taking a horseback ride in Midlothian,
Virginia, in 1980. Reagan began riding horseback in earnest when he
joined the National Guard in Des Moines while announcing sports for WHO.
Almost every day at Rancho El Cielo near Santa Barbara, he saddled up.
An extrovert in public, Reagan was actually a very private man who
usually enjoyed sports with a few close friends. Courtesy of Ronald
Reagan Presidential Library, Simi Valley, California.

trees in the afternoon. It was a happy time." In spite of the prying press, who set up cameras as close as possible, this private president had found a solitary refuge where he could be just plain "Dutch" or "Ronnie." In Reagan's words, "aside from Camp David, the ranch was the only place where we had any privacy—where we could just go for a walk and be ordinary people."[30]

His life in the late 1980s was a long way from Ronald Reagan, the twenty-nine-year-old actor who described himself as an ordinary guy. Or was it? He had now played major roles in politics as governor of California and president of the United States. To be sure, his accomplishments were far from ordinary. Yet the myths that grew up around this extraordinarily popular president were built on the fact that he was a hero that Main Street America could identify with.

★

A Seasoned Performer

Ronald Reagan was sixty-nine when he became president, making him the oldest chief executive (Ike had left office at sixty-nine). Understandably, he no longer played football or baseball—even his golfing, so long neglected, became a rarity. Only in 1984, when he presided over the Olympics, did he relive his celebrity as a sports figure or, periodically, when he visited Eureka and waxed nostalgic about his college years (Ralph McKinzie, his football coach, was still alive—and coaching), or when he invited a group of athletes to the White House. On March 27, 1981, Reagan invited thirty-two vintage baseball stars to the White House for a nostalgic luncheon. "Nostalgia bubbles within me and I might have to be dragged away," he declared. According to baseball historian Bill Mares, Joe DiMaggio observed, "I think the president enjoyed the visit even more than we did." Three days later, Reagan was the victim of an assassination attempt.[31]

Yet, there were echoes—even more distinct reminders—of his sports career. Above all things, Ronald Reagan was a performer who failed to see how you could be in politics and *not* be a performer. "Ronald Reagan is by profession a performer," Robert Lindsey has written, "and it is the single most important point about him." The roles began in acting, but were strengthened by his athletic experiences—his lifeguarding, football playing, and sports announcing. As a sports announcer, he learned to intonate subtly. "He likes his voice, treats it like a guest," someone later wrote. He learned to charm with his voice using just the right intensities to describe action, to enable the listener to imagine the game or to sit in the box seats at Wrigley Field absorbing sights, sounds, and movements that came, not from the game, but from Reagan's fertile imagination. Certainly "the great communicator" honed his skills in the sound booth.[32]

Reagan's ability to rise above what was expected of him in public forums, especially when he spoke or debated on television, confounded friends and foes. When he debated Jimmy Carter in October 1980, he was able to play the ordinary guy as he had so often in the past. He appeared relaxed before the cameras, made his points, and then good naturedly ribbed Carter. "There you go again," Reagan's one-liner made after a Carter statement on Medicare, probably did more to humanize Reagan and to brand Carter as a deadly dull, policy wonk than any response he could have made. Brilliantly, Reagan won points by ridiculing his opponent as too well informed and not the ordinary guy that Reagan prided himself on being. He would soon put the polishing touches on the TV presidency that had begun in earnest with John Kennedy and then was used with varying degrees of effectiveness by Richard Nixon. The presidency finally had an occupant who actively—and effectively—used television to bond with the public.[33]

Much of the criticism leveled at Reagan—his "reign of errors"—began with Dutch Reagan, the sports figure. Just as he ad-libbed in his tryout at WHO or while the telegraph line was dead, he had a sense of when to adorn an ordinary event or how to tell a story to make his point. More than a few times, the stories morphed into pure fiction. His biographer Lou Cannon recalls a Reagan story of a football game in his hometown of Dixon against nearby Mendota. In the story, a player confesses to the referee of a rules infraction that he committed, thereby costing his team the game. "By the time I heard the story in the late sixties," Cannon writes, "the hero was anonymous and the game was no longer set in Dixon." The player who called the penalty on himself had actually dropped a pass. "The story should have been suspicious on its face," Cannon reflects, "but I did not realize what Reagan had done until on one trip he lapsed into the old Mendota version [against Dixon] of the tale and made himself the hero." Cannon came to believe that the story was untrue, no matter what version Reagan told. He also contends that Reagan "had long ago convinced himself of its verity."[34]

Reagan's small-town sports version of an urban legend!

★

Playing in Real Time

His crowning triumph—and near-death experience—came on March 30, 1981, when a psychotic young man, John Hinckley, improbably seeking to impress movie actress Jody Foster, fired six shots at the president. One hit Reagan and another felled his press secretary, Jim Brady. Now it was time for someone to be the lifeguard for Reagan. The lifeguard—secret service agent Jerry Parr—shoved the president into his limousine. "You sonofabitch, you broke my ribs," Reagan exclaimed, not realizing that he had been shot. Instead of going to the White House—in which case he would have choked to death on his own blood—Agent Parr directed the driver to George Washington Hospital. Unknown to Parr, the bullet lodged an inch from Reagan's heart; it was because he saw blood pouring from the president's mouth that the agent redirected the limousine. Remarkably, Reagan walked into the emergency room, then collapsed.[35]

A seriously wounded president is hardly a sports hero, but Reagan came close. Ronald Reagan played the role of his life, even greater than lifeguarding at Lowell Beach, or improvising for six minutes when the wire went dead in Des Moines, or, for that matter, whispering a deathbed message in *Knute Rockne, All American*. His ability to defy the odds again—as if throwing that crucial block—made him seem tough and yet sympathetic (no other president who had been shot by an assassin had ever survived). Despite his wounds, he was irrepressible. "Honey, I forgot to duck," he remarked when he saw his wife Nancy. To the doctors who prepared him for surgery, he quipped: "Please tell me you're all Republicans." Despite his lengthy convalescence, the assassination attempt enabled his administration to get its tax cuts through Congress. His boys—and girls—went out and "won one for the Gipper."[36]

Ronald Reagan's political career has many facets totally unrelated to sports—he was president of the Screen Actors Guild in the 1940s, governor of California, and an eloquent spokesman for Barry Goldwater in 1964. Yet the "speech," as his plea for Goldwater became known, was a *High Noon* scenario that Reagan specialized in. The bad guys (the liberals) were coming to kill the marshal and destroy law and order (conservative values). The Republicans were feeling down, and the breaks (Goldwater's shoot-from-the-hip remarks) were going against them. Reagan delivered the message to the electorate, but his team lost anyway.

In politics, George Gipp didn't die. Even after Reagan lost to Ford in 1976 at the Republican convention, he did not leave politics as he and others had predicted. It was as if the Gipper played on and on—far beyond the point when his eligibility ran out—a fifth year, a sixth . . . and, when he left the presidency, he didn't exactly disappear either—he simply faded into the California sunset.

*Captain George H. W. Bush of the Yale baseball team in his college
uniform accepting the ghostwritten memoirs of an ailing Babe Ruth at
Yankee Stadium in 1948. An outstanding athlete, Bush demonstrated his
athleticism as a combat pilot in World War II and took his Yale team to the
finals of the college world series. As president, the hyperactive Bush set out to be
an "Oyster Bay kind of guy," but health problems forced him to cut back on
his numerous sports during the last two years of his presidency. Courtesy
of George H. W. Bush Presidential Library, College Station, Texas.*

George H. W. Bush
TR Revisited

When George H. W. Bush moved into the White House in 1989, he had the portrait of Calvin Coolidge replaced with one of Theodore Roosevelt.

"I'm an Oyster Bay type of guy," Bush told a visitor. "Maybe I'll turn out to be a Teddy Roosevelt."[1]

The two men did have a number of similarities. Born to the manor, both delighted in outdoor sports, and both had distinguished war records. As Roosevelt went west after his first wife Alice died, Bush migrated to Texas following his graduation from Yale. Though Bush made his fortune and began his political career in his newly adopted state, he never entirely shed his eastern image. Like TR, he had a resume of appointive positions—most of them more prestigious than Roosevelt's. Both men had served as vice-president—Teddy's eight months far briefer than Bush's eight years.

For all TR's bluster and gusto, George Bush was probably a better athlete, and he came by it naturally. His father, Senator Prescott Bush, at six foot four, played first base for Yale's baseball team as well as competing in golf and hockey. Prescott Bush had a scratch—zero—handicap (his score of 65 was a record at the Cape Arundel golf course near the family's vacation home in Maine). While senator from Connecticut in the 1950s, he was a favorite golf partner of President Dwight Eisenhower. Bush's mother, Dorothy Walker Bush, was a nationally ranked tennis player as a teenager who continued to play into her eighties. Once, George as a boy confided to her that he was having trouble with his tennis game. "You don't have a game," she scowled. "Get out and work harder and maybe someday you will."[2]

Poppy (Bush's nickname) learned to boat and fish with his grandfather, George Herbert Walker, who had bought Walker's Point near Kennebunkport, Maine. Like the Bushes, Walker was originally from the Midwest and had been the heavyweight boxing champion of Missouri. "He was a tough father, a tough old bastard," one of his grandchildren once remarked. The tough old bastard was also a sportsman who thrived on gambling, horses, yachts, fishing—and golf. At the suggestion of his friend Dwight Davis (father of the Davis Cup), he donated the Walker Cup to the winners of an amateur golf match between the British and Americans.[3]

At Andover, Poppy Bush captained both the soccer and baseball teams. When he attended Yale after World War II, he played soccer and, like his father, was first baseman on the baseball team. For the two years that Bush played, Yale went to the finals of the college world series. With his flawless play at first base, Bush briefly attracted the attention of major league scouts.

With his athletic and combat resume, it comes as a surprise that Bush as a presidential candidate was regarded as a "wimp." As a candidate in the primaries in 1980 and as the Republican nominee in 1988, the "wimp" factor was a drag on his candidacy—and it persisted as an undercurrent running through the four years of the Bush presidency.

Six years after leaving office, Bush made a parachute jump to celebrate his seventy-fifth birthday.

These two images were too disparate to describe a single individual. So, why was Bush—not only a talented schoolboy athlete but also an enthusiastic and active former president—imprinted as a political figure with the scarlet letters WIMP?

★

Preppy Poppy: A Study in Contrasts

George Bush's elite origins, never a problem for the Roosevelts or Kennedys, turned into a presidential liability; critics scoffed that he succeeded because of privilege, or, in sports lingo, because he had been born on third base. Yet his athletic credentials were genuine. He exhibited them in his sense of confidence, in his athletic demeanor, and in the way he related to both friends and to the public. In order to understand Bush the hyperactive sportsman, we have to begin with the schoolboy, the combat aviator, and collegiate athlete.

In his senior year at Phillips Andover Academy, Poppy Bush compiled a remarkable athletic record. As captain of "one of the most astounding soccer teams" in school history (from the Andover yearbook), Bush played every minute of every game. In addition to its prep school rivals, Andover defeated the freshmen teams of four colleges—Yale, Harvard, Dartmouth, and Tufts— and archrival Exeter. That winter, Bush was manager of the basketball team; he had been a super sub his junior year, entering the game at critical moments to supply the needed power surge. In the spring of his senior year, he was captain of a scrappy baseball team which won more than it lost. "Captain Poppy

Bush excelled on first base in every game," the Andover yearbook recorded in 1942, "and was a powerful batter when at the plate." Though he was always a slick fielding first baseman, this would be one of the last times that he won kudos for his hitting.[4]

In the life of the Bush males, and like many young men of his social class, there was a seemingly natural progression from sports to money and finally to public service. In ranking classmates, did Andover's class of 1942 expect Poppy to be a superstar in politics, business, or, for that matter, in academics? Not in the least. A poll of his class at Andover showed that he was both popular and respected. But most likely to succeed? Bush's name wasn't even listed in the top four. Nor did he appear in other categories such as most intelligent, most mature, or even among those who had done most for Andover. Most surprising, he failed to make the top five in "politics."[5]

Bush was a so-so student, one of "best all-around fellows," one of the "most respected"—and, as strongly suggested by his rankings in the class poll, a gifted leader.[6]

Less than a month after he graduated from Andover, Bush enlisted in the Navy and was trained as a naval aviator. Still a teenager, he became skilled at landing his aircraft on carrier decks, a difficult task that required precise timing, coordination, and nerves of steel. According to Bush's biographer Herbert Parmet, Bush made 116 successful landings in 1944, including three emergency landings. It was the two landings that he didn't make on the carrier decks, but in the South Pacific, that were his most memorable—and showed an athleticism that rivaled the combat performances of Washington, Grant, and Theodore Roosevelt.

Two days after his twentieth birthday, Bush and his crew were on a bombing mission in the *Barbara* (named after his fiancée, Barbara Pierce) when a cloud of black smoke began pouring out of the plane. Realizing that his engines were about to give out, Bush maneuvered the plane for a crash landing in the ocean. Still carrying two thousand pounds of explosives, he made a perfect landing, the tail hitting the water before the fuselage and skimming to a stop. That he was able to do this, inflate a life raft, and row quickly away from a potential explosion required perfect skill, timing, and endurance. In a brief letter to his parents (mail was censored), Bush wrote that he had forgotten to tell them that "3 days ago I had to make a forced landing in the water. I was a bit nervous. It went off o.k. however. All three of us got out safely and into our raft. We were rescued by a destroyer."[7]

The crash landing during the Great Turkey Shoot of the Marianas, as this massive sea battle was known, was Bush's warm-up for a far more serious encounter with the enemy. As the Navy pushed toward Iwo Jima, Admiral Chester Nimitz targeted the radio towers in the Chichi Jima harbor. On September 2, 1944, Bush piloted his Avenger, the *Barbara Two,* to the harbor and, as the plane dived, he released eight bombs on the radio station. Immediately, the plane was slammed by antiaircraft fire. Smoke enveloped the cabin, and flames spread across the wing toward the fuel tank. He yelled for his crew to prepare to bail out. Climbing on the wing at 2,500 feet, he pulled his ripcord prematurely. As he jumped, his head hit the side of the plane, and the parachute tore on the rear of the plane.

Remarkably Bush survived the fall and began a frantic swim toward the life raft that had luckily fallen within swimming distance (he had forgotten to attach it to his lifejacket). He reached the sea pack and inflated his raft. "I then realized that I had overexerted myself swimming, because suddenly I felt quite tired [and nauseated from ingesting sea water]," he wrote his parents. "It was a hell of a job to keep water out of the raft. . . . At first I was scared that perhaps a [enemy] boat would put out from the shore which was very close by, but I guess our planes made them think twice about that." He was lucky to be alive (the other members of the crew were never found). Three hours later, one of the nearby American subs threw him a line and then, once he was aboard, dived to avoid the enemy.[8]

The war was nearly over for George Bush. He was transferred stateside and arrived home just before Christmas 1944. On January 6 he and his fiancée of two years, Barbara Pierce, were married. A descendant of President Franklin Pierce, Barbara, like her husband, came from a midwestern family with impressive athletic credentials. Her father, Samuel Walker, graduated Phi Beta Kappa while working his way through Ohio's Miami University. "He also earned nine letters playing on all the athletic teams," she wrote in her autobiography. He played in the backfield and was captain of the football team in his senior year. Like George Bush's father (who began in Columbus, Ohio), he had migrated to the East and entered business, becoming the head of McCall publications in New York. Barbara herself played a strong game of tennis, though unlike Dorothy, she did not often play with her husband or sons.[9]

Discharged from the military, George Bush immediately enrolled at Yale. His record at Yale nearly matched his father's. To the surprise of his prep school friends, he sped through Yale in less than three years, graduating Phi Beta Kappa in economics. He also resumed his athletic career, playing one year of soccer and two of baseball. Yale's baseball team in 1947 went to the college world series where it lost to the University of California—the Yale coach ordered an intentional walk to set up a double play, and the next hitter, future major league slugger Jackie Jensen, hit a home run. In his final year, Bush was elected captain of the Yale team. His flawless play at first base once again helped propel Yale into the finals of the college world series in Kalamazoo, Michigan, where it lost to Southern California. While Bush was outstanding in the field, he was a mediocre hitter—usually. "Once after a particularly strong day at bat in Raleigh, N.C. [against North Carolina State]," he recalled, "I was 3-for-5 with a double and a triple, and a scout approached me as I left the field. That was the first and last nibble I ever got from the pros." Three members of the postwar Yale teams ended up playing in the major leagues, so he might have been better than he let on.[10]

His finest moment on the baseball diamond came, not in Raleigh or New Haven, but at Yankee Stadium, in 1948. He stood in his Yale baseball uniform on the playing field to accept the memoirs of Babe Ruth, which the Bambino had donated to the Yale library. Ravaged by cancer, with only two months to live, the once great Sultan of Swat handed the manuscript of his autobiography to a future president of the United States.

Bush's athletics may have played a role in his selection to Skull and Bones, the secret society at Yale to which his father had belonged. To be sure, Bush had distinguished himself academically and in extracurricular activities. Aside from the secret bonding rituals, the selectivity of Skull and Bones brought together some of the wealthiest, most privileged, and most powerful men of his generation, a "stepping stone" as Bush's biographer Herbert Parmet describes it. "Lifelong friends were made in that inner sanctum," Parmet writes, "which, along with the base that had already been built as early as Andover, formed the core of a network for his future career."[11]

★

Bush and the Athletic Thing

George Bush left for Texas and raised enough money to participate in the postwar oil boom in West Texas. Through a family friend, Neil Mallon, he went to work for Dresser Industries, and in 1951 he and a friend formed their own oil exploration company. When a property was sold or leased, they retained the rights to receive royalties. Because the government exempted oil royalties from taxes, it was a bonanza at government expense, and easterners flocked to the oil fields as they had to the plains of North Dakota in Teddy Roosevelt's day. Bush launched his Zapata Oil Company and, by the age of thirty-five, was a millionaire. In 1959 he moved Zapata from Odessa, Texas, to Houston, where he became a prominent leader of the then outnumbered Republicans in what was still largely a Democratic state.

Bush's sports also moved into their postcollegiate phase. Soon after arriving in Texas, he wrote to his parents from Odessa. "Speaking of Golf—they have a course here. The other day Bar [Barbara Bush] and I were driving by and we saw four players seated on a small jeep-like vehicle with an umbrella raised over it [an early golf cart]. It was so damned hot they really couldn't have made it around without this car." When he traveled to New York, he and Barbara attended baseball games. His Uncle Herbie Walker had pitched in to finance the start-up New York Mets. Once he moved to Houston, Bush began to hunt quail on large ranches such as the Lazy F Ranch owned by the Farish family (Bush was a dead-eye skeet shooter—he'd learned from shooting clay pigeons from the back of an aircraft carrier during the war).[12]

He also got to know James Baker, a Princeton graduate and Houston lawyer. The two played tennis together at the Houston Country Club and jogged in Memorial Park, forging a relationship that later blossomed into a political partnership. "We went on to win two club championships," Baker wrote, "his strong volley and net game complementing my steady baseline game and ability to lob." Baker would later serve as Ronald Reagan's chief of staff and secretary of state under Bush.[13]

And, of course, there were the yearly trips to Kennebunkport. "I can't thank you enough for the wonderful two days at K'port," he wrote to Uncle Herby. "It was great fun from the cunner fishing to the links to the boat to the tremendous chow and to seeing the family."[14]

After an unsuccessful run for the Senate in 1964, Bush served two terms in Congress and then suffered another defeat in 1970 in a race for a Senate seat against Lloyd Bentsen, who would run with Michael Dukakis against the Bush-Quayle ticket in 1988. But Bush's national career began to take off, and once again he settled in the East (though still a legal resident of Texas). He served as Richard Nixon's ambassador to the United Nations, head of the Republican National Committee, envoy to China, and director of the CIA, all in rapid succession from 1971 to 1976. When Gerald Ford was choosing a vice-president in 1974, George Bush was a strong contender (Governor Nelson Rockefeller of New York was chosen instead).

Between 1977 and 1979, to prepare for the next presidential campaign, he canvassed for the state primaries and especially for the Iowa caucuses. "I think I'm putting on a little weight," he wrote in his campaign diary, "I got to run only once this week, and that was in Iowa." Still, he managed to keep up the hectic pace, and it paid off in the Iowa caucuses where he nosed out front-runner Ronald Reagan—ironically, since Reagan had begun as a radio sportscaster in Des Moines.[15]

Bush had high hopes coming into the New Hampshire primary. But a slipup in a debate at Nashua first saddled him with the "wimp" label. Initially set up to be a one-on-one between Bush and Reagan, the FCC ruled that a newspaper could not foot the expense of the debate. Instead, Reagan's campaign agreed to pay the cost and invited the others to participate. The result was a confusing event, delayed by half an hour and then abruptly opened up by Reagan and the "Nashua four," who walked with the frontrunner to the stage, followed by more confusion when the moderator ordered that Reagan's microphone be turned off. In one of his perfectly timed spontaneous acts, Reagan grabbed the microphone and famously said, "I'm paying for this microphone, Mr. Green." Though he got the name wrong (it was Breen), the Reagan response landed a body blow to Bush's strategy for a one-on-one debate with Reagan and cast Bush as the spoilsport. The conservative editor of the *Manchester Union Leader*, William Loeb, notorious for his attacks on presidential hopefuls, wrote that Bush looked "like a small boy who had been dropped off at the wrong birthday party."[16]

The primary season continued to be a downhill slide. Though he won in Michigan and outpolled Reagan in Pennsylvania, Bush fell far behind Reagan in delegate count. By Memorial Day, as Reagan approached the number needed to win the nomination, Bush faced the decision of whether to drop out or to continue in a losing cause.

The possibility still remained that Reagan might offer Bush the second spot on the ticket, but Bush hesitated. After having devoted so much money and energy to his campaign, he was reluctant to drop out. On a Saturday morning of a holiday weekend, he and his son Jeb (and a secret service agent) went jogging in Houston's Memorial Park. "After about two miles, Jeb and the security man had had enough," Herbert Parmet writes. "They fell by the wayside, as the candidate went on, completing the course."[17]

To complete the course politically, he realized, would embitter Reaganites and doom any possibility that he might get the vice-presidential nomination. Reluctantly, Bush folded up his campaign two days later on Memorial Day and went to work paying off the $400,000 in campaign debts.

Briefly, the Reagan campaign staff flirted with the possibility of selecting former president Gerald Ford as Reagan's vice-presidential candidate, but Ford quickly fell from favor. That left George Bush. In truth, Reagan didn't particularly like Bush—he too considered him a "wimp." Nancy Reagan also resented Bush's labeling of Reagan's economic plan as "voodoo economics." But the "wimp" was just too prominent to disregard; after all, he came in second in the delegate count.

Bush proved to be a loyal and hard-working vice-president—just as he had been the flawless first baseman. Indeed, his loyalty was such that it bred suspicion that he was involved with the Iran-Contra scandal, the low point of the Reagan presidency. Criticized by Democrats as a Reagan clone and by some conservatives as the button-down Ivy League wimp, he still managed to become the best-known contender for the 1988 nomination. Once again, he launched a jogging campaign in Iowa (which he lost to Robert Dole) and then proceeded to sop up the delegates. The photo of his opponent, Democratic nominee Michael Dukakis, waving from the turret of an M-1 tank as he circled the parking lot at General Dynamics helped to lift the lingering curse of the effete, buttoned-down Ivy Leaguer from his shoulders—if he was a wimp, he was running against a worse, more comical wimp (of course, the label applied to neither candidate).

One drag on Bush's candidacy proved to be his choice for vice-president, the youthful Senator Dan Quayle of Indiana (he looked much younger than his forty years). Handsome and athletic, Quayle's single major accomplishment might have been his golf game. An outstanding golfer with a seven handicap at DePauw University, Quayle led his golf team to an undefeated season. His college coach believed that he could have turned pro (Quayle modestly denied it). In a pro-am tournament, he nearly matched the massive drives of golfer John Daly, then in his prime—and he did defeat his partner in the Kemper Open, a touring professional. Shepherd Campbell and Peter Landau in *Presidential Lies* have written that "Dan Quayle . . . was beyond question the best golfer that the country had yet elected on a national ticket."[18]

If Quayle had been as strong a candidate as a golfer, Bush might have saved himself some embarrassments. Unfortunately, the vice-presidential debate with Senator Lloyd Bentsen branded Quayle as a "political lightweight." Asked why he was qualified to be vice-president, Quayle replied that he had as much experience in Congress as JFK did when he became a candidate. Quayle might have been able to defeat a touring pro, but he could not outdrive a legend. "Senator, I served with Jack Kennedy," Bentsen famously replied. "I knew Jack Kennedy. Jack Kennedy was a friend of mine. Senator, you're no Jack Kennedy."[19]

Richard Nixon, who had quit golf, told Quayle to stay off the golf courses. "The average guy is not on the golf course, the tennis court or a speedboat because he doesn't have one," Nixon counseled. Quayle disregarded the advice.[20]

Despite the Quayle handicap, Bush won decisively with 53 percent of the popular vote. But was Bush, the Republican, simply the "least worst"? In spite of his experience and proven abilities, Bush failed in the Ronald Reagan department of charm and enthusiasm. Bush was often described as "ungainly," and when he fell in a bowling alley on a campaign stop, it seemed to confirm the worst. "They kept showing it in slow motion, this spastic-looking fall when he's really such a good athlete," his daughter Dorothy said in anguish.[21]

After his election, the president-elect attempted to unveil the real George Bush, including his athletic interests and attainments. Writer George Plimpton, a Harvard graduate who could match elite credentials with the president-elect, visited the Bush clan at Kennebunkport to research an article for *Sports Illustrated*. Plimpton participated in the frenetic Bush athletics from doubles on the tennis court to the president-elect's passion for horseshoes. Reporting on his tennis, Plimpton stated that while Bush's backhand was almost nonexistent, "the net is where the President-Elect is utterly at home." Bush is, he wrote, "fast of reflex and aggressive and he will come in at every opportunity, even behind a second serve or a falling-leaf return."[22]

Plimpton pitched horseshoes at Walker's Point (a journalistic Walter Mitty, Plimpton in the 1960s played quarterback for the Detroit Lions in an exhibition game, hockey for the Boston Bruins, and even struck the gong for Leonard Bernstein's New York Philharmonic—all of which became raw material for books and articles). Why did the elite George Bush so gleefully play such a plebian sport as horseshoes? Plimpton reported that Bush had come up with the sport to keep the secret service agents amused. Now an aficionado, he planned to install his own pits on the South Lawn of the White House. Good-natured games between the Bush Whackers (the Bush clan) and the Agent Busters (the secret service agents) became standard fare.

Plimpton described the lexicon of Bush sportspeak. One of the favorite terms for golf and tennis was "power outage"—a weak serve or a limp-wristed putt. "Unleash Chiang," when a player called for a powerful serve, harkened back to the 1950s when Republicans demanded that Generalissimo Chiang Kai-shek be allowed to invade mainland China and vanquish the Communists. In horseshoes, SDI (strategic defense initiative) referred to a toss with a high arc—as if missiles were raining from outer space—and "ugly pit" meant that no horseshoes had landed in the pit. Other varieties of Bushspeak such as "Arnold Farmer" (a play on Arnold Palmer, meaning a mediocre golfer), "Vic Damone" (named after the singer, it was shorthand for a winning round or match), and "wedge city" (golf balls in the sand trap) might well have been Esperanto to outsiders.[23]

Plimpton also glimpsed the hyperactive approach to sports that would stamp the Bush presidency. Almost every sport was played on fast forward.

Take golf. "It's not what you make on a hole," the local golf pro at Cape Arundel Golf Club told Plimpton, "but how many ticks on the stopwatch it's taken you to hole out." Most golfers took four hours or more; not so the Bushes, who tore around the course in two-and-a-half hours or less. Of course, as Bush rose higher politically, fewer foursomes were permitted to impede their whirlwind rounds. "Cart polo," the pro called it. "We've done eighteen holes in two hours and twenty minutes."[24]

Bush's sports had a Kennedyesque flavor. Unlike the hobbled JFK, George Bush as president eagerly played tennis and golf as well as engaging in outdoor sports such as hunting and fishing, which Kennedy had seldom engaged in. Critics of Bush in 1988 said that he was running on his resume—the appointive offices he had held rather than on his accomplishments. Certainly the array of sports that he played had the character of, well, a resume. No question, the "Oyster Bay kind of guy" participated in more sports than any of his predecessors, including (possibly) Teddy Roosevelt.

As Herbert Parmet has noted, the articles on Bush's sports had a political subtext. Their purpose: to show that the president was an ordinary guy, to make him more likable than Bush the candidate, and to demolish what was left of his reputation as a wimp. Plimpton's article in *Sports Illustrated* as well as a front-page spread in the *New York Times* also introduced readers to George Bush, the fisherman, who pursued bluefish off Walker's Point as well as bonefish, tarpons, and sailfish in the waters off the Florida keys—and Bush, the dead-eye shot who hunted quail in Texas.[25]

Sports brought him into frequent contact with average Joes or Bobs. He had a local Kennebunkport pal, Bob Boilard, fishing adviser to the vice-president and now to the president. A few years earlier, while out on the water, Boilard, a retired Navy yard employee, turned to see a formidable flotilla coming his way. It included the Vice-President George Bush's Cigarette boat closest to him, a secret service boat close enough to speed to Bush's rescue, and a Coast Guard cutter hanging back a little. "It was quite a sight," Boilard recalled. "He called out and asked me what I was catching them [the bluefish] on." Bush followed Boilard out and soon Boilard was Bush's northeastern fishing guru. When Bush fished in Florida, he used a celebrity fishing guide, one hired by big names like Ted Williams and Jack Nicklaus.[26]

Sports Illustrated had a subhead to its story that suggested great things from a Bush administration—from its sports and, yes, from its statesmanship: "After pitching a ringer in November's election, George Bush will bring to the White House a rich athletic heritage." Certainly Bush's sporting pedigree and triumphs suggested an administration that was supple and talented, perhaps more than that headed by Ronald Reagan, the often forgetful senior citizen who would soon depart for California.[27]

The articles could not airbrush one attribute—a political and sporting resume like George Bush's almost had to come from a background of wealth and privilege. That meant prep schools, elite country clubs, and well-positioned friends. Could sports endear Bush to the American public—in a downward way—as Ronald Reagan had always found ways to charm those who were a notch or two above him?

★

The Decline—and Falls—of a Hyperactive Sportsman

In his *Sports Illustrated* article, George Plimpton asked the president-elect if he thought that his presidential duties would interfere with his sports. No, Bush responded, he didn't think so—sports were such an important part of his life.

For slightly over two years, Bush managed to carry off the "Oyster Bay thing." He jogged, golfed, fished, pitched horseshoes, and played tennis. "It's a Rare Sport That Bush Doesn't Like," the *New York Times* headlined in a front-page article about Bush and sports. Still another news story told of Bush abruptly deciding to change into his bright orange running pants and heading for Fort McNair for a jog, throwing the press corps into confusion.[28]

During Bush's presidential honeymoon with the press, a story in the *New York Times* ran with a banner headline, "Living the Life That Reagan Only Talked About," and referred to Bush as a "regular guy." "Now the public has a clearer picture," Maureen Dowd wrote, "having been exposed to his assurance, his athletic skills, and his all-American family."[29]

But sports and sporting vacations were double-edged swords. The Bush presidency would test whether it was still possible to be an Oyster Bay guy in the 1990s.

Teddy Roosevelt, who often had days with an empty desk calendar, undoubtedly found more time for sports than he would have in George Bush's day. Moreover, he seldom faced the barbs of the press. In 1990 Bush tried to spend his August vacation at Walker's Point only to find that the press expected him to be on duty. Saddam Hussein, the thief of Baghdad, had invaded and annexed Kuwait with its rich oil deposits. With the fourth-largest army in the world, Saddam dared his weak-kneed neighbors or Western powers to roll back his conquest of Kuwait.

Immediately after the invasion, Bush met with Prime Minister Margaret Thatcher of Great Britain, the "the Iron Maiden," at the Aspen Institute in

Colorado. Thatcher's close relationship with Ronald Reagan—and her own success in the Falklands War—made her unwilling to compromise. Later reports suggested that Mrs. Thatcher had stiffened Bush's spine ("remember, George, this is no time to go wobbly," so the Iron Maiden was reported to have said). Herbert Parmet believes that Bush had already made up his mind to oppose Saddam. Whatever went on within the meeting, Bush found time to sneak off for a brief interlude of trout fishing and hooked a brook trout. "Not a bad-sized little guy," Bush commented. "Fly-casting on a wet fly—it was fun." Reminders of FDR and Winston Churchill fishing before the Quebec Conference.[30]

A week later, Bush took off for his annual vacation at Kennebunkport. His advisers wondered if he was making a mistake in leaving Washington. Troops were departing for the Middle East. Americans were being detained in Kuwait and Iraq. Why wasn't Bush at his desk? Even Bush worried that his vacation might seem frivolous. He went out of the way to assure the press corps on *Air Force One* that he would remain in contact—and in control.

It wasn't much of a vacation, but rather an absence from Washington. As Jean Smith in *George Bush's War* has pointed out, Bush's vacation gave him wiggle room. "In a curious way, by going ahead with his vacation, Bush enhanced his control of the situation," Smith writes. "By leaving Washington, the president dissipated public pressure for an instant solution to the crisis." Bush was constantly on the phone to world leaders, including his friend, President Hosni Mubarak of Egypt. When Mubarak last visited Washington, the two presidents attended a Baltimore Orioles baseball game together. King Hussein of Jordan and the foreign minister of Saudi Arabia helicoptered into the Bush compound. With the weight of the Persian Gulf on his shoulders, Bush appeared weary.[31]

To make matters worse, the weather at Kennebunkport and the president's golf game were equally poor. "The course was so soaked," wrote Maureen Dowd, "that when his ball landed in a sand trap, the President had to ask Ken Raynor, the club's pro and his regular partner, if he should play it or count it as a water hazard and take a penalty stroke." He played even when it rained so hard that the course was closed to other golfers. "The President doesn't even seem to be having fun racing around the golf course," one Bush aide confided. "It's almost as though he's on some sort of driven mission." It was the frenetic Bush style of sports, as if he were a hyperactive child wanting to play with every toy.[32]

He fished a little, golfed a little, and worried a lot. He kept a telephone in his golf cart and in his Cigarette boat. During his absence from Washington,

Bush put together by telephone and negotiations the coalition that would liberate Kuwait in 1991.

The coalition's victory in the Persian Gulf War vindicated the president in the short term. Desert Storm proved to be a remarkably well-orchestrated operation, from the broad UN coalition to the careful military buildup. (Columnist Andy Valeur pointed out that golf, after all, glistened with patriotic terms such as "eagle" and hitting the ball "close to the flag.") Bush briefly enjoyed an 89 percent approval rating. So what if the president played a round of cart golf, jogged for two miles, and caught a bluefish while the Middle East was in turmoil? Maybe that was the way to manage a foreign crisis. Just as he had won at almost everything he ever attempted, George Bush put together a UN coalition, led by the American military, and thumped Saddam with a "Vic Damone."[33]

Unfortunately for Bush, the "splendid little war" proved to be the high point of his ratings in voter approval polls and of his presidential sporting image. That spring, while jogging at Camp David, the president complained of feeling tired and wisely suggested to his secret service agent to make arrangements to check with a physician. Normally, the sixty-six-year-old Bush jogged two or three miles a day. Two days before his episode at Camp David, he had participated in a number of vigorous activities—aerobics, weight lifting, basketball, and soccer—as part of the Great American Workout with actor Arnold Schwarzenegger, an event sponsored by the President's Council on Physical Fitness (of which "Conan the Barbarian" was the head).

Something was surely wrong. The president was suffering from irregular heartbeat, leading to rumors of a heart attack. The brief episode caused more headlines than headaches. Later in the month, his physicians diagnosed Bush's condition as an overactive thyroid or Graves' disease (oddly, Barbara Bush suffered from the same condition)—and radiation treatment had to be applied to his thyroid. Still, the media wondered if the stress of the Persian Gulf War might have contributed to his medical problem. Media-wise, his workouts suddenly appeared to be more damaging than helpful in much the same way as Jimmy Carter's had.

But Bush did not intend to let this small health problem interfere with his athletics. By the end of May, he resumed a full athletic regimen—in spite of his doctors' advice. At Kennebunkport over Memorial Day, he went on two fishing expeditions and golfed as if he were on the pro tour. After church, he reeled off twenty-seven holes of golf—then played with grandchildren and pitched horseshoes. "Tired of looking tired," the headlines read, "Bush relaxes like mad." He had lost ten pounds and did look tired. While half-blind, rheumatic TR could scramble anonymously in Rock Creek Valley, Bush was scrutinized daily by the White House press corps. Though he was in better shape than Teddy at fifty, the Bush athletic presidency as monitored by the media reflected badly on the state of his administration.[34]

Hit by a post-Reagan recession, Bush's approval ratings dropped precipitously. Conservative Republicans were livid when he agreed to an omnibus tax bill that went against his promise to resist higher taxes in 1988—"read my lips," as he had said in the campaign. Once, confronted by reporters while jogging, he responded pointing to his partner, "read my hips," which certainly seemed to mock his sacred pledge.[35]

In January 1992 his health once again made the national—and international—news when he became sick to his stomach at a state dinner in Tokyo. Not only that, he threw up on the Japanese prime minister who was sitting next to him. Worse yet, the momentary horror of the American president collapsed on the Japanese prime minister's lap was captured on videotape and appeared on the nightly news in the United States. While Bush was rushed back to his quarters, Barbara Bush carried off the toasts flawlessly. Burton Lee, Bush's physician, concluded that "she [Barbara Bush] took over and gave her great performance that saved the day."[36]

All of this was part of an eleven-day, four-nation tour of Asia. A day before in Singapore, Bush appeared tired, barely able to stay awake at a banquet. He had already played tennis with the Emperor Akihito only hours before he went to dinner. Realizing that the president was ill, Dr. Lee warned him not to attend, but Bush was as stubbornly determined as if he were playing cart golf in the rain—he was certain that he could see it through. What alarmed the Japanese and the Americans was no more than intestinal flu. The image of a stricken Bush at the banquet was far worse than a brief if violent malady.

At Kennebunkport that spring, the president seemed to have curtailed his activities, taking a power walk down the beach. A sore right hip had forced him to abandon jogging. "Mr. Bush under doctor's orders to get rest," the New York Times reported, "said he hoped to have Walker's Point fixed up by summer." (A hurricane had badly damaged the buildings and seafront.) In a campaign year, it might not have been politically savvy to vacation in an upscale resort town, especially when many voters were still suffering from the economic downturn. During his walk, he kept up his usual "patter through his panting to show that the First Sportsman was unfazed by the exercise"—even though his hip was still hurting. "Whether the vacation in the upscale setting might damage him politically in the fall," the Times mused, "would turn largely on how much the voters blame the President for their hard times."[37]

Appearing at major league baseball's All-Star Game in July 1992, Bush was booed. The boos were reminiscent of Herbert Hoover's experience at the World Series in 1931 when the voters began to chant, "we want beer." Only Hoover, Truman, and Bush suffered such ignominy while watching the "Presidents' Game."[38]

Apparently, the booing did reflect dissatisfaction with the economy. In November the voters handed Bush and Quayle their walking papers. Biographers and editors later speculated that Bush's lackluster and passive campaign—in marked contrast to his energetic campaigning in 1988—was related to his thyroid condition. Far from becoming an "Oyster Bay type of guy," Bush's campaign to match TR's sporting presidency failed to materialize. The bouts with Graves' disease and intestinal flu, so widely reported and viewed, undermined his hyperactive sports regimen—and made his sporting image seem more of a liability than an asset.

Not that Bush abandoned sports. He boasted to George Plimpton that he and the Kennebunkport club pro had played the course in one hour and twenty minutes. If Prescott Bush held the course record for the fewest strokes, his son held it for the fewest minutes taken for an eighteen-hole round.

When Plimpton and his son visited "the country squire" (Plimpton's words) at Camp David early in his term, they participated in a smorgasbord of sports. One sport that was not reported in the *Sports Illustrated* article was tiddlywinks, a Bush family favorite. Plimpton wrote: "The president agreed instantly—with no sense that he was being asked to indulge in a game that could hardly be called . . . well, *presidential*. He oversaw setting everything up. The table had to be the right height. . . . A blanket produced and spread over the table. Various glasses and cups into which to chip the little disks, or winks, were brought in by the stewards and discarded as too tall or too shallow."[39]

The president and Plimpton lost both games to Jonathan Bush, a brother, and thirteen-year-old Taylor Plimpton.

"Not my day, I guess," the president said to Plimpton. "I let you down."[40]

And, not his year, 1992. After he left the White House, Plimpton asked Bush if he missed the presidency—and if so, what?

"The decision-making, the actual involvement, and trying to make things happen," he said. "I like that. I liked that a lot." After the election, he had gone to Maine. To play cart golf or fish in his Cigarette boat? No. "In Maine, I just sat there and watched the tide come in and go out."[41]

In other words, the sports had gone hand-in-hand with the adrenaline surge from calling world leaders, orchestrating a coalition in the Persian Gulf, and even engaging in an ill-fated campaign against Bill Clinton and Al Gore.

Bush did adjust to a less active role. He enjoyed the trips to Fenway Park and an occasional celebrity golf tournament. Power walks and cart golf continued after his presidency. Unlike TR, he did not go big-game hunting in Africa or explore in the Amazon Basin. Nor did he use the post-presidency to lobby for the environment. Yet he did skydive, no mean feat for a seventy-five-year-old.

George H. W. Bush, now referred to as Bush Number One or the first Bush, came from a winning pedigree; he exhibited athleticism of a high order in his fighter pilot days as well as in the more conventional role as Yale first baseman. High-speed golf, tenacious horseshoes, consistent jogging, aggressive tennis, fishing with the best, hunting, even tiddlywinks. He played most of the games that twentieth-century presidents have played—and then some—with his own inimitable idiom and flavor.

Move over, TR.

VI

New Players, Old Games

President Bill Clinton putting with "Buddy" on his private putting green on the South Lawn of the White House. Clinton had a passion for golf usually associated with Republican presidents. His Republican opponents and golf purists criticized his mulligans and billigans as well as scores that just didn't add up. Critics suggested that his golfing character was a mirror image of his behavior in the Monicagate-impeachment episode. Courtesy of William Jefferson Clinton Presidential Library, Little Rock, Arkansas.

22

Bill Clinton
Oh, How He Played the Game

Bill Clinton's sports stirred more controversy, provoked more curiosity, caused more disdain, and even created more humor—surely more than George Bush and Gerald Ford, possibly more than Richard Nixon, and definitely more than Dwight Eisenhower.

A big man at six foot three and 230 pounds, he was taller and heavier than his predecessors, including George Bush and Gerald Ford. He could drive a golf ball 300 yards—or more—and ran eight-minute miles when he jogged. His bowling average was 230, and he had played basketball and rugby at Oxford.

But was he a natural athlete? Not by a long shot! His athletic ability tended to be an outgrowth of his ability to finesse the rules, the scores, and his own image. A test case occurred in 1995 when President Clinton played a round with two of the best presidential athletes in history. That collector of presidential golfers, comedian Bob Hope, corralled Clinton, George Bush, and Gerald Ford to play in the same foursome (actually a fivesome) for Hope's pro-am tournament. In the interviews before teeing off, Clinton remarked to announcer Dick Enberg, "We are as nervous as cats." Clinton had just spent a half hour warming up on the practice tee, something he seldom did.[1]

Measured by golf handicaps, Clinton played better golf than either of the former presidents. He listed his handicap as 11 while his senior partners had handicaps of 18. Of course, Clinton made no secret that he played by his own rules. He took mulligans or "billigans," as they were sometimes called—extra shots when he didn't like his drives or even his approach shots and sometimes just because he felt like it. He normally practiced while he was on the fairways, a violation of rule 7-2 of the United States Golf Association. He also took long gimmes, putts that his partners conceded to him. These gifts from Bill to himself or by his partners to the president were based on the assumption that he could make these putts, by no means as certain as he made them seem.

On that day, there would be no mulligans and certainly none off the fairway—gimmes, well, that depended on the other players.

The presidential golf match was clearly a landmark for televised presidential sports. It was nearly half a century, after millions of television antennas sprouted across America and thirty years since televised sports had become a staple of American life. Seldom had presidents allowed themselves to be televised playing golf or, for that matter, any sport. Here, on network TV, were three presidents playing a game once regarded as frivolous. One might call it the unveiling of the sports presidency.

But was it a victory for the youngest of the three, the man then occupying the Oval Office? Clinton won in only one category—he was the only one who didn't hit a spectator. Bush hit two (one required ten stitches across her face and another was hit in the rump). The seventy-nine-year-old Ford grazed the pinkie of one bystander. Clinton, fortunately, missed the onlookers, but he didn't win the match. Bush won a squeaker, 92 to Clinton's 93 (not such a great score for a golfer with an 11 handicap).

A stickler for putting every putt, Ford shot a score of 100. Scores and injuries aside, the match was more comical—or entertaining—than the ever-so-clever newspaper headlines were able to convey. It took the three presidents six-and-a-half hours to play eighteen holes; the speedy Bush and the elderly Ford were perhaps thrown off their game a little by the 91-year-old Bob Hope who slowed the pace. In addition to the shots that hit spectators, all three of the players hit a number of balls out of bounds. In spite of Ford's rectitude, there were reports of the presidents giving each other generous gimmes to speed up play. Clinton, facing reelection in 1996, even charged into the galleries to greet his constituents. ,

Getting beat by George Bush didn't really hurt Clinton's image or his ego. After all, both Bush and Ford were known for their athletics—and Republican presidents were notorious for spending a lot of time on well-groomed courses playing with corporate executives and celebrity golfers.

During their student days, both Ford and Bush played intercollegiate sports at a high level. Clinton played the saxophone. The press criticized Republican presidents for the time they spent at plush country clubs playing tennis or golf, not to mention skiing or flying off to crown national champions (as Nixon did in 1969 at the Texas-Arkansas game). Somehow, Bill Clinton never faced the criticism normally leveled at Republicans when they hit the links, which he did even more often than Ford or Bush. Call it personality or political savvy—as of 1995, Bill Clinton was, like Ronald Reagan, a Teflon president, at least on the links. So far, his golfing had not become an issue.

Who would have guessed that the fat boy (his words) who won a band scholarship rather than an athletic scholarship would not be called a wimp or that he would end up as the most obsessive golfer, the most knowledgeable spectator, and possibly the most dedicated jogger of all Democrats occupying the White House? Or that, during his presidency, the South Lawn would then incorporate a practice green and jogging track?

But then who would have divined in 1995 that those gimmes and billi- gans of President William Jefferson Clinton would hint at the dark side of his presidency?

★

A World-Class Spectator

Few stories emerge of Bill Clinton's youthful athletics. Growing up in Hot Springs, Arkansas, he caddied and taught himself to play on the local courses but gave it all up at sixteen. Though he played church league basketball, even at his height he didn't play high school ball. In fact, he played no varsity sports in high school or college.

As a student at Georgetown University, he had had little time and little in- terest in sports. The games that he normally played had something to do with politics. Clinton joined the games of touch football popularized by the Ken- nedy clan; unlike JFK, he was better known for his skill in arguing the rules than for throwing or catching passes. When he decided to try for the pres- tigious Rhodes scholarship, he had to assemble a barebones sports resume (Rhodes scholars were expected to be well rounded). As his biographer David Maraniss has pointed out, Clinton's occasional bowling seemed a bit plebian for a tweedy Oxfordian. So he "maneuvered" himself into the chairmanship of Student Athletic Commission, which rounded out his resume and, along with his superior academic record, won him the coveted scholarship.[2]

At Oxford, the gregarious Clinton took time to go out for basketball and made the second team. "Which shows you how weak basketball was at Ox- ford," he modestly—and accurately—pointed out. He recalled that he was overweight and slow. "It was a period in my life when I didn't have the disci- pline to show up and do the practice," he reflected, then adding, "What I really liked was rugby."[3]

He went out for rugby—and, here too, he made the second team. His en- thusiasm, according to Maraniss, made more of an impression than his rugby skills. "Once he flattened a guy who didn't have the ball," the team's star told

Maraniss. "When the ref said 'you don't do that,' I had to explain, 'Sorry he's from America where you can flatten anyone.'" Clinton once received a concussion playing against Cambridge. Since there were no substitutions, the coach told him to get back on the playing field. "I asked what I was supposed to do since I was dizzy," Clinton recalled. "He said, 'Just get in somebody's way.'" Clinton concluded: "I think it's a terrific game. I just loved it."[4]

In 1969 Clinton and a fellow Rhodes Scholar rented a short-wave radio to listen to the Arkansas-Texas game, dubbed the "game of the century" (after which President Richard Nixon crowned the Longhorns). Years later, when Clinton was running for Congress, this so-called game of the century re-emerged as a campaign issue. According to his opponent, a photo existed of Clinton perched in a tree above the stadium—in some versions, stark naked—among antiwar demonstrators. "In 1979, my first year as governor, and ten years after the Game," Clinton recounts in his memoirs, "when I was answering questions at a high school assembly . . . a student asked me whether I had really been in that tree." When the governor asked how many had heard the story, the hands of half the students and three-quarters of the faculty shot up. This patently false story was the prelude to the many rumors that would dog Clinton during his campaign for the White House and his eight years in the presidency.[5]

The tree incident aside, sports—initially—had little to do in shaping Clinton's adult political career. He never played or coached football nor was he known for his enthusiasm for the outdoors. Nor did he worship a coach who served as a mentor, imposing strict discipline and instilling a code of values. Nevertheless, he remained a sports fan, both in terms of enthusiasm and knowledge.

When he taught law briefly at the University of Arkansas, he cultivated the basketball coach, Eddie Sutton. "In Arkansas when I was a kid," he recalled, "everybody loved football. Basketball didn't really catch on until I was a young man, not until Eddie Sutton came up and decided to coach basketball. He and his wife became friends of Hillary's and mine, and I learned most of what I know about basketball from him."[6]

Twenty years later, Bill Clinton became the first president to attend college basketball games. He was a diehard Arkansas Razorback fan who seemed to know everything about the game. "He has taken to basketball like most subjects," wrote Alexander Wolff in *Sports Illustrated*, "with a thoroughness that's dazzling, perhaps a little eye-glazing." Wolff noted that Clinton broke down the points that Georgia and Arkansas scored off of turnovers as he watched a tape of the game in his bedroom at the White House. Clinton pointed out the

Razorbacks' mastery of the half-court trap in the final minutes of the game. "As the tape continued," Wolff wrote, "the President's . . . command of X's and O's astonished several White House aides who had never seen him turn his attention to this particular subject."[7]

Whether on the bench or in the stands, his attentive and nimble mind could see beyond mere shots and scores—not unlike a political strategist who must look beneath the surface and beyond the present. Occasionally, his sports appeared frivolous, as when he played hearts with the White House staff. John F. Harris in *The Survivor: Bill Clinton in the White House*, describes his "Bush Sr." cart-golf approach to cards. "Let's deal 'em up," he ordered his staff when he had the time and the partners to play a game. Aboard a helicopter, on his way from the White House to Andrews Air Force Base, "Clinton was always trying to set a new record for the number of hands that could be played during the chopper's ten-minute hop, as the cards were picked up and thrown down in a frenzy." Once on board *Air Force One*, Harris relates, Clinton would continue the games whether on domestic or international flights. "Clinton could remember the cards in his hand and everyone else's, and the precise sequence in which they had been played," Harris comments. And Bill frequently took the players to task for misplaying their hands. All of this might occur while the president was reading a book or even talking on the phone to heads of state.[8]

As with basketball, though, Clinton rarely played the game; rather, he was a politically active "player." Take college football, for example. He once operated as the twelfth man on the Arkansas team during a postseason crisis. When Clinton was attorney general of Arkansas in 1979, Coach Lou Holtz suspended three Razorback players—the three best offensive players—for an episode that involved a woman in the football dormitory. The players never faced criminal charges, but Holtz suspended them because they violated his "do right" rule. Arkansas was playing in the Orange Bowl against Oklahoma, and the absence of the offensive trio undermined the Razorbacks' odds of winning.

Nevertheless, Clinton backed Holtz when the players went to court seeking reinstatement. For Holtz and Clinton (who planned a run for governor in 1980), the case was difficult because the players were black and the woman was white. From Florida, where he had gone to see the game, Clinton orchestrated the defense. Holtz's predicament grew worse when nine other players refused to play unless the three were back on the team. Clinton recruited a member of his staff, a friend of Hillary, to argue against reinstatement. After spending several days on the phone with the attorney and athletic director

Frank Broyles, the Razorback predicament was resolved. The three players withdrew from the lawsuit, and the team members dropped their boycott. "With smothering defense and a record-setting 205 yards rushing from reserve back Roland Sales," Clinton proudly writes in My Life, "the Razorbacks routed Oklahoma 31-6, perhaps the biggest and certainly the most unlikely victory in the storied history of Arkansas football."[9]

As with his other sports friendships, nonathlete Clinton was also proud that he got to know a nationally known coach like Lou Holtz. "I was grateful that this bizarre episode gave me the chance to know him well," he writes. "He's brilliant and gutsy, perhaps the best on-the-field coach in America."[10]

The Razorback victory on New Year's Day 1980 made up for the defeat by Texas in 1969 when Clinton was in London. And this time no one could say he was in a tree overlooking the stadium.

But it was Arkansas basketball that created the sports thrills during his presidency.

In 1994 Clinton watched his team go the distance in March Madness, as the postseason NCAA basketball tournament is known. Coach Nolan Richardson led Arkansas to a victory over Duke, 76-72, in the NCAA championship game. In the tradition of Richard Nixon, Clinton visited both locker rooms. Consoling Duke, he readily agreed to shake hands with Coach Mike Krzyewski's players. The "master of spin," both a political and basketball skill, was able to congratulate, console, and do a little politicking all at the same time.

What about his own sports? He had begun jogging at Georgetown in the 1960s, initially to keep off the fat and make himself a little more athletic before the Rhodes competition. That continued. Hillary Clinton played tennis, and Bill tried to learn the game. "But I just wasn't very good at it," he told George Plimpton. "Hillary's always been a better tennis player; she's quit playing, which I think is a great mistake, because she has a gift for it. I've been trying to get her to start playing again."[11]

Did Hillary play golf? A photo of the president and first lady in 1995 had a caption: "President Clinton drove a golf cart yesterday as the First Lady Hillary Rodham Clinton walked alongside after they played nine holes of golf in Arlington, Virginia." In fact, Hillary took golf lessons several times. She played with Bill at his urging on Martha's Vineyard in 1994. She dabbled at putting. So, did the photo in 1995 indicate that Hillary was a golfer in the making? Not really. Hillary simply didn't enjoy golf. It was enough that she realized that her husband needed golf as personal and presidential therapy.[12]

Bill resumed playing golf when he returned to Little Rock as attorney general and governor. He played at the Country Club of Little Rock with Hillary's associates in the Rose Law Firm, Webster Hubbell (Clinton's attorney general, who was later convicted and jailed for "billing irregularities" in his law practice) and Vince Foster, whose suicide was forever coupled with the flood of allegations against the pre-presidential and presidential Clinton.

In the 1980s, he frequently took part in the Renaissance Weekend at Hilton Head, South Carolina, where the nation's best and the brightest gathered around the New Year holiday. Besides the distinguished panels and discussions, the more than a thousand invitees could participate in an array of sports. Clinton golfed, played touch football and volleyball, and bicycled with Hillary and his young daughter Chelsea. For Clinton, politics was never far away. Here at Hilton Head, the governor of a small southern state could get to know members of state legislatures and Congress who would help him in his bid for the presidency in 1992.

★

Presidential Sports

When William Jefferson Clinton took the oath of office in 1993, he first made news with his jogging. In a phrase, he jogged religiously. Not only did he run for exercise, but his jogs also suggested that he was running for more than exercise. "Politicians find jogging with Clinton is no stroll in the park," the *New York Times* headlined. Clinton jogged eight-minute miles, a pace that exhausted those who were merely looking for photo ops. "It's a status thing," Representative Bob Filmer of California declared. "I thought there'd be some interesting pictures I could use to talk about in a fun way with my constituents." Filmer dropped out after a mile.[13]

Jogging with the president even became an international attraction. In Seoul, President Kim Young-sam insisted on joining Clinton for his morning jog through the streets of Seoul. Out of deference to his jogging partner, the president substituted a jogging suit for his usual baggy shorts. At home, the president used jogging as an opportunity to schmooze with political and military figures. Before a budget vote, he ran with Senator Bob Kerry of Nebraska discussing economic policy and Vietnam. He joined General Barry McCafferty on a run in Vancouver, Canada, to smooth over strained relations between the military and the White House.

Friends of Bill (FOBs) built him a $30,000 running track on the South Lawn of the White House, which he used when he had to stay near home. "The track is very good in bad weather," the president commented. "It's also very good for me at night or after dark, if I want to run." Otherwise he took secret service agents on less predictable routes around the capital.[14]

Clinton had grown up following baseball when the St. Louis Cardinals were the closest team to Arkansas. When he married Hillary (a native of the Chicago area), he became a fan of the Chicago Cubs—a popular though star-crossed franchise. When in 1995 he intervened in a major league baseball strike, most Americans were unaware of Clinton's interest in baseball. The players had gone on strike the previous August, prematurely ending the season and eliminating the World Series. The owner-player deadlock persisted into the new year and threatened to eliminate spring training, normally beginning in February.

"Americans have been living without baseball for too long," Clinton announced and, in February, he insisted that both parties end the strike. A more compelling reason for his interest was that spring training camps were located in two politically vital states: Florida and Arizona. Each would suffer economically if spring training succumbed to the strike. But probably the most important, vote-rich Florida was key to Clinton's reelection campaign in 1996.[15]

Clinton became the first president to intervene in a labor dispute involving sports. "Clinton [Casey] at the Bat," read the New York Times headlines. "At least baseball has finally returned to Washington," Clare Smith wrote. The Washington Senators had moved to Texas in 1971 becoming the Texas Rangers (owned by Governor George W. Bush of Texas—among others—when Clinton stepped to the plate). Briefly the president had brought major league baseball back to the nation's capital, even if only for high level talks.[16]

Clinton summoned the mediator, Bill Usery, along with representatives of the club owners and players to the White House. For five hours, the owners and players were held "hostage" at the White House—all to no avail. "I have done everything I could to change the situation," Clinton declared in frustration.

Next, he would recommend that Congress pass legislation mandating binding arbitration to settle the strike. "It was not exactly the spanking the two sides deserved," wrote George Vecsey in the New York Times. "Instead it was a lecture on separation of powers."[17]

To his dismay, Congress refused to field the ball—sports simply wasn't a winning issue when it came to running for reelection to Congress. Soon after, the game returned to the ball parks; the strike ending before it eroded salaries and gate receipts. The National Labor Relations Board issued an injunction against the owners, just in time for spring training and the start of the 1995 season. Once again, a president had learned, as Teddy Roosevelt had in 1905, that sports disputes did not lend themselves to presidential intervention in the same way that other national crises did.

★

Golf as a Presidential Looking Glass

Bill Clinton loved golf. He played at least twice a week in good weather and bad. Like Woodrow Wilson, he played in chill, rain, and sleet. Not only did he have a practice green installed on the South Lawn, but he also used the green as if it were the first hole on a White House course. Sometimes he and a friend would hit long, approach shots across the lawn toward the practice green as if they were playing the final shots of the hole on a conventional course. He avoided Camp David because there was no eighteen-hole golf course there.

He wasn't a bad golfer. When he walloped a drive, his ball sometimes flew 300 long yards off the tee. Occasionally, as in the three presidents' round, they flew long and out of bounds. His weakness was his chips or delicate shots from just off the green, which might scud along the ground either going only a few yards (chili-dips) or tear across the green and into the same approach area on the other side. All golfers, except those with really low handicaps, periodically face this problem. In other words, Bill Clinton was a so-so golfer who claimed to have a lower handicap than he could demonstrate. But he was improving so rapidly, he asserted, that he would soon break 80. That would make him a 7 or 8 handicapper—a very good golfer indeed.

Clinton was fun to play with—most of the time. Like JFK, he kept up a constant, entertaining banter. According to golf historian Don Van Natta Jr., who played a round with him, he could talk endlessly about the hundreds of old clubs that he owned or used (he was given a putter that once belonged to President John Kennedy). He described playing with Arnold Palmer, Jack Nicklaus, Greg Norman, well-known professional Amy Alcott (who, he never stopped telling, shot thirty-three holes in his company), and Michael Jordan. He could describe rounds played years before in microscopic detail. "On the golf course," Van Natta wrote in *Sports Illustrated*, "he was as easily distracted as he was in the Oval Office, his mind zigzagging from subject to subject."[18]

There were also flashes of temper when he messed up. Usually, he turned it inward on himself. "Billy, Billy, Billy," he railed. The anger quickly disappeared with a decent shot, but he continued to talk to himself—or to the ball ("whoa, Momma"). Clinton's rounds were the opposite of Bush's cart golf. Van Natta called it a "plodding pace." On one Memorial Day weekend, Clinton's party "bumped" the other foursomes off the Robert Trent Jones course in northern Virginia, playing very slowly, thoroughly enjoying themselves, and roadblocking the club members. A presidential prerogative perhaps, but irritating to club members and political fodder for Clinton-haters.

One reason for Clinton's sluggish play was the number of shots that he took. For starters, he sometimes carried nineteen clubs (fourteen allowable). Worse yet, he used those clubs to take a few practice shots on the fairway, which is strictly against the rules. And bending the rules even further, instead of the occasional freebie that weekend golfers sometimes take on the first hole, he hit those mulligans from the fairway as well as off the tee, sometimes repeatedly. Then, by taking the best of the two or three or more balls that he hit, he surely improved his score. In fairness to Clinton, however, he was equally generous to his golfing partners. To Vernon Jordan, after Jordan's ball wound up behind a tree, Clinton said, "You've got to get a good shot on the first tee, Vernon." Then there were the short garden-variety gimmes and long Clinton-variety grand-slam gimmes. The comeback kid made his comebacks on the putting green and not because he was a great putter. Normally, he played with one partner who was a better golfer—or at least a better putter. When one of those FOBs made their putt, Clinton picked up his own ball as if the hole were over for him too. Of course, the president recorded the strokes on his card, added the total, and then presented it as his actual score—and these 80s and 82s established his handicap or, more precisely, his pronounced status as a golfer. All in a day's work.[19]

If accounts of golf with Bill were accurate—there's no reason to think they weren't—almost any putt, chip, or even a long approach to the green was a potential gimme. But to be fair, while invoking presidential privilege, he always included his partners. Rick Reilly, a columnist for *Sports Illustrated* who played with the president, admitted that he wasn't opposed to the freebees— Clinton didn't have to invoke "presidential privilege." One of their playing partners was an excellent golfer who normally would not give "downhill, side-hill, six footers to an opponent, but I'm sure he wasn't eager to get audited for the next twenty years," Reilly wrote.[20]

Then there was the highly public drama of the president's struggle to break a magic golfing number of 80 (remember Richard Nixon retiring his clubs for good with a 79?). At the Coronado Golf Course in San Diego, Clinton announced that he had finally broken 80, actually, a 78. "I was hot. I was smoking 'em," he modestly told reporters. Then he added more modestly: "Even a blind pig finds an acorn sometimes."[21]

Then the unofficial recount began. It appeared that the president did bend a few rules. He hit two balls on the first tee—he hadn't practiced. He took a gimme on another hole, then putted it anyway, missed, and gave himself the conceded putt. And how about the other holes where no one was watching? That magic moment seemed highly political, designed to make news at the beginning of a presidential campaign. Again, the number 80 seemed to hang like an albatross around Clinton's neck. In 1997 the president reported that he had scored a 79 at the Farm Neck course on Martha's Vineyard. Despite the skepticism, none of his partners or sidekicks contradicted him—they formed a remarkably closed-mouthed bunch. Anyone who watched him on the first tee saw him take three shots—mulligan and billigan. Yet he denied that he had played "Billy Ball." Asked if he played the ball where it landed, playing partner Vernon Jordan wisely nodded. General Electric chairman Jack Welch was equally unwilling to testify.

By this time, the whole world—at least those who understood golf—knew that Clinton stood accused of playing fast and loose with the rules. Why had he never broken 90 when he played in a tournament, that is, played by the rules? The Republicans and Bob Dole, at a loss for big issues to campaign on, accused Clinton of exaggerating his scores, of taking mulligans and billigans, gimmes, and the whole enchilada—the first time golf scores had ever become a political issue.

To be sure, it was "slick Willie" all over again. Did it matter? Not to the American public, which gave him a thumping victory over Senator Bob Dole (who couldn't play golf because of war injuries which left him with a mis-shapen hand). The economy was humming, and the nation was truly at peace for the first time in fifty years. Who cared what President Clinton did on the golf course? After Bush's quirky Boy Scout sporting persona, Clinton's roguish behavior made for a refreshing change—for a while, that is.

After his reelection, Clinton suffered an improbable, quasi-golf injury when he fell down some stairs and tore his quadriceps tendon. Staying with his old pal Greg Norman, a touring pro from Australia nicknamed the "Shark," Clinton had come to play in Norman's pro-am tournament. He was on crutches for six weeks following surgery. Then came Monicagate and all the "I told you so's." To those who followed his golf game, his way of addressing the charges ("I did not have sex with that woman, Miss Lewinsky") had a familiar—and hollow—ring. When he admitted that he had lied, Clinton's golf critics merely clucked louder. The sleazy, immoral, presidential behavior that the whole country had to bear witness to seemed part and parcel with his approach to golf.

Clinton found few people who sympathized with his predicament, leading up to his impeachment trial. In the meantime, he developed a shank (whereby the golfer hits the ball nearly at right angles to his target). The Ken Starr shank, as it was dubbed (after the independent counsel who sought to dig up dirt on all the Clinton mischief), took the spotlight away from Clinton's golf. Columnist Maureen Dowd reported that one Sunday evening, the president "was hitting balls in a gray drizzle at a suburban country club, his white sports hat dripping wet." She added: "The most gregarious of presidents was playing solo."[22]

As Clinton seemingly shrugged off the impeachment, still more questions arose when the president left office. The shower of presidential pardons in the final hours of his presidency reminded the Clinton golf critics of all those mulligans and gimmes. Again, the question arose, Was the president merely being generous or was he bending the rules in a self-serving—and unpresidential—way? Of course, if he could pardon bad golf shots, he had every reason to pardon and seek to rehabilitate those who were friends, donors, or political associates who had, so to speak, hit their personal drives out of bounds or into impossible lies.

Nothing surpasses golf as offering a unique and crystalline view into presidential character and thus into presidential administrations. Clinton, a highly competitive golfer whose self-promoted image surpassed his actual ability at golf, struggled mightily to break 80. Like many of us who play golf, he ran up against a wall, or, more precisely, his own limitations. For every golfer, the Hamlet-like or Clintonian dilemma appears: Should we take or should we not take mulligans and gimmes? What if our friends offer gimmes—and we honestly don't know if we can make the putts? Or, worse yet, if we pick up the ball and give others their putts? The seduction of golf is that a new sphere is entered, one where everything is at stake (one's own image) or where nothing is at stake (it's just a social outing and a sporting pastime).

Lest this seem like an indictment, let it be said that President Bill Clinton was wonderfully knowledgeable and enthusiastic about sports. He thoroughly loved watching games and was expert at analyzing them. In fact, he was far more adept as a sports spectator than as a participant. The remarkable intellect that he displayed, his knowledge and his way of putting facts into contexts, was never better demonstrated than by his grasp of sports.

What about golf and lying under oath? After Monicagate, few would deny that Clinton's performance before the American public resembled his dissembling on the golf course. Some observers of the president's golf were, from the start, pretty sure the truth lay somewhere else.

Clinton played many games while he was president, and most of them with cleverness and skill. Even when he was cornered by adversaries and critics, he was able to extricate himself—and he probably would have been reelected had he been eligible to run for a third term.

But, oh, the games he played. Even his worst enemies found him the most newsworthy of presidents—in games and in politics.

George W. Bush
From Bush Leagues to the Majors

In October 2004 the hapless Montreal Expos moved to the nation's capital where they were christened the Washington Nationals. In January 2005 President George W. Bush invited the team's manager, Frank Robinson, to dine at the White House. Bush, a Houston Astros' fan, told Robinson that while he would gladly go to RFK Stadium to watch the Nationals, he worried that his presence would inconvenience the fans.

"I understand," Robinson said, "but don't let that stop you from seeing us, Mr. President."[1]

It had been more than three decades earlier, during the first term of Richard Nixon, when the old Washington Senators moved to Texas. Like the Expos, the newly christened Texas Rangers brought with them a reputation as losers ("first in war, first in peace, and last in the American League," had been the Senators' byword). For the most part, that tradition persisted in Texas.

Twenty years after the franchise was moved, a syndicate headed by George W. Bush purchased the struggling Rangers. This had provided Bush, a passionate baseball fan, with a jump-start for his public career. Moreover, sports proved to have more of an impact on Bush's rise than on any other pre-presidential career since Teddy Roosevelt.

Bush's first experience with a Washington (or former Washington) franchise had come just as unexpectedly. It had rescued the career of an ambitious "First Son" who had little going for him except his father's name and his family contacts.

Would a Washington franchise once again boost Bush out of a public-relations predicament? Or, would the tattered Expos-Nationals symbolize a president destined to lose his luster in his second term?

Baby-faced George W. Bush on the baseball field when he pitched for the Yale freshmen. A jock at heart, Bush the younger simply lacked his father's athletic ability and switched from baseball to rugby. His love of baseball and the opportunity to own a major league team led him to be the managing partner of the Texas Rangers in 1989. Through ownership of the Rangers, Bush managed to get his name before the public, which led to his decision to run for governor of Texas in 1994. Courtesy of George H. W. Bush Presidential Library, College Station, Texas.

★
Stranded on the Sidelines

On January 22, 1989, the day before his father was inaugurated, the *Washington Post* ran a brief story that the president-elect's son, George W. Bush, was heading a group seeking to purchase major league baseball's Texas Rangers. Two days earlier, the wire services had reported that the younger Bush might be a candidate for governor of Texas.

George W. Bush—the name was familiar, but the man was not. Presidents' sons and daughters normally remain anonymous until the famous parent takes office, but, after all, the *Washington Post* had news to sell. Few people knew that George W. Bush was a partner in a Texas oil company—or that he had played an important role in his father's election campaign. For most Americans, including a majority of Texans, George Bush was the name of the president. Until January 23, 1989, George W. was off the media radar.

Born in Connecticut while his father was a student at Yale, George W. grew up in Midland, Texas, after George the first had relocated to the Texas oil fields. As a teenager, he moved to Houston when his father transferred his oil interests and entered politics.

Like the elder Bush, he graduated from Phillips Andover Academy and Yale—and, after two years at Harvard Business School—began his own oil firm.

It sounded a lot like his father's career. The only difference was that George W., unlike his father, grew up in Texas. After his schooling in the East, he returned to the Lone Star State and married Laura Welch of Midland, a graduate of Southern Methodist University who had worked as a schoolteacher and librarian in Houston.

George W. Bush badly needed to create an identity separate from his father's if he wanted to enter politics—he had yet to find an answer, as he later remarked, to his own question: "What's the boy ever done?"[2]

Now he had a game plan. If he and his group bought the baseball franchise, he could finally emerge from his father's shadow. And he might be able to make the money necessary to launch a political career.

But the "boy" needed help. Bidding for a big-league franchise depended on more than Bush's gritty determination and brassy confidence. And on more than his lifelong interest in Little League Baseball, collecting baseball cards, and pitching for the Yale freshman team. The price of the team might run $70 to $90 million, more than he had in his natural-gas piggy bank. He would have to rely on his wealthy friends and family connections.

On January 23 he stood in the reviewing stand as the inaugural parade honored his father. As the colorful Texas floats passed by, he doffed his hat, a ten-gallon Texas special. Soon afterward, he left for Dallas to pursue his gold-plated dream.

So far, George W. Bush's athletic career had not been memorable, at least in the way that his father's had been.

At Andover, George hung around with the athletic elite. He was a pitcher on the baseball team and won his varsity letter, but he never starred as his father had. He was known as a junk ball pitcher who threw an assortment of breaking and offspeed pitches; he didn't have a sizzling fastball or a baffling curve.

Though not a star player himself, baseball was his passion. He had begun playing as a Little Leaguer in Midland, Texas. When he was a boy visiting New York, his Uncle Buck took him to see the New York Giants play. At the age of fifty, he could still remember the lineup of the 1954 World Champion New York Giants. Like Bill Clinton, Bush's favorite player was Willie Mays.

His Uncle Herbie Walker had been co-owner of the startup New York Mets—as awful as the Mets were in those days, he had a personal connection with a major league team. His uncle took him to the Mets dugout where he shook hands with manager Casey Stengel and hall-of-famer Rogers Hornsby. A boy's dream, for sure, and a far cry from Jimmy Carter's being ordered off the field by one of those he had asked for an autograph.

In his senior year at Andover, Bush not only won his letter in baseball but was also chosen high commissioner of stickball, a variety of street baseball. Dressed in a top hat and mounted on a high chair, it was the job of "Tweeds" (after the infamous Boss Tweed of New York) to hand down the rules and officiate at the games. In addition, he was the head cheerleader who boomed out the school yells through his megaphone at football games (joining Woodrow Wilson, Franklin Roosevelt, and Dwight Eisenhower who led cheers for their college teams).[3]

At Yale, he pitched for the freshmen but lacked the talents to make the varsity. He later told the story that the coach once yanked the starting pitcher after a particularly bad outing. Bush thought then that his moment had arrived, only to have the coach call in the second baseman as a relief pitcher. "That's when I figured my aspirations of becoming a big-league pitcher might not be achieved," he wrote.[4]

As a junior, he quit baseball and, like Bill Clinton, took up rugby, making the first team his senior year. "Rugby is a great game," he once declared, "a game of speed and hard knocks with a tradition of postgame camaraderie." He was also at Yale when its football team boasted two outstanding players, Brian Dowling and Calvin Hill, and beat Princeton to win the Ivy League championship. Bush and several friends rushed onto the field at Princeton to tear down the goalposts, an expression of unbridled enthusiasm that landed them in jail.[5]

While he won no academic honors, Bush became president of his fraternity. Once as a pledge, called upon to name his pledge brothers, he reeled off the names of all fifty—others could only remember a handful. His inventive, bon vivant personality earned him notoriety if not distinction. Once he organized a game of football of fraternity members to play against the freshman team—without helmets. Like his father, he was tapped as a member of Skull and Bones, the third generation of Bushes to join the secret society of elite and well-connected young men. Like his father and grandfather, George would find that the contacts would prove helpful in business and politics. Unlike the previous generations, the honor was based on neither grades nor athletics.

★

Pickup Games

Being a Bush, George W. participated in plenty of family games and sports. He fished for bluefish and bonefish, hunted quail, and played tennis and golf. His golf handicap may not have matched his father's in his prime, but he boasted a respectable game. Don Van Natta quotes golfer Ben Crenshaw, who has played with the Bush family: "He's very athletic and very strong. He's a pretty good driver and he hits some good shots."[6]

Bush pursued distance running more consistently than any other sport. He began running several miles each day in his twenties and continued into the presidency. He ran a ten-mile race along with his brother Jeb while Mom and Dad looked on. Although his larger brother Jeb outpaced him, Bush moved more swiftly than Bill Clinton, averaging three miles in twenty minutes.

He also worked out almost every day. While he was governor, he spent time in the gym at the nearby University of Texas. "That was a place I could go out and be alone," he declared. "And I got to know [football coach] Mack Brown and Jeff (Mad Dog) Madden, the strength coach. I got to see the insides of the program and became very fond of the men that were involved with the program." As president, Bush continued to run "six-minute miles," usually running on the treadmill and cycling on exercise machines. Some reporters suggested that he made sure that those who surrounded him, such as Secretary of State Condoleezza Rice, shared his athletic interests, and perhaps physical fitness was a requirement for appointees to top posts.[7]

How athletic was George W. Bush, the son who never matched his father's varsity attainments? Competitive like Bill Clinton and, unlike his predecessor, a deceptively good athlete. Roger Staubach, the Hall of Fame quarterback for the Dallas Cowboys and a Bush family friend, once played basketball with some friends against the Bush brothers (Bush Sr. even watched the contest). Staubach and his pals won the first game, the Bushes the second, and "we won the third," Staubach recalled. How good was Bush's game? "Good jump shot—good dribbler. He ran the game. He's a very good athlete."[8]

Sparring with words comes naturally to George W. (some say he takes after his mother Barbara). And never was he more voluble than on the basketball court. Asked if the president was a "trash talker," Staubach laughed. "You know the President is a very confident guy. So when he won the second game, well, he definitely inspired us to play better in the third game."[9]

When "Forty-Three" (as he was first called to distinguish him from his father, president "Forty-One") went on his first-term vacations to his Texas ranch, he golfed—and, like Ronald Reagan, he cleared brush. Here, we're not talking about the gentle sea breezes that swept up the mountain at Reagan's El Cielo. This was very deep in the heart of Texas in mid-August. "He jogs prairies, spits, hunts the odd dove, and hosts the occasional world leader or economic forum," Mark Leibovich wrote in the *Washington Post*. "But 'clearing brush,' is, hands down, George W.'s most cherished form of recreation, at least measured by how often you hear about it."[10]

What was the attraction of clearing brush—and why do it on a summer vacation in Texas? Ronald Reagan's press secretary, Marlin Fitzwater, once declared that "if you're president, you have control over worldwide movements. But you often feel out of control of the little things." Clearing brush, like playing basketball, made the Andover and Yale grad, the imperial president, into a regular guy who spends his time working in the back forty. As Bush himself famously commented, "most Americans don't sit in Martha's Vineyard, swilling white wine." Or even on the ocean at Kennebunkport where Bush normally spent a few days. Of course, Bill Clinton never cleared brush, spending a lot of idyllic hours on the Farm Neck golf course on Martha's Vineyard—but probably not guzzling wine.[11]

In a turnabout of party stereotypes, Bush the Republican played less golf than President Bill Clinton—and was rarely photographed when he did. Of course, this was largely due to the press of presidential business after the attacks on September 11, 2001. But Bush seemed to understand from his father's experience that in TR's words "golf is fatal" (especially if widely publicized). Golf has proved historically unhealthy for presidents, raising endless nitpicking questions rather than endearing them to the voters.

His father's "cart golf" was out, while brush clearing and workouts were in.

Bush and the Business of Baseball

Baseball catapulted George Bush from the son and namesake of a president to the governor of Texas and a presidential hopeful.

When he returned from his father's inauguration, he was about to put the finishing touches on his purchase of the Texas Rangers. His friend Bill DeWitt, whose family had owned the Cincinnati Reds, whetted George's appetite when he told him that Eddie Chiles was trying to sell the team. Chiles, who had owned the team since the early 1980s, had taken a hit when oil prices collapsed in 1986. In addition, he was suffering from incipient Alzheimer's.

Bush had long dreamed of owning a baseball team and sometimes shared his fantasy with DeWitt. He had watched baseball in Texas as a teenager: "Shortly after my family moved to Houston, baseball expanded to our new city. The Colt 45s [later the Astros] came to town, and I became their number one fan. I sweltered through day games in the Houston summers, days in which the temperature and humidity were ninety-eight."[12]

In 1971 baseball came to Dallas as the expansion Washington Senators abandoned the nation's capital and moved to Arlington, Texas, next to Dallas–Fort Worth. But the Rangers were major-league losers. In its first two years in Texas, the team lost 100 and 105 ball games. Two years later, the feisty manager Billy Martin briefly turned the Rangers into winners, but they quickly faded. The Rangers tended to wilt in the Texas heat. In 1988 the team's abominable pitching and mediocre hitting relegated it to a sixth-place finish in a seven-team division.

Bush's net worth of roughly half a million was hardly adequate to buy the team. Already the baseball owners had turned down Eddie Gaylord who owned the second largest stake in the team, because they were fearful that he would use his radio and TV stations to invade their media fiefdoms. In addition to DeWitt, Bush had recruited his fraternity brother Roland Betts, an entrepreneur who had financed some of the most gruesome movies of the 1970s. Bush needed to get Dallas financing, and the men with big bucks, Rusty Rose and Richard Rainwater, were not interested. Financiers didn't want the spotlight that ownership in the Rangers would bring.

Bush did have an ally in high places, baseball commissioner Peter Ueberroth, the bright young man who put together the 1984 Los Angeles Olympics—and a Republican eager for a cabinet position with the Bush administration. To keep the Rangers in Texas and purchase the team, Ueberroth assured Rose that Bush would be suitable as the out-front, glad-handing partner. And with Rose and then Rainwater in the fold, Ueberroth could assure the owners that this group of local buyers would not move the team.

Bush himself had to pledge his Harken Energy stock shares to secure a $500,000 bank loan. His percentage of ownership was small—1.8 percent when he later upped his investment—but he stood to benefit when the team was sold. His stake, if he raised attendance and got a new stadium, would jump 10 percent.

George Bush boasted with some justification that "I was the pit bull on the pant leg of opportunity. I wouldn't let go." Yet, without being the president's son or without the help of Ueberroth and the help of the elder Bush's friend, American League president Dr. Bobby Brown, upstart George W. probably wouldn't have reached first base.[13]

This would have been unfortunate for George W. Bush because he proved to be a natural as a managing partner. The Rangers were fast out of the gate in the spring of 1989. Pitcher Charlie Hough, described by columnist George Will as looking "like Lyndon Johnson with a secret sorrow," shut out the Detroit Tigers on opening day with his "meandering, maddening knuckleball." In April, the Rangers held onto first place in the Western Division of the American League. Bush convinced his mother Barbara, the first lady, to throw out the first ball of the season. Crowds flocked through the turnstiles. "Rangers Bandwagon, Stadium Getting Crowded," proclaimed the *Dallas Morning News*. The Rangers jammed 40,429 fans into Arlington Stadium on April 30 when the legendary strike-out king Nolan Ryan outdueled Roger Clemens, 2-1.[14]

Though the team was unable to maintain its momentum, it would end the season with a winning record at 83-79, finishing squarely in the middle of its division—and it repeated this better-than-expected performance in 1990. In Bush's years as managing partner, the team would never produce a contender, yet he received credit for improving the team and setting the stage for later successes. Bush became the team's most visible booster, speaking endlessly to civic groups and giving banquet speeches. A virtuoso in dealing with the press, his image contrasted favorably with Jerry Jones, the new owner of the Dallas Cowboys. Jones fired the coaching icon Tom Landry and made insulting remarks about team personnel. In contrast, Bush reassured the team personnel that their jobs were not in jeopardy (two years later, he fired the manager, Bobby Valentine, and then general manager Tom Grieve).

George, Laura, and their twin daughters, Barbara and Jenna, according to his count, logged fifty to sixty games each year, sitting in their box next to the dugout. Here, Bush kidded with the players and conversed with fans, always giving them autographed copies of his own specially designed baseball cards. He learned the names of ticket-takers and hot-dog vendors. He sat proudly beside Bart Giamatti, the new commissioner of baseball and former president of Yale, as Nolan Ryan struck out batter number 5,000. Giamatti died later that summer, thrusting Bush family friend Fay Vincent into the hot seat as commissioner.

Best of all, he and Laura had time between the taunts of irate fans and the cracking of George's peanut shells to spend time together. They talked of family, of baseball, and of "life." According to Bush's campaign autobiography, it strengthened their marriage. "I always say if you're going to a baseball game, you had better go with someone you like, because you have ample time to talk," Bush wrote. "I went with someone I loved."[15]

The visibility of his job was worth millions politically. He confided to his friend Roland Betts that until he became a partner he was only "a media creation"—or, more accurately, a name. Now, he had added flesh to his bones. He was not only a public figure, but also a successful businessman.

When he solicited Betts as a partner, he assured him that he wouldn't run for governor. Yet rumors continued to surface in the spring of 1989 as the Rangers surged, and *Time* featured an article on Bush, "another winner for the Bush family," and suggested that "George the Younger" was pondering a race for the Texas statehouse. "He says that the media attention he's getting as managing partner will help him 'overcome the image problem,' meaning most Texans know little about him," *Business Week* reported. About this time, Barbara Bush gave one of her frank interviews, stating flatly that son George was not ready to become governor—he should concentrate on his job in baseball. Furious at first, Bush had to concede that Barbara had trumped him, even though he felt like a small child. "My mother's always been a very outspoken person who vents very well," he confided. "Once it's over, you know exactly where you stand and that's it."[16]

Barbara Bush knew better than her son. George W. had found his niche. Not only was he popular in Dallas, but he also won the respect of the owners. Nowhere was this better demonstrated than when family friend Fay Vincent ran athwart of the major league owners. As the majority of owners planned to fire him, Bush gave a spirited defense of Vincent and pleaded with his fellow owners to retain him.

Bush's speech did not keep the owners from firing Vincent, but neither did it diminish George W's popularity with them. In fact, the onetime Andover stickball commissioner had dreams of becoming baseball commissioner. With Vincent now out of the picture, George went to Bud Selig, acting commissioner, letting him know that he himself would one day like to become commissioner. Selig did nothing to discourage him, though the owner of the Milwaukee Brewers had his eye on the job himself—and eventually got it.

George W. Bush had to settle for governor of Texas and president of the United States.

★

An Aging Bandbox

The Bush syndicate trained its sights on obtaining a new stadium—at public expense—to replace "the aging bandbox," as an article in *Business Week* called it. The owners' trump card was the implicit threat to move the team out of Arlington, say to Dallas, if the city didn't find a way to pay for a new stadium. To be sure, the stadium at Arlington was a white elephant, a minor league ball park, upgraded when the team moved from Washington. Achieving its break-even goal of 2 million fans per season, not to mention revenue from luxury boxes and other amenities, the team needed a state-of-the-art stadium—at least for starters.[17]

Bush worked with the mayor of Arlington, Richard Green, to hammer out a deal that would be profitable to the owners and would keep the Rangers in Arlington. The plan called for the voters to foot the bill—municipal bonds totaling $135 million would get the job done. In turn, a hike in the sales tax of a half percent and a surcharge of $1 per ticket sold would enable the city to pay off the bonds. The owners would pay only $30 million toward the cost of construction.

In return, the owners stood to profit handsomely. The Bush syndicate would pay rent of $5 million a year, and after $60 million, the Rangers would own the stadium and receive all the revenues from ticket sales (minus the surcharge).

Bush mounted a campaign to convince the voters—he even trotted out future hall-of-famer Nolan Ryan. In January 1991 almost two-thirds of Arlington's voters approved the proposal. A year later, George Bush, aboard a front loader, broke ground for the new stadium. He achieved something most owners of sports franchises dreamed about—to get the public to finance the hometown stadium.

Much of the controversy and criticism surrounding the stadium arose from the land next to the stadium. A bill enabling the city of Arlington to issue bonds also included a clause allowing it to secure land by eminent domain. The owners wanted the 12.8 acres adjacent to the stadium belonging to the Mathes family to develop restaurants, stores, and office buildings. When the Mathes family spurned the owners' lowball offer, the Rangers seized the land for $3.16 per square foot, far less than the land was worth. Eventually, the courts awarded $7.2 million for the land or more than $11 per square foot (the sports authority had paid only slightly more than $800,000).

By that time, not only had the stadium been built, but the owners had sold out as well. George W. Bush, the aggressive deal maker (with the 10 percent jump, his share was worth slightly more than 11 percent), had parlayed around $600,000 into $16 million.

But it had not been without a downside. To purchase the Rangers, Bush had pledged his stock in Harken Energy, where he was a consultant and a member of the board. In 1991 Bush sold his Harken stock and used the proceeds to repay the loan to the Midland Bank. Only days later, Harken shares tumbled on news of substantial losses, a result of failed schemes for offshore drilling in Kuwait, which Bush had opposed. Rumors of "insider trading" shadowed George W. when he entered politics. He had neglected to file a form required of those with internal connections to the firm—until eight months after the sale. Though the SEC eventually dropped the investigation, Bush's explanation that he simply wanted to pay back his Rangers loan provided great material for his critics and political opponents (his critics were dismissive of the SEC decision because his father was still president).

Baseball was good to Bush. It allowed him to become independently wealthy, to burnish his image, and to engage in sports, next to politics the endeavor he most enjoyed. Just as his father had, he graduated from youthful sports, to business (with a youthful flavor), then to public service. No president in American history derived more from employment in sports than George W. Bush— not Andrew Jackson, TR, Ford, or Reagan.

But his sojourn in the world of baseball, so crucial to his political career, proved to be a double-edged sword—entertaining and upbeat on the surface, troubling and paradoxical underneath.

Critics would label the stadium project as the "Governor's Sweetheart Deal." They would point out that the opponent of public welfare had been the recipient of corporate welfare. How else would the stadium in Arlington have been built? But was Bush operating unethically? "Well, you have to say that at that point," his friend and fellow investor Roland Betts has observed, "George wasn't the governor of Texas. He was a general partner, he was a fiduciary, and a fiduciary's obligations are to perform well for investors. And that's what he did."[18]

Within a decade, Bush straddled the oil business, major league baseball, and national politics. And, as much as baseball boosted the career of George W. Bush, winning baseball games was far less messy than running for president.

In his campaign biography, *A Charge to Keep,* George W. Bush makes one heartfelt statement against baseball's wild-card system, whereby an extra team with a strong win-loss record gets to participate in the playoffs and, occasionally, to play its way into the World Series. "I'm a traditionalist when it comes to our national sport," Bush wrote. "I voted against wild-card play, because I didn't believe baseball should reward a second-place finish."[19]

Many Bush opponents felt that the Republican candidate in 2000 had a second-place finish because he garnered fewer popular votes than his opponent Al Gore. Declared winner in the state of Florida, Bush barely eked out a victory in the Electoral College, but unlike baseball, the title to the presidency was not clear-cut. Problems with voting machines in the key state of Florida led to court appeals. Eventually, the Supreme Court served as the referee of last resort, rendering a 5-4 decision in favor of Bush and the Republicans. Everything from the pregnant and hanging chads (disputed ballots resulting from the use of voting machines) to the attempted recounts and court decisions was far messier than wild-card finishes in major league baseball.

★

From Tee-Ball to Terror

George Bush's love of baseball in all shapes and forms did not stop with his becoming president. In May 2001 he inaugurated tee-ball on the South Lawn of the White House. Here, the president was in his element, back as the commissioner. To avoid the endless foul balls and wild pitches, the youngsters would hit the ball off a tee, hurry-up baseball patterned after cart golf.

In the first game, a seven-year-old hit a hard liner to right field. An extra base hit, the spectators thought, until an outfielder lunged and caught it. President Bush, seated near first base, sprang to his feet. "What a catch," he yelled, as he applauded the young prodigy. The president seemed more excited than the parents.[20]

When he was commissioner of stickball at Andover decades earlier, he stopped a game when one of the players, a klutz when it came to catching the ball, had clasped a pop fly—and led the applause.

The summer of 2001 was the calm before the storm. Larry Sabato, the political pundit from the University of Virginia, would refer to Bush's tee-ball as restoring "honor, integrity, and the 1950s to the White House." Columnist Maureen Dowd referred to Bush as "Eisenhower with hair."[21]

All of the 1950s analogies changed abruptly when Al Qaeda terrorists flew planes into the twin World Trade Center towers and the Pentagon—the infamous 9/11 attack.

Two days later, the president with a megaphone would lead cheers for his country on the rubble of the twin World Trade Center towers. "We can't hear you," workers yelled to Bush. "I can hear you," he shouted. "The rest of the world hears you. And the people who knocked these buildings down will hear all of us soon."[22]

Those halcyon summer days of the 1950s had suddenly taken on a darker hue and led into the first decade of the twenty-first century—and Bush, still controversial, had become the cheerleader for the War on Terror.

Bush's subsequent invasion of Iraq would become a controversial second chapter in his War on Terror, and its lengthy and grim aftermath undermined his post-9/11 popularity. Big-league baseball in nearby RFK Stadium could not hoist George W. from his decline in the polls, as it had rescued him from obscurity in 1989. Yet it did provide relief from the dreary litany of roadside bombs and suicide bombers in Iraq and Afghanistan.

In the fall of 2004, as Bush fought John Kerry for a second term, the hapless Montreal Expos, virtually a pariah in Quebec, moved with fanfare—and controversy—to the nation's capital. By defeating John Kerry, Bush became the first president, in April 2005, to preside at the opening-day baseball game in Washington since Richard Nixon's first term.

The Nationals then surprised baseball prognosticators by surging into first place in their division in June. Not since 1933 had a Washington baseball team won a pennant or found themselves in postseason play. Unfortunately, the team went into a nosedive during the second half of the season.

Tee-ball had morphed into major league baseball in Washington. Was George Bush simply fortune's child or was this merely a distraction from the struggles over court appointees and social security reform? Did he really care about the Nationals as he had the Rangers and the Astros? Did baseball in the nation's capital deserve a fraction of the inches that newspapers devoted to the economy and the war?

If the Nationals—and baseball—were a sideshow in Washington, one fact remained. A former sports owner had parlayed his notoriety into winning two campaigns for the White House. Was George W. Bush unique, or was this part of a trend? Would a sports performer—a former star like movie actor Ronald Reagan with name recognition from earlier playing days—one day occupy the Oval Office?

One conclusion seems evident. A background in sports has already become a credential for being elected president.

★ ★ ★

Conclusion

Since Theodore Roosevelt descended from Mount Marcy in 1901, sports have been a small but growing facet of the American presidency. How important? That depends on the president, his interests, temperament, talent, and his needs—and on the nature of the presidency and when he served. Roosevelt could hike through Yellowstone practically unprotected and "scramble" and swim in the wilds of Rock Creek Valley. He also used sporting ops to burnish his macho image and promote his interest in conservation of wildlife and natural resources. When he climbed the precarious cliffs along Rock Creek, barely a stone's throw from the White House, each step was progressively "bully" and "bullier."

By contrast, when George W. Bush was asked if he would like to ride in a race car at the Daytona 500 in February 2004, he had to beg off: "I'd like to, but I'm afraid the [Secret Service] agents wouldn't let me."[1]

When George W. Bush flew to Florida for the Daytona 500, he aimed his political radar at the second-largest sporting event (second only to the Super Bowl) and an extremely popular spectator sport. In addition to the 180,000 race fans in the grandstands and infield, the Daytona 500 had a television audience of 35 million. Faced with declining presidential ratings, he chose a sporting event that had a conservative fan base and friendly competitors. Brian Z. France, NASCAR chairman and chief executive, had contributed $2,000 to the Bush campaign and the president had entertained the previous year's winner, Tony Stewart, at the White House.

As the racers were being introduced on a grand stage, *Air Force One* eased into view and, after landing, Bush approached in an impressive twenty-car motorcade. After climbing out of his black limousine, he waved to the cheering crowd. He and Laura Bush chatted with several drivers and admired their cars. The president boasted that he liked "speed," reminding the drivers that he had flown fighter jets in the Air National Guard.

The Bushes stayed for half of the 200 laps and then departed. The television cameras interrupted their coverage to focus on *Air Force One* as it winged over the track and vanished into the clouds. The *Washington Post* called the presidential appearance a "shot of publicity that no opponent could buy."[2]

★
What Do Sports Reveal?

If we begin with Theodore Roosevelt in 1901, eighteen men have made the presidential sporting team. While none of them equaled TR, most of them had sporting interests before and during their presidencies. Some have been expert athletes, some merely spectators or occasional sportsmen.

With the recent explosion of sports and especially televised sports, have our expectations for presidents changed? Governor Al Smith of New York famously said of Franklin Roosevelt when FDR was running for governor of New York: "We do not elect him for his ability to do a double back-flip or a handspring." It's safe to say that we still don't.[3]

The question is not whether to exercise, but how to integrate sports with the duties of the presidency. We do *not* expect our presidents to be sports fanatics or to spend their afternoons playing golf and their evenings watching baseball or football. As with Eisenhower's golf, a president who spends too much time at sport creates the impression that he is neglecting matters of state. Sports and exercise carried to extreme may endanger the health and well-being of the president. Even if the president merely faints or feels dizzy while jogging, the news media blows these events far out of proportion.

But, given the choice, we prefer our presidents to be vigorous and outgoing. We expect them to keep themselves in shape. More to the point, we don't want them alcoholic, obese, or ashen in complexion. Occasionally, a nonathletic president has come to office after the death of his predecessor—Calvin Coolidge, Harry Truman, or Lyndon Johnson. We tolerate—sometimes even admire and enjoy—these chief executives as we get to know them. But would they have been nominated by their party, much less elected president? We don't want wimps or couch potatoes leading the nation.

But, if we elect a sporting president, can we predict what type of president and administration we will get?

We historians don't have to be Monday morning quarterbacks to make judgments about a president's sporting enthusiasms. Presidential sports may be a means of politicking, relaxing, self-promotion, or simply indulging sports interests. The president is the "sportsperson in chief." When he calls a coach, the coach listens. If he admires a golf club, the club soon becomes his. If he says he shot a 79 (or 93 in a three-way contest), he gets credit for doing just that. At least, no one contradicts him to his face.

Dig a little deeper, and you may find more pay dirt—pre-presidential pay dirt or just weird stuff. Teddy Roosevelt on a youthful hunting trip in Montana not only downed a bird by barely grazing it, but then also tried to make it appear that he had shot its head off. His guide came upon him, his foot on the bird's head, pulling it by the legs, "with the intention of pulling its head off and making it appear that it [the head] had been shot off." Richard Nixon wandered among students on the Mall in Washington during a war protest trying to talk professional football with them. Dwight Eisenhower played baseball as a professional in Kansas and passed himself off as an amateur at West Point when he went out for football. His adversary in one memorable game, Jim Thorpe of Carlisle, was not so lucky. He had his Olympic gold medals stripped for playing summer baseball for pay.[4]

Not every presidential observer should be taken at face value.

Take football star O. J. Simpson who stated that golf was a way of assessing presidential character. Only months before the murder of Nicole Simpson and Ron Goldman, Simpson played golf with President Bill Clinton and came away with a self-serving message. After the round, the former football superstar effused to the press: "You learn more about a guy after one round of golf than you'd learn doing business with him for a month. I didn't vote for him, but now I'm a big fan."[5]

Sports may be a way of reading—and misreading—presidential character, but it is also a way to interpret administrative style. Most crucial is the way in which presidents organize their administrations. Do they prefer to delegate, to organize their administrations as teams, or to orchestrate the presidency much as they might give detailed advice to a partner in golf or tennis?

How to Organize the Presidency: A Sports Analysis

Are presidents who played team sports more likely to be team players? So it seems. These chief executives delegate and orchestrate their administrations much as the coach of a football team might. Dwight Eisenhower had already learned to delegate broadly as allied commander in World War II. But before Ike became a colonel or general or president, he played—and coached—football. He credits football for laying the foundation for teamwork, leadership, and military success. What he said about football sums up his convictions about the educational role of sports: "I believe that football, perhaps more than any other sport, tends to instill in men the feeling that victory comes through hard—almost slavish—work, team play, self-confidence, and an enthusiasm that amounts to dedication."[6]

Richard Nixon played third-string at Whittier College, serving as a punching bag in practice for the starting team, but then acting as morale builder for the team on the bench and in the locker room. His hero and practically the only teacher he mentions in his autobiography was his coach, Wallace Newman, who "drilled into me a competitive spirit and the determination to come back after you have been knocked down or after you lose."[7]

Nixon, it is true, did not spend hours on the golf course, but he did delegate—too much, if he is to be judged by the Watergate scandal that came back to bite him. Gerald Ford, who played big-time college football at Michigan and coached at Yale, needed no convincing that his administration should function like a team. His high school coach described him as "one of the hardest working kids who ever played football for me, and totally dependable in every game." Ford learned that the team was more important than the individual, and he absorbed his coach's view that "you play to win," though only by the rules.[8]

Ronald Reagan, who played football, preferred individual, even solitary, sports as he grew older. Yet he functioned more like the athletic director, delegating to his chiefs of staff, who in turn delegated to staff. From his teamwork as an athlete and an actor, Reagan was well disciplined; he knew how to follow orders or directions when he needed to be coached for a TV appearance.

The list continues with the first George Bush, who was captain of the baseball team at Andover and Yale—and who was a loyal subordinate as CIA director, UN ambassador, and as vice-president under Ronald Reagan. And George W. Bush, who badly needed coaching, had played on baseball and rugby teams before becoming the managing owner of a major league baseball team. Lacking a presidential persona and close knowledge of the issues, he listened to advice, worked closely with his advisers, and learned on the job.

What about the president who has never played on a team? A test case might be Woodrow Wilson, who coached football but never played it. Indeed, he preferred to participate in individual sports such as bicycling, tennis, billiards, and golf. Wilson was a hands-on president who specialized in hands-on foreign policy, even typing dispatches on his own typewriter. Perhaps typical of a president who imposed his managerial style on football teams at Princeton and Wesleyan, President Wilson chalked up a mixed record when he had to lead his presidential team.

To be sure, Wilson consulted with members of his cabinet and usually left technical matters to experts. Unlike Jimmy Carter, he did not try to micromanage the trivia of the presidency. He carefully consulted members of his cabinet and, in his first term, worked with Congress to put through progressive legislation. He was cautious about leading the country into World War I and in concert with public opinion. For more than two years, he kept tensions with Germany at a manageable level. Even during the controversies following the war, he tried to sound out some members of Congress and potential allies.

That said, Wilson had a remarkably small circle of counselors, one of whom was his second wife, Edith Wilson. If he did not micromanage, he often conducted foreign policy in a highly personal manner. A quick study, he had only grudging respect for those whom he consulted on foreign policy, especially during World War I. More solitary than the flamboyant TR, he often neglected to solicit the opinions of those who could have helped him the most. With the stress of peace negotiations and the ravages of illness, he became less and less willing to compromise. If he wasn't exactly an autocratic coach, he often found it difficult to accept advice or to engage in give-and-take. As he drew up his beloved covenant of the League of Nations, he shared few of its details. In the words of John Milton Cooper, a Wilson scholar, "the Draft Covenant also expressed Wilson's lone handed, radically executive approach to foreign policy."[9]

Convinced that he had world opinion—and right—on his side, his capacity for teamwork diminished. Once reminded that there were two sides to every question, he responded, "Yes, the right and the wrong." Another time he told a political colleague, "I am sorry for those who disagree with me." Why? "Because they are wrong."[10]

Would he have learned the give-and-take of teamwork had he actually played a team sport? Or could he have accommodated those who disagreed with him? Or if he had been more comfortable with the political maneuvers necessary to achieve consensus, especially in foreign policy?

Most tragically, he tried to ramrod his simon-pure version of the Versailles peace treaty through the Senate and rejected any form of compromise. "Anyone who disagrees with me," he told a Democratic senator, "I'll crush." While Wilson's health undoubtedly made him more obstinate, his experience in sports and in the classroom had programmed him to ignore those who suggested different strategies. When pressures mounted, so did Wilson's tendency to go it alone.[11]

Does the tendency to delegate freely and effectively appear only among Republicans? Certainly almost all of the pigskin presidents came from the Republican side. The presidents who emphasized individual sports—Wilson, Franklin Roosevelt, John Kennedy, Jimmy Carter, and Bill Clinton—were mostly Democrats. Which is *not* to say that none of these presidents played team sports. John Kennedy played football at prep school and junior varsity football at Harvard. Like Ronald Reagan, he was a swimmer and, like the Republican presidents, a golfer. And Reagan, who played football in high school and college also thrived as a solitary lifeguard and equestrian.

One Republican president who did not play team sports was Herbert Hoover. The thirty-first president preferred individual sports like fishing or low-profile exercise regimens, notably medicine ball. True, Hoover managed the football and baseball teams at Stanford, business positions that required more individual initiative than teamwork. Put simply, Hoover preferred individual sports like fishing to golf or tennis where this shy, unathletic man would not have to show his weaknesses. Fishing was the silent sport. "One of the few opportunities given a President for the refreshment of his soul and the clarification of his thoughts by solitude lies through fishing," he wrote.[12]

His hideaway in the Blue Ridge Mountains was just that: a place to hide. Not that Hoover did not enjoy reading the sports pages or attending baseball games—though the reception that he and Lou Hoover received at the World Series in 1931 might have disheartened a less stalwart soul. Hoover may have delegated too much when he ordered Douglas MacArthur to disperse the bonus army, but mostly he remained burrowed in the Oval Office. Had the Depression not struck when it did, he probably would have traveled more (as he and Lou Hoover did to South America before his inauguration) and appeared at more public events.

Another lover of the outdoors, Jimmy Carter, epitomizes the president who preferred individual to team sports. Not that Carter ignored team sports, either as a basketball player in high school and junior college or as a sports spectator who followed college and professional teams. Possibly because of the notoriety surrounding Nixon and Ford, he attended fewer sporting events. He preferred running, mainly for relaxation and exercise, as well as fishing, hiking, and cross-country skiing. As a hands-on administrator, he ran the presidency like his peanut warehouse. Most famously, he supervised the scheduling of the White House tennis courts. Carter's hands-on approach and its drawbacks resembled Hoover's. Despite his patented smile and charm in solo or in small group settings, he did not always do well in public forums, often coming across as aloof and opinionated. More than for any other president, sports combined with other events to detract from Carter's standing, notably his near collapse while running in a six-mile race near Camp David. Like Hoover, Carter lost to a former governor, Ronald Reagan, who had a winning smile and seemed to be saying, like FDR, that "happy days are here again."

And Taft, the president with the elephantine girth, enjoyed walking golf courses and spending afternoons at baseball games. Taft, like later Republicans, delegated far more than TR. (His presidency is reminiscent of Eisenhower's and his propensity for long afternoons on golf courses, but without the ability to make tough decisions.) Taft did not have the experience of team play that Ike so valued. Hence, the hours spent on the golf course—not really that many—did more damage to Taft than to Wilson or Eisenhower, or, for that matter, to Bill Clinton.

Would "Big Bill" Taft have delegated more effectively if he had played football? Probably not. Teddy Roosevelt didn't play team sports and still was able to delegate as well as to act independently. TR boxed, wrestled, hunted, scrambled, and played tennis—mostly individual sports. Roosevelt had an ability to delegate when necessary and yet to play a starring role as he did in the coal strike in 1903 and in mediating the Russo-Japanese War in 1905. His brief attempt to solve football's problems, when he assembled the gridiron experts at the White House in 1905, proved to be the least successful of his interventions. No doubt chastened, he refused to dive into the Olympic controversy with the British in 1908 except to congratulate the American Olympians and the "winner" of the marathon—pointedly—when the president was vacationing at Oyster Bay.

★

Athlete in Chief

Before Teddy Roosevelt, the public had few sporting expectations of its presidents. Nineteenth-century presidents were cautious about sports, at least when they were in the White House. Because many sports were regarded as children's pastimes or undignified, lower-class pursuits through much of the nineteenth century, presidents felt more comfortable participating in or simply observing sports out of the public eye.

When Grover Cleveland fished in the 1880s, he disappeared into the wilderness of the Adirondack Mountains in July and August (leaving the government in the hands of a single cabinet member). When Cleveland was in Washington, he rejected the offer to attend a professional baseball game. What would the voters think, he asked, if they knew he was wasting his time watching baseball?

TR changed all that. He did not have to live up to expectations; he created his own sporting culture. He did it in the White House, in Rock Creek Valley, and in the parks and wilderness areas where he went to hunt and hike. He rode horseback, wrestled, boxed, scaled cliffs, played tennis, and roughhoused with his children. He created his own sporting persona—his own way of using sports politically and personally, not to mention indulging his bent for risk taking. His approach to sports would never be matched and not only because he was the first. No modern president could have deftly avoided the press or secret service agents as he scrambled, swam, and scaled cliffs within miles of the White House; none of his successors have had TR's rare opportunity to translate outdoor sports into a public legacy.

This is not to say that TR's successors did not share his interest and enthusiasm for sports. Since World War II, presidents have introduced their own variations of Teddy's sporting presidency. They have golfed, run, skied, and gone to sporting events like baseball games and NASCAR races. None of them has had the time, the boundless energy, the commitment, or the privacy to repeat Roosevelt's sporting regime. Even Teddy, had he served in the late twentieth century, would probably have adjusted his sporting manias to the intrusive urban landscape and more rapid forms of transportation.

After Roosevelt, sports were no longer taboo. Disregarding TR's advice, Taft played golf. Woodrow Wilson—out of public view—played golf almost every day. Harding golfed, wagered, and hobnobbed with sports celebrities. Calvin Coolidge fished and attended baseball games, though he preferred to sleep. With TR's successors, the public still did not expect the president to spend time playing sports. If the public approved of the president, his sporting interests were tolerated, even approved and admired. Nor did the voters object to a few games of baseball, or an exercise regimen like Hoover's medicine ball, or Harding's hobnobbing with sports celebrities in the 1920s.

Since midcentury, a revolution in presidential sports has occurred. Midcentury would include Harry Truman, but old Harry was an anomaly since he did not golf or play tennis and, besides walking, merely swam to stay in shape. To be sure, he had far more to worry about than sports. So much was expected of FDR's successor, and so much criticism was heaped on Truman, that sports, other than the morning walks, hardly mattered. Yet Truman pioneered a big change in the way presidents chose to vacation—when he flew to Key West. Since Truman's presidency, air travel has freed the presidents to do their sports any time and anywhere they elect. It has also created disagreements as to how much is too much and how far is too far.

The flying White House has created new expectations as well.

Truman's successor Dwight Eisenhower became the storm center of controversies over the flying carpet approach to sport. His golfing at Augusta National and in Colorado, not to mention on the South Lawn of the White House, gave the Democrats one issue that they could use against the president in 1956. His opponent Adlai Stevenson, so utterly unathletic as to have a pasty, slightly effete look, had difficulty making his case. Even if Stevenson had won the U.S. Open, he probably couldn't have defeated the popular war hero. Yet the contrast between Stevenson in the 1950s and John F. Kennedy in 1960—disparities in age and appearance—would define a new attitude toward presidential sports. Television as well as the availability of *Air Force One* would make the president's athletic image far more useful as a political tool.

Though golf got the Democrats few votes in the 1950s, Ike's continued health problems coupled with his time away from Washington did create concern during his second term. Should the president absent himself from the White House to play golf, shoot, and fish with wealthy business friends? By 1960 Kennedy could present himself as healthy and vigorous while criticizing the older gentleman in the White House who retired to the golf course, having lost his grip as a decision maker and having allowed the country to lag behind the Soviet Union.

Kennedy barely eked out a victory over Nixon who, though hardly an athlete like Eisenhower, showed enthusiasm for sports and presided briefly over the newly created President's Council on Physical Fitness.

JFK legitimized sports, even though his health did not permit him to golf or play tennis through much of his presidency. That he was considered fit and athletic (though he really wasn't) created the expectation that presidents should display an athletic veneer. Kennedy added to his sports persona by beefing up the President's Council on Physical Fitness—as if saying the country should be as fit and vigorous as he himself was. Unlike Eisenhower, he did not play golf with celebrities, but he invited celebrities both in sports and entertainment to the White House, some of them athletic standouts like the first African American Heisman Trophy winner, Ernie Davis. Hollywood even immortalized his athletic feats in PT-109, thereby boosting his prospects for the forthcoming presidential election in 1964.

Not that President Kennedy was merely a sports enthusiast who liked to golf and watch football. JFK was born to the manor in a way that neither Truman, Eisenhower, or Kennedy's opponent in 1960, Richard Nixon, were. Because he and his wife Jackie were glamorous, they were able to defuse the issue of we and they—the very wealthy and the very ordinary folks. After Kennedy, the Republican presidents (and occasional Democrats) tried to emulate the sporting persona—including the myth of presidential health and vigor—that Kennedy had so effortlessly created. As they sought it, they established the boundaries of the modern sporting presidency. They tested the limits of what the American public would accept—and what the public would respond to.

Lyndon Johnson was not a sporting president nor did he pretend to be. He assumed that his legislative record would move the voters—and, for a time, it did. But not for long, as the Vietnam War so engulfed his presidency that he dared not play golf even when he wanted to. Nevertheless, LBJ continued the President's Council on Physical Fitness, incorporating fitness into the Great Society programs. He invited athletes and coaches to the White House. He congratulated his friend Darrell Royal when the University of Texas won the national championship. When he bowed out of the presidential race in 1968, the frontrunner for the Democratic nomination was JFK's brother Bobby—until he was assassinated. RFK was vigorous, healthy, youthful, and athletic. If he had lived to run and won, he might well have claimed the mantle of his brother's athletic presidency—and probably have been an athletic president in the tradition of TR. Bobby was one of the few administration officials who completed the fifty-mile hike from Washington to Camp David—a standard of military fitness that originated with Theodore Roosevelt.

Did the American public want a president who spouted sportspeak, attended sporting events, suggested plays to NFL coaches, crowned national champion teams, and invented all-star baseball teams? And made fun of his own puny exploits as a third-string football player? And used this in place of his own athletic endeavors other than occasional bowling and golf? And, occasionally, spoke to the TV cameras at sporting events? Richard Nixon tested the public's tolerance of a president who used sports more openly for political purposes than any other chief executive since TR.

Nixon faced a steep incline as he tried to create his own sports presidency. He won a close victory in 1968 over Hubert Humphrey (moderately nonathletic). The public had formed a strong divide between Nixon-haters or those who admired his political skills and toughness toward communism. The Vietnam War persisted through his first term, leading to protests in the nation's capital and on college campuses. Still, Nixon soldiered on, flying to all-star baseball games, high-profile sports banquets, championship football games, and then forging a friendship with Coach George Allen of the popular Washington Redskins—possibly calculated to divert attention from the war. And, of course, the sports did not hurt him in his landslide victory against George McGovern, which he would have won even without his hyperactive sports schedule.

The Nixon presidency did accelerate the bonding between spectator sports and the presidency. The president's use of sports to indulge his own interests, to show off his knowledge of football, and to reinvent himself as a regular guy became part of his imperial presidency. Probably Nixon believed that the country was more interested in his sporting jaunts than it really was. But it was another way to get his name, face, and message before the American public.

Awkward as Nixon's forays into sports proved, they did break new ground—and, except for Jimmy Carter, post-Nixon presidents have stepped up their sports appearances and participation. Gerald Ford, the accidental president but a big-time athlete, seamlessly entertained sports celebrities and made calls to sports victors. That he looked like and talked like an athlete made him more convincing than Nixon. However, when Ford played golf or skied, he had far less latitude than Eisenhower or Nixon (in his first term) to counter criticism that he played golf with lobbyists or took golfing and skiing vacations when he should have remained at the White House.

With Ford, the athlete in the presidency took a strange turn. Because he stumbled and bumped his head, he appeared bumbling and uncoordinated. Almost every week, comedian Chevy Chase lampooned him on *Saturday Night Live,* refining the stumbles and bumps into an art form. When Teddy Roosevelt fell off a cliff or was thrown from his horse, no one outside the White House knew. With the scrutiny of the president by the White House press corps and TV news anchors, presidents have been subjected to criticism or ridicule because they have failed to live up to the graceful image of John F. Kennedy. Even the first George Bush, an outstanding athlete, fell victim to athletic expectations that had nothing to do with his ability to perform on the campaign trail or in office—and became live meat for comedians and hosts of late-night talk shows.

The athletic image of Ronald Reagan, combined with his communication skills gained in his movie and TV career, contributed to his popularity. That a president in his seventies could survive a near-fatal assassination attempt gave him temporarily an aura of invincibility. After that event, the members of his staff began to talk about "winning one for the Gipper," and the Gipper became more Ronald Reagan than George Gipp. This is not to say that Reagan himself did not spend his valuable time hosting athletes and conferring awards within the confines of the White House—he did. He further became the first president to preside over the opening of an Olympics, the Los Angeles games in 1984—and the first to attend a NASCAR event. Trim and tanned at six feet, Reagan constantly drew on his experience in sportscasting and in the movies. He was still proud—even vain—about the physique that he developed as a football player and swimmer. That he was still vigorous was demonstrated by his horseback rides with the First Lady—and clearing brush—when he vacationed at Rancho El Cielo. No one doubted that Reagan was a regular guy.

The first George Bush's athleticism was *not* well known when he ran for president. Instead, the athletic image that he conveyed in person was confused with an Ivy League, buttoned-down, effeteness—the wimp factor—when he was captured on newsreel, lampooned on television, written up in the press, or attacked by his fellow Republicans. When he was elected, Bush went overboard to demonstrate that he was an athlete—and a regular guy. At first, the press was interested, but four years later his cart golf and horseshoes were merely, well, Bushisms. He lost to a taller man—a tendency in presidential elections—but not to a better athlete.

A cursory look at Bill Clinton's administration might suggest that sports didn't matter. Tall as he was, he had never shown much athletic talent, and his sports were seldom in public view—in 1992 he and vice-presidential nominee Al Gore confined themselves to putt-putt golf. Yet President Bill Clinton managed to engage the public, for a time, with his golf just as he did with his saxophone. Even his mulligans and gimmes proved to be either entertaining to supporters or subject to offhand ridicule by opponents. How much did his talk of breaking 80 or his 11 handicap hurt him? Probably not as much as having a sport helped him. Clinton was the most knowledgeable spectator since Richard Nixon. Only when politics, like art, imitated life, did golf damage his presidential image. And probably the downside did not hurt him as much as golf with lobbyists, businessmen, and plutocrats undermined Republican presidents.

George W. Bush pushed the sporting presidents into still another realm—the jock presidency. While the president himself never equaled his father's sports achievements, he managed to have more sports enthusiasts surrounding him than his predecessors. He watched pro football with Secretary of State Condoleezza Rice, who seldom missed a Super Bowl and whose father coached football. Rice herself was a champion ice skater. Donald Rumsfeld, secretary of defense, was a wrestling champion, and the leaders of the Republican congress, Bill Frist and Dennis Hastert, were standout athletes in high school.

When Bush made his first Supreme Court nomination, he selected John Roberts, a onetime captain of his high school football team. Geoff Earle in the *Washington Post* observed that, "after long deliberations and an exhaustive background check, Bush—an avid runner and cyclist—picked the jock." Earle contrasted Bush's appointee with Clinton's "geeks" such as Secretary of State Warren Christopher and Supreme Court Justice Ruth Bader Ginsburg. Bush even warned a potential nominee, Judge J. Harvie Wilkinson, of "impending doom" (the judge's words) for failing to do enough cross-training. When he fired one economic adviser, the president privately grumbled about "his failure to exercise physically."[13]

Republicans have often chosen more conventional sporting presidents and candidates for high office. The country-club connection has become so well known as not to need elaboration. The political downside for Republican athletes has been far greater than for Democrats. Not only have we expected Republicans to be athletes, but we have also harbored the suspicion that they waste precious hours, days, or weeks or allow golfing cronies and lobbyists to get special favors. A Democrat rarely spends too much time at the Burning Tree or Congressional golf courses—or plays in the wrong company, even if it's similar to a Republican foursome.

Old media attitudes die hard. From Bush to Rumsfeld, Rice, and Frist, the Republican team features a remarkable number of former jocks and even professional athletes. Do American voters and pundits respond to robust specimens who look like the athletes we all remember from high school and college? And will the Democrats have to recruit a team that can vie with the Republicans for the best touch football team in the nation's capital—all of this in order to enhance their image?

Unlike European voters, Americans expect their presidents to be the people's representative and to project a nonpolitical persona—engaging heads of state as well as political chieftains. Presidents need to be like us, only more intelligent, better informed, and more experienced. That said, the president should look presidential—even if, like Warren Harding, they have little else to offer. And Harding, like George W. Bush, enjoyed the company of athletes.

More to the point, former athletes often look and act like the leaders they were on the playing field. As a result, a winnowing process takes place whereby nonathletes—the small and unimpressive males—simply never seem to reach the point where they can win presidential primaries and rarely are they chosen to run as vice-presidential candidates. Who would expect to see a rotund, stunted scarecrow—a political Truman Capote—running for the presidency? Or a candidate who did not have some background in sports and appreciation of the outdoors? Even a big, imposing, telegenic figure like Bill Clinton, who could smash a golf ball three hundred yards, won easily over a candidate of lesser stature, Bob Dole, who had suffered a disabling wound in World War II and compensated by delivering stinging—sometimes damaging to himself—verbal shots rather than booming drives. Or a vice-presidential candidate, Senator Joseph Lieberman, not physically impressive or athletic, who spent months in a fruitless attempt to convince the voters in the Democratic 2004 primaries that he was presidential material. Could Calvin Coolidge or Harry Truman be elected to the presidency in the twenty-first century?

Finally, let's not forget the first ladies. The first sixty years of the twentieth century produced several first ladies with athletic talents and interests, namely Edith Roosevelt, Grace Coolidge, Lou Hoover, Bess Truman, Jackie Kennedy, and even Eleanor Roosevelt. Based on their pioneering tradition, shouldn't the wives of recent presidents spend time on golf links, tennis courts, or on horseback and trailside? Alas, the women of the past forty years appear less athletic.

Since JFK's assassination, the women in the White House have demonstrated less enthusiasm for sports than Edith Roosevelt, who rode horseback with TR every day or Grace Coolidge who attended major league baseball games. To be sure, a younger Betty Ford was a dancer and skier, and Rosalynn Carter participated in some of her husband's outdoor activities. Yet they are the exceptions. The absence of women's presence on the sporting turf flies in the face of the sporting enthusiasms of recent presidents. Do we still expect our first ladies to be more traditional, less active politically and physically? When Eleanor Roosevelt and Hillary Clinton breached the traditional political boundaries, a storm of criticism resulted. Will it require a female president to eliminate this taboo or simply a highly athletic (and photogenic) first lady?

★

Do's and Don'ts

Sports and the presidency may be joined at the hip, but presidents need to tread cautiously when they embrace a particular sport. TR could do whatever he wanted as long as he did not embarrass himself by being photographed in a tennis outfit. Since the electorate consisted of male voters, he was able to win votes by appealing to the male sporting ego. In the twenty-first century, TR might well travel to Daytona for NASCAR; as a young legislator, he attended cockfights in Albany and, on his stopover at Yellowstone in 1903, hunted "varmints" on the sly.

Teddy Roosevelt is our yardstick for presidential sports—even though no president will likely match his sporting presidency. He did more than any other president and did it more effectively. Other presidents such as George H. W. Bush have equaled or exceeded him in the number of sports, games, and outdoor activities; none has combined sports and politics for nearly two terms and done it with such panache.

That said, macho sports exemplified by TR (as opposed to more conventional sports) may have less appeal for today's voters. Despite George W. Bush's success at the Daytona 500, sports appearances don't always generate cheers from the fans or handshakes from the players. Bill Clinton visited the Darlington speedway in South Carolina in 1992, but he had a far less friendly reception than Bush. These Reagan Democrats and "NASCAR Dads," as they were later called, wanted no part of the Arkansas Democrat. "Not only did stock-car racing fans roundly boo when Clinton waved to the grandstands," the *Washington Post* recalled, "NASCAR officials also had trouble persuading drivers to pose for pictures with the Arkansas governor or show him around." Nevertheless, he defeated George H. W. Bush who (like his son) attended the Daytona 500 before the 1992 presidential election.[14]

Which brings us back to our presidents and their active sports. Or to presidents in the twentieth century (plus twenty-first-century George W. Bush).

Here are some do's and don'ts.

1. "Golf is fatal," Teddy Roosevelt famously said, and he was right. Golf has caused more problems for more presidents than any other sport. Taft, Ike, Ford, and even the first Bush, not to mention Vice-President Dan Quayle and Bill Clinton, have taken political hits because they either played too much golf or played it in an unacceptable way or with the wrong partners.

If you must play golf, avoid the paparazzi. Be wary of the television cameras and telescopic lenses. Presidential foursomes on plush courses, especially if they are Republicans, immediately raise red flags. Recall the best piece of advice that Richard Nixon ever gave—to Dan Quayle: Leave your clubs at home (Quayle finally got the message, because he never mentions golf in his autobiography).

Oh yes, avoid pro-am tournaments where you might wing a spectator— and that applies to former presidents as well.

2. Sports and public policy don't ordinarily mix. Teddy Roosevelt was able to make outdoor sports and conservation dovetail. One might argue that Jimmy Carter had no choice but to boycott the Moscow Olympics—Gerald Ford told me that he probably would have as well.

But it didn't work.

3. Don't play poker. Oh, I know that every president from Taft to Nixon played poker—or poker, bridge, and even hearts. Despite poker's newfound popularity, the game evokes unsavory presidential images of smoke-filled rooms in the Harding White House or a clueless William Howard Taft playing at Henry Frick's mansion. Though the stories of Harry Truman's poker are amusing, remember that he was the Bill Clinton of poker. To be sure, he never cheated, but he did include Chief Justice Fred Vinson of the Supreme

Court along with his Missouri cronies. Not only did he violate separation of powers, but he nearly fleeced Winston Churchill on the "Iron Curtain" train trip to Missouri.

No one wants a president who has a gambling problem or who, just to ante-up, loses a set of official White House china. Wait until you're out of the White House and then go to a Native American casino. You'll be righting some past wrongs, especially if you lose.

4. Try to exercise in natural settings; go hiking or fishing. The TR ethos has blossomed into militant environmentalism (even though Teddy still reigns as the "hunter in chief"). That said, let me add a note of caution to presidents in the twentieth-first century: Don't hunt, or if you must, don't let anyone know. Disappear into the wilderness as TR did at Yellowstone. Be forewarned: Hunt openly and the chorus of protests from Bambi-huggers and birders will drown out your dialogue with the voters. You don't need that static.

5. Don't do more than you're capable of. Medical events such as the mini-crises suffered by Jimmy Carter or George H. W. Bush raise doubts about the president's long-term health, let alone his ability to govern. Suppose you should sustain a heart attack as Ike did after playing golf—better take a stress test!

6. Don't use sports to be one of the guys if you aren't. Richard Nixon invaded locker rooms. He called coaches. He suggested plays. If anything, he managed to distract the public momentarily from the war in Vietnam—and from his own stilted personality. Still his sports—both as a participant and a spectator—lacked the grace of a John Kennedy or the effortlessness of a Ronald Reagan or even a Bill Clinton. Nixon's "silent Americans," let alone the Vietnam protesters with whom he talked football on the Washington Mall, didn't really care that he was a macho guy—when he really wasn't.

Avoiding phony publicity and photo-ops goes for military maneuvers such as landing on aircraft carriers. Don't do it unless you're a highly decorated veteran. But be sure to go to military bases whenever possible—our military personnel, often the silent Americans, need to know that somebody cares.

7. Invite sporting groups and sports figures to the White House, but try to vary the mix. People may have poked fun at Richard Nixon's all-star baseball teams, but they did not object to Ronald Reagan's baseball dinner with old-time all-stars. Make calls to victors or greet them at the White House, but keep it from being patently self-serving. Above all, don't waste your precious presidency schmoozing with athletes.

8. When you retire or are retired by the voters, you are now responsible for your post-presidency. Let 'er rip. But, if you're trying to win points with future

sportspersons and historians, keep in mind that both Herbert Hoover and Jimmy Carter wrote books on outdoor sports that made them seem more like great sportsmen, thinkers, and, well, just regular guys.

9. If you know deep down that you are not a particularly good or even interested athlete, then let your wife's sporting interests bring you some good press. Bring the first lady along. When Calvin Coolidge did, he avoided leaving the World Series with the score tied in the ninth inning—and risking the displeasure of Washington Senators fans (many of whom, as District residents, couldn't vote).

10. If you are the first female president, you cannot approach sports in the same way as your male counterparts, at least not at first. A woman may play tennis, do aerobics, run on mechanical tracks, or even play a few rounds of golf, appropriately dressed, with few photo-ops.

But keep in mind that expectations will be different. A female version of the hyperactive George H. W. Bush would invite unflattering humor on late-night talk shows, if not outright ridicule on *Saturday Night Live*. The same with a woman who takes up fly casting or bowling. The "good ol' boy" culture of Bill Clinton and George W. Bush would seem inappropriate, even for a "good ol' girl" president. In spite of our efforts at gender correctness, a double standard in sports—and politics—persists.

Where should you look for cues? Let Harry Truman serve as a model. I don't mean that you should hold rollicking poker games or fast-walking, fast-talking press conferences. Simply remember that old Harry never pretended to be a sports person, and it never hurt his political standing. You might also look to several first ladies who pioneered in sports: Grace Coolidge, Bess Truman, and Lou Hoover.

Your time is coming, and whoever you are, better give presidential sport some thought.

The games presidents have played—or embraced—encompass both sports, exercise, and less physically active outlets (such as poker and bridge). They have included sports in tranquil settings or among throngs of spectators, seeing and being seen, playing for votes and voting for (football) plays. Sporting pursuits include tennis and tiddlywinks, horseshoes and hiking, college football and major league baseball, entertaining athletes or letting athletes provide the entertainment, fishing for votes or fishing in solitude, golfing publicly in pro-ams or anonymously on out-of-the-way courses. As much as we may watch with interest or dismay, our presidents need their sports and daily exercise. If the past half century is a guide, we will see more presidential sports, more athletes visiting the White House, more first-ever presidential sports or sports appearances, more elaborate White House workout spas, and possibly a one-time professional athlete at the helm.

In the end, what purpose is—or should be—served by presidential sports?

Let us assume that presidents want a way to refresh and restore themselves or just plain indulge an athletic interest. What Herbert Hoover wrote about fishing might apply to other presidential sports as well.

> Fishing [substitute sports] seems to be one of the few avenues left to Presidents through which they may escape to their own thoughts, may live in their own imaginings, find relief from the pneumatic hammer of constant personal contacts, and refreshment of mind in rippling waters. Moreover, it is a constant reminder of the democracy of life, of humility and of human frailty. It is desirable that the President of the United States should be periodically reminded of this fundamental fact—that the forces of nature discriminate for no man.[15]

Step aside, Imperial Presidency, Hoover says; the games played by presidents should be just that—games.

Alas, history tells me that they will continue to be both public and political.

★ ★ ★

Appendix: Ranking the Presidents

Presidential Rankings

The Great, the Good, and the Awful

Who were the best—and the worst? Just as a refresher: Here are the presidents since 1901 with a capsule description of their sporting interests and sporting abilities.

Presidents number 26 to 43, 1901–2005

Number	Name	Nickname	Known For
26	Theodore Roosevelt	Tee Dee, Teddy	Sports presidency

Father of sports presidency; TR was a good if not great athlete. Versatile, energetic, and astute, he converted interest in outdoor sports into public policy. A failed bear hunt was responsible for the Teddy Bear.

| 27 | William Howard Taft | Will/Big Bill | Heaviest president |

Size and lethargy were handicaps, but he was the first golfer in the presidency and starred as a baseball fan.

| 28 | Woodrow Wilson | Tommy | Closet athlete |

Wilson lacked athletic ability and stamina, but loved sports, especially when he was in control; he coached football, bicycled, played tennis, billiards, and golf, but his participation was often based on health considerations.

| 29 | Warren G. Harding | Warren | Wagered on games |

Harding was not particularly talented, but liked to play golf and poker and enjoyed the company of sports figures.

| 30 | Calvin Coolidge | Silent Cal | Awful athlete |

Coolidge was almost less than zero when it came to sports, but he knew how to use sports and sports figures to his political advantage. His wife Grace lived up to her name, graceful and interested in sports.

| 31 | Herbert Hoover | Bert | Followed sports, fished |

Hoover enjoyed keeping fit and fishing but hated to be on display, so he did his sports in private or, as with medicine ball, in small, friendly groups.

Number	Name	Nickname	Known For

32   Franklin D. Roosevelt   Frank/FDR   Individual sports, rehab
FDR was an excellent athlete and sportsman, but it's hard to know how good. Two lives—pre- and post-polio—were both marked by tremendous energy and discipline. He preferred individual or small-group sports like sailing and golf.

33   Harry S Truman   Harry   Nonathlete who kept fit
Harry never had a chance to develop sports, but he kept fit by walking and swimming, and he occasionally fished, rode horseback, and followed college football. His wife, Bess, was far more athletic and interested in sports.

34   Dwight D. Eisenhower Ike   Top-notch athlete, sportsman
Ike played sports and games with skill and brains—he could have been as good in football as Ford. His football injury hampered participation in more active sports, but he was an enthusiastic flycaster and bridge player, and was a golfer with an attitude.

35   John F. Kennedy   Jack   Natural athlete, prone to disability
JFK had as much talent as any president, maybe more. His World War II swim was the greatest presidential feat. His infirmities got in the way of athletics. Glamour of presidency overlapped into sporting presidency, even when he was hurting.

36   Lyndon B. Johnson   LBJ   Unnatural athlete, uninterested
LBJ does not offer much to evaluate. He did invite athletes to White House, kept Ike and JFK's President's Council on Physical Fitness, and followed University of Texas football.

37   Richard M. Nixon   Dick   Hard worker, gifted spectator
"Tricky Dick" was not much on playing fields, but enjoyed sports and knew enough about them that he could schmooze intelligently with coaches and players. He used sports in tricky, dramatic, and heavy-handed political ways, but his analytical mind made him a canny spectator.

38   Gerald R. Ford   Jerry   Top college athlete, multitalented
Ford may have been "accidental president," but sports were no accident. He talked the talk and walked the walk. He not only played football, but also skied, golfed, and swam and, for a very brief time, modeled sportswear.

39   James Earl Carter Jr.   Jimmy   Best at outdoor sports since TR
Jimmy Carter preferred tennis, fishing, hiking, and cross-country skiing. Like TR, he was committed to outdoors and environmentalism, and also followed professional and college sports. He launched an Olympic boycott in 1980.

| Number | Name | Nickname | Known For |

40   Ronald W. Reagan   Dutch, Gipper   Athletic, fit, gifted swimmer

Reagan's sports have to be approached on several levels: youth, myth, and presidential. He was interested in sports, though not much of a spectator, and was the most enthusiastic White House equestrian since Taft.

41   George H. W. Bush   Bush Sr.,   Highly athletic
                                      Forty-One

The first George Bush succeeded at everything athletically, played college sports at highest level, and for two years his hyperactive sports presidency made him an "Oyster Bay kind of guy."

42   William Jefferson Clinton   Bill   Nonathlete, enjoyed golf,
                                                     super fan

Always entertaining, Clinton's golf became known for billigans, mulligans, and gimmes; a basketball fanatic, he shared with Nixon a remarkable knowledge, grasp, and ability to analyze sports.

43   George W. Bush   George, W,   Athletic, running, fitness
                                      Forty-Three

Not as talented as Forty-One, George W. is still a competent athlete. His lifelong addiction to baseball is reflected in his ownership of the Texas Rangers. A competitive runner, W also managed early workouts in the White House gym.

Presidential Rankings

Since 1948, historians have been ranking—and reranking—presidents, based on their performance in office and on their impact as presidents. Except for ratings of presidential golfers, no presidential poll has dealt with presidents as athletes, as sportsmen, as spectators, and even as presidents who used sports for political gain. No easy chore, these rankings, but I have decided to let my gentle readers—as nineteenth-century writers called them—judge for themselves how well I put these gentlemen in order or, in the case of the All-Presidential Dream Team, how appropriate my choices.

All-Time Presidential Dream Team—
Presidential Athletes/Sportsmen, 1789–2005 (alphabetical order)

George H. W. Bush

Grover Cleveland

Gerald Ford

Dwight Eisenhower

Benjamin Harrison

John F. Kennedy

Abraham Lincoln

Theodore Roosevelt

Franklin Roosevelt

George Washington

Honorable Mention:

John Quincy Adams, George W. Bush,
Ulysses Grant, Andrew Jackson, Ronald Reagan

Best Natural Athletes, 1901–2005

Number One	George H. W. Bush	Master sportsman and athlete
Number Two	John F. Kennedy	Nothing that he couldn't do, effortless
Number Three	Dwight D. Eisenhower	Excelled at several sports, a natural
Number Four	Gerald Ford	Virtually a pro in football, versatile
Number Five	Theodore Roosevelt	Master of many sports, energetic
Number Five (tie)	Ronald Reagan	Good athlete—remarkable swimmer
Number Seven	Jimmy Carter	Small but fast—deceptively good

Other Categories

Best All-Around Sportsmen, 1901–2005

First: Theodore Roosevelt

Second: George H. W. Bush

Third: Dwight D. Eisenhower

Fourth: Jimmy Carter

Fifth: Franklin D. Roosevelt

Honorable Mention: Ronald Reagan, Gerald Ford

Presidential Sports Spectators, 1901–2005

First: Richard M. Nixon

Second: Bill Clinton

Third: Jimmy Carter

Fourth: George W. Bush

Fifth: William Howard Taft

Best at Using Sports to Advance Their Presidencies, 1901–2005

First: Theodore Roosevelt	The macho man always on the go; created sports imagery
Second: Ronald Reagan	Myth combined with reality
Third: John F. Kennedy	Looked and acted athletic; urged nation to become fit
Fourth: Richard Nixon	Employed sports often and in novel ways
Fifth: Dwight Eisenhower	Used sports to overcome problems stemming from heart attack and stroke

Worst Natural Athletes, 1901–2005

First and Worst	Calvin Coolidge	Athletically challenged
Next to Worst	Harry Truman	Good president, just not athletic
Third Worst	Lyndon Johnson	Big but uninterested and not too good
Fourth Worst	Richard Nixon	Tried hard, but simply didn't have it
Fifth Worst	Woodrow Wilson	Played tennis and billiards, but lacked body coordination and strength

Author's Note

When I began this study, I knew the sports reputations of Ford, Reagan, Bush the elder, Clinton, and Theodore Roosevelt. TR's story, however, is so varied and multi-faceted that I needed to separate the myth from reality, sports from the "strenuous life." I also needed to bring the lesser known sports of presidents such as Woodrow Wilson, Calvin Coolidge, and Jimmy Carter into focus.

I found that assessing the natural ability of the presidents is especially difficult. After all, how does one quantify sport and the ability to do sport? Put simply, sports such as baseball, football, and even TR's scrambling all require hand-eye-body coordination as well as strength and agility. If I had my top five contenders together for field trials, I could assess those abilities, allowing for age, size, and the context of their sporting experiences. As a sports historian, I glean my opinions from others' reports and by digging into presidential archives and published accounts.

My greatest difficulty came when I tried to rank the top five twentieth-century athletes. Four athletes cluster near the top and seem at times interchangeable in their sporting abilities. George H. W. Bush ranks first among presidential athletes. Not only did he master a variety of sports, but he also played college baseball at an extremely high level. Being captain of a Yale baseball team that made it twice to the finals of the college world series makes him unique among presidents. John F. Kennedy was an outstanding athlete, but his health and size never allowed him to play varsity sports. (The one exception came when he swam on the best freshman swimming team in Harvard's history.) His swimming at Harvard combined with his PT-109 swims and his effortless conquest of individual or pickup sports gives him a slight edge over the three others in the top five—but a very slight edge. Dwight Eisenhower and Gerald Ford were fine athletes whose accomplishments in college and semiprofessional sports outrank Kennedy's. That said, neither matched Kennedy's golf or swimming or ability to play almost any sport effortlessly. I stand by my ranking of those four.

Teddy Roosevelt proves a quandary because he told a journalist that he was an ordinary athlete who enjoyed sports—an uncharacteristically modest statement. Obviously he was good at a lot of sports, though never the college boxing champion whom others claimed him to be. Still, he could wrestle, box, and do martial arts with the best of them; he could swim frigid rivers and ride horseback like a pro. Given the physical handicaps that crept into his life, he had to be athletic to ride a hundred miles in a winter storm and to clamber up cliffs in Rock Creek Valley, not to mention riding, roping, and using his fists during his ranching days in the Dakota Territory.

Ronald Reagan also poses a challenge. To be sure, he was a good athlete, though not as great as Bush, Eisenhower, and Ford. He was versatile, but not as versatile as Kennedy. Only in swimming did Reagan have a remarkable talent, but so did JFK. Much of Reagan's sporting reputation is based on stories he told or on his Gipp portrayal in the film *Knute Rockne, All American*. When the myth is stripped away, Reagan emerges as a fine natural athlete, probably as good as Teddy Roosevelt, perhaps even better.

Yet Teddy was so active and accomplished in so many sports that he has exhausted this reviewer's attempts to dislodge him from the top five.

The Worst-Ever was again a guess, but easier to make. As for categories such as sports spectators and political sportsman, they flowed more easily out of my research and writing.

I wouldn't want to compete against any of the top seven on my A-list. They could hold their own with the best of athletes and sportspersons, yet I'd enjoy an outing with these sports figures and surely would learn from them. Who knows? Scrambling with TR, an evening of poker with Truman, fly casting with Carter, cart golf with the elder George Bush, jogging at dawn with Clinton? I might learn a lot—if I could keep up.

After watching the top presidential athletes at play—as well as the others—I have an abiding admiration for our "athletes in chief."

Not only could they hold their own, but they also had other things to occupy their minds during their time in office. Since 1901, consider the historical record—wars, strikes, racial strife, depressions and recessions, landings on the moon, global boycotts, and terrorists. And that's just a trifle compared to any complete listing. The games presidents played, whether frivolously or assiduously, may have kept a lid on things.

Play on, Mr. (or Ms.) President.

Notes

Chapter 1. In the Beginning

1. C. Brian Kelly, "Young George Washington Would Bury the British Major Who Stubbornly Rejected His Advice," *Military History* 18, 6 (February 2002): 74.

2. Frank E. Grizzard Jr., *George Washington: A Biographical Companion* (Santa Barbara, Calif.: ABC-CLIO, 2002), 35.

3. *Washington Post*, February 23, 1936.

4. Donald Jackson, ed., *The Diaries of George Washington*, 6 vols. (Charlottesville: University Press of Virginia, 1976), 3:56. The quote is from the letters of a British customs official, William Eddis.

5. Theodore Roosevelt, *The Wilderness Hunter*, vol. 1 of *The Works of Theodore Roosevelt*, ed. Hermann Hagedorn, 20 vols. (New York: Charles Scribner's, 1926), 362.

6. George Washington Parke Custis, *Recollections and Private Memoirs of Washington, By His Adopted Son, George Washington Parke Custis, with a Memoir of the Author by his Daughter; and Illustrative and Explanatory Notes by Benson J. Lossing* (New York: Derby and Jackson, 1860), 459–61.

7. Grizzard, *George Washington*, 84.

8. Ibid.

9. Joseph J. Ellis, *His Excellency: George Washington* (New York: Alfred A. Knopf, 2004), 225.

10. "Some Jefferson Ideas on Exercise, Guns and Games," Thomas Jefferson, Information Files, Personal Life—Exercise Folder, Monticello Library, Charlottesville, Virginia. Jefferson to Peter Carr, August 19, 1785, in Julian Boyd, ed., *Papers of Thomas Jefferson*, 30 vols. (Princeton: Princeton University Press, 1953), 8:406–8.

11. Jefferson to Peter Carr, August 19, 1785, in Boyd, *Papers of Thomas Jefferson*, 8:406–8; cartoon, *Potomac Times*, October 10, 1990.

12. Jefferson to George Gilmer, December 16, 1788, in Boyd, *Papers of Thomas Jefferson*, 14:360–62.

13. Jefferson to John Adams, August 15, 1822, in Albert E. Bergh, ed., *The Writings of Thomas Jefferson*, 20 vols. (Washington, D.C.: Thomas Jefferson Memorial Association, 1907), 15:269.

14. Douglas L. Wilson, *A Mystery Solved* (Charlottesville, Va.: Thomas Jefferson Memorial Foundation, 1995), 1–12. From the Monticello Keepsake Collection, courtesy of Thomas Jefferson Foundation, Inc.

15. Thurlow Weed, *The Autobiography of Thurlow Weed*, 2 vols. (Boston: 1883–84), 1:179.

16. John Quincy Adams, *The Diary of John Quincy Adams, 1794–1845: American Political, Social, and Intellectual Life from Washington to Polk*, ed. Allan Nevins (New York: Longmans, Green, 1928), 297, entry for August 9, 1823.

17. Ibid., 349, entry for June 13, 1825.

18. Paul F. Boller Jr., *Presidential Anecdotes* (New York: Oxford University Press, 1981), 63–64.

19. Lynn Hudson Parsons, *John Quincy Adams* (Madison, Wis.: Madison House, 1998), 266.

Chapter 2. The Sporting Frontier

1. Paul F. Boller Jr., *Presidential Anecdotes* (New York: Oxford University Press, 1981), 73.

2. Robert Remini, *The Life of Andrew Jackson* (New York: Harper and Row, 1988), 53.

3. Ibid.

4. Robert Routledge to William Herndon, [ca. November 1, 1866]; Henry McHenry Interview, October 10, 1866, both in Douglas L. Wilson and Rodney O. Davis, eds., *Herndon's Informants: Letters, Interviews, and Statements about Abraham Lincoln* (Urbana: University of Illinois Press, 1988), 386, 369.

5. Andrew S. Kirk Interview, March 7, 1887, in ibid., 603.

6. William Miller statement, no date, in ibid., 366.

7. Samuel L. Treat Interview, [1883], in ibid., 725.

8. Charles S. Zane Interview, [1865–66], in ibid., 492.

9. Jean Edward Smith, *Grant* (New York: Simon & Schuster, 2001), 27–28.

10. Ulysses S. Grant, *Personal Memoirs of U.S. Grant*, 2 vols. (New York: Charles Webster, 1885), 1:116.

11. Ibid., 581.

12. Diary of Dr. Cary Grayson, January 21, 1919, in Arthur Link, ed., *Papers of Woodrow Wilson*, 69 vols. (Princeton: Princeton University Press, 1966–94), 54:175–76; Don Van Natta Jr. describes this incident somewhat differently in *First Off the Tee: Presidential Hackers, Duffers, and Cheaters from Taft to Bush* (New York: Public Affairs, 2003), 114.

Chapter 3. Barely Visible to Press and Public

1. Charles Richard Williams, ed., *Diaries and Letters of Rutherford B. Hayes, Nineteenth President of the United States*, 7 vols. (Columbus: Ohio State Archaeological and Historical Society, 1922), 1:253.

2. John F. Reiger, *American Sportsmen and the Origins of Conservation* (Corvallis: Oregon State University Press, 2001), 108.

3. Thomas C. Reeves, *Gentleman Boss* (New York: Alfred A. Knopf, 1975), 362.

4. "Seeing Grand Scenes," August 19, 1884, clipping files, Chester Arthur Papers, Library of Congress, Washington, D.C. (The name of the newspaper is missing.)

5. Allan Nevins, *Grover Cleveland: A Study in Courage* (New York: Dodd, Mead, 1932), 244–45.

6. Ibid.

7. *New York Times*, June 9, 1886.

8. *New York Times*, August 12, 1886.

9. Paul F. Boller Jr., *Presidential Anecdotes* (New York: Oxford University Press, 1981), 184.

10. Don Van Natta Jr., *First Off the Tee: Presidential Hackers, Duffers, and Cheaters from Taft to Bush* (New York: Public Affairs, 2003), 115.

11. Jack Level Presidents Collection, draft manuscript, 78, Joyce Sports Research Collection, Special Collections, University Libraries of Notre Dame, South Bend, Indiana. Level wrote drafts of a book of sports and recreations of the presidents. He also collected materials such as newspaper clippings and briefly corresponded with presidential aides as well as former First Lady Grace Coolidge.

12. Boller, *Presidential Anecdotes*, 193.

13. Ibid., 207.

Chapter 4. Theodore Roosevelt

1. Theodore Roosevelt, *Theodore Roosevelt's Diaries of Boyhood and Youth* (New York: Charles Scribner's, 1928), 363–64.

2. Ibid., 365.

3. Roosevelt to Anna Roosevelt, August 22, 1880, in E. Morison, ed., *The Letters of Theodore Roosevelt*, 8 vols. (Cambridge: Harvard University Press, 1952), 1:46.

4. Edmund Morris, *The Rise of Theodore Roosevelt* (New York: Modern Library, 2001), 109. This book was originally published in 1979 by Coward, McCann and Geoghegan in slightly different form.

5. Paul Grondahl, *I Rose like a Rocket: The Political Education of Theodore Roosevelt* (New York: Free Press, 2004), 83.

6. Nathan Miller, *Theodore Roosevelt: A Life* (New York: William Morrow, 1992), 158; Kathleen Dalton, *Theodore Roosevelt: A Strenuous Life* (New York: Alfred Knopf, 2002), 90.

7. Herman Hagedorn, *Roosevelt in the Bad Lands* (Boston: Houghton Mifflin, 1921), 208.

8. Theodore Roosevelt, *The Autobiography of Theodore Roosevelt* (New York: Charles Scribner's, 1958), 79–80.

9. Theodore Roosevelt, *Hunting Trips of a Ranchman: Sketches of Sport on the Northern Cattle Plains* (New York: G. P. Putnam's Sons, 1885), 240.

10. Morris, *Rise of Theodore Roosevelt*, 681.

11. Richard Harding Davis, *The Cuban and Puerto Rican Campaigns* (New York: Charles Scribner's, 1904), 217.

12. Paul F. Boller Jr., *Presidential Anecdotes* (New York: Oxford University Press, 1981), 197.

13. Theodore Roosevelt, *The Rough Riders* (New York: Charles Scribner's, 1899), 136.

Chapter 5. Sports and the Presidency

1. John Sayle Watterson, *College Football: History, Spectacle, Controversy* (Baltimore: Johns Hopkins University Press, 2000), 65; Theodore Roosevelt, *The Strenuous Life: Essays and Addresses* (New York: Century, 1901), 20.

2. Theodore Roosevelt to Philip Bathell Stewart, November 24, 1902, in Elting E. Morison, ed., *The Letters of Theodore Roosevelt*, 8 vols. (Cambridge: Harvard University Press, 1952), 3:378.

3. Edward J. Renehan Jr., *John Burroughs: An American Naturalist* (Post Mills, Vt.: Chelsea Green Publishing, 1992), 243.

4. John Burroughs, *Camping and Tramping with Roosevelt* (New York: Houghton Mifflin, 1907), 6.

5. Roosevelt, "The American Boy," in Roosevelt, *The Strenuous Life*, 164.

6. Watterson, *College Football*, 66–68.

7. Roosevelt, "The Function of a Great University," in *The Works of Theodore Roosevelt*, ed. Hermann Hagedorn, 20 vols. (New York: Charles Scribner's, 1926), 12: 324–35.

8. Roosevelt to Walter Camp, March 11, 1895, Walter Camp Papers, Yale University Archives, New Haven, Connecticut.

9. Ronald A. Smith, ed., *Big-Time Football at Harvard, 1905: The Diary of Coach Bill Reid* (Urbana: University of Illinois Press, 1994), 193–94.

10. *New York Times*, October 10, 1905.

11. Roosevelt to George Candee Buell, August 18, 1908, in Morison, *Letters of Theodore Roosevelt*, 6:1183.

12. Roosevelt to James Bryce, November 25, 1908, in ibid., 6:1382.

13. Allen Guttman, *The Olympics: A History of the Modern Games* (Urbana: University of Illinois Press, 2002), 30.

14. Theodore Roosevelt to James Franklin Bell, April 20, 1907, in Morison, *Letters of Theodore Roosevelt*, 5:651.

15. Archie Butt to Clara Butt, November 8, 1908, in Archibald W. Butt, *The Letters of Archie Butt, Personal Aide to President Roosevelt* (New York: Doubleday, Page, 1924), 168. Clara Butt was his sister-in-law.

16. Nicholas Roosevelt, *Theodore Roosevelt: The Man as I Knew Him* (New York: Dodd, Mead, 1967), 71.

17. Archie Butt to Clara Butt, January 14, 1909, in Butt, *Letters of Archie Butt*, 286.

18. Ibid., 293.

19. Ibid., 297.

20. Edward Wagenknecht, *The Seven Worlds of Theodore Roosevelt* (New York: Longmans, Green, 1958), 17.

21. William H. Harbaugh, *Power and Responsibility: The Life and Times of Theodore Roosevelt* (New York: Farrar, Straus and Cudahy, 1961), 328.

Chapter 6. Inside TR's Sporting Presidency

1. Theodore Roosevelt to John Burroughs, July 6, 1903, in Elting E. Morison, ed., *The Letters of Theodore Roosevelt*, 8 vols. (Cambridge: Harvard University Press, 1951), 3:510–11.

2. Edward Wagenknecht, *The Seven Worlds of Theodore Roosevelt* (New York: Longmans, Green, 1958), 13.

3. Archibald W. Butt, *The Letters of Archie Butt, Personal Aide to President Roosevelt* (New York: Doubleday, Page, 1924), 37–38.

4. Jack Willis (as told to Horace Smith), *Roosevelt in the Rough* (New York: Ives Washburn, 1931), 13. The author thanks Michael Lansing for calling his attention to this episode. See also Wagenknecht, *Seven Worlds*, 15. According to Wagenknecht, Roosevelt was lowered to slightly over thirty feet above the stream and then he was dropped (it was his idea) into the water below where he was hauled onto a raft, stiff and half-frozen.

5. Roosevelt to Kermit Roosevelt, December 4, 1902, in Morison, *Letters of Theodore Roosevelt*, 3:389.

6. William Bayard Hale, *A Week in the White House* (New York: G. P. Putnam's, 1908), 88; Paul F. Boller Jr., *Presidential Anecdotes* (New York: Oxford University Press, 1981), 206–7.

7. Boller, *Presidential Anecdotes*, 207.

8. Butt, *The Letters of Archie Butt*, 121.

9. Ibid., 122.

10. Ibid., 123.

11. William H. Harbaugh, "The Theodore Roosevelts' Retreat in Southern Albemarle: Pine Knot, 1905–1908," *Magazine of Albemarle County History* 51 (1993): 27.

12. Ibid., 27–28.

13. Sylvia Jukes Morris, *Edith Kermit Roosevelt: Portrait of a First Lady* (New York: Modern Library, 1980), 294.

14. Ibid.

15. Mike Donovan, *The Roosevelt That I Know: Ten Years of Boxing with the President—and Other Memories of Famous Fighting Men* (New York: B. W. Dodge, 1909), 8–9.

16. Edmund Morris, *Theodore Rex* (New York: Random House, 2001), 696.

17. Roosevelt to Henry Cabot Lodge, August 6, 1906, in Morison, ed., *Letters of Theodore Roosevelt*, 5:346–47.

18. Hale, *A Week in the White House*, 88–89.

Chapter 7. William Howard Taft

1. Paul F. Boller Jr., *Presidential Anecdotes* (New York: Oxford University Press, 1981), 215.

2. Carl Sferrazza Anthony, *Nellie Taft: The Unconventional First Lady of the Ragtime Era* (New York: HarperCollins, 2005), 213.

3. Ibid., 210.

4. Archibald W. Butt, *Taft and Roosevelt: The Intimate Letters of Archie Butt*, 2 vols. (Garden City, N.Y.: Doubleday, Doran, 1930), 1:92.

5. Ibid., 81.

6. Ibid., 81–82.

7. Jack Level Presidents Collection, draft manuscript, 84, Joyce Sports Research Collection, Special Collections, University Libraries of Notre Dame, South Bend, Indiana. Level gives Taft's score as an 88; more likely, it was a 98.

8. Butt, *Taft and Roosevelt*, 2:503.

9. Ibid., 1:163.

10. William Manners, *TR and Will: A Friendship That Split the Republican Party* (New York: Harcourt, Brace, 1969), 102.

11. Ibid., 119.

12. Butt, *Taft and Roosevelt*, 1:174.

13. Ibid., 2:703.

14. William B. Mead and Paul Dickson, *Baseball: The Presidents' Game* (Washington, D.C.: Farragut Publishing, 1993), 12.

15. Charles Alexander, *Our Game: An American Baseball History* (New York: Henry Holt, 1991), 68.

16. Mead and Dickson, *Baseball: The Presidents' Game*, 24.

17. Butt, *Taft and Roosevelt*, 1:105.

18. Ibid.

19. Ibid., 106–7.

20. Ibid., 107.

21. Ibid., 190–91.

22. Ibid., 192.

23. Ibid., 2:439.

24. Ibid., 470.

25. Ibid., 460.

26. Ibid., 848.

27. Manners, *TR and Will*, 221.

28. Butt, *Taft and Roosevelt*, 2:601.

Chapter 8. Woodrow Wilson

1. Phyllis Lee Levin, *Edith and Woodrow: The Wilson White House* (New York: Scribner, 2001), 131.

2. Stockton Axson, *Brother Woodrow: A Memoir of Woodrow Wilson*, ed. Arthur S. Link (Princeton: Princeton University Press, 1993), 38–39.

3. Ibid., 37.

4. Henry W. Bragdon, *Woodrow Wilson: The Academic Years* (Cambridge: Harvard University Press, 1967), 39–40.

5. Ibid.

6. John Sayle Watterson, *College Football: History, Spectacle, Controversy* (Baltimore: Johns Hopkins University Press, 2000), 26–27.

7. Watterson, "The Football Crisis of 1909–1910: The Response of the Eastern 'Big Three,'" *Journal of Sport History* 8, 1 (Spring 1981): 33–49.

8. Edwin A. Weinstein, *Woodrow Wilson: A Medical and Psychological Biography* (Princeton: Princeton University Press, 1981), 166.

9. Ibid., 168.

10. Kenneth R. Crispell and Carlos F. Gomez, *Hidden Illnesses in the White House* (Durham: Duke University Press, 1988).

11. Copy of diary kept by head usher at White House, I. D. Hoover, March 4, 1913 to March 4, 1921, Edith Bolling Galt Wilson Papers, Library of Congress, Washington, D.C. This is the same collection cited for Taft papers, and the same material can be found on microfilm for the Wilson years. Don Van Natta Jr., *First Off the Tee: Presidential Hackers, Duffers, and Cheaters from Taft to Bush* (New York: Public Affairs, 2003), 138. Van Natta speculates that the figure may be closer to sixteen hundred.

12. Interview, Samuel G. Blythe, December 5, 1914, in Arthur Link, ed., *Papers of Woodrow Wilson*, 69 vols. (Princeton: Princeton University Press, 1966–94), 31: 394–95.

13. Irwin H. Hoover, *Forty-two Years in the White House* (Boston: Houghton Mifflin, 1934), 61.

14. Edward T. Brown to Mary Celeste Mitchell Brown, June 8, 1915, in Link, *Papers of Woodrow Wilson*, 33:374.

15. C. Brian Kelly, *Best Little Stories of the White House* (Nashville: Cumberland House, 1999), 288–89.

16. Edward Mandell House Papers, 1885–1938, vol. 3, 230, Manuscripts and Archives, Yale University Archives, New Haven, Connecticut (volume 3 is on reel 2 of the microfilmed papers of Edward House).

17. Wilson to Edith Bolling Galt, August 3, 1915, in Link, *Papers of Woodrow Wilson*, 34:72–73, 127.

18. Edmund Starling, *Starling of the White House* (New York: Simon & Schuster, 1946), 66.

19. From the Diary of Dr. Grayson, February 28, 1919, in Link, *Papers of Woodrow Wilson*, 55:308.

20. Ray Stannard Baker, *Woodrow Wilson and the World Settlement*, 2 vols. (Garden City, N.Y.: Doubleday, Page, 1922), 2:43.

21. Starling, *Starling of the White House*, 145–46.

22. Cary T. Grayson, *Woodrow Wilson: An Intimate Memoir* (New York: Holt, Rinehart and Winston, 1959), 100; Diary of Cary Grayson, entry for September 26, 1919, in Link, *Papers of Woodrow Wilson*, 63:519. The quote is from Grayson's memoir.

23. Wilson to Williamson Updike Vreeland, January 25, 1922, in Link, *Papers of Woodrow Wilson*, 67:524.

24. Newton D. Baker to Wilson, April 2, 1917, in ibid., 41:527–28.

Chapter 9. Warren Harding

1. Joel T. Boone, Memoirs, XVII-72–73, Joel T. Boone Papers, Library of Congress, Washington, D.C.

2. Paul F. Boller Jr., *Presidential Anecdotes* (New York: Oxford University Press, 1981), 230. On Sundays, Harding also rode horseback.

3. Evalyn Walsh McLean, "Father Struck It Rich," unpublished manuscript, 356, Evalyn Walsh McLean Papers, Library of Congress. Because of the sensitive material (for that era) on the Hardings and Ned McLean, the *Saturday Evening Post*, which was excerpting the book, asked to have those pages cut from the manuscript. The title of the manuscript should not be confused with the bowdlerized version published in 1936 under the same title.

4. Alice Roosevelt Longworth, *Crowded Hours: Reminiscences of Alice Roosevelt Longworth* (New York: Charles Scribner's, 1938), 325; McLean, "Father Struck It Rich," 356.

5. Longworth, *Crowded Hours*, 324.

6. Boller, *Presidential Anecdotes*, 231.

7. Edmund W. Starling, *Starling of the White House* (New York: Simon and Schuster, 1946), 180. McLean recalled that Harding was not present when the fight movie was shown at Friendship, but Harding biographer Francis Russell states that Harding did see it at the McLean House on I Street. McLean, "Father Struck It Rich," 364.

8. Francis Russell, *The Shadow of Blooming Grove: Warren Harding and His Times* (New York: McGraw-Hill, 1968), 472.

9. Starling, *Starling of the White House*, 177.

10. Ibid., 189; Robert H. Ferrell, *The Strange Deaths of President Harding* (Columbia: University of Missouri Press, 1996), 6–9; *New York Times*, July 24, 1922.

11. "Training on the Links," *New York Times*, March 28, 1923.

12. Starling, *Starling of the White House*, 193.

13. McLean, "Father Struck It Rich," 396.

14. Boone, Memoirs, XIX-20, Boone Papers, Library of Congress.

15. Ibid.

16. Boone, Memoirs, XIX-106–7, Boone Papers, Library of Congress.

Chapter 10. Calvin Coolidge

1. Shepherd Campbell and Peter Landau, *Presidential Lies: The Illustrated History of White House Golf* (New York: Macmillan, 1996), 75.

2. Paul F. Boller Jr., *Presidential Anecdotes* (New York: Oxford University Press, 1981), 241.

3. John M. Carroll, *Red Grange and the Rise of Modern Football* (Urbana: University of Illinois Press, 1999), 114.

4. Hendrik Booraem V, *The Provincial: Calvin Coolidge and His World, 1885–1895* (Lewisburg, Pa.: Bucknell University Press, 1994), 188.

5. Ibid.

6. Grace Coolidge to Jack Level, June 23, 1945, Jack Level Presidents Collection, Joyce Sports Research Collection, Special Collections, University Libraries of Notre Dame, South Bend, Indiana.

7. Ishbel Ross, *Grace Coolidge and Her Era: The Story of a President's Wife* (New York: Dodd, Mead, 1962), 136–37.

8. Joel T. Boone, Memoirs, XXI-895–96, Joel T. Boone Papers, Library of Congress, Washington, D.C.

9. Edmund W. Starling, *Starling of the White House* (New York: Simon and Schuster, 1946), 206.

10. Campbell and Landau, *Presidential Lies,* 71. Evalyn Walsh McLean, "Father Struck It Rich," unpublished manuscript, Evalyn Walsh McLean Papers, Library of Congress.

11. McLean, "Father Struck It Rich," 358.

12. Ross, *Grace Coolidge,* 136.

13. Ibid., 135; *New York Times,* July 12, 1925.

14. Boone, Memoirs, XXI-854, Boone Papers, Library of Congress.

15. Alice Roosevelt Longworth, *Crowded Hours: Reminiscences of Alice Roosevelt Longworth* (New York: Charles Scribner's, 1938), 337. Actually Alice Longworth says that she got the phrase from her doctor, who heard it from a patient, but Princess Alice told it so often that her name became associated with it.

16. *New York Times,* February 12, 1925. Author's conversation with Cynthia Bittinger, August 12, 2005.

17. Irwin Hoover Papers, microfilm reel 8, Library of Congress, Washington, D.C.

18. Ross, *Grace Coolidge,* 119.

19. Calvin Coolidge, *The Autobiography of Calvin Coolidge* (New York: Cosmopolitan Book Corporation, 1929), 190.

20. Starling, *Starling of the White House,* 224.

21. Ibid., 242–43.

22. A. Scott Berg, *Lindbergh* (New York: G. P. Putnam's, 1998), 154–55.

23. Irwin H. Hoover, *Forty-two Years in the White House* (Boston: Houghton Mifflin, 1934), 131; Hal Elliott Wert, *Hoover, the Fishing President: Portrait of the Private Man and His Life Outdoors* (Mechanicsburg, Pa.: Stackpole Books, 2005), 155. Wert describes the laborious process whereby a persistent guide on the Brule taught Coolidge to cast with a fly.

24. Ross, *Grace Coolidge*, 231–32; Starling, *Starling of the White House*, 252–53.

25. Boone, Memoirs, XXXI-839, Boone Papers, Library of Congress.

26. *New York Times*, July 7, 1927.

27. *New York Times*, August 8, 1927.

28. Boller, *Presidential Anecdotes*, 234.

29. Grace Coolidge to Maude Trumbull, January 30, 1933, CCMF, President Coolidge State Historical Site, as quoted in Cynthia D. Bittinger, *Grace Coolidge: Sudden Star* (Huntington, N.Y.: Nova Publishers, 2005), 100.

Chapter 11. Herbert Hoover

1. Herbert Hoover, *The Memoirs of Herbert Hoover: Years of Adventure, 1874 to 1920*, 3 vols. (New York: Macmillan, 1951), 1:21–22.

2. William B. Mead and Paul Dickson, *Baseball: The Presidents' Game* (New York: Walker, 1997), 60.

3. Robert W. Creamer, *Babe: The Legend Comes to Life* (New York: Simon and Schuster, 1974), 351.

4. Joel T. Boone Notes, 1930–33, Joel T. Boone Papers, Library of Congress, Washington, D.C.

5. Joel T. Boone, Memoirs, XXII-55–56, Boone Papers, Library of Congress.

6. Ibid.

7. Ibid., XXII-57 a–h, 76, Boone Papers, Library of Congress.

8. Anne Beiser Allen, *An Independent Woman: The Life of Lou Henry Hoover* (Westport, Conn.: Greenwood Press, 2000), 11.

9. Ibid., 97–98; *New York Sun*, April 6, 1925.

10. Laurel A. Racine, *Historic Furnishings Report, Rapidan Camp: "The Brown House," Shenandoah National Park* (Washington, D.C.: National Park Service, 2001), 26.

11. Irwin H. Hoover, *Forty-two Years in the White House* (Boston: Houghton Mifflin, 1934), 190–91. Just as he disliked Calvin Coolidge, Ike Hoover did not care for Herbert and Lou Hoover.

12. Ibid.

13. Joel T. Boone, notes on draft of booklet on Camp Hoover, April 2, 1968, Boone, Memoirs, XXII-147c, 232, Boone Papers, Library of Congress.

14. J. Russell Young, "When the President Takes a Vacation," *Sunday Star Magazine* (Washington), April 19, 1931, 1–2.

15. Ibid.

16. William M. Garland to Herbert Hoover, July 6, 1932, Herbert Hoover Papers, Herbert Hoover Presidential Library, West Branch, Iowa.

17. Lawrence Richey to Garland, July 15, 1932, Hoover Papers, Hoover Presidential Library.

18. Richard Norton Smith, *An Uncommon Man: The Triumph of Herbert Hoover* (New York: Simon & Schuster, 1984), 139.

19. Hoover, *Fishing for Fun and to Wash Your Soul* (New York: Random House, 1963), 76.

Chapter 12. Franklin Delano Roosevelt

1. Jean Gould, *A Good Fight: The Story of FDR's Conquest of Polio* (New York: Dodd, Mead, 1960), 191.

2. Diary, June 22, 1903, Franklin Delano Roosevelt Papers, Franklin Delano Roosevelt Presidential Library, Hyde Park, New York.

3. Theo Lippmann Jr., *The Squire of Warm Springs: FDR in Georgia, 1924–1945* (n.p., n.d.), 82–83.

4. Kenneth S. Davis, *FDR: The Beckoning of Destiny, 1882–1928* (New York: G. P. Putnam's, 1972), 683.

5. Dore Schary, *Sunrise at Campobello: A Play in Three Acts* (New York: Random House, 1957), 100–101.

6. Hugh G. Gallagher, *FDR's Splendid Deception: The Moving Story of Roosevelt's Massive Disability and the Intense Efforts to Conceal It from the Public* (New York: Dodd, Mead, 1985), 62.

7. Gould, *A Good Fight*, 198.

8. Michael F. Reilly and William J. Slocum, *Reilly of the White House* (New York: Simon & Schuster, 1947), 98–100.

9. Lippmann, *The Squire of Warm Springs*, 180; Bernard Heigh to Roosevelt, April 25, 1933, Roosevelt Papers, Roosevelt Presidential Library.

10. Robert F. Cross, *Sailor in the White House: The Seafaring Life of FDR* (Annapolis, Md.: Naval Institute Press, 2003), 88.

11. Bill Mares, *Fishing with the Presidents: An Anecdotal History* (Mechanicsburg, Pa.: Stackpole Books, 1999), 38.

12. *New York Times*, April 1, 1933.

13. The Cruise of President Franklin D. Roosevelt to South America and the Inter-American Conference for the Maintenance of Peace, November 18, 1936 to December 15, 1936, Roosevelt Papers, Roosevelt Presidential Library.

14. Elliott Roosevelt, *As He Saw It* (Westport, Conn.: Greenwood Press, 1945), 20–21.

15. Franklin D. Roosevelt to Anna Roosevelt Boettiger, August 10, 1943, in Elliott Roosevelt, ed., *F.D.R.: His Personal Letters, 1928–1945*, 2 vols. (New York: Duell, Sloan and Pearce, 1950), 2:1438.

16. Gallagher, *FDR's Splendid Deception*, 207.

17. *Washington Post*, March 2, 1945.

18. Russell Freedman, *Eleanor Roosevelt: Life of Discovery* (New York: Clarion, 1993), 45.

19. Blanche Wiesen Cook, *Eleanor Roosevelt, 1884–1933* (New York: Viking, 1992), 182.

20. Eleanor Roosevelt, *The Autobiography of Eleanor Roosevelt, 1884–1933* (New York: DaCapo, 1992), 121.

21. Cook, *Eleanor Roosevelt, 1884–1933*, 431.

22. Ibid.

23. Blanche Wiesen Cook, *Eleanor Roosevelt, 1933–1938* (New York: Viking, 2000), 204–6.

24. Roosevelt to Kenesaw M. Landis, January 15, 1942, Roosevelt Papers, Roosevelt Presidential Library; *New York Times*, April 13, 1933, and January 6, 1943.

Chapter 13. Harry S Truman

1. Paul F. Boller Jr., *Presidential Anecdotes* (New York: Oxford University Press, 1981), 278.

2. Interview with Henry P. Chiles, November 1, 1961, and August 14, 1962, Harry S Truman Presidential Library, Independence, Missouri.

3. Mary Paxton Keely, "Bess Wallace Played Basketball after 'Phog' and Brothers Began It," *Examiner Suburban Life* (Independence, Mo.), May 6, 1988.

4. Margaret Truman, *Bess W. Truman* (New York: Macmillan, 1986), 35; Harry S Truman to Bess Wallace, September 9, 1912, in Robert H. Ferrell, ed., *Dear Bess: The Letters from Harry to Bess Truman, 1910–1959* (New York: W. W. Norton, 1983), 96.

5. Truman to Bess Wallace, August 14, September 2, 5, 1911, in Ferrell, *Dear Bess*, 43–45.

6. Ibid.

7. Helen Thomas, "Physical Fitness Becomes Way of Life at White House," *Examiner Suburban Life* (Independence, Mo.), June 26, 1985.

8. Harry H. Vaughan to Richard K. Goodman, September 30, 1946, Sports, Truman Presidential Library.

9. Drew Pearson, "Presidential Poker," *Washington Merry-Go-Round*, [1950], Truman Presidential Library.

10. Clark M. Clifford, *Counsel to the President: A Memoir* (New York: Random House, 1991), 102–4.

11. Boller, *Presidential Anecdotes*, 280–81; David McCulloch, *Truman* (New York: Simon & Schuster, 1992), 829.

12. *New York Times*, November 14, 19, 1951.

13. "Hayes: 'Truman Would Have Been a Great Coach,'" *Long Beach Press Telegram*, December 27, 1972; "Sad Hayes Praises Truman: A Man Who Could Take It," *Chicago Sun-Times*, December 27, 1972.

Chapter 14. Dwight D. Eisenhower

1. Clarence G. Lasby, *Eisenhower's Heart Attack: How Ike Beat Heart Disease and Held on to the Presidency* (Lawrence: University Press of Kansas, 1997), 70–78.

2. Ibid.

3. Dwight D. Eisenhower to Earl E. Hazlett, March 2, 1956, Eisenhower Papers, Dwight D. Eisenhower Presidential Library, Abilene, Kansas.

4. Dwight D. Eisenhower, *At Ease: Stories I Tell to Friends* (Garden City, N.Y.: Doubleday, 1967), 15–16.

5. Ibid., 23.

6. Ibid., 198.

7. Stephen E. Ambrose, *Eisenhower: Soldier of the Army, President-Elect, 1890–1952* (New York: Simon & Schuster, 1983), 51; Eisenhower, *At Ease*, 16.

8. Eisenhower, *At Ease*, 15.

9. John S. D. Eisenhower, *Strictly Personal: A Memoir* (Garden City, N.Y.: Doubleday, 1974), 8.

10. Susan Eisenhower, *Mrs. Ike: Memories and Reflections on the Life of Mamie Eisenhower* (New York: Farrar, Straus and Giroux, 1996), 144–45, 152.

11. Interview with Clifford Roberts, Eisenhower Presidential Library, recorded as part of Columbia University Oral History Project, September 12, 1968.

12. Priscilla Slater Diary, Thanksgiving 1953, in Ellis D. Slater, *The Ike I Knew* (Palm Desert, Calif.: Ellis D. Slater Trust, 1980), 57.

13. *New York Times*, February 14, 1957.

14. Dwight Eisenhower to Earl E. Hazlett, July 21, 1953, Eisenhower Papers, Eisenhower Presidential Library.

15. Slater, *The Ike I Knew*, diary, February 27, 1953, 38; diary, April 24, 1957, 151.

16. Interview with Charles R. Yates, August 10, 1970, Eisenhower Presidential Library.

17. *New York Times*, March 25, 1954.

18. *New York Times*, June 20, 1954.

19. *New York Times*, February 26, 1956.

20. Interview with Clifford Roberts, Eisenhower Presidential Library; Clifford Roberts, *The Story of the Augusta Country Club* (Garden City, N.Y.: Doubleday, 1976), 169–70.

21. Interview with Clifford Roberts, Eisenhower Presidential Library.

22. Diary of Howard Snyder, April 11, 1959, Howard Snyder Papers, Eisenhower Presidential Library.

23. Stephen E. Ambrose, *Eisenhower, the President* (New York: Simon & Schuster, 1983), 655.

24. William E. Leuchtenburg, *A Troubled Feast: American Society since 1945* (Boston: Little, Brown, 1973).

25. Slater, *The Ike I Knew*, 162.

Chapter 15. John F. Kennedy

1. John F. Kennedy, *Profiles in Courage* (New York: Harper and Row, 1955), 75.

2. Nigel Hamilton, *JFK: Reckless Youth* (New York: Random House, 1992), 104.

3. Joan Blair and Clay Blair Jr., *The Search for JFK* (New York: Berkeley Publishing, 1976), 32.

4. Hamilton, *JFK*, 228.

5. Robert Dallek, *An Unfinished Life: John F. Kennedy, 1917–1963* (New York: Little, Brown, 2003), 76.

6. Hamilton, *JFK*, 605.

7. Blair and Blair, *The Search for JFK*, 305.

8. John F. Kennedy, "The Soft American," *Sports Illustrated*, December 26, 1960, 15.

9. *New York Times*, March 31, June 28, 1960.

10. John F. Kennedy, "The Vigor We Need," *Sports Illustrated*, July 16, 1962, 12–15.

11. Pierre Salinger, *With Kennedy* (Garden City, N.Y.: Doubleday, 1966), 239.

12. *New York Times*, March 29, 1961.

13. Salinger, *With Kennedy*, 239; Benjamin C. Bradlee, *Conversations with Kennedy* (New York: W. W. Norton, 1975), 210–11.

14. Bradlee, *Conversations*, 210–11.

15. Sally Bedell Smith, *Grace and Power: The Private World of the Kennedy White House* (New York: Random House, 2004), 115, 136.

16. Bradlee, *Conversations*, 211–12.

17. Smith, *Grace and Power*, 123.

18. Charles K. Ross, *Outside the Lines: African-Americans and the Integration of the National Football League* (New York: New York University Press, 2003), 153.

19. Dallek, *An Unfinished Life*, 562.

20. A. E. Housman, "To an Athlete Dying Young," *A Shropshire Lad* (New York: Henry Holt, 1924), 27.

Chapter 16. Lyndon Johnson

1. Sally Bedell Smith, *Grace and Power: The Private World of the Kennedy White House* (New York: Random House, 2004), 13.

2. Interview with Richard S. "Cactus" Pryor, September 10, 1968, Archives, Lyndon Baines Johnson Library and Museum, Austin, Texas.

3. Interview with Lorena D. Hughes and Allie T. Hughes, April 30, 1965, Archives, Johnson Library.

4. Robert Dallek, *Lone Star Rising: Lyndon Johnson and His Times, 1908–1960* (New York: Oxford University Press, 1991), 91; Irwin Unger and Debi Unger, *LBJ: A Life* (New York: John Wiley, 1999), 33.

5. Merle Miller, *Lyndon: An Oral Biography* (New York: G. P. Putnam's, 1980), 175.

6. Interview with Eugene "Sam" Worley, October 16, 1968, Archives, Johnson Library.

7. Ibid.

8. Ibid.

9. "The Senator's Senator," *Sports Illustrated*, September 29, 1955, 1.

10. Hal K. Rothman, *LBJ's Texas White House: "Our Heart's Home"* (College Station: Texas A&M Press, 2001), 95; Alfred Steinberg, *Sam Johnson's Boy: A Close-Up of the President from Texas* (New York: Macmillan, 1968), 297.

11. Interview with Walter Heller, December 21, 1971, Archives, Johnson Library; Rothman, *LBJ's Texas White House*, 208.

12. Marie Hanlon to Lyndon Baines Johnson, January 5, 1964, Archives, Johnson Library.

13. Paul R. Henggeler, *In His Steps: Lyndon Johnson and the Kennedy Mystique* (Chicago: Ivan R. Dee, 1991), 142.

14. Ibid.

15. Philip Knollmueller to Johnson, February 23, 1964, Archives, Johnson Library.

16. Author's interview with Darrell Royal, February 1, 2002, Johnson Library.

17. Ibid.; Rothman, *LBJ's Texas White House*, 245; Jimmy Banks, *The Darrell Royal Story* (Austin, Tex.: Eakin Press, 1973), 140.

18. Author's interview with Darrell Royal, February 1, 2002.

19. Ibid.

20. Ibid.

21. Ibid.

Chapter 17. Richard Nixon

1. Incident Recalled by Harrison McCall, January 3, 1959, Richard Nixon Pre-Presidential Papers, National Archives, Pacific Region, Laguna Niguel, California; "Dick Nixon Likes to Write Sports," *Washington Post*, August 15, 1959.

2. Stephen E. Ambrose, *Nixon: The Education of a Politician, 1913–1962* (New York: Simon & Schuster, 1987), 65.

3. Interview with James Graves, May 13, 1970, in Rennee K. Schulte, ed., *The Young Nixon: An Oral Inquiry* (Fullerton: California State University, Fullerton, Oral History Program, 1978), 102.

4. Richard M. Nixon, *RN: The Memoirs of Richard Nixon* (New York: Simon & Schuster, 1978), 20.

5. Interview with Charles Kendle, April 17, 1970, in Schulte, *The Young Nixon*, 187.

6. Fawn M. Brodie, *Richard Nixon: The Shaping of His Character* (New York: W. W. Norton, 1981), 112.

7. Quoted in Ambrose, *Nixon: The Education of a Politician*, 112.

8. UPI-150, Richard Nixon, Pre-Presidential Papers, National Archives, Pacific Region.

9. Ambrose, *Nixon: The Education of a Politician*, 671.

10. Richard M. Nixon to Woody Hayes, January 2, 1973, Richard Nixon Papers, National Archives, College Park, Md.

11. *New York Times*, January 3, 1969.

12. Terry Frei, *Horns, Hogs, and Nixon Coming: Texas vs. Arkansas in Dixie's Last Stand* (New York: Simon and Schuster, 2002), 259.

13. *New York Times*, December 8, 1969.

14. *New York Times*, December 7, 1969.

15. *New York Times*, December 10, 1969.

16. Ibid.

17. *New York Times*, November 24, 1971.

18. "The President and the Play," *Post Standard*, April 23, 1994, Richard M. Nixon Presidential Library and Museum, Yorba Linda, California.

19. *New York Times*, December 26, 1971.

20. *New York Times*, January 4, 1972.

21. *New York Times*, January 17, 1972.

22. *New York Times*, January 15, 1971.

23. *New York Times*, February 2, 1972.

24. *New York Times*, August 15, 1959.

25. *New York Times*, August 18, 1971.

26. Address by David Eisenhower, April 19, 1995, Hofstra University, Hempstead, New York.

27. Red Smith, "New, Slow Boy on the Baseball Beat," *New York Times*, July 3, 1972.

28. *New York Times*, July 4, 1972.

29. Address by Richard Nixon to the American Football Coaches Association, January 18, 1958, Nixon Pre-Presidential Papers, National Archives, Pacific Region.

30. Richard M. Nixon, *In the Arena: A Memoir of Victory, Defeat, and Renewal* (New York: Simon and Schuster, 1990), 163; *Los Angeles Examiner*, April 21, 1955.

31. *New York Times*, September 17, 1971.

32. *New York Herald-Tribune*, September 12, 1953; Don Van Natta Jr., *First Off the Tee: Presidential Hackers, Duffers, and Cheaters from Taft to Bush* (New York: Public Affairs, 2003), 228; Nixon, *In the Arena*, 161.

33. Van Natta, *First Off the Tee*, 232.

34. Stephen E. Ambrose, *Nixon: Ruin and Recovery, 1974–1990* (New York: Simon and Schuster, 1991), 33.

35. Nixon, *In the Arena*, 165.

36. Address by David Eisenhower, April 29, 1995, Hofstra University.

37. Ambrose, *Nixon: Ruin and Recovery*, 467.

Chapter 18. Gerald Ford

1. Memorandum, V. L Nicholson to Eliska Hasek, December 14, 1974, President's Council on Physical Fitness and Sports, Gerald R. Ford Papers, Gerald R. Ford Presidential Library, Ann Arbor, Michigan.

2. *Grand Rapids Press*, November 29, 1974.

3. James Cannon, *Time and Change: Gerald Ford's Appointment with History* (New York: HarperCollins, 1994), 5.

4. Gerald R. Ford, *A Time to Heal: The Autobiography of Gerald K. Ford* (New York:

Harper and Row, 1979), 52–53. Author's interview with President Gerald R. Ford, August 8, 2002.

5. Jan Hemming, "Yale Professors Recall Ford as Mild-Mannered Gentleman," undated newspaper article in Vertical File Folder, Ford, Gerald—Sports—Football—Yale, Ford Presidential Library.

6. Ibid.

7. Edward L. Schapsmeier and Frederick H. Schapsmeier, *Gerald R. Ford's Date with Destiny: A Political Biography* (New York: Peter Lang, 1989), 13.

8. Memorandum of conversation, July 14, 1976, National Security Adviser, Memoranda of Conversations, 1973–77, Ford Papers, Ford Presidential Library.

9. Memorandum, Tod Hullin to Ken Cole, January 7, 1975, Sexual Equality, Title IX, 1975, Ford Papers, Ford Presidential Library.

10. Glenn Schembechler to Gerald Ford, July 14, 1975, White House Central File Name File, Ford Papers, Ford Presidential Papers.

11. James H. Cavanaugh to Bryce N. Harlow, November 11, 1974, Ford Papers, Ford Presidential Library.

12. Ford, *A Time to Heal*, 112.

13. "What's Going On Here?" April 7, 1975, Sheila Weidenthal Papers, Golf, Ford Papers, Ford Presidential Library.

14. Author's interview with Gerald R. Ford, August 8, 2002.

15. Ford, *A Time to Heal*, 205.

16. Howard Erickson, "Skiing," *Rocky Mountain News*, December 25, 1974.

17. Elizabeth Kolbert, "Stooping to Conquer, Why Politicians Mock Themselves," *New Yorker*, April 19 and 26, 2004, 88 [combined issue].

18. President Ford Committee, Records, 1973–77, Transcripts, Grand Rapids Interview, Ford Family, 13, Ford Presidential Library.

19. "Face the Nation," [Muhammad Ali], May 2, 1976, Ronald A. Nessen File, Ford Papers, Ford Presidential Library; *New York Times*, April 28, 1976; Scores, Summary Lists, President's Daily Diary, Ford Papers, Ford Presidential Library.

20. Recommended Telephone Call, July 6, 1976, Public Relations—Press Conferences, Ford Papers, Ford Presidential Library.

21. Presidential Remarks for the Lee Elder Testimonial, December 1, 1974; Golf lists, President's Daily Diary, Golf, 1974–76, Ford Papers, Ford Presidential Library.

22. "Mrs. Ford Gains a Campaign Style," October 18, 1976, Weidenthal Papers, Ford Presidential Library; "Betty vs. Rosalynn, Life on the Campaign Trail," *U.S. News and World Report*, October 18, 1976, 22.

23. Ford, *A Time to Heal*, 430, 435–36.

Chapter 19. Jimmy Carter

1. Jimmy Carter, *An Hour before Daylight: Memories of a Rural Boyhood* (New York: Simon & Schuster, 2001), 101.

2. Jimmy Carter, *An Outdoor Journal: Adventures and Reflections* (Fayetteville: University of Arkansas Press, 1988), 15.

3. Ibid., 10.

4. Carter, *An Hour before Daylight,* 122.

5. Ibid., 123.

6. Ibid., 105.

7. Kenneth E. Morris, *Jimmy Carter: American Moralist* (Athens: University of Georgia Press, 1986), 67.

8. Carter, *An Hour before Daylight,* 107.

9. Ibid., 97. Also see Peter G. Bourne in *Jimmy Carter: A Comprehensive Biography from Plains to Post-Presidency* (New York: Scribner, 1997), 210. Bourne relates that the Carters learned that they were expelled from the Americus Country Club when Rosalynn took son Chip for a golf lesson.

10. Bourne, *Jimmy Carter,* 210.

11. Carter, *Outdoor Journal,* 159.

12. James Fallows, "The Passionless Presidency: An Insider's Report on the Trouble with the Carter Administration," *Atlantic* 243, 5 (May 1979): 38. A second part appeared in the June issue.

13. Carter, *Outdoor Journal,* 114.

14. Ibid.

15. *New York Times,* December 28, 1980.

16. *New York Times,* September 16, 1979; Bourne, *Jimmy Carter,* 449. Carter resumed his daily running, usually fifty to sixty miles each week.

17. Bourne, *Jimmy Carter,* 449; Bill Mares, *Fishing with the Presidents: An Anecdotal History* (Mechanicsburg, Pa.: Stackpole Books, 1999), 131–33.

18. Carter, *Outdoor Journal,* 54.

19. Allen Guttmann, *The Olympics: A History of the Modern Games* (Urbana: University of Illinois Press, 1992), 150.

20. *New York Times,* February 23, 1980.

21. *Columbus Dispatch,* April 5, 1980. Bert Shaw, chairman of the American water polo governing body, used the phrase "political hostages."

22. Jimmy Carter, *Keeping Faith: Memoirs of a President* (New York: Bantam Books, 1982), 543.

23. Fallows, "The Passionless Presidency," 35.

24. Douglas Brinkley, *The Unfinished Presidency: Jimmy Carter's Quest for Global Peace* (New York: Penguin Group, 1999).

Chapter 20. Ronald Reagan

1. Lou Cannon, *Reagan* (New York: G. P. Putnam's, 1982), 59.

2. *Knute Rockne, All American,* Warner Brothers, 1940.

3. Murray Sperber, *Shake Down the Thunder: The Creation of Notre Dame Football* (New York: Henry Holt, 1993), 110.

4. Bill Adler and Bill Adler Jr., *The Reagan Wit: The Humor of the American President* (New York: William Morrow, 1998), 81; Ronald Reagan, *Where's the Rest of Me?* (New York: Dell, 1965), 95.

5. Reagan to Chet Sampson, May 22, 1986, in Kiron K. Skinner, Annelise Anderson, and Martin Anderson, eds., *Reagan: A Life in Letters* (New York: Free Press, 2003), 130.

6. Lou Cannon, *President Reagan: The Role of a Lifetime* (New York: Public Affairs, 1991), 112.

7. *Prism* (Eureka College Yearbook), 1930, 63.

8. Ronald Reagan, *An American Life* (New York: Simon and Schuster, 1990), 52. Reagan says that the team was staying in Dixon, but other sources indicate that it was in Aurora fifty-eight miles away and McKinzie may have given them money for cab fare to Dixon.

9. Ibid.

10. Ibid., 29.

11. Anne Edwards, *Early Reagan: The Rise to Power* (New York: William Morrow, 1987), 64.

12. *The Eureka Pegasus*, March 29, 1930; Edwards, *Early Reagan*, 87–88.

13. Reagan, *An American Life*, 58.

14. Ibid., 64.

15. Reagan to Ron Cochran, May 12, 1980, in Skinner, Anderson, and Anderson, *Reagan: A Life in Letters*, 29.

16. Reagan, *An American Life*, 73.

17. Ibid.

18. Edwards, *Early Reagan*, 141.

19. Reagan, *An American Life*, 81.

20. Adler and Adler, *The Reagan Wit*, 47.

21. Reagan to Rudolph Hines, August 14, 1986, in Skinner, Anderson, and Anderson, *Reagan: A Life in Letters*, 803; Doug McClelland, *Hollywood on Ronald Reagan: Friends and Enemies Discuss Our President, the Actor* (Winchester, Mass.: Faber and Faber, 1983), 18.

22. Larry Speakes, *Speaking Out: Inside the Reagan White House* (New York: Charles Scribner's, 1988), 92; Nancy Reagan, *My Turn: The Memoirs of Nancy Reagan* (New York: Random House, 1989), 106.

23. *Knute Rockne, All American*, Warner Brothers, 1940.

24. Cannon, *Reagan*, 29.

25. Ronald Reagan to Bob Feller, August 11, 1948, File, Baseball, Softball, box 2 RE 0001, Ronald Reagan Presidential Library, Simi Valley, California. Feller did send an autographed ball.

26. Reagan, *Where's the Rest of Me?*, 239.

27. Ibid., 238; Nancy Reagan, *My Turn*, 66.

28. Speakes, *Speaking Out*, 110.

29. Reagan, *An American Life,* 387.

30. Ibid., 503.

31. William B. Mead and Paul Dickson, *Baseball: The Presidents' Game* (New York: Walker, 1997), 170.

32. Robert Lindsey, "Creating the Role," in Hedrick Smith, Adam Clymer, Leonard Silk, Robert Lindsey, and Richard Burt, *Reagan: The Man, the President* (New York: Macmillan, 1980), 21; Cannon, *Reagan,* 45.

33. Cannon, *Reagan,* 114.

34. Ibid., 187.

35. Ibid., 402.

36. Adler and Adler, *The Reagan Wit,* 179–80.

Chapter 21. George H. W. Bush

1. *New York Times,* March 29, 1989.

2. Pamela Killian, *Matriarch of a Family* (New York: St. Martin's Press, 2002), 25.

3. Mickey Herskowitz, *The Life and Legacy of Prescott Bush* (Nashville: Rutledge Hill Press, 2003), 42.

4. *Pot Pouri,* 1942 (Andover Yearbook), "Varsity Baseball," 128–29.

5. *Pot Pouri,* 1942, "The 1942 Class Poll," 80–81.

6. Ibid.

7. George Bush to Prescott and Dorothy Bush, June 22, 1944, in George Bush, ed., *All the Best: George Bush; My Life in Letters and Other Writings* (New York: Scribner, 1999), 44.

8. Bush to Prescott and Dorothy Bush, September 3, 1944, in Bush, ed., *All the Best,* 51.

9. Barbara Bush, *A Memoir* (New York: Charles Scribner's, 1994), 8.

10. William B. Mead and Paul Dickson, *Baseball: The Presidents' Game* (New York: Walker, 1997), 175–78.

11. Herbert S. Parmet, *George Bush: The Life of a Lone Star Yankee* (New York: Scribner, 1997), 65.

12. Bush to Fitzgerald Bemiss, August 28, 1948, in Bush, *All the Best,* 63.

13. James A. Baker, *The Politics of Diplomacy, Revolution, War, and Peace* (New York: G. P. Putnam's, 1995), 18.

14. Bush to G. H. Walker Jr., August 22, 1951, in Bush, *All the Best,* 72.

15. Campaign Diary, September 29, 1979, in ibid., 282.

16. Parmet, *George Bush,* 229.

17. Ibid., 235.

18. Shepherd Campbell and Peter Landau, *Presidential Lies: The Illustrated History of White House Golf* (New York: Macmillan, 1996), 214.

19. Dan Quayle, *Standing Firm: A Vice-Presidential Memoir* (New York: Harper Collins, 1994), 64; Parmet, *George Bush,* 354.

20. Byron York, "Bill's Bad Lie," *American Spectator,* September 1996, 45.

21. *New York Times*, January 2, 1989.

22. George Plimpton, "Sportsman Born and Bred," *Sports Illustrated*, December 26–January 2, 1989, 156.

23. Ibid.

24. Ibid., 158.

25. Parmet, *George Bush*, 357.

26. Plimpton, "Sportsman Born and Bred," 148.

27. Ibid., 141.

28. *New York Times*, January 2, 1989.

29. Maureen Dowd, "A Regular Guy Goes to the White House," *New York Times*, January 15, 1989.

30. Parmet, *George Bush*, 453.

31. Jean Edward Smith, *George Bush's War* (New York: Henry Holt, 1992), 129.

32. *New York Times*, August 19, 1990.

33. Andy Valeur, "The Golf Crisis: It's Getting Rough," *New York Times*, August 25, 1990.

34. *New York Times*, August 27, 1991.

35. Parmet, *George Bush*, 469.

36. Burton J. Lee III, "The Bush Presidency and Presidential Liability," in Kenneth W. Thompson, ed., *The Bush Presidency: Ten Intimate Perspectives of George Bush* (Lanham, Md.: University Press of America, 1997), 170–71.

37. *New York Times*, April 20, 1992.

38. Mead and Dickson, *The President's Game*, 179.

39. George Plimpton, *The X Factor: A Quest for Excellence* (New York: W. W. Norton, 1995), 153–54.

40. Ibid.

41. Ibid., 161.

Chapter 22. Bill Clinton

1. *New York Times*, February 16, 1995; Don Van Natta Jr., *First Off the Tee: Presidential Hackers, Duffers, and Cheaters from Taft to Bush* (New York: Public Affairs, 2003), 5.

2. David Maraniss, *First in His Class: A Biography of Bill Clinton* (New York: Simon & Schuster, 1995), 101.

3. George Plimpton, "Jock Talk," *New Yorker*, August 12, 1996, 22.

4. Ibid.

5. Bill Clinton, *My Life* (New York: Alfred A. Knopf, 2004), 165.

6. Plimpton, "Jock Talk," 23.

7. Alexander Wolff, "The First Fan," *Sports Illustrated*, March 21, 1994, 26.

8. John F. Harris, *The Survivor: Bill Clinton in the White House* (New York: Random House, 2005), 57–58.

9. Clinton, *My Life*, 254.

10. Ibid.

11. Plimpton, "Jock Talk," 23.

12. *New York Times*, January 9, 1995.

13. *New York Times*, July 26, 1993.

14. Ibid.

15. *New York Times*, January 27, 1995.

16. Clare Smith, "Well, Mr. President, Baseball Hasn't Caved," *New York Times*, February 4, 1995.

17. George Vecsey, "White House Couldn't Hit Loud Foul," *New York Times*, February 8, 1995.

18. Don Van Natta Jr., "The Rights of Bill," *Sports Illustrated*, March 21, 2003, 98.

19. *New York Times*, August 23, 1993; Van Natta, "The Rights of Bill," 100.

20. Rick Reilly, "President Clinton," *Sports Illustrated*, June 12, 1995, 53.

21. Byron York, "Bill's Bad Lie," *American Spectator*, September 1996, 38.

22. Maureen Dowd, "President Lonely Guy," *New York Times*, October 20, 1999.

Chapter 23. George W. Bush

1. Michael Bamberger, "Whole New Ball Game," *Sports Illustrated*, March 14, 2005, 42.

2. Lois Romano and George Lardner Jr., "Moving Up to the Big Leagues," *Washington Post*, July 31, 1999.

3. *The Phillipian*, 1963 (Phillips Andover Academy), 56.

4. "The Road to Politics Ran Directly through a Ballpark in Texas," *New York Times*, September 24, 2000.

5. George W. Bush, *A Charge to Keep* (New York: William Morrow, 1999), 47.

6. Don Van Natta Jr., *First Off the Tee: Presidential Hackers, Duffers, and Cheaters from Taft to Bush* (New York: Public Affairs, 2003), 307.

7. "Q&A: George W. Bush," *Sports Illustrated*, September 29, 2003, 45–46.

8. "Q&A: Roger Staubach, *Sports Illustrated*, February 2, 2004, 25.

9. Ibid.

10. *Washington Post*, August 21, 2002.

11. Ibid.

12. Bush, *A Charge to Keep*, 202.

13. "The Road to Politics Ran Directly through a Ballpark in Texas," *New York Times*, September 24, 2000.

14. George Will, *Men at Work* (New York: Macmillan, 1990), 65; *Dallas Morning News*, May 1, 1989.

15. Bush, *A Charge to Keep*, 206.

16. Elizabeth Mitchell, *"W": Revenge of the Bush Dynasty* (New York: Penguin, 2000), 252; "Another Winner for the Bush Family," *Business Week*, May 22, 1989, 166.

17. "Another Winner for the Bush Family," *Business Week*, May 22, 1989, 166.

18. "The Road to Politics Ran Directly through a Ballpark in Texas," *New York Times*, September 24, 2000.

19. Bush, *A Charge to Keep*, 207.

20. Byron York, "Bush to Tee," *National Review* 53, 17 (September 3, 2001), 30.

21. Ibid., 32.

22. David Frum, *The Right Man: The Surprise Presidency of George W. Bush* (New York: Random House, 2003), 140.

Conclusion

1. *Washington Post*, February 16, 2004.

2. Ibid.

3. Jean Gould, *A Good Fight: The Story of FDR's Conquest of Polio* (New York: Dodd, Mead, 1960), 191.

4. Jack Willis (as told to Horace Smith), *Roosevelt in the Rough* (New York: Ives, Washburn, 1931), 13. Roosevelt had been told by his guide to shoot the bird in the head because a shot into the body would cause this species to fly apart.

5. Byron York, "Bill's Big Lie," *American Spectator*, September 1996, 38. More can be found about the Clinton-Simpson round in Alan Schroeder, *Celebrity-in-Chief: How Show Business Took Over the White House* (Boulder, Colo.: Westview Books, 2004), 52.

6. Dwight Eisenhower, *At Ease: Stories I Tell to Friends* (Garden City, N.Y.: Doubleday, 1967), 16.

7. Richard M. Nixon, *RN: The Memoirs of Richard Nixon* (New York: Simon & Schuster, 1978), 19–20.

8. James Cannon, *Time and Change: Gerald Ford's Appointment with History* (New York: HarperCollins, 1994), 15.

9. John Milton Cooper Jr., *Breaking the Heart of the World: Woodrow Wilson and the Fight for the League of Nations* (Cambridge: Cambridge University Press, 2001), 54.

10. Paul F. Boller Jr., *Presidential Anecdotes* (New York: Oxford University Press, 1981), 218.

11. John A. Garraty, *The American Nation* (New York: Harper and Row, 1979), 2:615.

12. Herbert Hoover, *Fishing for Fun and to Wash Your Soul* (New York: Random House, 1963), 76.

13. Geoff Earle, "Forget His Resume, What's His Regimen?" *Washington Post*, July 31, 2005.

14. *Washington Post*, February 16, 2004.

15. Hoover, *Fishing for Fun*, 76–77.

★ ★ ★
Suggested Reading

If readers want to immerse themselves in the sports of the presidents, where should they begin? Not with the presidents. Few have shared their sporting experiences in the White House (though several have written articles and books about outdoor pursuits before and after they held office). Serious readers must be prepared to read books both big and small. Many of the big books contain interesting background on presidential sports. Short of this, I would advise beginning with Paul F. Boller Jr.'s *Presidential Anecdotes* (New York: Oxford University Press, 1981), a sparkling collection of personal tidbits, like so many needles in a biographical haystack. Some of the anecdotes, such as Teddy Roosevelt's hunting, wrestling, and scrambling, cover the presidential sports.

My book deals primarily with twentieth-century presidents while other books cover the entire list of presidents. Some authors have taken a particular sport or a slice of presidential life, beginning with George Washington onward. *Presidents at Play* by George Sullivan (New York: Walker, 1995), for example, is a well-written, easy-to-read volume containing essays on each of nine sports. From equestrians to runners, Sullivan has a mixed bag of presidential characters from Grant to Clinton in this recreational history of the presidents. The book's appendix details the sports of presidents from Washington to Clinton.

One unpublished collection of articles and anecdotes on presidential sports is worth mentioning. Jack Level, a New York book dealer, accumulated scrapbooks and folders of clippings, letters, and notes on presidential recreation and athletics. He also wrote rough drafts of the book he envisioned. Unfortunately, he died before he could wrestle his vast and disorganized collection into a book. Now the Jack Level Presidents Collection resides in the Joyce Sports Research Collection in the Special Collections at the University Libraries of Notre Dame. Some of the material is useful and some difficult to corroborate.

To read about the health of the presidents, I would suggest going to Dr. Rudolph Marx's *The Health of the Presidents: The 41 United States Presidents through 1993 from a Physician's Point of View* (Jefferson, N.C.: McFarland, 1993). Marx gives capsule accounts, such as Grover Cleveland's secret surgery for mouth cancer aboard the presidential yacht. As interesting as these studies are, biographies and group studies that cover the heath of recent presidents such as Dwight Eisenhower and John F. Kennedy go into medical problems in far more detail—and relate them to presidential sports. Or, occasionally, a book discusses a single president's disability, such as Franklin Delano Roosevelt's struggle with the ravages of polio.

For those who want to read about a single sport, *First Off the Tee: Presidential Hackers, Duffers, and Cheaters from Taft to Bush,* by Don Van Natta Jr. (New York: Public Affairs, 2003) is amusing, if slightly unfair to the hackers and duffers. Van Natta's book is notable for two reasons: he actually played a round of golf with Bill Clinton, in which he recorded Clinton's unique approach to the rules. Van Natta also writes with panache about hilarious bloopers of the presidential threesome, Ford, Bush Sr., and Clinton, who played together with Bob Hope in 1994. Shepherd Campbell and Peter Landau wrote a more conventional history of presidential golf in *Presidential Lies: The Illustrated History of White House Golf* (New York: Macmillan, 1996). For comparison, Campbell and Landau's book offers a more balanced view of presidential golfers.

For the past twenty years, the books on the presidents have parsed their lives in minute detail. Now you can ride across the ranches of LBJ and Ronald Reagan; sail and fish with FDR; hunt, ranch, and explore with Teddy Roosevelt. The big biography is still alive and well, but so are the smaller volumes with a more limited focus.

The biographies of George Washington are too numerous to catalog here. One useful work is Frank E. Grizzard Jr., *George Washington: A Biographical Companion* (Santa Barbara, Calif.: ABC-CLIO, 2002). Grizzard's highly readable paperback volume includes sections on Washington's athletic prowess, including the story of the silver dollar hurled across the Rappahannock. I particularly like Joseph J. Ellis, *His Excellency: George Washington* (New York: Alfred A. Knopf, 2004), even though you will find precious little having to do with Washington's physical prowess. For a hands-on account of Washington's role in the battle at the Monongahela, C. Brian Kelly's "Young George Washington Would Bury the British Major Who Stubbornly Rejected His Advice" (*Military History* 18, 6 [February 2002]: 74) gives a workable account of Washington's military athleticism.

Surprisingly, many biographers of Jefferson have barely mentioned his wrist injury or accepted Jefferson's report of a dislocated wrist. For a more detailed account of the wrist injury, read Lyman H. Butterfield, "Jefferson's Earliest Note to Maria Cosway and Some New Facts and Conjectures on His Broken Wrist," which can be found in *William and Mary Quarterly,* 3rd ser., 5, 1 (1948): 26–33.

To get a firsthand account of John Quincy Adams's early morning plunges into the Potomac, readers should consult his diary for his years in Washington (Allan Nevins, ed., *The Diary of John Quincy Adams, 1794–1845: American Political, Social, and Intellectual Life from Washington to Polk* [New York: Longmans, Green, 1928]). To learn of Jackson as a young sport, either see Boller, *Presidential Anecdotes,* or Hendrik Booraem V, *Young Hickory: The Making of Andrew Jackson* (Dallas: Taylor Trade Publishing, 2001).

Nineteenth-century presidents rarely left accounts of their youthful sports and games. So it is notable that William Herndon, Lincoln's law partner, collected oral histories of the martyred president soon after his death. These accounts (*Herndon's Informants: Letters, Interviews, and Statements about Abraham Lincoln* [Urbana: University of Illinois Press, 1988]) suggest that young Lincoln had varied athletic interests. Unlike the presidential Lincoln, who had little time for sports, some nineteenth-century presidents and ex-presidents hunted and fished while in office. Thomas C. Reeves tracks Chester Arthur on his trip to Yellowstone in "President Arthur in Yellowstone National Park," *Montana, the Magazine of Western History* 19, 3 (July 1969): 18–29. John F. Reiger's ground-breaking book, *American Sportsmen and the Origin of Conservation* (Corvallis: Oregon State University Press, 2001), explains the influence of sportsmen such as George Bird Grinnell on Benjamin Harrison's contributions to conservation, not to mention Grinnell's impact on the youthful Theodore Roosevelt. A less ambitious volume by a gentleman sportsman is Grover Cleveland's *Fishing and Shooting Sketches* (New York: Outing Publishing, 1907). Cleveland's chapters reflect on fishing and hunting rather than merely narrating a specific experience. It's a landmark book because Cleveland was the first president, though hardly the last, to write on sports.

As presidential personalities, Grover Cleveland and Theodore Roosevelt had some notable similarities—both were sportsmen and both wrote about sports. The best way to understand Roosevelt, the athlete and sportsman, is by reading his prolific writings. For TR's account of his colorful and muscular youth, read *The Autobiography of Theodore Roosevelt* (New York: Charles Scribner's, 1958). Roosevelt's *Hunting Trips of a Ranchman: Sketches of Sport on the Northern Cattle Plains* (New York: G. P. Putnam's Sons, 1885) is one of several books about his life on the plains. If you want to see where it all began, read *Theodore Roosevelt's Diaries of Boyhood and Youth* (New York: Charles Scribner's, 1928). Roosevelt's *Rough Riders: An Autobiography* (New York: Charles Scribner's, 1899) gives a self-serving, though fairly accurate account of that remarkable saga. Many of Roosevelt's writings have been reissued in paperback, making them easily accessible.

Almost any biography of Roosevelt will include the story of the asthmatic youth who became the muscular boxer and rancher. One recent book that includes his athletic activities is Paul Grondahl's *I Rose like a Rocket: The Political Education of Theodore Roosevelt* (New York: Free Press, 2004). True, Grondahl takes the TR story only up to 1901, but his well-researched and nicely written volume includes accounts of Roosevelt's boxing, wrestling, and shooting, not to mention his interest in conservation as a legislator and governor. A well-illustrated fifty-page account highlighting his Dakota experience is Chester L. Brooks and Ray H. Mattison's *Theodore Roosevelt and the Dakota Badlands* (Washington, D.C.: National Park Service, 1958).

The array of Roosevelt's athletics and sports as president is almost too diverse to survey in this brief essay. Nevertheless, Edward Wagenknecht's *The Seven Worlds of Theodore Roosevelt* (New York: Longmans, Green, 1958) captures TR's universe of athletic interests. Edward J. Renehan's *John Burroughs: An American Naturalist* (Post Mills, Vt.: Chelsea Green, 1992) describes Burrough's trip with TR to Yellowstone, warts and all; the naturalist's own account, *Camping and Tramping with Roosevelt* (New York: Houghton Mifflin, 1907), might be read alongside. Paul Russell Cutright's *Theodore Roosevelt: The Making of a Conservationist* (Urbana: University of Illinois, 1985) brings to light the magnitude of TR's contribution to saving the natural environment. My research on Roosevelt's role in the 1905 football controversy may be found in *College Football: History, Spectacle, Controversy* (Baltimore: Johns Hopkins University Press, 2000).

Roosevelt's private life in the White House—and his sporting activities—are chronicled in *Edith Kermit Roosevelt: Portrait of a First Lady* by Sylvia Jukes Morris (New York: Modern Library, 1980). We get a clear view of the formidable First Lady who made TR's active life possible and shared a few of his outdoor pursuits. For a firsthand account of scrambling with the president, read Archibald W. Butt, *The Letters of Archie Butt, Personal Aide to President Roosevelt* (New York: Doubleday, Page, 1924). William H. Harbaugh chronicles the saga of the first presidential Camp David in "The Theodore Roosevelts' Retreat in Southern Albemarle: Pine Knot, 1905–1908," a sparkling essay in the *Magazine of Albemarle County History* 51 (1993): 1–50. The first chapter of Wagenknecht's *Seven Worlds of Theodore Roosevelt* mentions the impact of TR's physical activities on his deteriorating health. Joseph R. Ornig's *My Last Chance to Be a Boy: Theodore Roosevelt's South American Expedition of 1913–1914* (Baton Rouge: Louisiana State University Press, 1998) shows how Roosevelt's declining health and physical problems, some of them sustained as president, nearly killed him in his attempt to explore an uncharted river in Brazil. A superbly researched and riveting account of the same expedition is Candice Millard's *The River of Doubt: Theodore Roosevelt's Darkest Journey* (New York: Doubleday, 2005), which should be read for its description of the menacing tropical rain forest as well as its historical narrative. For further information and insights on Roosevelt and Taft, I strongly recommend *When Trumpets Call: Theodore Roosevelt after the White House* by Patricia O'Toole (New York: Simon & Schuster, 2004).

From TR through FDR, sports were, as part III suggests, "acceptable but not required." Yet presidents from Taft through FDR played golf or fished or, in the case of FDR, not only fished but also rebuilt the upper portion of his wasted body. Entertaining chapters on William Howard Taft's leisurely golf games, often at the expense of presidential business, may be found in Campbell and Landau's *Presidential Lies* and Van Natta's *First Off the Tee*. Serious readers may want to go to the memoirs of those who knew these two presidents. Archie Butt, who became Taft's military aide, describes his golf—and other sporting activities—in the two-volume *Taft and Roosevelt: The Intimate Letters of Archie Butt* (Garden City, N.Y.: Doubleday, Doran, 1930), in letters that were not published until after Taft's death. For Taft's pioneering trips to the ball park, I would recommend William B. Mead and Paul Dickson's *Baseball: The Presidents' Game* (Washington, D.C.: Farragut Publishing, 1993).

Woodrow Wilson's sports are crucial because his health may have been related to his choice of outdoor sports. Until his second marriage to Edith Bolling Wilson, Wilson's closest golfing companion was his physician, Dr. Cary Grayson. Grayson recalled his life with the president in *Woodrow Wilson: An Intimate Memoir* (New York: Holt, Rinehart and Winston, 1959), including their daily golf outings.

Secret service agent Edmund Starling, who was assigned to four presidents, describes Wilson and Edith's golf in *Starling of the White House* (New York: Simon &

Schuster, 1946). Phyllis Lee Levin's *Edith and Woodrow: The Wilson White House* (New York: Scribner, 2001) gives a complete account of Wilson's second marriage and weaves sports and recreations into the account. For a firsthand account of Wilson's billiards, tennis, and bicycling, see his brother-in-law Stockton Axson's *Brother Woodrow: A Memoir of Woodrow Wilson* (Princeton: Princeton University Press, 1993). For anyone who wishes to dig deeper, Henry W. Bragdon illuminates Wilson's gridiron activities—and ill health—in *Woodrow Wilson: The Academic Years* (Cambridge: Harvard University Press, 1967), a book that helped me to appreciate Woodrow Wilson's temperament and talents.

Certainly the 1920s offer less to read on specific presidential sports. Readers who want to skim the sporting activities of Harding, Coolidge, or Hoover would do well to consult Bill Mares, *Fishing with the Presidents: An Anecdotal History* (Mechanicsburg, Pa.: Stackpole Books, 1999); Mead and Dickson, *Baseball: The Presidents' Game;* or the two books on presidential golf cited previously. Once again, Edmund Starling who guarded the presidents—and tutored Calvin Coolidge on his fishing—gives a sympathetic view of the sporting presidency. Irwin (Ike) H. Hoover also had a bird's-eye (if sometimes skewed) view of the presidents, which he recorded in *Forty-two Years at the White House* (Boston: Houghton Mifflin, 1934). The best work on all three presidents—and their sporting interests—is unpublished. Dr. Joel Boone, who spent time with the three presidents and their families, left hefty diaries and memoirs that now reside in the Library of Congress. His son-in-law, Milton Heller Jr., published a readable version of Boone's experiences based on the diaries, *The Presidents' Doctor: An Insider's View of Three First Families* (New York: Vantage, 2000); while there is no substitute for the drama of firsthand accounts, Heller makes it possible for readers to get the gist of Boone's White House career. Readers who want the raw diary entries would do well to go to the Manuscript Reading Room of the Library of Congress. Be prepared. The second phase of his career as an inspector of coal mines pales by comparison to such experiences as tending to the dying Warren Harding and the doomed Calvin Coolidge Jr., or to the daily checkups of President Herbert Hoover before going outside to play medicine ball.

In spite of his reclusive nature, Hoover's outdoor sports and recreation hint at the later uses presidents and ex-presidents made of sport. Like Jimmy Carter, Hoover wrote a delightful book on his favorite sport late in his life, *Fishing for Fun and to Wash Your Soul* (New York: Random House, 1963). His retreat, Camp Rapidan, has been the subject of two books, predecessors to books on the LBJ Ranch and Ronald Reagan's El Cielo. The most detailed as to the architecture and activities at the Hoovers' retreat is Laurel A. Racine, *Historic Furnishings Report, Rapidan Camp: "The Brown House"* (Washington, D.C.: National Park Service, 2001). A less detailed but readable account of Camp Hoover is Darwin Lambert, *Herbert Hoover's Hideaway: The Story of Camp Hoover on the Rapidan River in Shenandoah National Park* (Luray, Va.: Shenandoah Natural History Association, 1971). An extremely detailed and well-researched volume is Hal Elliott Wert's *Hoover, the Fishing President: Portrait of the Private Man and His Life Out-*

doors (Mechanicsburg, Pa.: Stackpole Books, 2005), which is a biography of Hoover's life approached through his fishing and other outdoor activities.

Among presidential wives, several biographies give brief glimpses of their athletic interests and occasionally those of their husbands. Anne Beiser Allen's *An Independent Woman: The Life of Lou Henry Hoover* (Westport, Conn.: Greenwood Press, 2000) demonstrates convincingly the role played by athletics in the life of this first lady. Other biographies of presidential wives contain only cursory, though interesting, sections on their sporting activities. Readers who want to plumb the depths might look at Ishbel Ross's *Grace Coolidge and Her Era: The Story of a President's Wife* (New York: Dodd, Mead, 1962) or Blanche Wiesen Cook's *Eleanor Roosevelt, 1884–1933* (New York: Viking, 1992), especially the section on her bodyguard and athletic tutor, Earl Miller. A recent—and thorough—biography of Grace Coolidge that not only gives a far clearer understanding of Grace but also of her husband is Cynthia D. Bittinger's *Grace Coolidge: Sudden Star* (Huntington, N.Y.: Nova Publishers, 2005). Readers may also want to look at *Nellie Taft: The Unconventional First Lady of the Ragtime Era* by Carl Sferrazza Anthony (New York: HarperCollins, 2005), which gives a detailed account of Nellie's life and some intriguing details about her gambling, usually at poker, where she was far superior to her husband. An earlier work by the same author, *Florence Harding: The First Lady, the Jazz Age, and the Death of America's Most Scandalous President* (New York: William Morrow, 1998), may be the best researched account of President Harding's wayward behavior, not to mention the conflicting details of his death. For a briefer treatment of the Hardings, see John W. Dean, *Warren G. Harding* (New York: Henry Holt, 2004).

The life of Franklin Roosevelt has been so exhaustively researched that almost any standard biography contains accounts of his youthful sailing, golf, fishing, hunting, and hiking. I found Geoffrey Ward's *Before the Trumpet: Young Franklin Roosevelt, 1882–1905* (New York: Harper and Row, 1985) the most informative and readable. His life after polio is well documented. Take, for example, Hugh G. Gallagher, *FDR's Splendid Deception: The Moving Story of Roosevelt's Massive Disability and the Intense Efforts to Conceal It from the Public* (New York: Dodd, Mead, 1985). For a good read, I strongly recommend Robert F. Cross's *Sailor in the White House: The Seafaring Life of FDR* (Annapolis, Md.: Naval Institute Press, 2003), which covers his fishing, sailing, and cruises. A book that is available at Warm Springs is *The Squire of Warm Springs: FDR in Georgia, 1924–1945* by Theo Lippmann Jr., which unfortunately lacks information about date and place of publication. Still this well-researched little paperback manages to capture the story of Warm Springs and the important part it played in FDR's post-poliomyelitis quest for health.

Harry Truman, a nonathlete, still left us a trove of pithy stories and quotes, some of them sports-related. Once again, Boller's *Presidential Anecdotes* offers amusing and interesting thumbnail sketches of the independent man from Independence. Robert H. Ferrell collected some of his most interesting correspondence; read his *Dear Bess: The Letters from Harry to Bess Truman, 1910–1959* (New York: W. W. Norton, 1983). A brief but fascinating publication is *Harry Truman and the Little White House in Key West* by Arva Moore Parks (Miami: Centennial Press, 1999). Want to read and see the first flying destination of a midcentury president, the curtain raiser on the ranches, golf resorts, and beach houses of his successors? This richly illustrated oversized pamphlet is filled with stories and little-known facts of Truman's 175 halcyon days in Key West. It also says a great deal about the character of this "uncommon, common man."

The literature on the final nine presidents of the twentieth century, while as different as the men themselves, has common threads. Most wrote memoirs for posterity and profit (Truman, the last ex-president without a pension wrote his memoirs while living in genteel poverty, holes in the linoleum and leaks in the roof, both lovingly preserved by the National Park Service). Dwight Eisenhower published a best seller, a delightful little volume, *At Ease: Stores I Tell to Friends* (Garden City, N.Y.: Doubleday, 1967). Some of the stories about sports in his youth indeed tell of his football ambitions and the disheartening knee injury in 1912 (the book contains some references to his next obsession, playing cards, notably poker).

In his dogged effort to redeem himself, Richard Nixon published an account of his life after the presidency—*In the Arena: A Memoir of Victory, Defeat, and Renewal* (New York: Simon & Schuster, 1990). The memoir of the "new Nixon" features the role that golf played in his rehabilitation and his friendships (at least that was what he called them) with members of the California Angels and New York Mets. In a somewhat different vein, Jimmy Carter—easily the most prolific presidential writer since Theodore Roosevelt—has given us numerous books including a book of poetry and a historical novel. The two books that describe his early and later sports are *An Hour before Daylight: Memories of a Rural Boyhood* (New York: Simon & Schuster, 2001) and *An Outdoor Journal: Adventures and Reflections* (Fayetteville: University of Arkansas Press, 1988).

Accounts of these presidents as young men tell more about sports than, say, lengthy biographies of Millard Fillmore or James Garfield. A book about the youthful Calvin Coolidge includes some of the few sports, or, more precisely, physical activities of his early life. I refer to Hendrik Booraem V, *The Provincial: Calvin Coolidge and His World, 1885–1895* (Lewisburg, Pa.: Bucknell University Press, 1994). One of the most fascinating of this genre is a biography of John Kennedy by Nigel Hamilton, *JFK: Reckless Youth* (New York: Random House, 1992). Here he is, the sickly but athletic kid with all of his randy ramblings to his friend Lem Barker, ending with his heroic swim after the PT-109 disaster. Not nearly as randy, but just as fascinating is Anne Edwards's *Early Reagan: The Rise to Power* (New York: William Morrow, 1987). Edwards covers the sporting phases of Dutch's early life and career—his years as a lifeguard in Dixon, Illinois, his football and swimming at Eureka College, sportscasting for WHO in Des Moines, and *Knute Rockne, All American*, the movie role that stuck with him the longest. Fragments from David Maraniss's *First in His Class: The Biography of Bill Clinton* (New York: Simon & Schuster, 1995) help define the nonsporting persona of a young Bill Clinton.

Two books less obviously related to sports still describe the alpha and omega of young presidential sportsmen. Edward R. Renehan Jr.'s *The Kennedys at War, 1937 to 1945* (New York: Doubleday, 2002) gives a portrait of the military and nonmilitary family at crisis points in its own and the nation's history. Sports—military and otherwise—make their appearance. An oral history published at California State University, Fullerton, provided me with useful background on Richard Nixon's self-destructive football ambitions. *The Young Nixon: An Oral Inquiry,* edited by Renee K. Schulte (Fullerton: California State University, Fullerton, Oral History Program, 1978), incorporates interviews with Nixon's teammates on high school and college football teams. And, of course, there is much more than sports in both books.

The ranches and vacation homes of presidents have become grist for writers' mills. I've noted Hoover's and Truman's recreational settings—Camp Rapidan and the Little White House in Key West. One of the best treatments of a presidential retreat is Hal Rothman, *LBJ's Texas White House: "Our Heart's Home"* (College Station: Texas A&M Press, 2001). This book is important because it explains the image-creating function of Johnson's ranch. Johnson used the ranch to transform himself from a southern to a southwestern politician and also used it to entertain colleagues and dignitaries. Was Johnson merely a scheming politician? The story of his ranch helps to fill in the picture that mega-biographies by Robert Caro and Robert Dallek have told in exquisite detail.

Ronald Reagan's El Cielo was probably the best known ranch after LBJ's Texas White House. Almost every book about Reagan touches upon the ranch, where the Reagans spent 345 days of his eight presidential years. Peter Hannaford offers up light reading on the Reagan ranch and other presidential retreats in *Ronald Reagan and His Ranch: The Western White House, 1981–1989* (Bennington, Vt.: Tordis Ilg Isselhardt, Publisher, 2002). Yet the door is wide open for books about other presidential retreats from Jefferson's Poplar Forest to Dwight Eisenhower's Gettysburg farm or from JFK's Hyannisport to George H. W. Bush's Kennebunkport.

Speaking of JFK, one hardly needs to remind readers of the cottage industry of books spawned by John F. Kennedy and First Lady Jackie, from the scholarly to the popular, some of them already noted. An outstanding account of JFK's presidency is Sally Bedell Smith's *Grace and Power: The Private World of the Kennedy White House* (New York: Random House, 2004). Superbly researched and written, this gem of a book not only details the sports of Jack and Jackie in the White House years, but also describes Jack's daily swims (sometimes with girlfriends) and how important the Glen Ora estate in the fox country of Virginia was to Jackie. Another book worth mentioning is *The Search for JFK* (New York: Berkeley Publishing, 1976) by Joan and Clay Blair Jr. It first brought Kennedy's ailments into public and scholarly discussion—and, by implication, his sporting persona.

A recent book that made the best-seller lists is Brian Kilmeade, *The Games Do Count: America's Best and Brightest on the Power of Sports* (New York: Regan Books, 2004). Kilmeade's oral history includes presidents who offered their stories—Gerald Ford, George H. W. Bush, and George W. Bush—on the impact of sports on their lives

(John Kerry was included just in case Bush lost). The seventy brief chapters, including other political figures such as Henry Kissinger, Gray Davis, Bob Kerrey, Joe Biden, Condoleezza Rice, John McCain, and Dennis Hastert, give some feeling for the power of sports in shaping political lives. A book less related to sports but containing sports anecdotes, some of them hilarious, is Alan Schroeder, *Celebrity-in-Chief: How Show Business Took Over the White House* (Boulder, Colo.: Westview Press, 2004).

Bill Clinton and George Bush are almost too contemporary and controversial to get a fair reading of their sports. Even Don Van Natta Jr.'s *First Off the Tee* and his lively account of his golf game with Bill ("The Rights of Bill," *Sports Illustrated*, March 21, 2003, 98) pull no punches. George W. Bush has taken bruising criticism, but rarely for his golf, which he has kept relatively private. Both Bush and Clinton do refer to sports, pre-presidential and presidential, in their autobiographies. Bush's light memoir, *A Charge to Keep* (New York: William Morrow, 1999), gives one version of his pre-gubernatorial years as managing partner of the Texas Rangers. A more interesting article on the same subject is "The Road to Politics Ran Directly through a Ballpark in Texas," *New York Times*, September 24, 2000. Clinton's memoir may weigh four or five times as much as Bush's brief narrative; maybe that's why sporting experiences are harder to find in *My Life* (New York: Alfred A. Knopf, 2004). Though sporting experiences are few and far between, I did find a few episodes, such as the account of Clinton "assisting" Lou Holtz and the Arkansas Razorbacks before the Orange Bowl on January 1, 1980.

Do sports form a necessary resume for a candidate? Have wannabe candidates in the twentieth century highlighted them in their campaign biographies? Yes, but there are exceptions. Take former Vice-President Dan Quayle's autobiography, *Standing Firm: A Vice-Presidential Memoir* (New York: HarperCollins, 1994). Written after he left the vice-presidency, there is nary a mention of his golf game. Evidently, Quayle, who still had presidential ambitions, went out of his way to avoid golf. His sport had become a liability—as even fatherly Richard Nixon counseled him. The public was more aware of his golfing proficiency than his claim to be presidential timber. The absence of information on Quayle the golfer is unfortunate. He mastered his game as superbly as any president or vice-president has done with any sport. Campbell and Landau in *Presidential Lies* devote several pages to what they call "Dan Quayle's Game: '100 Percent Silk.'" It would be interesting to have a book on golf by Quayle similar to Herbert Hoover's *Fishing for Fun and to Wash Your Soul*, a reflective book on politics, golf, and the fickle nature of public opinion. To paraphrase Brian Kilmeade, even if the games count against you, defend your turf.

Is there any reason why we should not have more books on sports by the presidents and vice-presidents—to let us know what their recreations meant to them when they were in office? None of our presidents has written an account *exclusively* about what sports meant to him when he was in the White House. This includes the priceless books by Hoover and Carter about their love for outdoor sports.

Let this essay end with a plea for such a book.

★ ★ ★

Index

Adams, John, 15–16
Adams, John Quincy, 16–19
Ali, Muhammad, 256–57, 271
Allen, George, 1, 236–39, 346
Amateur Athletic Act, 250–51
Augusta National (golf club), 2, 76, 122, 189, 191, 193–94, 196, 198, 254, 284, 344
Arthur, Chester, 28–29, 52, 162
Axson, Stockton, 91, 93, 101

Baker, Newton, 108–9
Bell, J. Franklin, 58–59
Bentsen, Lloyd, 298, 300
Boone, Joel, 107, 116–17, 121, 124–25, 131, 136–37, 143
Braddock, Edward, 9–10
Brown, Phyllis, 248–49
Brown vs. Board of Education of Topeka, 197, 220, 265
Burroughs, John, 51–52, 61, 68–69, 113, 167
Bush, Barbara P., 295–96, 298, 305–6, 328, 331
Bush, Barbara P. (daughter of George W.), 331
Bush, Dorothy (mother of George H. W.), 293
Bush, Dorothy (daughter of George H. W.), 301
Bush, George H. W. (elder Bush), 71, 292, 311–12, 321, 325; Asian trip, 306; attends Daytona 500, 330, 350–51; baseball, 292, 294–95, 296–97, 304;

booed at baseball game, 307; bumbling image of, 301, 347; election campaigns, 298–300; fishing, 293, 302; golf, 302–5, 308, 312; Gulf War, 304–5; health problems, 305–7, 352; horseshoes, 301, 303; hunting, 298, 302; jock presidency, 297, 301–3; military service, 294–96; oil business, 297; "Oyster Bay thing," 292–93, 302–3, 307; post-presidency, 308; presidential golf match, 311–12; President's Council on Physical Fitness, 305; running, 303, 306; teamwork and presidency, 340; receives memoirs of Babe Ruth, 292; soccer, 294, 296; tennis, 298, 301; tiddlywinks, 307–8; walking, 306; wimp factor, 299–300, 347–48
Bush, George W., ix, x, 147, 324; athletic ability, 326; attends Daytona 500, 337, 350; baseball, 336, 329–34, 335–36; baseball politics, 331–32; basketball, 328; cheerleader, 326; clearing brush, 328; early years, 325; financial arrangements, 329–30, 332–34; fishing, 327; football, 327; golf, 327–29; as governor of Texas, 327; Harken Energy, 333; hunting, 327–28; insider trading, 333; macho presidency, 348–49; reaction to 9/11, 335; rugby, 326; running, 327; stickball at Andover, 326, 334; tee ball, 334–35; tennis, 327; weight training, 327
Bush, Jeb, 299, 327
Bush, Jenna (daughter of George W.), 331

Bush, Laura, 325, 331, 337
Bush, Prescott (father of George H. W.), 293
Butt, Archie, 59, 64, 67–68, 76–78, 80–82, 84–89
Butt, Clara, 77, 89

Camp, Walter, 54, 104, 157
Camp David ("Shangri-la"), 3, 60, 68–69, 173, 193, 262, 267–68, 288, 305, 342, 346
Carter, Earl (father of Jimmy), 263–65
Carter, James Earl, Jr., "Jimmy," 1, 2, 4, 57, 256, 258–59, 326; "banzai bunny" story, 269–70; baseball, 263–64; basketball, 265; Camp David Accords, 262; and conservation, 267; cooperates with Ford, 260; cross-country skiing, 269; delegating and team sports, 342; exhausted in road race, 269; fishing, 261–64, 266–69; golf, 265–66; health, 263; hunting, 261–64; image of, 269; micromanaging, 267, 342; Naval Academy, 265; Nobel Peace prize, 273; Olympic boycott, 57, 262, 270–73; outdoor sports, 261; post-presidency, 273; presidential debates, 256, 289; race relations, 265–66; and Soviet invasion of Afghanistan, 270; square dancing, 260; stock car racing, 266; tennis, 262–63, 266, 267; track events, 265, 269; as writer, 265, 353
Carter, Lillian (mother of Jimmy), 263–64
Carter, Rosalynn, 1, 262, 264, 265, 359
Cheney, Richard, 256–57
Chiang Kai-shek, 251, 301
Churchill, Winston, 162–64, 179–80, 352
Cleveland, Frances Folsom, 30
Cleveland, Grover, 29–31, 40, 83
Clemenceau, Georges, 101–2

Clifford, Alice and Bede, 162
Clifford, Clark, 179–82
Clinton, Chelsea (daughter of Bill), 317
Clinton, Hillary Rodham, 316–17, 350
Clinton, William Jefferson, "Bill," ix, 4, 57, 109, 327–28, 339, 352–53; athletic ability of, 311; attends NASCAR event, 351; baseball, 57, 318; basketball, 313–15; bowling, 313; as card player, 315; election campaigns, 321; football, 313, 317; golf, 311–13, 316–17, 319–22; impeachment, 321–22; invitational tournament injury, 321; physique, 311; plays putt-putt golf, 348; presidential golf match, 311–12; renaissance weekends, 317; rugby, 313–14; running, 313, 316–17; as sports spectator, 314–15, 348; tennis, 316; tree rumor, 314
Cobb, Ty, 83–84
Coolidge, Calvin, 107, 338, 349, 353; attends baseball games, 120–21; athletic limitations of, 119, 222; character and image, 119; entertains Al Smith, 128; fishing, 127–28, 130, 344; football, 120; golf, 122, 132; hosts Charles Lindbergh, 128–29; plays outdoor sports as youth, 120, 127; presidential yacht, 122–23, 127; reprimand of wife, 121; reputation, 119, 131–32; son's death, 124–27, 131; summer in South Dakota, 129–31; third term rejected, 131; vacation in Wisconsin, 130; wife and Jim Haley, 130
Coolidge, Calvin, Jr., 124–27, 131
Coolidge, Grace, 119–24, 126, 128–32, 147, 287, 350, 353

Davis, Ernie, 213–14, 345
Davis, John W., 127
Davis, Richard Harding, 44–45
Dewey, Thomas, 174
Dole, Robert, 321, 349

Donovan, Mike, 70
Dukakis, Michael, 299–300

Edison, Thomas, 113, 136
Eisenhower, David (grandson of
    Dwight D.), 239–40, 243
Eisenhower, Dwight D., 2, 4, 147, 229,
    311, 345; at Augusta National, 189,
    193–94, 198; baseball, 186, 194;
    bridge, 190, 193, 197; cheerleader,
    326; and civil rights, 197–98; cooking,
    190–91; criticism of, 194–96, 343;
    diplomatic initiatives, 198–99;
    fishing, 190–91; football, 186–88;
    golf, 185, 188–89, 192–95, 199, 347;
    heart attacks, 185, 195, 352; hunting,
    191–92; President's Council on Physi-
    cal Fitness, 209–10; poker, 189–90;
    second term issue, 195–96; sporting
    diplomacy, 195; squirrel controversy,
    194–95; stroke, 198; use of Camp
    David, 193
Eisenhower, John (son of Dwight D.),
    188–89, 194
Eisenhower, Julie Nixon. See Nixon, Julie
Eisenhower, Mamie, 189–90, 194,
    197–99
Elder, Lee, 254, 257
Elizabeth II (queen of England), 287

female president, 353
first ladies and sports, 349–50
Ford, Betty, 249, 252, 257–58, 350
Ford, Gerald R., 2, 298–99, 340, 347;
    African American teammate of, 247–
    48; bumbling image of, 245, 256;
    coach at Yale, 248; drafted by NFL
    teams, 247; early years, 246–47; elec-
    tion campaign, 257–58; football, 245–
    48, 282; golf, 245, 254, 257–58, 347;
    as law student, 248; modeling, 249;
    Olympics, 250–51; Nixon pardon, 245;

presidential debates, 256; presidential
    golfing match, 311–12; role of sports
    celebrities, 256–58; skiing, 255; swim-
    ming, 255; as team player, 258–59,
    340; and Title IX, 252–53; World War
    II service, 249
Ford, Susan (daughter of Gerald),
    256–57
Frick, Henry, 86–88, 351

Garagiola, Joe, 256, 258
Garfield, James, 64–65, 79
Gipp, George, 275, 277
Goldwater, Barry, 234, 291
Gore, Albert, 334
Graham, Martha, 257
Grange, Harold "Red," 104, 108, 120
Grant, Ulysses S., 2, 24–27, 31–33, 63,
    83, 295
Grayson, Cary, 96–97, 99–103
Grinnell, George Bird, 32, 43, 50

Harding, Florence, 112, 114–15, 117
Harding, Warren G., 3, 139, 152, 162;
    baseball, 110, 117; boxing, 112–13;
    camping, 113–14; celebrities and, 107–
    8, 110; common touch, 108; drinking
    illegally, 110; extramarital affairs, 109;
    golf, 106–9, 112, 114–15, 211; medical
    condition, 114, 116; poker, 111–12, 117,
    351; presidential yacht Mayflower, 123;
    racial stance, 112–13; role of media,
    117; scandals, 115; signs peace treaty,
    107; temperament, 108; vacations,
    108, 114–15; trip to Alaska, 115–16;
    visit to Vancouver, 116, 162; wagering,
    109–12
Harrison, Benjamin, 31–32, 43, 83
Hayes, Rutherford B., 27
Hayes, Woody, 184, 233–34
Holtz, Lou, 315–16
Hoover, Herbert, 2, 3, 111–12, 167, 190;

Hoover, Herbert (*continued*)
booed at World Series game, 135, 183, 307, 342; criticized for using federal funds to build Rapidan Camp, 159; dam building, 142–43; fishing, 134, 139, 142, 147; football, 133; Great Depression, 135; hounded by FDR, 167; interest in sports scores, 137; jibe by Babe Ruth, 135; medicine ball, 136–37; Olympics, 1932, 145–46; outraged by gambling, 111–12; personality traits, 134, 136; Rapidan Camp, 69, 134, 140–41, 159; sports and presidential attributes, 341–42; treatment of bonus marchers, 146–47; tributes to fishing and sports, 147, 353; trips to Caribbean, South America, 144–45, 342
Hoover, Irwin (Ike), 98–99, 125, 130, 141
Hoover, Lou, 139–41, 342, 350, 353
Hope, Bob, 180, 242–43, 311–12, 325
Humphrey, Hubert, 218, 234, 346
Hussein, Saddam, 303

Jackson, Andrew, 2, 5, 20–22, 33, 333
Jefferson, Thomas, 2, 13–16, 33, 69
Johnson, Andrew, 25, 33, 83, 333
Johnson, Jack, 112–13, 175
Johnson, Lady Bird, 220
Johnson, Lynda Bird (daughter of Lyndon B.), 222
Johnson, Lyndon B., 245, 338; baseball, 217–19; college politics, 218; debate coach, 218; early political career, 219; football, 218, 255–56; golf, 219, 224; Great Society, 346; heart attacks, 222, 224, 226; hunting, 217–18, 220, 222; imperial presidency of, 167; invites athletes and coaches to White House, 223; Kennedy assassination, 215, 217, 222; lack of interest in athletics, 345–46; LBJ ranch, 216–17, 220–22, 224–

25; and Pakistani camel driver, 221; physical attributes, 223–24; post-presidency, 224–26; President's Council on Physical Fitness, 346; swimming, 222; and Vietnam War, 224, 346; view of Gerald Ford, 245; visits racetrack, 219; western image, 220–21
Johnson, Walter, 10, 84, 121
Jones, Robert Tyre (Bobby), 108, 189, 193
Jusserand, Jules, 64, 66–67

Kennedy, Jacqueline, 208–9, 212, 345, 350
Kennedy, John F., 2, 4, 17, 60, 153, 233, 300, 302, 346; assassination of, 215, 217, 222; athletic ability, 202, 205, 345; baseball, 201; and Cuban missile crisis, 211, 214–15; disabilities of, 60, 201–3, 224; 50-mile hike, 60, 210–11; football, 201, 203, 208, 213–14; Glen Ora, 212; golf, 201, 204, 211–13; greets Ernie Davis, 213; healthy appearance, 201–2; hunting, 217; image of, 201, 209, 223–24, 347, 352; military career, 201, 204; physical condition, 201, 204; President's Council on Physical Fitness, 210, 345; *Profiles in Courage*, 203; PT-109, 202, 205–7; sailing, 201, 204; staunch anti-Communism, 209; swimming, 203, 213, 215; televised debates, 201, 209; Washington Redskins, 213–14; *Why England Slept*, 204
Kennedy, Joseph P., Sr. (father of John F.), 201, 204, 206–7
Kennedy, Joseph P., Jr. (brother of John F.), 204, 207
Kennedy, Robert F., 60, 208, 210, 214, 221, 224, 346
Kerry, John, 335
Khrushchev, Nikita, 198–99, 214–15, 233
King, Martin Luther, Jr., 197, 213–14, 230

Landis, Kenesaw Mountain, 167–68
Lewis and Clark expedition, 2, 15
Lincoln, Abraham, 5, 22–24, 33, 37, 254
Lindbergh, Anne, 129, 142
Lindbergh, Charles, 128–29, 135, 142, 167
Lloyd-George, David, 97, 101
Lodge, Henry Cabot, 71
Lodge, Henry Cabot, Jr., 207
Longworth, Alice Roosevelt. *See* Roosevelt, Alice (daughter of TR)

MacArthur, Douglas, 111, 147, 181, 183, 342
Mayflower (presidential yacht), 122–23, 127, 143
McGovern, George, 241, 346
McKinley, William, 32–33, 46–47, 83
McKinzie, Ralph, 278–80, 289
McLean, Edward (Ned), 109, 112–13
McLean, Evalyn, 109, 122
Miller, Earl, 166–67
Morrow, Dwight, 129, 135
Muir, John, 53, 61, 167

NASCAR, 337, 344, 347, 350–51
Newman, Wallace, 230–31, 234, 236, 244, 340
Nicklaus, Jack, 254, 302
Nixon, Frank (father of Richard M.), 230
Nixon, Julie (daughter of Richard M.), 239
Nixon, Patricia, 232
Nixon, Richard M., 4, 311, 345; admiration for college coach, 230–31, 234, 236; advice to Dan Quayle, 300, 351; baseball, 229, 239–41, 243; bonding between sports and presidency, 229, 234, 346–47; bowling, 241; delegating, 340; election campaigns, 232–33, 240–41; fishing, 229, 241; football, 228–32, 235–38, 339; golf, 241–43,

320; imperial presidency of, 167; and Jackie Robinson, 229–30; pardoned, 245; pep talks, 231; Ping Pong match, 3; poker, 232, 351; President's Council on Physical Fitness, 233; SALT talks, 236; sports spectator, 53–54, 239–41, 285, 346; sportswriter wish, 239–40; suggests plays for coaches, x, 1, 237–38; talks football to protesters, 352; televised debate, 201; Texas-Arkansas game, 235, 314; trip to China, 236, 238; as vice-president, 229, 242; and Vietnam War, 234–37, 346; Watergate break-in, 236, 240–43
Noble, John, 32, 43
Norman, Greg, 321

Olympic Games, 2, 57–58, 145–46, 250–52, 270–73

Palmer, Arnold, 256, 301
Patterson, Joseph, 159
Philip (duke of Edinburgh), 287
Pinchot, Gifford, 50–51, 53, 64–65, 79–80
Pine Knot, 68–70, 191
Player, Gary, 256
Plimpton, George, 301–2, 307
President's Council on Physical Fitness, 209–10, 223, 233, 345–46
presidential golfing match, 311–12
presidential yachting and sailing, 122–23, 153, 160–62, 173–74, 204

Quayle, Dan, 299, 300, 307, 351

Rayburn, Sam, 178, 221
Reagan, Jack (father of Ronald W.), 278
Reagan, Nancy, 284–85, 287–88, 291, 299
Reagan, Neil ("Moon," brother of Ronald W.), 278

Reagan, Nelle (mother of Ronald W.), 278–79

Reagan, Ronald W., 4, 262, 333, 336, 342, 352; as actor, 275, 277–78, 280, 284–86; African American teammates, 279; assassination attempt, 290–91; baseball, 281–82, 286, 289; childhood and youth, 278; "Dutch," 278, 284; Eureka College, 278–80; first president to attend NASCAR event, 348; football, 278–79, 290; "Gipper," 275, 277, 286, 291, 347; golf, 284–85; *Knute Rockne, All American*, 275, 277, 291; lifeguarding, 276, 279–80, 285; "Nashua Four," 298–99; personality traits, 285, 340; presidential style of, 340; radio announcer, 280–83; Rancho El Cielo, 287–88; "reign of errors," 290; riding, 285–89; swimming, 279–80; telegraph goes dead incident, 282; television, 285, 289–90

Rice, Condoleezza, 328, 348

Richardson, Nolan, 316

Robb, Lynda Bird. *See* Johnson, Lynda Bird

Roberts, Clifford, 189, 198

Robinson, Jackie, 229–30, 264

Rockne, Knute, 275, 277

Roosevelt, Alice (daughter of TR), 36, 41, 63, 109–11

Roosevelt, Alice Lee (first wife of TR), 39, 41, 43, 63

Roosevelt, Archie (son of TR), 50, 63

Roosevelt, Edith (second wife of TR), 43, 53, 56, 63, 68–69, 71

Roosevelt, Eleanor, 151–54, 165–67, 350

Roosevelt, Elliott (brother of TR), 39, 53, 165

Roosevelt, Elliott (son of FDR), 156–57, 162–63

Roosevelt, Franklin D., 2, 53–54, 57, 342;
athletic ability, 152; Atlantic Charter, 163; baseball, 168; Campobello Island, 150, 152–54, 161; childhood, 151–52; cover-up of disability, 151, 157–58, 164; death of, 164; fall before speech, 158–59; fishing, 153, 155, 159–64; golfing, 150, 152; Hundred Days, 161; nominates Al Smith, 155–56; polio, 149–51, 153–58, 163, 167; Roosevelt Memorial, 149, 168–69; sailing and yachting, 153, 159–62; sports and delegating, 341–42; swimming, 152–53, 155, 159–60, 164, 173; trip on *Amberjack II*, 161; trips to Latin America, 162; Warm Springs, 150, 155–56, 158–59, 163; World War II, 162–64, 168

Roosevelt, James (father of FDR), 152

Roosevelt, James (son of FDR), 156, 158

Roosevelt, Kermit (son of TR), 55, 62, 63, 66, 70

Roosevelt, Quentin (son of TR), 63–64

Roosevelt, Theodore, ix, 3, 4, 34, 91, 101, 151, 167, 283, 293, 295, 297, 302, 306, 308, 318, 323, 337–38, 344; ability to delegate, 343; asthma, 38; Battle of San Juan Hill, 45–46, 205; boxing and wrestling, 37–38, 41, 47, 70; childhood, 37–38; and conservation, 2, 37, 42, 50–51, 53, 61–62, 352; Dakota badlands, 40–41, 43; death of, 71; death of wife and mother, 41; discourages Taft from playing golf, 74–75, 329, 351; energetic children, 63; first marriage, 39; football reform, 54–57, 318; hunting, 37, 39–40, 42, 47, 49–50, 71; as naturalist, 38; Olympics, 57–58; outdoor sports, 47; photo of waterfalls, 66; physical ailments, 43, 70–71; Pine Knot, 68–69; presidential yacht *Mayflower*, 123; ride to Warrenton, Virginia, 59–60; Rough Riders, 42, 44–45, 53; scrambling in Rock Creek

Valley, 1, 58–59, 62, 64–65; second marriage, 43; self-defense, 39–42, 69; sets bar for presidential sports, 71; "strenuous life," 43, 54, 70; takes oath of office, 47; Teddy Bear, 48–50; tennis, 39, 46, 64–66; transformation of sporting presidency, 37, 46–47, 72; trip with John Burroughs, 51–52; trolley accident, 48, 66; visits Panama Canal, 162

Roosevelt, Theodore, Jr., "Ted," 36, 55–56, 63, 65, 71, 111, 145

Root, Elihu, 55, 75

Royal, Darrell, 225–26, 235, 346

Ruth, Babe, 108, 110, 119, 121, 135, 292, 297

Ryan, Nolan, 330, 332

Salinger, Pierre, 210–11

Schwarzenegger, Arnold, 305

Shula, Don, 238

Simpson, O. J., 234, 339

Skyline Drive, 2, 141

Smith, Al, 124, 127–28, 150, 155–56, 168, 338

Starling, Edmund, 100, 110, 112–14, 126–28

Stevenson, Adlai, 192, 196, 345

Stone, Harlan, 137

Sunrise at Campobello, 156

Taft, Nellie, 75–76, 86–87, 90

Taft, Robert, "Bob" (son of William Howard), 81, 191–92, 232

Taft, William Howard, 53; automobile excursions, 77, 81; baseball, 82–86; exercising, 78; golf, 74–79, 342–43; health, 78; hobnobs with businessmen, 86–88; horseback rides, 75–77, 81; lacks TR flair, 77; Pinchot-Ballinger dispute, 79–80; poker, 87–88; Taft-Roosevelt feud, 79, 88–

89; team sports and delegating, 343; *Titanic* sinking, 80, 89; trip to Manassas, 81–82; wife's stroke, 76

television, 201, 256, 258, 312, 337, 347

Texas Rangers, ix, 318, 324–25, 329–34

Thatcher, Margaret, 303–4

Title IX, 223, 252–53

Truman, Bess, 172, 174–76, 184, 350

Truman, Harry S, 2, 3, 172, 338, 345, 349; air travel, 174; athletic interests of, 173, 175–77, 349; booed at baseball game, 183; bowling, 177; builds tennis court, 175–76; compares himself to Jack Johnson, 175; courts Bess Wallace, 175–76; desegregation orders, 180; farming, 174–75; fires Douglas MacArthur, 183; fishing, 172, 174, 176; football, 183; greets "negro" athletes at White House, 180–81; horseback riding, 177; Key West, 178, 181–82; Korean War, 183; letter to music critic, 182; 1948 election, 174, 176; as nonathletic, 173; physical condition, 173; poker, 177, 179–80, 184, 351; praised by Woody Hayes, 184; "Shangri-la" (Camp David), 173; sports and presidency of, 353; swimming, 173, 176–77; trip to Missouri with Churchill, 179–80; trip to South America, 181; visits LBJ ranch, 221; walking, 176, 178; presidential yacht *Williamsburg*, 173–74

Truman, Margaret, 182

Vaughan, Harry, 177, 179

Vinson, Fred, 177, 351

Ward, Willis, 247–48

Warm Springs, Georgia, 150, 155–56, 158–60, 163–64

Washington, Booker T., 47, 69

Washington, George, 2, 5, 9–13, 33, 45, 202–3, 295

Wilson, Edith (Wilson's second wife), 98, 100–103, 147, 341
Wilson, Ellen (Wilson's first wife), 95–96, 99
Wilson, Woodrow, 107, 151, 167, 239, 341; ambidextrous, 95; Archie Butt's view of, 89; attends horse races, 102; baseball, 93, 98; bicycling in England, 95; billiards and pool, 91, 93; death of first wife, 99; early strokes, 92, 95–96, 101; football, 2, 33, 93–95, 99, 103–5, 233, 326; golf, 1, 91–92, 96–99, 100–102, 105, 319, 340, 343; ill-nesses in Paris, 102; lack of team-work, 340; motoring, 96–97, 99, 103; Paris Peace Conference, 102, 162; political skills, 89; presidential yacht *Mayflower*, 122–23; romantic therapy, 100; sports and policymaking, 340–41; as sports spectator, 239; stroke in 1919, 103; tennis, 91, 93; walking, 101–2; World War I, 100–101
Wood, Leonard, 44, 66

Yellowstone National Park, 28–29, 43, 50–53, 352